enVision Mathematics
Common Core

Volume 2 Topics 7–13

Authors

Robert Q. Berry, III
Professor of Mathematics Education, Department of Curriculum, Instruction and Special Education, University of Virginia, Charlottesville, Virginia

Zachary Champagne
Assistant in Research Florida Center for Research in Science, Technology, Engineering, and Mathematics (FCR-STEM) Jacksonville, Florida

Eric Milou
Professor of Mathematics Rowan University, Glassboro, New Jersey

Jane F. Schielack
Professor Emerita Department of Mathematics Texas A&M University, College Station, Texas

Jonathan A. Wray
Mathematics Supervisor, Howard County Public Schools, Ellicott City, Maryland

Randall I. Charles
Professor Emeritus Department of Mathematics San Jose State University San Jose, California

Francis (Skip) Fennell
Professor Emeritus of Education and Graduate and Professional Studies, McDaniel College Westminster, Maryland

SAVVAS
LEARNING COMPANY

ISBN-13: 978-0-7685-7880-5
ISBN-10: 0-7685-7880-9
8 2023

CONTENTS

TOPICS

DIGITAL RESOURCES

Go Online

INTERACTIVE STUDENT EDITION
Access online or offline

VISUAL LEARNING
Interact with visual learning animations

ACTIVITY
Use with *Solve & Discuss It, Explore It,* and *Explain It* activities and Examples

VIDEOS
Watch clips to support *3-Act Mathematical Modeling* Lessons and *enVision® STEM Projects*

PRACTICE
Practice what you've learned and get immediate feedback

TUTORIALS
Get help from *Virtual Nerd* any time you need it

MATH TOOLS
Explore math with digital tools

GAMES
Play math games to help you learn

KEY CONCEPT
Review important lesson content

GLOSSARY
Read and listen to English and Spanish definitions

ASSESSMENT
Show what you've learned

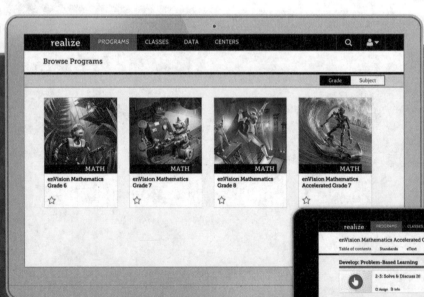

realize.
Everything you need for math anytime, anywhere.

Use Sampling to Draw Inferences About Populations

TOPIC 9 Probability

TOPIC 10 Solve Problems Involving Geometry

TOPIC 11

Congruence and Similarity

TOPIC 12

Understand and Apply the Pythagorean Theorem

TOPIC 13

Solve Problems Involving Surface Area and Volume

Standards for Mathematical Content

RATIOS AND PROPORTIONAL RELATIONSHIPS

7.RP.A Analyze proportional relationships and use them to solve real-world and mathematical problems.

1. Compute unit rates associated with ratios of fractions, including ratios of lengths, areas and other quantities measured in like or different units. *For example, if a person walks $\frac{1}{2}$ mile in each $\frac{1}{4}$ hour, compute the unit rate as the complex fraction $\frac{\frac{1}{2}}{\frac{1}{4}}$ miles per hour, equivalently 2 miles per hour.*

2. Recognize and represent proportional relationships between quantities.

   a. Decide whether two quantities are in a proportional relationship, e.g., by testing for equivalent ratios in a table or graphing on a coordinate plane and observing whether the graph is a straight line through the origin.

   b. Identify the constant of proportionality (unit rate) in tables, graphs, equations, diagrams, and verbal descriptions of proportional relationships.

   c. Represent proportional relationships by equations. *For example, if total cost t is proportional to the number n of items purchased at a constant price p, the relationship between the total cost and the number of items can be expressed as t = pn.*

   d. Explain what a point (x, y) on the graph of a proportional relationship means in terms of the situation, with special attention to the points (0, 0) and (1, r) where r is the unit rate.

3. Use proportional relationships to solve multistep ratio and percent problems. *Examples: simple interest, tax, markups and markdowns, gratuities and commissions, fees, percent increase and decrease, percent error.*

THE NUMBER SYSTEM

7.NS.A Apply and extend previous understandings of operations with fractions to add, subtract, multiply, and divide rational numbers.

1. Apply and extend previous understandings of addition and subtraction to add and subtract rational numbers; represent addition and subtraction on a horizontal or vertical number line diagram.

   a. Describe situations in which opposite quantities combine to make 0. *For example, a hydrogen atom has 0 charge because its two constituents are oppositely charged.*

   b. Understand p + q as the number located a distance |q| from p, in the positive or negative direction depending on whether q is positive or negative. Show that a number and its opposite have a sum of 0 (are additive inverses). Interpret sums of rational numbers by describing real-world contexts.

   c. Understand subtraction of rational numbers as adding the additive inverse, $p - q = p + (-q)$. Show that the distance between two rational numbers on the number line is the absolute value of their difference, and apply this principle in real-world contexts.

   d. Apply properties of operations as strategies to add and subtract rational numbers.

Standards for Mathematical Content

2. Apply and extend previous understandings of multiplication and division and of fractions to multiply and divide rational numbers.

   a. Understand that multiplication is extended from fractions to rational numbers by requiring that operations continue to satisfy the properties of operations, particularly the distributive property, leading to products such as $(-1)(-1) = 1$ and the rules for multiplying signed numbers. Interpret products of rational numbers by describing real-world contexts.

   b. Understand that integers can be divided, provided that the divisor is not zero, and every quotient of integers (with non-zero divisor) is a rational number. If p and q are integers, then $-\left(\frac{p}{q}\right) = \frac{(-p)}{q} = \frac{p}{(-q)}$. Interpret quotients of rational numbers by describing real-world contexts.

   c. Apply properties of operations as strategies to multiply and divide rational numbers.

   d. Convert a rational number to a decimal using long division; know that the decimal form of a rational number terminates in 0s or eventually repeats.

3. Solve real-world and mathematical problems involving the four operations with rational numbers.[1]

EXPRESSIONS AND EQUATIONS

7.EE.A Use properties of operations to generate equivalent expressions.

1. Apply properties of operations as strategies to add, subtract, factor, and expand linear expressions with rational coefficients.

2. Understand that rewriting an expression in different forms in a problem context can shed light on the problem and how the quantities in it are related. *For example, $a + 0.05a = 1.05a$ means that "increase by 5%" is the same as "multiply by 1.05."*

7.EE.B Solve real-life and mathematical problems using numerical and algebraic expressions and equations.

3. Solve multi-step real-life and mathematical problems posed with positive and negative rational numbers in any form (whole numbers, fractions, and decimals), using tools strategically. Apply properties of operations to calculate with numbers in any form; convert between forms as appropriate; and assess the reasonableness of answers using mental computation and estimation strategies. *For example: If a woman making \$25 an hour gets a 10% raise, she will make an additional $\frac{1}{10}$ of her salary an hour, or \$2.50, for a new salary of \$27.50. If you want to place a towel bar $9\frac{3}{4}$ inches long in the center of a door that is $27\frac{1}{2}$ inches wide, you will need to place the bar about 9 inches from each edge; this estimate can be used as a check on the exact computation.*

4. Use variables to represent quantities in a real-world or mathematical problem, and construct simple equations and inequalities to solve problems by reasoning about the quantities.

   a. Solve word problems leading to equations of the form $px + q = r$ and $p(x + q) = r$, where p, q, and r are specific rational numbers. Solve equations of these forms fluently. Compare an algebraic solution to an arithmetic solution, identifying the sequence of the operations used in each approach. *For example, the perimeter of a rectangle is 54 cm. Its length is 6 cm. What is its width?*

   b. Solve word problems leading to inequalities of the form $px + q > r$ or $px + q < r$, where p, q, and r are specific rational numbers. Graph the solution set of the inequality and interpret it in the context of the problem. *For example: As a salesperson, you are paid \$50 per week plus \$3 per sale. This week you want your pay to be at least \$100. Write an inequality for the number of sales you need to make, and describe the solutions.*

Standards for Mathematical Content

GEOMETRY

7.G.A Draw, construct, and describe geometrical figures and describe the relationships between them.

1. Solve problems involving scale drawings of geometric figures, including computing actual lengths and areas from a scale drawing and reproducing a scale drawing at a different scale.

2. Draw (freehand, with ruler and protractor, and with technology) geometric shapes with given conditions. Focus on constructing triangles from three measures of angles or sides, noticing when the conditions determine a unique triangle, more than one triangle, or no triangle.

3. Describe the two-dimensional figures that result from slicing three-dimensional figures, as in plane sections of right rectangular prisms and right rectangular pyramids.

7.G.B Solve real-life and mathematical problems involving angle measure, area, surface area, and volume.

4. Know the formulas for the area and circumference of a circle and use them to solve problems; give an informal derivation of the relationship between the circumference and area of a circle.

5. Use facts about supplementary, complementary, vertical, and adjacent angles in a multi-step problem to write and solve simple equations for an unknown angle in a figure.

6. Solve real-world and mathematical problems involving area, volume, and surface area of two- and three-dimensional objects composed of triangles, quadrilaterals, polygons, cubes, and right prisms.

STATISTICS AND PROBABILITY

7.SP.A Use random sampling to draw inferences about a population.

1. Understand that statistics can be used to gain information about a population by examining a sample of the population; generalizations about a population from a sample are valid only if the sample is representative of that population. Understand that random sampling tends to produce representative samples and support valid inferences.

2. Use data from a random sample to draw inferences about a population with an unknown characteristic of interest. Generate multiple samples (or simulated samples) of the same size to gauge the variation in estimates or predictions. *For example, estimate the mean word length in a book by randomly sampling words from the book; predict the winner of a school election based on randomly sampled survey data. Gauge how far off the estimate or prediction might be.*

7.SP.B Draw informal comparative inferences about two populations.

3. Informally assess the degree of visual overlap of two numerical data distributions with similar variabilities, measuring the difference between the centers by expressing it as a multiple of a measure of variability. *For example, the mean height of players on the basketball team is 10 cm greater than the mean height of players on the soccer team, about twice the variability (mean absolute deviation) on either team; on a dot plot, the separation between the two distributions of heights is noticeable.*

4. Use measures of center and measures of variability for numerical data from random samples to draw informal comparative inferences about two populations. *For example, decide whether the words in a chapter of a seventh-grade science book are generally longer than the words in a chapter of a fourth-grade science book.*

Standards for Mathematical Content

7.SP.C **Investigate chance processes and develop, use, and evaluate probability models.**

5. Understand that the probability of a chance event is a number between 0 and 1 that expresses the likelihood of the event occurring. Larger numbers indicate greater likelihood. A probability near 0 indicates an unlikely event, a probability around $\frac{1}{2}$ indicates an event that is neither unlikely nor likely, and a probability near 1 indicates a likely event.

6. Approximate the probability of a chance event by collecting data on the chance process that produces it and observing its long-run relative frequency, and predict the approximate relative frequency given the probability. *For example, when rolling a number cube 600 times, predict that a 3 or 6 would be rolled roughly 200 times, but probably not exactly 200 times.*

7. Develop a probability model and use it to find probabilities of events. Compare probabilities from a model to observed frequencies; if the agreement is not good, explain possible sources of the discrepancy.

   a. Develop a uniform probability model by assigning equal probability to all outcomes, and use the model to determine probabilities of events. *For example, if a student is selected at random from a class, find the probability that Jane will be selected and the probability that a girl will be selected.*

   b. Develop a probability model (which may not be uniform) by observing frequencies in data generated from a chance process. *For example, find the approximate probability that a spinning penny will land heads up or that a tossed paper cup will land open-end down. Do the outcomes for the spinning penny appear to be equally likely based on the observed frequencies?*

8. Find probabilities of compound events using organized lists, tables, tree diagrams, and simulation.

   a. Understand that, just as with simple events, the probability of a compound event is the fraction of outcomes in the sample space for which the compound event occurs.

   b. Represent sample spaces for compound events using methods such as organized lists, tables and tree diagrams. For an event described in everyday language (e.g., "rolling double sixes"), identify the outcomes in the sample space which compose the event.

   c. Design and use a simulation to generate frequencies for compound events. *For example, use random digits as a simulation tool to approximate the answer to the question: If 40% of donors have type A blood, what is the probability that it will take at least 4 donors to find one with type A blood?*

---

[1]Computations with rational numbers extend the rules for manipulating fractions to complex fractions.

COMMON CORE STATE STANDARDS

Standards for Mathematical Content

THE NUMBER SYSTEM

8.NS.A Know that there are numbers that are not rational, and approximate them by rational numbers.

1. Know that numbers that are not rational are called irrational. Understand informally that every number has a decimal expansion; for rational numbers show that the decimal expansion repeats eventually, and convert a decimal expansion which repeats eventually into a rational number.

2. Use rational approximations of irrational numbers to compare the size of irrational numbers, locate them approximately on a number line diagram, and estimate the value of expressions (e.g., π^2).

EXPRESSIONS & EQUATIONS

8.EE.A Work with radicals and integer exponents.

1. Know and apply the properties of integer exponents to generate equivalent numerical expressions.

2. Use square root and cube root symbols to represent solutions to equations of the form $x^2 = p$ and $x^3 = p$, where p is a positive rational number. Evaluate square roots of small perfect squares and cube roots of small perfect cubes. Know that $\sqrt{2}$ is irrational.

3. Use numbers expressed in the form of a single digit times an integer power of 10 to estimate very large or very small quantities, and to express how many times as much one is than the other.

4. Perform operations with numbers expressed in scientific notation, including problems where both decimal and scientific notation are used. Use scientific notation and choose units of appropriate size for measurements of very large or very small quantities (e.g., use millimeters per year for seafloor spreading). Interpret scientific notation that has been generated by technology.

Standards for Mathematical Content

8.EE.B Understand the connections between proportional relationships, lines, and linear equations.

5. Graph proportional relationships, interpreting the unit rate as the slope of the graph. Compare two different proportional relationships represented in different ways.

6. Use similar triangles to explain why the slope m is the same between any two distinct points on a non-vertical line in the coordinate plane; derive the equation $y = mx$ for a line through the origin and the equation $y = mx + b$ for a line intercepting the vertical axis at b.

8.EE.C Analyze and solve linear equations and pairs of simultaneous linear equations.

7. Solve linear equations in one variable.

   a. Give examples of linear equations in one variable with one solution, infinitely many solutions, or no solutions. Show which of these possibilities is the case by successively transforming the given equation into simpler forms, until an equivalent equation of the form $x = a$, $a = a$, or $a = b$ results (where a and b are different numbers).

   b. Solve linear equations with rational number coefficients, including equations whose solutions require expanding expressions using the distributive property and collecting like terms.

GEOMETRY

8.G.A Understand congruence and similarity using physical models, transparencies, or geometry software.

1. Verify experimentally the properties of rotations, reflections, and translations:

   a. Lines are taken to lines, and line segments to line segments of the same length.

   b. Angles are taken to angles of the same measure.

   c. Parallel lines are taken to parallel lines.

2. Understand that a two-dimensional figure is congruent to another if the second can be obtained from the first by a sequence of rotations, reflections, and translations; given two congruent figures, describe a sequence that exhibits the congruence between them.

3. Describe the effect of dilations, translations, rotations, and reflections on two-dimensional figures using coordinates.

4. Understand that a two-dimensional figure is similar to another if the second can be obtained from the first by a sequence of rotations, reflections, translations, and dilations; given two similar two-dimensional figures, describe a sequence that exhibits the similarity between them.

5. Use informal arguments to establish facts about the angle sum and exterior angle of triangles, about the angles created when parallel lines are cut by a transversal, and the angle-angle criterion for similarity of triangles.

Standards for Mathematical Content

8.G.B Understand and apply the Pythagorean Theorem.

6. Explain a proof of the Pythagorean Theorem and its converse.

7. Apply the Pythagorean Theorem to determine unknown side lengths in right triangles in real-world and mathematical problems in two and three dimensions.

8. Apply the Pythagorean Theorem to find the distance between two points in a coordinate system.

8.G.C Solve real-world and mathematical problems involving volume of cylinders, cones, and spheres.

9. Know the formulas for the volumes of cones, cylinders, and spheres and use them to solve real-world and mathematical problems.

Math Practices and Problem Solving Handbook

The **Math Practices and Problem Solving Handbook** is available online.

MP.1 Make sense of problems and persevere in solving them.

MP.2 Reason abstractly and quantitatively.

MP.3 Construct viable arguments and critique the reasoning of others.

MP.4 Model with mathematics.

MP.5 Use appropriate tools strategically.

MP.6 Attend to precision.

MP.7 Look for and make use of structure.

MP.8 Look for and express regularity in repeated reasoning.

Jordan helps his uncle set up for an event. Jordan's uncle drew a diagram to show Jordan how he wants the tables set up. Jordan needs to set up enough tables for 42 guests. How can Jordan figure out how many tables to set up?

Enough tables for 42 Guests

Can I see a pattern or structure in the problem or solution strategy? I can see that each end table has 5 seats and each middle table has 4 seats. Each additional table increases the number of seats by 4.

How can I use the pattern or structure I see to help me solve the problem? I can write an equation that includes a term for the two end tables and a term for the middle tables.

Do I notice any repeated calculations or steps? Each additional table adds 4 seats.

Are there general methods that I can use to solve the problem? I can multiply the number of middle tables by 4 and then add the seats on the two end tables.

Other questions to consider:
- Are there attributes in common that help me?
- Can I see the expression or equation as a single object? Or as a composition of several objects?

Other questions to consider:
- What can I generalize from one problem to another?
- Can I derive an equation from a series of data points?
- How reasonable are the results that I am getting?

Standards for Mathematical Practice

MP.1 Make sense of problems and persevere in solving them.

Mathematically proficient students:
- can explain the meaning of a problem
- look for entry points to begin solving a problem
- analyze givens, constraints, relationships, and goals
- make conjectures about the solution
- plan a solution pathway
- think of similar problems, and try simpler forms of the problem
- evaluate their progress toward a solution and change pathways if necessary
- can explain similarities and differences between different representations
- check their solutions to problems.

MP.2 Reason abstractly and quantitatively.

Mathematically proficient students:
- make sense of quantities and their relationships in problem situations:
  - They *decontextualize*—create a coherent representation of a problem situation using numbers, variables, and symbols; and
  - They *contextualize* – attend to the meaning of numbers, variables, and symbols in the problem situation
- know and use different properties of operations to solve problems.

MP.3 Construct viable arguments and critique the reasoning of others.

Mathematically proficient students:
- use definitions and problem solutions when constructing arguments
- make conjectures about the solutions to problems
- build a logical progression of statements to support their conjectures and justify their conclusions
- analyze situations and recognize and use counterexamples
- reason inductively about data, making plausible arguments that take into account the context from which the data arose
- listen or read the arguments of others, and decide whether they make sense
- respond to the arguments of others
- compare the effectiveness of two plausible arguments
- distinguish correct logic or reasoning from flawed, and—if there is a flaw in an argument—explain what it is
- ask useful questions to clarify or improve arguments of others.

MP.4 ▸ Model with mathematics.

Mathematically proficient students:
- can develop a representation—drawing, diagram, table, graph, expression, equation–to model a problem situation
- make assumptions and approximations to simplify a complicated situation
- identify important quantities in a practical situation and map their relationships using a range of tools
- analyze relationships mathematically to draw conclusions
- interpret mathematical results in the context of the situation and propose improvements to the model as needed.

MP.5 ▸ Use appropriate tools strategically.

Mathematically proficient students:
- consider appropriate tools when solving a mathematical problem
- make sound decisions about when each of these tools might be helpful
- identify relevant mathematical resources, and use them to pose or solve problems
- use tools and technology to explore and deepen their understanding of concepts.

MP.6 ▸ Attend to precision.

Mathematically proficient students:
- communicate precisely to others
- use clear definitions in discussions with others and in their own reasoning
- state the meaning of the symbols they use
- specify units of measure, and label axes to clarify their correspondence with quantities in a problem
- calculate accurately and efficiently
- express numerical answers with a degree of precision appropriate for the problem context.

MP.7 ▸ Look for and make use of structure.

Mathematically proficient students:
- look closely at a problem situation to identify a pattern or structure
- can step back from a solution pathway and shift perspective
- can see complex representations, such as some algebraic expressions, as single objects or as being composed of several objects.

MP.8 ▸ Look for and express regularity in repeated reasoning.

Mathematically proficient students:
- notice if calculations are repeated, and look both for general methods and for shortcuts
- maintain oversight of the process as they work to solve a problem, while also attending to the details
- continually evaluate the reasonableness of their intermediate results.

TOPIC 7

ANALYZE AND SOLVE LINEAR EQUATIONS

? Topic Essential Question

How can we analyze connections between linear equations, and use them to solve problems?

Topic Overview

7-1 Combine Like Terms to Solve Equations

7-2 Solve Equations with Variables on Both Sides

7-3 Solve Multistep Equations

7-4 Equations with No Solutions or Infinitely Many Solutions

3-Act Mathematical Modeling: Powering Down

7-5 Compare Proportional Relationships

7-6 Connect Proportional Relationships and Slope

7-7 Analyze Linear Equations: $y = mx$

7-8 Understand the y-Intercept of a Line

7-9 Analyze Linear Equations: $y = mx + b$

Topic Vocabulary

- slope of a line
- slope-intercept form
- y-intercept

Lesson Digital Resources

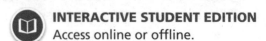

INTERACTIVE STUDENT EDITION
Access online or offline.

VISUAL LEARNING ANIMATION
Interact with visual learning animations.

ACTIVITY Use with *Solve & Discuss It, Explor* and *Explain It* activities, and to explore Exam

VIDEOS Watch clips to support *3-Act Mathematical Modeling Lessons* and *STEM P*

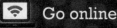 Go online

Powering Down

Powering Down

Do you know that feeling when you realize you left your charger at home?
Uh-oh. It's only a matter of time before your device runs out of power.
Your battery percentage is dropping, but you still have so much left to do.
Think about this during the 3-Act Mathematical Modeling lesson.

PRACTICE Practice what you've learned.

TUTORIALS Get help from *Virtual Nerd*, right when you need it.

MATH TOOLS Explore math with digital tools.

GAMES Play Math Games to help you learn.

KEY CONCEPT Review important lesson content.

GLOSSARY Read and listen to English/Spanish definitions.

ASSESSMENT Show what you've learned.

:ënVision® STEM Project

Did You Know?

Demography is the study of changes, such as the number of births, deaths, or net migration, occurring in the human population over time.

Births Worldwide in 2015 (estimated)

13,760,000 in more developed countries

132,213,000 in less developed countries

145,973,000

57,052,000

44,769,000 in less developed countries

12,283,000 in more developed countries

Deaths Worldwide in 2015 (estimated)

Emigration is the act of leaving one's country to settle elsewhere. In 2015, 244 million people, or 3.3% of the world's population, lived outside their country of origin.

Immigration is the act of entering and settling in a foreign country. The United States has the largest immigrant population in the world.

Emigration

Immigration

Your Task: Modeling Population Growth

Human population numbers are in constant flux. Suppose a country has a population of 20 million people at the start of one year and during the year there are 600,000 births, 350,000 deaths, 100,000 immigrants, and 5,000 emigrants. You and your classmates will determine the total population at the end of the year and then model expected change over a longer period.

Review What You Know!

Vocabulary

Choose the best term from the box to complete each definition.

inverse operations
like terms
proportion
variables

1. In an algebraic expression, _____ are terms that have the same variables raised to the same exponents.

2. Quantities that represent an unknown value are _____.

3. A _____ is a statement that two ratios are equal.

4. Operations that "undo" each other are _____.

Identify Like Terms

Complete the statements to identify the like terms in each expression.

5. $4x + 7y - 6z + 6y - 9x$

$4x$ and ☐ are like terms.

$7y$ and ☐ are like terms.

6. $\frac{1}{2}s - (6u - 9u) + \frac{1}{10}t + 2s$

$\frac{1}{2}s$ and ☐ are like terms.

$6u$ and ☐ are like terms.

Solve One-Step Equations

Simplify each equation.

7. $2x = 10$

8. $x + 3 = 12$

9. $x - 7 = 1$

Simplify Fractions

10. Explain how to simplify the fraction $\frac{12}{36}$.

Language Development

Fill in the Venn diagram to compare and contrast linear equations of the form $y = mx$ and $y = x + b$.

$y = mx$ $y = x + b$

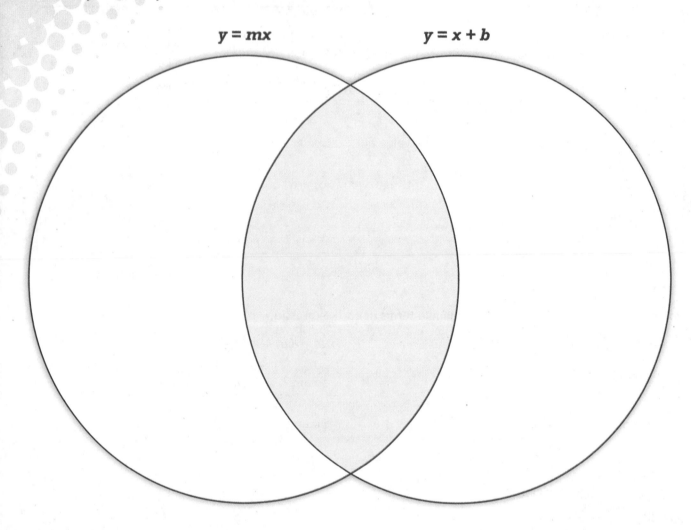

In the box below, draw graphs to represent each form of the linear equations.

PROJECT 7A

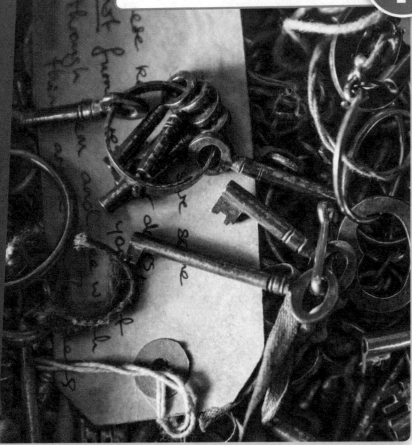

If you had to escape from a locked room, how would you start?

PROJECT: DESIGN AN ESCAPE-ROOM ADVENTURE

PROJECT 7B

What animal would you most like to play with for an hour? Why?

PROJECT: PLAN A PET CAFÉ

PROJECT 7C

If you wrote a play, what would it be about?

PROJECT: WRITE A PLAY

PROJECT 7D

How many tiny steps does it take to cross a slack line?

PROJECT: GRAPH A WALKING PATTERN

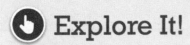 **Explore It!**

 ACTIVITY

A superintendent orders the new laptops shown below for two schools in her district. She receives a bill for $7,500.

I can...
solve equations that have like terms on one side.

Common Core Content Standards
8.EE.C.7b

Mathematical Practices
MP.1, MP.2, MP.4, MP.7

A. Draw a representation to show the relationship between the number of laptops and the total cost.

B. Use the representation to write an equation that can be used to determine the cost of one laptop.

Focus on math practices

Reasoning Why is it important to know that each laptop costs the same amount?

? Essential Question How do you solve equations that contain like terms?

  VISUAL LEARNING ASSESS

EXAMPLE 1 ◉ **Combine Like Terms to Solve Addition Equations**   Scan for Multimedia

Gianna has 36 yards of fabric to make sets of matching placemats and napkins. How many matching sets can she make?

Look for Relationships Why can you use the same variable to represent the number of placements and to represent the number of napkins?

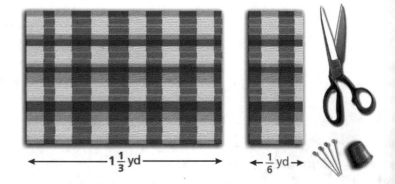

$1\frac{1}{3}$ yd — $\frac{1}{6}$ yd →

Draw a bar diagram to show how the quantities are related.

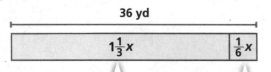

36 yd

$1\frac{1}{3}x$ $\frac{1}{6}x$

Yards of fabric needed to make x placemats

Yards of fabric needed to make x napkins

Use the diagram to write and solve an equation.

$$1\frac{1}{3}x + \frac{1}{6}x = 36$$
$$\frac{8}{6}x + \frac{1}{6}x = 36$$
$$\frac{9}{6}x = 36$$ ← Combine like terms.
$$\frac{6}{9} \cdot \left(\frac{9}{6}\right)x = \frac{6}{9} \cdot (36)$$
$$x = 24$$

Gianna has enough fabric to make 24 matching sets of placemats and napkins.

☑ **Try It!**

Selena spends $53.94 to buy a necklace and bracelet set for each of her friends. Each necklace costs $9.99, and each bracelet costs $7.99. How many necklace and bracelet sets, s, did Selena buy?

Selena buys necklace and bracelet sets for ☐ friends.

☐ s + ☐ s = 53.94

☐ s = 53.94

s = ☐

Convince Me! Suppose the equation is $9.99s + 7.99s + 4.6 = 53.94$. Can you combine the s terms and 4.6? Explain.

Selene bought a computer screen on sale for 35% off the original price. What was the price of the computer screen before the sale?

Draw a bar diagram to represent the situation.

> Let p be the price of the screen before the sale.

SALE PRICE
$130

p	
$130	$0.35p$

Use the bar diagram to write an equation. Then solve.

$$p - 0.35p = 130$$
$$0.65p = 130 \quad \longleftarrow \text{Combine like terms.}$$
$$\frac{0.65p}{0.65} = \frac{130}{0.65}$$
$$p = 200$$

> **Look for Relationships** How do the original price and the sale price relate?

The price of the computer screen before the sale was $200.

 **Try It!**

Nat's grocery bill was $150, which included a 5% club discount. What was Nat's bill before the discount? Write and solve an equation.

EXAMPLE 3 **Combine Like Terms with Negative Coefficients to Solve Equations**

Solve the equation $-3.5y - 6.2y = -87.3$.

$$-3.5y - 6.2y = -87.3$$
$$-9.7y = -87.3$$
$$\frac{-9.7y}{-9.7} = \frac{-87.3}{-9.7}$$
$$y = 9$$

> To combine like terms with negative coefficients, use the rules that you learned for adding and subtracting rational numbers.

Try It!

Solve for d.

a. $-\frac{1}{4}d - \frac{2}{5}d = 39$

b. $-9.76d - (-12.81d) = 8.54$

In an equation with variable terms on one side, you can combine like terms before using inverse operations and properties of equality to solve the equation.

$$0.8n + 0.6n = 42$$

$$1.4n = 42 \quad \text{Combine like terms.}$$

$$\frac{1.4n}{1.4} = \frac{42}{1.4}$$

$$n = 30$$

Do You Understand?

1. **Essential Question** How do you solve equations that contain like terms?

2. **Look for Relationships** How do you recognize when an equation has like terms?

3. **Make Sense and Persevere** In the equation $0.75s - \frac{5}{8}s = 44$, how do you combine the like terms?

Do You Know How?

4. Henry is following the recipe card to make a cake. He has 95 cups of flour. How many cakes can Henry make?

CAKE RECIPE
FLOUR NEEDED FOR EACH CAKE

$2\frac{2}{3}$ CUPS FOR THE BATTER

$\frac{1}{2}$ CUP FOR THE TOPPING

5. A city has a population of 350,000. The population has decreased by 30% in the past ten years. What was the population of the city ten years ago?

6. Solve the equation $-12.2z - 13.4z = -179.2$.

Practice & Problem Solving

Scan for
Multimedia

Leveled Practice In **7** and **8**, complete the steps to solve for *x*.

7. $\frac{4}{5}x - \frac{1}{4}x = 11$

$$\frac{\boxed{}}{20}x = 11$$

$$\frac{\boxed{}}{\boxed{}}\left(\frac{\boxed{}}{20}x\right) = \frac{\boxed{}}{\boxed{}}(11)$$

$$x = \boxed{}$$

8. $-0.65x + 0.45x = 5.4$

$$\boxed{}x = 5.4$$

$$x = \frac{5.4}{\boxed{}}$$

$$x = \boxed{}$$

In **9–12**, solve for *x*.

9. $\frac{4}{9}x + \frac{1}{5}x = 87$

10. $-3.8x - 5.9x = 223.1$

11. $x + 0.15x = 3.45$

12. $-\frac{3}{5}x - \frac{7}{10}x + \frac{1}{2}x = -56$

13. A contractor buys 8.2 square feet of sheet metal. She used 2.1 square feet so far and has $183 worth of sheet metal remaining. Write and solve an equation to find out how much sheet metal costs per square foot.

14. Make Sense and Persevere Clint prepares and sells trail mixes at his store. This week, he uses $\frac{3}{8}$ of his supply of raisins to make regular trail mix and $\frac{1}{4}$ of his supply to make spicy trail mix. If Clint uses 20 pounds of raisins this week, how many pounds of raisins did he have at the beginning of the week?

15. Make Sense and Persevere A submarine descends to $\frac{1}{6}$ of its maximum depth. Then it descends another $\frac{2}{3}$ of its maximum depth. If it is now at 650 feet below sea level, what is its maximum depth?

650 ft

16. Model with Math Write an equation that can be represented by the bar diagram, then solve.

```
          ┌───────── −3.78 ─────────┐
          ┌──────┬───────────────────┐
          │ −1.2y│      −4.2y         │
          └──────┴───────────────────┘
```

17. Higher Order Thinking Solve $\frac{2}{3}h - 156 = 3\frac{13}{24}$.

18. Model with Math Nathan bought one notebook and one binder for each of his college classes. The total cost of the notebooks and binders was $27.08. Draw a bar diagram to represent the situation. How many classes is Nathan taking?

Notebook $0.95   Binder $5.82

✓ Assessment Practice

19. Construct Arguments Your friend incorrectly says the solution to the equation $-\frac{3}{5}y - \frac{1}{7}y = 910$ is $y = 676$. What error did your friend make?

Ⓐ Added $-\frac{1}{7}$ to $-\frac{3}{5}$

Ⓑ Subtracted $\frac{1}{7}$ from $-\frac{3}{5}$

Ⓒ Multiplied 910 by $\frac{26}{35}$

Ⓓ Multiplied 910 by $\frac{35}{26}$

20. A 132-inch board is cut into two pieces. One piece is three times the length of the other. Find the length of the shorter piece.

PART A

Draw a bar diagram to represent the situation.

PART B

Write and solve an equation to find the length of the shorter piece.

Solve & Discuss It!  ACTIVITY

Jaxson and Bryon collected an equal amount of money during a car wash. They collected cash and checks as shown below. If each check is written for the same amount, *x*, what is the total amount of money collected by both boys? Explain.

I can...
solve equations with variables on both sides of the equal sign.

© Common Core Content Standards
8.EE.C.7b

Mathematical Practices
MP.2, MP.4

Reasoning How can you use an equation to show that expressions are equal?

Focus on math practices

Model with Math What expressions can you write to represent the amount of money collected by each boy? How can you use these expressions to write an equation?

? Essential Question How do you use inverse operations to solve equations with variables on both sides?

VISUAL LEARNING   ASSESS

EXAMPLE 1 **Solve Equations with Fractional Coefficients**

Scan for Multimedia

Jonah and Lizzy are making smoothies that have the same number of fluid ounces. Jonah uses 4 containers of yogurt to make his smoothie. Lizzy uses $2\frac{1}{2}$ containers of yogurt to make her smoothie. How many ounces of yogurt, x, are in each container?

Jonah's Smoothie

6 ounces of juice →

yogurt →

Lizzy's Smoothie

← 12 ounces of juice

← yogurt

ONE WAY Draw a bar diagram to represent the situation. Use the diagram to solve for x.

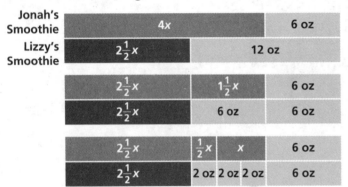

The bar for x is equal to the two bars of 2.

ANOTHER WAY Write an equation and use inverse operations to solve for x.

$$4x + 6 = 2\frac{1}{2}x + 12$$

$$4x - 2\frac{1}{2}x + 6 = 2\frac{1}{2}x - 2\frac{1}{2}x + 12$$

$$1\frac{1}{2}x + 6 = 12$$

$$1\frac{1}{2}x + 6 - 6 = 12 - 6$$

$$1\frac{1}{2}x = 6$$

$$\frac{2}{3} \cdot \frac{3}{2}x = \frac{2}{3} \cdot 6$$

$$x = 4$$

There are 4 ounces of yogurt in each container.

Subtract $2\frac{1}{2}x$ from both sides to get the variable terms on one side of the equation.

Subtract 6 from both sides to get all of the constant terms on one side of the equation.

✓ Try It!

Class A was given a sunflower with a height of 8 centimeters that grows at a rate of $3\frac{1}{2}$ centimeters per week. Class B was given a sunflower with a height of 10 centimeters that grows at a rate of $3\frac{1}{4}$ centimeters per week. After how many weeks are the sunflowers the same height?

Let w = the number of weeks.

☐ $w + 8 =$ ☐ $w + 10$

☐ $w + 8 = 10$

☐ $w =$ ☐

$w =$ ☐

Convince Me! How can you check your work to make sure the value of the variable makes the equation true? Explain.

The sunflowers are the same height after ☐ weeks.

EXAMPLE **2** Solve Equations with Decimal Coefficients

  ACTIVITY   ASSESS

Teresa earns a weekly salary of $925 and a 5% commission on her total sales. Ramón earns a weekly salary of $1,250 and a 3% commission on sales. What amount of sales, x, will result in them earning the same amount for the week?

0.05x	925
0.03x	1,250

$$0.05x + 925 = 0.03x + 1,250$$

$$0.05x - 0.03x + 925 = 0.03x - 0.03x + 1,250$$

$$0.02x + 925 = 1,250$$

$$0.02x + 925 - 925 = 1,250 - 925$$

$$0.02x = 325$$

$$0.02x \div 0.02 = 325 \div 0.02$$

$$x = 16,250$$

> Use inverse operations to combine like terms on both sides of the equals sign.

Teresa and Ramón each need $16,250 of sales in order to earn the same amount for the week.

EXAMPLE **3** **Solve Equations with Negative Coefficients**

Kelsey withdraws $25 per week from her bank account. Each week, Kris deposits $15 of his allowance and $20 earned from dog walking into his bank account. After how many weeks will they have the same amount of money in the bank?

Bank Statement

Name : Kelsey Jones

Saving Account Number
012 000 054 2036

DATE	DESCRIPTION	WITHDRAWAL	DEPOSIT	BALANCE
	PREVIOUS BALANCE			$550.00
WEEK 1	WITHDRAWAL	−$25.00		$525.00
WEEK 2	WITHDRAWAL	−$25.00		$500.00
WEEK 3	WITHDRAWAL	−$25.00		$475.00

Bank Statement

Name : Kris Jones

Saving Account Number
012 000 054 3169

DATE	DESCRIPTION	WITHDRAWAL	DEPOSIT	BALANCE
	PREVIOUS BALANCE			$10.00
WEEK 1	DEPOSIT		$35.00	$45.00
WEEK 2	DEPOSIT		$35.00	$80.00
WEEK 3	DEPOSIT		$35.00	$115.00

> Kelsey's amount after x weeks

> Kris's amount after x weeks

$$550 - 25x = 10 + 15x + 20x$$

$$550 - 25x = 10 + 35x$$

> Combine like terms.

$$550 - 25x + 25x = 10 + 35x + 25x$$

$$550 = 10 + 60x$$

$$550 - 10 = 10 - 10 + 60x$$

$$540 = 60x$$

$$540 \div 60 = 60x \div 60$$

$$9 = x$$

After 9 weeks, Kelsey and Kris will have the same amount of money in their bank accounts.

 Try It!

Solve the equation $96 - 4.5y - 3.2y = 5.6y + 42.80$.

When two expressions represent equal quantities, they can be set equal to each other. Then you can use inverse operations and properties of equality to combine like terms and solve for the unknown.

$$3x + 15 = 4x + 12$$
$$3x - 3x + 15 = 4x - 3x + 12$$
$$15 = x + 12$$
$$15 - 12 = x + 12 - 12$$
$$3 = x$$

Do You Understand?

1. **Essential Question** How do you use inverse operations to solve equations with variables on both sides?

2. **Reasoning** Why are inverse operations and properties of equality important when solving equations? Explain.

3. **Model with Math** Cynthia earns $680 in commissions and is paid $10.25 per hour. Javier earns $410 in commissions and is paid $12.50 per hour. What will you find if you solve for x in the equation $10.25x + 680 = 12.5x + 410$?

Do You Know How?

4. Maria and Liam work in a banquet hall. Maria earns a 20% commission on her food sales. Liam earns a weekly salary of $625 plus a 10% commission on his food sales. What amount of food sales will result in Maria and Liam earning the same amount for the week?

5. Selma's class is making care packages to give to victims of a natural disaster. Selma packs one box in 5 minutes and has already packed 12 boxes. Her friend Trudy packs one box in 7 minutes and has already packed 18 boxes. How many more minutes does each need to work in order to have packed the same number of boxes?

6. Solve the equation $-\frac{2}{5}x + 3 = \frac{2}{3}x + \frac{1}{3}$.

7. Solve the equation $-2.6b + 4 = 0.9b - 17$.

Practice & Problem Solving

Scan for
Multimedia

Leveled Practice In **8** and **9**, solve each equation.

8. $6 - 4x = 6x - 8x + 2$

$6 - 4x = \boxed{} + 2$

$6 = \boxed{} + 2$

$\boxed{} = \boxed{}$

$\boxed{} = x$

9. $\frac{5}{3}x + \frac{1}{3}x = 13\frac{1}{3} + \frac{8}{3}x$

$\boxed{}x = 13\frac{1}{3} + \frac{8}{3}x$

$\boxed{} = \frac{8}{3}x - \boxed{}x$

$-\frac{40}{3} = \boxed{}x$

$\boxed{} \cdot \left(-\frac{40}{3}\right) = \boxed{} \cdot \frac{2}{3}x$

$\boxed{} = x$

---

10. Two towns have accumulated different amounts of snow. In Town 1, the snow depth is increasing by $3\frac{1}{2}$ inches every hour. In Town 2, the snow depth is increasing by $2\frac{1}{4}$ inches every hour. In how many hours will the snowfalls of the towns be equal?

Town 2

Town 1

6 inches

5 inches

---

11. Solve the equation $5.3g + 9 = 2.3g + 15$.

a. Find the value of g.

b. Explain how you can check that the value you found for g is correct. If your check does not work, does that mean that your result is incorrect? Explain.

12. Solve the equation $6 - 6x = 5x - 9x - 2$.

---

13. Model with Math The population of one town in Florida is 43,425. About 125 people move out of the town each month. Each month, 200 people on average move into town. A nearby town has a population of 45,000. It has no one moving in and an average of 150 people moving away every month. In about how many months will the population of the towns be equal? Write an equation that represents this situation and solve.

14. Veronica is choosing between two health clubs. After how many months will the total cost for each health club be the same?

Yoga Studio A
Membership $22.00
Monthly Fee $24.50

Yoga Studio B
Membership $47.00
Monthly Fee $18.25

15. Higher Order Thinking The price of Stock A at 9 A.M. was $12.73. Since then, the price has been increasing at the rate of $0.06 per hour. At noon, the price of Stock B was $13.48. It begins to decrease at the rate of $0.14 per hour. If the stocks continue to increase and decrease at the same rates, in how many hours will the prices of the stocks be the same?

Market Watch

Stock A + 0.06
History: 9 AM
              ▲ $12.73

Stock B − 0.14
History: 12 PM
              ▼ $13.48

Buy

☑ Assessment Practice

16. In an academic contest, correct answers earn 12 points and incorrect answers lose 5 points. In the final round, School A starts with 165 points and gives the same number of correct and incorrect answers. School B starts with 65 points and gives no incorrect answers and the same number of correct answers as School A. The game ends with the two schools tied.

PART A

Which equation models the scoring in the final round and the outcome of the contest?

Ⓐ $12x + 5x − 165 = −12x + 65$

Ⓑ $12x − 5x + 165 = 12x + 65$

Ⓒ $5x − 12x + 165 = 12x + 65$

Ⓓ $12x − 5x − 165 = 12x + 65$

PART B

How many answers did each school get correct in the final round?

Solve & Discuss It!

ACTIVITY

A water tank fills through two pipes. Water flows through one pipe at a rate of 25,000 gallons an hour and through the other pipe at 45,000 gallons an hour. Water leaves the system at a rate of 60,000 gallons an hour.

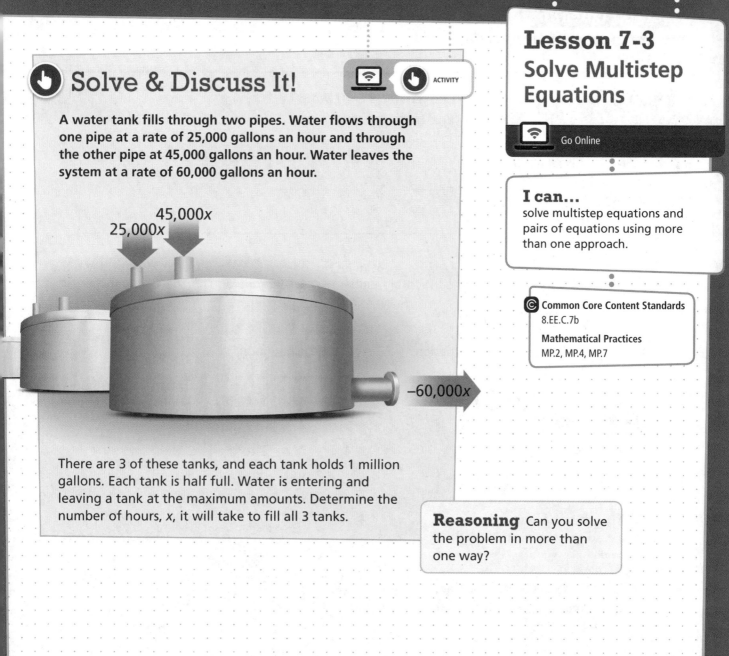

45,000x
25,000x

−60,000x

There are 3 of these tanks, and each tank holds 1 million gallons. Each tank is half full. Water is entering and leaving a tank at the maximum amounts. Determine the number of hours, x, it will take to fill all 3 tanks.

I can...
solve multistep equations and pairs of equations using more than one approach.

© **Common Core Content Standards**
8.EE.C.7b

Mathematical Practices
MP.2, MP.4, MP.7

Reasoning Can you solve the problem in more than one way?

Focus on math practices

Use Structure What are two different ways to simplify the expression $4(3x + 7x + 5)$ so that it equals $40x - 20$? Explain.

EXAMPLE 1 **Use the Distributive Property to Solve a Multistep Equation**

Scan for Multimedia

A math teacher recorded the distances he rode his bike last week. He challenged his class to find the number of miles he rode on Thursday. How far did he ride on Thursday?

Monday	Tuesday	Wednesday	Thursday	Friday	Saturday
←	$4x + 3$	→	x	$x + 7$	$x + 7$

The total number of miles he rode on Monday through Wednesday is the same as the total number of miles he rode on Thursday through Saturday.

Draw a bar diagram to represent the situation, and use it to write an equation

$4x + 3$		
x	$x + 7$	$x + 7$

$$4x + 3 = x + 2(x + 7)$$

The quantity $x + 7$ appears twice, so you can write $2(x + 7)$.

Model with Math How can you find the solution of the equation using the bar diagram?

Solve the equation.

$$4x + 3 = x + 2(x + 7)$$
$$4x + 3 = x + 2 \cdot x + 2 \cdot 7$$
$$4x + 3 = x + 2x + 14$$
$$4x + 3 = 3x + 14$$
$$4x - 3x + 3 = 3x - 3x + 14$$
$$x + 3 = 14$$
$$x + 3 - 3 = 14 - 3$$
$$x = 11$$

Distribute the 2 to the terms inside the parentheses.

Check your answer.

$$4(11) + 3 \stackrel{?}{=} 11 + 2(11 + 7) \longrightarrow 47 = 47 \checkmark$$

The teacher rode 11 miles on Thursday.

☑ Try It!

Solve the equation $3(x - 5) - 5x = -25 + 6x$.

$$3\boxed{} + 3 \cdot \boxed{} - 5x = -25 + 6x$$

$$\boxed{} - 5x = -25 + 6x$$

$$\boxed{}x - 15 = -25 + 6x$$

$$-15 = -25 + \boxed{}x$$

$$\boxed{} = \boxed{}x$$

$$x = \boxed{} \text{ or } \boxed{}$$

Convince Me! Can you add x to $-5x$ on the left side of the equation as the first step? Explain.

 EXAMPLE 2 **Distribute a Negative Coefficient to Solve Equations**

Solve each equation.

A. $-5(x - 2) = -25$

$-5 \cdot x + -5 \cdot -2 = -25$ — Distribute the -5 to the terms inside the parentheses.

$-5x + 10 = -25$

$-5x + 10 - 10 = -25 - 10$

$-5x = -35$

$\dfrac{-5x}{-5} = \dfrac{-35}{-5}$

$x = 7$

B. $3 - (x - 3) = 25$

$3 + -1 \cdot x + -1 \cdot -3 = 25$ — Distribute the -1 to the terms inside the parentheses.

$3 - x + 3 = 25$

$-x + 6 = 25$

$-x + 6 - 6 = 25 - 6$

$-x = 19$

$\dfrac{-x}{-1} = \dfrac{19}{-1}$

$x = -19$

EXAMPLE 3 **Use the Distributive Property on Both Sides of an Equation**

Solve the equation $\frac{1}{4}(x + 3) = \frac{1}{2}(x + 2)$.

$\frac{1}{4}(x + 3) = \frac{1}{2}(x + 2)$

$\frac{1}{4} \cdot x + \frac{1}{4} \cdot 3 = \frac{1}{2} \cdot x + \frac{1}{2} \cdot 2$ — Use the Distributive Property on both sides.

$\dfrac{x}{4} + \dfrac{3}{4} = \dfrac{x}{2} + 1$

$\dfrac{x}{4} - \dfrac{x}{2} + \dfrac{3}{4} = \dfrac{x}{2} - \dfrac{x}{2} + 1$

$-\dfrac{x}{4} + \dfrac{3}{4} = 1$

$-\dfrac{x}{4} + \dfrac{3}{4} - \dfrac{3}{4} = 1 - \dfrac{3}{4}$

$-\dfrac{x}{4} = \dfrac{1}{4}$

$-4 \cdot -\dfrac{x}{4} = -4 \cdot \dfrac{1}{4}$

$x = -1$

Use Structure Be sure to use the Distributive Property on both sides of the equation.

☑ **Try It!**

Solve the equation $-3(-7 - x) = \frac{1}{2}(x + 2)$.

When solving multistep equations, sometimes you distribute first, and then combine like terms.

$$7(5 + 2x) + x = 65$$

$$35 + 14x + x = 65$$

Sometimes you combine like terms first, and then distribute.

$$8(5x + 9x + 6) = 160$$

$$8(14x + 6) = 160$$

Do You Understand?

1. **Essential Question** How can you use the Distributive Property to solve multistep equations?

2. **Reasoning** What is the first step when solving the equation $3(3x - 5x) + 2 = -8$?

3. **Use Structure** How can you use the order of operations to explain why you cannot combine the the variable terms before using the Distributive Property when solving the equation $7(x + 5) - x = 42$?

Do You Know How?

4. Solve the equation $3x + 2 = x + 4(x + 2)$.

5. Solve the equation $-3(x - 1) + 7x = 27$.

6. Solve the equation $\frac{1}{3}(x + 6) = \frac{1}{2}(x - 3)$.

7. Solve the equation $0.25(x + 4) - 3 = 28$.

Practice & Problem Solving

Scan for
Multimedia

Leveled Practice In **8–10**, find the value of *x*.

8. Lori bought sunglasses and flip-flops at a half-off sale. If she spent a total of $21 on the two items, what was the original price of the sunglasses?

$\frac{1}{2}(\boxed{} + 24) = 21$

$\frac{1}{2}x + \boxed{} = 21$

$\frac{1}{2}x = \boxed{}$

$x = \boxed{}$

The original price of the sunglasses was $\boxed{}$.

9. Use the Distributive Property to solve the equation $28 - (3x + 4) = 2(x + 6) + x$.

$28 - \boxed{}x - \boxed{} = 2x + \boxed{} + x$

$24 - \boxed{}x = \boxed{}x + \boxed{}$

$24 - \boxed{}x = \boxed{}$

$\boxed{}x = \boxed{}$

$x = \boxed{}$

10. Use the Distributive Property to solve the equation $3(x - 6) + 6 = 5x - 6$.

$\boxed{}x - \boxed{} + 6 = 5x - \boxed{}$

$\boxed{}x - \boxed{} = 5x - \boxed{}$

$\boxed{}x - \boxed{} = \boxed{}$

$\boxed{}x = \boxed{}$

$x = \boxed{}$

11. What is the solution to $-2.5(4x - 4) = -6$?

12. What is the solution to the equation $3(x + 2) = 2(x + 5)$?

13. Solve the equation $\frac{1}{6}(x - 5) = \frac{1}{2}(x + 6)$.

14. Solve the equation $0.6(x + 2) = 0.55(2x + 3)$.

15. Solve the equation $4x - 2(x - 2) = -9 + 5x - 8$.

16. Use the Distributive Property to solve the equation $2(m + 2) = 22$. Describe what it means to distribute the 2 to each term inside the parentheses.

17. What is Peter's number?

If you subtract 12 from my number and multiply the difference by -3, the result is -54.

18. Higher Order Thinking Use the Distributive Property to solve the equation $\frac{4x}{5} - x = \frac{x}{10} - \frac{9}{2}$.

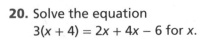

Assessment Practice

19. How many solutions does the equation $-2(x + 4) = -2(x + 4) - 6$ have?

20. Solve the equation $3(x + 4) = 2x + 4x - 6$ for x.

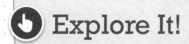 Explore It!   ACTIVITY

The Great Karlo called twins Jasmine and James onto the stage.

Jasmine, multiply your age by 3 and add 6. Then multiply this sum by 2. James, multiply your age by 2 and add 4. Then multiply this sum by 3. I predict you will both get the same number!

I can...
determine the number of solutions an equation has.

© **Common Core Content Standards**
8.EE.C.7a

Mathematical Practices
MP.1, MP.2, MP.3, MP.4, MP.7

A. Write expressions to represent Great Karlo's instructions to each twin.

B. Choose 4 whole numbers for the twins' age and test each expression. Make a table to show the numbers you tried and the results.

C. What do you notice about your results?

Focus on math practices

Make Sense and Persevere Choose three more values and use them to evaluate each expression. What do you notice? Do you think this is true for all values? Explain.

Essential Question Will a one-variable equation always have only one solution?

  VISUAL LEARNING ASSESS

EXAMPLE 1 · Solve an Equation with Infinitely Many Solutions

Scan for Multimedia

For what values of *x* will the rectangle and triangle have the same perimeter?

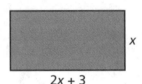

> **Model with Math** How can you use bar diagrams to represent the equal perimeters?

ONE WAY Draw bar diagrams to represent the perimeters. Then decompose and reorder the bar diagrams to solve for *x*.

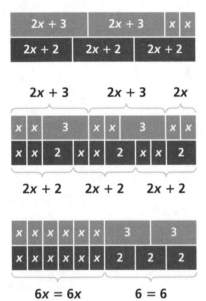

The expressions $6x = 6x$ and $6 = 6$ are true for any value of *x*. This equation has infinitely many solutions.

ANOTHER WAY Write an equation to represent the equal perimeters. Then use inverse operations and properties of equality to solve.

$$2x + 3 + 2x + 3 + x + x = 2x + 2 + 2x + 2 + 2x + 2$$

$$6x + 6 = 6x + 6$$

$$6x - 6x + 6 = 6x - 6x + 6$$

$$6 = 6$$

> For what values of *x* will $6x + 6 = 6x + 6$?

> Because $6 = 6$ is always true, all values of *x* will make the equation true.

This equation has infinitely many solutions.

☑ Try It!

How many solutions does the equation

$3x + 15 = 2x + 10 + x + 5$ have?

The equation has [ ] solutions.

Convince Me! If the value of *x* is negative, would the equation still be true? Explain.

$$3x + 15 = 2x + 10 + x + 5$$

$$3x + 15 = \boxed{}x + \boxed{}$$

$$3x - \boxed{} + 15 = 3x - \boxed{} + 15$$

$$\boxed{} = \boxed{}$$

EXAMPLE 2   ACTIVITY ASSESS

EXAMPLE 2 — Solve an Equation with One Solution

Anna and Lee played soccer for the same number of hours one week. How many hours did Lee play on Sunday?

ONE WAY Use bar diagrams to solve.

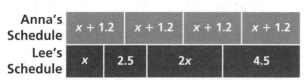

Anna's Schedule	$x + 1.2$	$x + 1.2$	$x + 1.2$	$x + 1.2$
Lee's Schedule	x	2.5	$2x$	4.5

x	x	x	x	4.8
x	x	x	2.2	4.8

$$x = 2.2$$

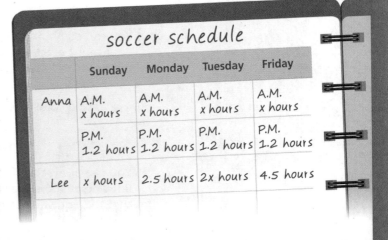

soccer schedule

		Sunday	Monday	Tuesday	Friday
Anna	A.M.	x hours	x hours	x hours	x hours
	P.M.	1.2 hours	1.2 hours	1.2 hours	1.2 hours
Lee		x hours	2.5 hours	2x hours	4.5 hours

ANOTHER WAY Write and solve an equation.

$$4(x + 1.2) = x + 2.5 + 2x + 4.5$$
$$4x + 4.8 = x + 2.5 + 2x + 4.5$$
$$4x + 4.8 = 3x + 7.0$$
$$4x - 3x + 4.8 = 3x - 3x + 7.0$$
$$x + 4.8 - 4.8 = 7.0 - 4.8$$
$$x = 2.2$$

> This equation has one solution, $x = 2.2$.

Lee played soccer for 2.2 hours on Sunday.

EXAMPLE 3 — Solve an Equation with No Solution

Gil makes 3 bracelets and Mika makes 2 bracelets. They both use the same number of string colors. How many colors should they use to make the same amount of money?

Write an equation to represent this situation. Then solve.

Let $x =$ the number of string colors.

$$3(2x + 5) = 2(3x + 3)$$
$$6x + 15 = 6x + 6$$
$$6x - 6x + 15 = 6x - 6x + 6$$
$$15 \neq 6$$

> Because 15 can never equal 6, this equation has no solution.

Because $15 \neq 6$, there is no number of string colors that results in Gil and Mika making the same amount of money.

Gil's Bracelets
$5 per bracelet plus $2 for each string color

Bracelets by Mika
$3 per bracelet and $3 for each string color

✓ Try It!

How many solutions does the equation $4x + 8 = 0.1x + 3 + 3.9x$ have? Explain.

EXAMPLE 4 Determine the Number of Solutions by Inspection

How can you determine the number of solutions each equation has without solving?

a. $x + 3 + 7 = 2x - 10 - x$

$x + 10 \neq x - 10$

> You can combine like terms mentally. The equivalent expressions $x + 10$ and $x - 10$ are not true for any values of x.

The equation $x + 3 + 7 = 2x - 10 - x$ has no solutions.

- -

b. $3(x + 4) = 3x + 12$

$3x + 12 = 3x + 12$

> You can apply the Distributive Property on the left side of the equation mentally. It is easy to see that the equivalent equation $3x + 12 = 3x + 12$ is true for all values of x.

The equation $3(x + 4) = 3x + 12$ has infinitely many solutions.

- -

c. $5x + 8 = 2x - 1$

$3x = -9$

> Notice that the coefficients of the variable terms are different. When like terms are collected and combined, the result will be a unique value of x.

The equation $5x + 8 = 2x - 1$ has one solution.

☑ Try It!

Determine the number of solutions each equation has without solving. Explain your reasoning.

a. $3x + 1.5 = 2.5x + 4.7$ **b.** $3(x + 2) = 3x - 6$ **c.** $9x - 4 = 5x - 4 + 4x$

A one-variable equation has **infinitely many solutions** when solving results in a true statement, such as $2 = 2$.	A one-variable equation has **one solution** when solving results in one value for the variable, such as $x = 2$.	A one-variable equation has **no solution** when solving results in an untrue statement, such as $2 = 3$.

Do You Understand?

1. **? Essential Question** Will a one-variable equation always have only one solution?

2. **Use Structure** Kaylee writes the equation $6x + 12 = 2(3x + 6)$. Can you find the number of solutions this equation has without solving for x? Explain.

3. **Construct Arguments** The height of an experimental plant after x days can be represented by the formula $3(4x + 2)$. The height of a second plant can be represented by the formula $6(2x + 2)$. Is it possible that the two plants will ever be the same height? Explain.

Do You Know How?

4. How many solutions does the equation $3(2.4x + 4) = 4.1x + 7 + 3.1x$ have? Explain.

5. How many solutions does the equation $7x + 3x - 8 = 2(5x - 4)$ have? Explain.

6. Todd and Agnes are making desserts. Todd buys peaches and a carton of vanilla yogurt. Agnes buys apples and a jar of honey. They bought the same number of pieces of fruit. Is there a situation in which they pay the same amount for their purchases? Explain.

Practice & Problem Solving

Leveled Practice In **7** and **8**, complete the equations to find the number of solutions.

7. Classify the equation $33x + 99 = 33x - 99$ as having one solution, no solution, or infinitely many solutions.

$$33x + 99 = 33x - 99$$

$33x - \boxed{} + 99 = 33x - \boxed{} - 99$

$99 \boxed{} - 99$

Since 99 is $\boxed{}$ equal to -99, the equation has $\boxed{}$ solution(s).

8. Solve $4(4x + 3) = 19x + 9 - 3x + 3$. Does the equation have one solution, no solution, or infinitely many solutions?

$$4(4x + 3) = 19x + 9 - 3x + 3$$

$4 \cdot \boxed{} + 4 \cdot \boxed{} = 19x + 9 - 3x + 3$

$16x + 12 = \boxed{} + \boxed{}$

$16x - \boxed{} + 12 = 16x - \boxed{} + 12$

$12 \boxed{} 12$

Since 12 is $\boxed{}$ equal to 12, the equation has $\boxed{}$ solution(s).

9. Generalize What does it mean if an equation is equivalent to $0 = 0$? Explain.

10. Solve $4x + x + 4 = 8x - 3x + 4$. Does the equation have one solution, no solution, or infinitely many solutions? If one solution, write the solution. Explain.

11. Reasoning Two rival dry cleaners both advertise their prices. Let x equal the number of items dry cleaned. Store A's prices are represented by the expression $15x - 2$. Store B's prices are represented by the expression $3(5x + 7)$. When do the two stores charge the same rate? Explain.

12. Reasoning How is solving an equation with no solution similar to solving an equation that has an infinite number of solutions?

13. Solve $0.9x + 5.1x - 7 = 2(2.5x - 3)$. How many solutions does the equation have?

14. Critique Reasoning Your friend solved the equation $4x + 12x - 6 = 4(4x + 7)$ and got $x = 34$.

What error did your friend make? What is the correct solution?

$$4x + 12x - 6 = 4 (4x + 7)$$
$$16x - 6 = 16x + 28$$
$$16x - 16x - 6 = 16x - 16x + 28$$
$$x - 6 = 28$$
$$x - 6 + 6 = 28 + 6$$
$$x = 34$$

15. Solve $49x + 9 = 49x + 83$.

a. Does the equation have one solution, no solution, or infinitely many solutions?

b. Write two equations in one variable that have the same number of solutions as this equation.

16. Classify the equation $6(x + 2) = 5(x + 7)$ as having one solution, no solution, or infinitely many solutions.

17. Solve $6x + 14x + 5 = 5(4x + 1)$. Write a word problem that this equation, or any of its equivalent forms, represents.

18. Classify the equation $170x - 1,000 = 30(5x - 30)$ as having one solution, no solution, or infinitely many solutions.

19. Higher Order Thinking Write one equation that has one solution, one equation that has no solution, and one equation that has infinitely many solutions.

20. Solve $4(4x - 2) + 1 = 16x - 7$.

21. Solve $6x + 26x - 10 = 8(4x + 10)$.

22. Classify the equation $64x - 16 = 16(4x - 1)$ as having one solution, no solution, or infinitely many solutions.

23. Classify the equation $5(2x + 3) = 3(3x + 12)$ as having one solution, no solution, or infinitely many solutions.

✓ Assessment Practice

24. Which of the following best describes the solution to the equation $4(2x + 3) = 16x + 12 - 8x$?

- Ⓐ The equation has one solution.
- Ⓑ The equation has infinitely many solutions.
- Ⓒ The equation has no solution.
- Ⓓ The equation has two solutions.

25. Which of the following statements are true about the equation $10x + 45x - 13 = 11(5x + 6)$?

Select all that apply.

- ☐ The operations that can be used to solve the equation are addition and multiplication.
- ☐ The operations that can be used to solve the equation are multiplication and division.
- ☐ The equation has infinitely many solutions.
- ☐ The equation has a solution of $x = 53$.
- ☐ The equation has no solution.

1. Vocabulary How can you determine the number of solutions for an equation? *Lesson 7-4*

2. Solve the equation $-\frac{2}{3}d - \frac{1}{4}d = -22$ for d. *Lesson 7-1*

3. Edy has $450 in her savings account. She deposits $40 each month. Juan has $975 in his checking account. He writes a check for $45.45 each month for his cell phone bill. He also writes a check for $19.55 each month for his water bill. After how many months will Edy and Juan have the same amount of money in their accounts? *Lesson 7-2*

4. Which equation has infinitely many solutions? *Lesson 7-4*

Ⓐ $\frac{3}{4}x + x - 5 = 10 + 2x$

Ⓑ $3x - 2.7 = 2x + 2.7 + x$

Ⓒ $9x + 4.5 - 2x = 2.3 + 7x + 2.2$

Ⓓ $\frac{1}{5}x - 7 = \frac{3}{4} + 2x - 25\frac{3}{4}$

5. Solve the equation $-4(x - 1) + 6x = 2(17 - x)$ for x. *Lesson 7-3*

6. Hakeem subtracted 8 from a number, then multiplied the difference by $\frac{4}{5}$. The result was 20. Write and solve an equation to find the number, x. *Lesson 7-3*

How well did you do on the mid-topic checkpoint? Fill in the stars.

MID-TOPIC PERFORMANCE TASK

TOPIC 7

Hector is competing in a 42-mile bicycle race. He has already completed 18 miles of the race and is traveling at a constant speed of 12 miles per hour when Wanda starts the race. Wanda is traveling at a constant speed of 16 miles per hour.

PART A

Write and solve an equation to find when Wanda will catch up to Hector.

PART B

Will Wanda catch up to Hector before the race is complete? Explain.

PART C

At what constant speed could Wanda travel to catch up with Hector at the finish line? Explain.

3-ACT MATH

Powering Down

3-Act Mathematical Modeling: Powering Down

 Go Online

© **Common Core Content Standards**
8.EE.C.7a, 8.EE.C.7b

Mathematical Practices
MP.4, MP.2, MP.3, MP.7

ACT 1

1. After watching the video, what is the first question that comes to mind?

2. Write the Main Question you will answer.

3. Construct Arguments Predict an answer to this Main Question. Explain your prediction.

4. On the number line below, write a time that is too early to be the answer. Write a time that is too late.

Too early   **Too late**

←————————————————————————————————|——→

5. Plot your prediction on the same number line.

6. What information in this situation would be helpful to know? How would you use that information?

7. Use Appropriate Tools What tools can you use to solve the problem? Explain how you would use them strategically.

8. Model with Math Represent the situation using mathematics. Use your representation to answer the Main Question.

9. What is your answer to the Main Question? Is it earlier or later than your prediction? Explain why.

10. Write the answer you saw in the video.

11. Reasoning Does your answer match the answer in the video? If not, what are some reasons that would explain the difference?

12. Make Sense and Persevere Would you change your model now that you know the answer? Explain.

Reflect

13. Model with Math Explain how you used a mathematical model to represent the situation. How did the model help you answer the Main Question?

14. Look for Relationships What pattern did you notice in the situation? How did you use that pattern?

SEQUEL

15. Be Precise After 35 minutes, he started charging his phone. 21 minutes later, the battery is at 23%. Explain how you would determine when the phone will be charged to 100%.

Solve & Discuss It!

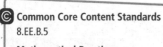 ACTIVITY

Mei Li is going apple picking. She is choosing between two places. The cost of a crate of apples at each place is shown.

Where should Mei Li go to pick her apples? Explain.

☺ Pick your own.
20 lb $7.25
Annie's Apple Orchard

🍎 Pick your own.
12 lb $5.00
Franklin's Fruit Orchard

I can...
compare proportional relationships represented in different ways.

© **Common Core Content Standards**
8.EE.B.5

Mathematical Practices
MP.1, MP.3, MP.4, MP.8

Construct Arguments
What information provided can be used to support your answer?

Focus on math practices
Model with Math Which representation did you use to compare prices? Explain why.

VISUAL LEARNING ASSESS

EXAMPLE 1 Compare Proportional Relationships Represented by Tables and Graphs

Scan for Multimedia

Meera is researching cruising speeds of different planes. Which airplane has a greater cruising speed?

Cessna 310

Time (min)	5	15	30	45	60
Distance (km)	40	120	240	360	480

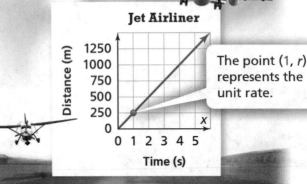

Jet Airliner

The point (1, *r*) represents the unit rate.

STEP 1 Find the cruising speed of the Cessna.

Distance (km)	40	120	240	360	480
Time (min)	5	15	30	45	60
$\frac{\text{Distance (km)}}{\text{Time (min)}}$	$\frac{40}{5}=8$	$\frac{120}{15}=8$	$\frac{240}{30}=8$	$\frac{360}{45}=8$	$\frac{480}{60}=8$

Find the constant of proportionality.

The Cessna has a cruising speed of 8 kilometers per minute.

STEP 2 Find the cruising speed of the Boeing 747.

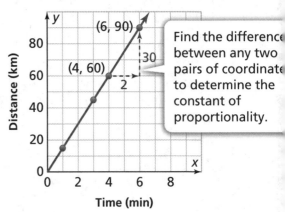

Find the difference between any two pairs of coordinate to determine the constant of proportionality.

The Boeing 747 has a cruising speed of 15 kilometers per minute. The Boeing 747 has a greater cruising speed than the Cessna.

✓ Try It!

The graph represents the rate at which Marlo makes origami birds for a craft fair. The equation $y = 2.5x$ represents the number of birds, y, Josh makes in x minutes. Who makes birds at a faster rate?

Convince Me! If you were to graph the data for Josh and Marlo on the same coordinate plane, how would the two lines compare?

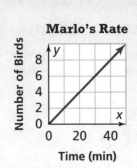

Marlo's Rate

EXAMPLE 2 — Compare Proportional Relationships Represented by Graphs and Equations

 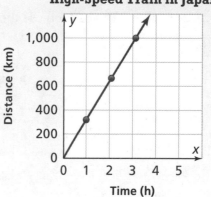

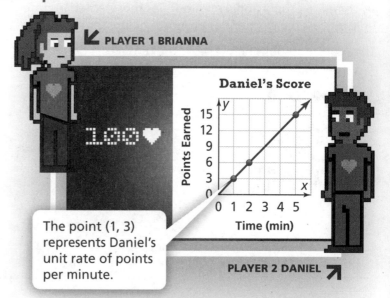

PLAYER 1 BRIANNA

The graph on the right represents the rate at which Daniel earns points in his video game. The rate at which Brianna earns points in her video game is represented by the equation $y = 2x$, where y is the number of points and x is the time in minutes. At these rates, who will earn 100 points first?

Daniel's Score

Find Brianna's rate.

$y = 2x$

$y = 2(1)$ ← Substitute 1 for x to find the unit rate.

$y = 2$

Brianna earns 2 points per minute.

The point (1, 3) represents Daniel's unit rate of points per minute.

PLAYER 2 DANIEL

Daniel earns 3 points per minute.
Daniel will earn 100 points first.

EXAMPLE 3 — Compare Proportional Relationships Represented by Graphs and Verbal Descriptions

The graph represents the cost per ounce of a granola cereal. A 15-ounce box of a raisin cereal costs $3.90. Which cereal costs more per ounce?

Use an equivalent ratio to find the cost per ounce of the raisin cereal.

$$\frac{\$3.90}{15 \text{ oz}} = \frac{\$0.26}{1 \text{ oz}}$$

The raisin cereal costs $0.26 per ounce.
The granola cereal costs $0.25 per ounce.

The raisin cereal costs more per ounce.

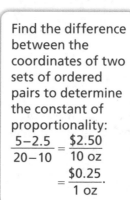

Find the difference between the coordinates of two sets of ordered pairs to determine the constant of proportionality:

$$\frac{5-2.5}{20-10} = \frac{\$2.50}{10 \text{ oz}}$$

$$= \frac{\$0.25}{1 \text{ oz}}.$$

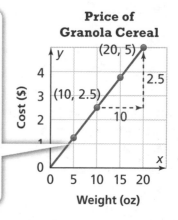

Price of Granola Cereal

(20, 5)

2.5

(10, 2.5)

10

Try It!

The distance covered by the fastest high-speed train in Japan traveling at maximum speed is represented on the graph. The fastest high-speed train in the United States traveling at maximum speed covers 600 kilometers in $2\frac{1}{2}$ hours. Which train has a greater maximum speed? Explain.

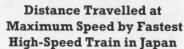

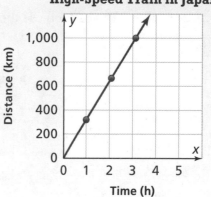

Distance Travelled at Maximum Speed by Fastest High-Speed Train in Japan

7-5 Compare Proportional Relationships   437

To compare proportional relationships represented in different ways, find the unit rate, or the constant of proportionality, for each representation.

The representations below show the rental cost per hour for canoes at three different shops.

Table

Rental Cost ($)	18	27	36	54
Time (hr)	$\frac{1}{2}$	$\frac{3}{4}$	1	$1\frac{1}{2}$
$\frac{\text{Rental Cost ($)}}{\text{Time (hr)}}$	$\frac{18}{0.5} = 36$	$\frac{27}{0.75} = 36$	$\frac{36}{1}$	$\frac{54}{1.5} = 36$

Graph

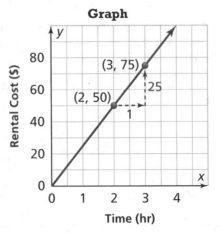

Equation

$c = 28t$

To find the unit cost, determine the value of c when $t = 1$.

Do You Understand?

1. **? Essential Question** How can you compare proportional relationships represented in different ways?

2. How can you find the unit rate or constant of proportionality for a relationship represented in a graph?

3. **Generalize** Why can you use the constant of proportionality with any representation?

Do You Know How?

4. Amanda babysits and Petra does yard work on weekends. The graph relating Amanda's earnings to the number of hours she babysits passes through the points (0, 0) and (4, 24). The table below relates Petra's earnings to the number of hours she does yard work.

Petra's Earnings

Hours	3	6	9
Earnings ($)	15	30	45

Who earns more per hour?

5. Milo pays $3 per pound for dog food at Pat's Pet Palace. The graph below represents the cost per pound of food at Mark's Mutt Market. At which store will Milo pay a lower price per pound for dog food?

Dog Food at Mark's Mutt Market

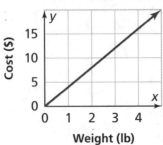

Practice & Problem Solving

Scan for
Multimedia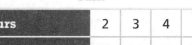

Leveled Practice For 6 and 7, complete the information to compare the rates.

6. Sam and Bobby want to know who cycled faster. The table shows the total miles Sam traveled over time. The graph shows the same relationship for Bobby. Who cycled faster?

Sam

Hours	2	3	4	5
Distance (miles)	20	30	40	50

Find the unit rate (constant of proportionality) for Sam.

$\dfrac{\text{distance}}{\text{time}} = \dfrac{20}{2} = \boxed{} \dfrac{\text{miles}}{\text{hour}}$

Find the unit rate (constant of proportionality) for Bobby.

Use ($\boxed{}$, $\boxed{}$) and ($\boxed{}$, $\boxed{}$) to find the constant of proportionality.

The unit rate (constant of proportionality) is $\boxed{}$ $\dfrac{\text{miles}}{\text{hour}}$.

So $\boxed{}$ cycled faster.

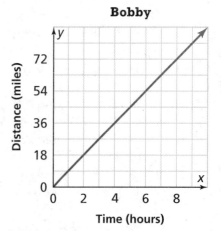

7. **Model with Math** The equation $y = 15x$ can be used to determine the amount of money, y, Pauli's Pizzeria makes by selling x pizzas. The graph shows the money Leo's Pizzeria takes in for different numbers of pizzas sold. Which pizzeria makes more money per pizza?

Pauli's Pizzeria takes in $\boxed{}$ per pizza.

Leo's Pizzeria takes in $\boxed{}$ per pizza.

$\boxed{}$'s Pizzeria takes in more money per pizza.

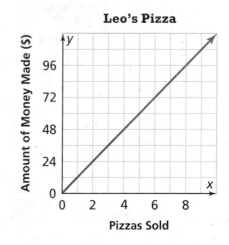

8. The graph shows the amount of savings over time in Eliana's account. Lana, meanwhile, puts $50 each week into her savings account. If they both begin with $0, who is saving at the greater rate?

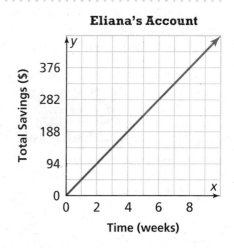

9. Make Sense and Persevere Beth, Manuel, and Petra are collecting sponsors for a walk-a-thon. The equation $y = 20x$ represents the amount of money Beth raises for walking x miles. The table shows the relationship between the number of miles Manuel walks and the amount of money he will raise. Petra will earn $15 for each mile that she walks.

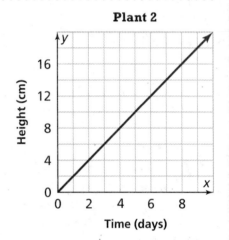

WALK-A-THON | **RUN OR WALK**
SPONSOR SHEET

NAME **Manuel**

MILES WALKED	MONEY RAISED
3	$45
5	$75
7	$105
9	$135

a. In order to compare the proportional relationships, what quantities should you use to find the unit rate?

b. Compare the amount of money raised per mile by the three people.

10. Higher Order Thinking Winston compares the heights of two plants to see which plant grows more per day. The table shows the height of Plant 1, in centimeters, over 5 days. The graph shows the height of Plant 2, in centimeters, over 10 days. Winston says that since Plant 1 grows 6 cm per day and Plant 2 grows 4 cm per day, Plant 1 grows more per day.

Plant 2

Plant 1

Days	2	3	4	5
Height (cm)	6	9	12	15

a. Do you agree with Winston? Explain your response.

b. What error might Winston have made?

✓ Assessment Practice

11. Ashton, Alexa, and Clara want to know who types the fastest. The equation $y = 39x$ models the rate at which Ashton can type, where y is the number of words typed and x is the time in minutes. The table shows the relationship between words typed and minutes for Alexa. The graph shows the same relationship for Clara. Who types the fastest?

Clara's Typing Rate

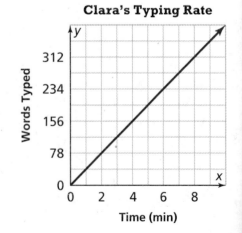

Alexa's Typing Rate

Minutes	2	3	4	5
Words Typed	78	117	156	195

Lesson 7-6
Connect Proportional Relationships and Slope

 Go Online

In the fall, Rashida earns money as a soccer referee for her town's under-10 soccer league. So far, she has worked 5 games and has been paid $98.50. She will work a total of 14 games this fall. How can Rashida determine how much she will earn refereeing soccer games this fall?

Look for Relationships
How is the number of games Rashida works related to her earnings?

I can...
understand the slope of a line.

Common Core Content Standards
8.EE.B.6

Mathematical Practices
MP.2, MP.3, MP.7

Focus on math practices

Reasoning How would Rashida's earnings change if she were paid by the hour instead of by the game?

Scan for
Multimedia

EXAMPLE 1   👁 Understand Slope

Maya and her father are building a tree house. The roof will have a 9:12 pitch; that is, for every 12 inches of horizontal distance, the roof rises 9 inches. How can Maya determine the height of the roof at its peak?

STEP 1 Make a table of values that show the 9 : 12 pitch.

Find the constant of proportionality.

Vertical distance	9	18	27	45
Horizontal distance	12	24	36	60
$\dfrac{\text{vertical distance}}{\text{horizontal distance}}$	$\dfrac{9}{12} = \dfrac{3}{4}$	$\dfrac{18}{24} = \dfrac{3}{4}$	$\dfrac{27}{36} = \dfrac{3}{4}$	$\dfrac{45}{60} = \dfrac{3}{4}$

STEP 2 Graph the ordered pairs from the table and draw a line to connect them. The line shows the steepness of the roof. The steepness is also called the slope of the line.

The **slope** of the line is the ratio $\frac{\text{rise}}{\text{run}}$.

Maya can use a graph to find that the roof is 54 inches in height at its peak.

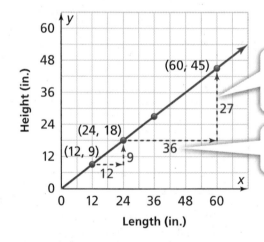

The change in vertical distance is the rise.

The change in horizontal distance is the run.

✔ Try It!

Jack graphs how far he plans to bike over a 3-day charity ride. Find the slope of the line.

slope: $\dfrac{\text{rise}}{\text{run}} = \dfrac{\boxed{}}{\boxed{}}$. The slope of the line is $\boxed{}$.

Jack's Charity Ride

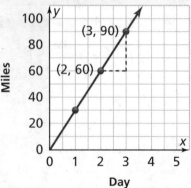

Convince Me! How do the unit rate and constant of proportionality relate to the slope of a line?

EXAMPLE **2** 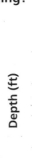 Find the Slope from Two Points

  ACTIVITY ✓ ASSESS

The graph represents the depth of a diving submarine over time. At what speed is the submarine descending?

Find the slope of the line.

slope: $\frac{\text{rise}}{\text{run}} = \frac{y_2 - y_1}{x_2 - x_1}$

> Find the rise and run using the *x*- and *y*-coordinates from two points on the line.

$= \frac{-800 - (-400)}{10 - 5}$

$= \frac{-400}{5}$

$= -80$

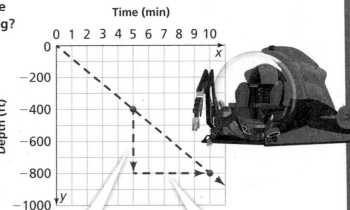

The slope of the line is −80. The submarine is decending at a rate of 80 feet per minute.

> The rise is the change in the *y*-coordinates or $y_2 - y_1$.

> The run is the change in the *x*-coordinates or $x_2 - x_1$.

> **Reasoning** How do the *x*- and *y*-coordinates relate when the slope is negative?

EXAMPLE **3** Interpret Slope

The graph shows the distance a car travels over time. Find the slope of the line. What does it mean in the problem situation?

slope: $\frac{\text{rise}}{\text{run}} = \frac{y_2 - y_1}{x_2 - x_1}$

$= \frac{220 - 110}{4 - 2}$

$= 55$

The slope of the line is 55.

The car travels 55 miles per hour.

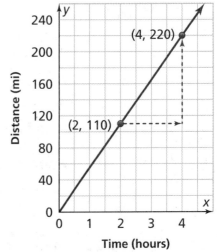

Distance Travelled

(4, 220)

(2, 110)

✓ **Try It!**

The graph shows the proportions of red and blue food coloring that Taylor mixes to make purple frosting. What is the slope of the line? Tell what it means in the problem situation.

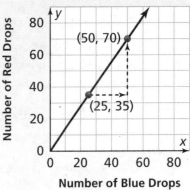

Purple Food Coloring

(50, 70)

(25, 35)

Slope is the measure of the steepness of a line. It represents the ratio of the rise (that is, the vertical distance) to the run (the horizontal distance) between two points on the line. In proportional relationships, slope is the same as the unit rate and constant of proportionality.

$$\text{slope} = \frac{\text{rise}}{\text{run}}$$

$$= \frac{\text{change in } y\text{-coordinates}}{\text{change in } x\text{-coordinates}}$$

$$= \frac{y_2 - y_1}{x_2 - x_1}$$

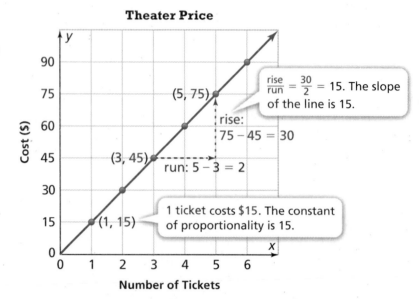

Theater Price

$\frac{\text{rise}}{\text{run}} = \frac{30}{2} = 15$. The slope of the line is 15.

rise: $75 - 45 = 30$

run: $5 - 3 = 2$

1 ticket costs $15. The constant of proportionality is 15.

Cost ($)

Number of Tickets

Do You Understand?

1. **Essential Question** What is slope?

2. **Reasoning** How is the slope related to a unit rate?

3. **Look for Relationships** Why is the slope between any two points on a straight line always the same?

Do You Know How?

4. What is the slope of the line?

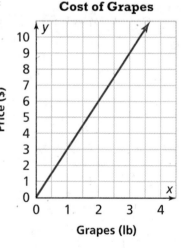

Cost of Grapes

Price ($)

Grapes (lb)

5. The scale of a model airplane is shown in the graph.

a. Find the slope of the line using $\frac{y_2 - y_1}{x_2 - x_1}$.

b. What does the slope mean in the problem situation?

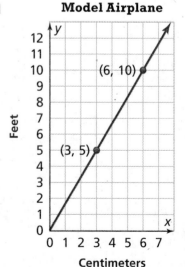

Model Airplane

Feet

Centimeters

Name: _____

Practice & Problem Solving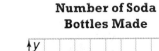

Leveled Practice In 6 and 7, find the slope of each line.

6. The graph shows the number of soda bottles a machine can make over time. Use the two points shown to find the number of soda bottles the machine can make per minute.

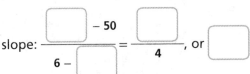

slope: $\dfrac{\boxed{} - 50}{6 - \boxed{}} = \dfrac{\boxed{}}{4}$, or $\boxed{}$

The machine can make $\boxed{}$ soda bottles each minute.

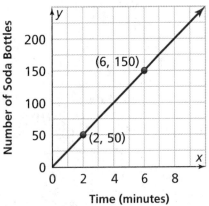

Number of Soda Bottles Made

(6, 150)

(2, 50)

Number of Soda Bottles

Time (minutes)

7. Find the slope of the line.

slope = $\dfrac{\text{rise}}{\text{run}}$

$= \dfrac{\boxed{}}{\boxed{}}$, or $\boxed{}$

The slope is $\boxed{}$.

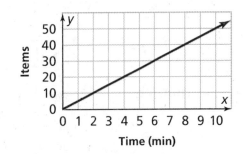

Items

Time (min)

8. **Reasoning** How can you find the slope of the line that passes through the points (0, 0) and (2, 4)? Explain.

9. The points (2.1, −4.2) and (2.5, −5) form a proportional relationship. What is the slope of the line that passes through these two points?

10. Find the slope of the line.

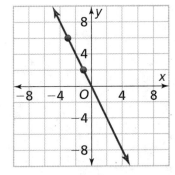

11. The graph shows the number of Calories Natalia burned while running.

a. What is the slope of the line?

b. What does the slope tell you?

Calories Burned

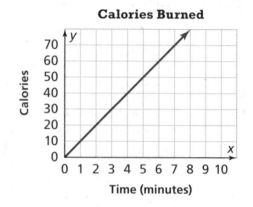

12. Critique Reasoning A question on a test provides this graph and asks students to find the speed at which the car travels. Anna incorrectly says that the speed of the car is $\frac{1}{64}$ mile per hour.

a. What is the speed of the car?

b. What error might Anna have made?

Speed of a Car

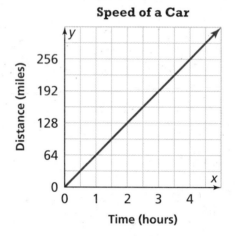

13. Higher Order Thinking You use a garden hose to fill a wading pool. If the water level rises 11 centimeters every 5 minutes and you record the data point of (10, y), what is the value of y? Use slope to justify your answer.

Rises 11 cm every 5 min

14. The points (15, 21) and (25, 35) form a proportional relationship.

a. Find the slope of the line that passes through these points.

b. Which graph represents this relationship?

Ⓐ
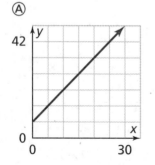

Ⓑ
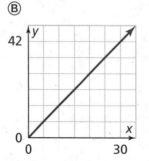

Ⓒ
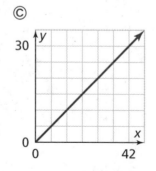

Ⓓ
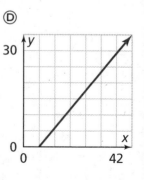

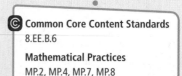
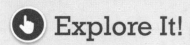
Explore It!

ACTIVITY

A group of college students developed a solar-powered car and entered it in a race. The car travels at a constant speed of 100 meters per 4 seconds.

I can...
write equations to describe linear relationships.

© **Common Core Content Standards**
8.EE.B.6

Mathematical Practices
MP.2, MP.4, MP.7, MP.8

A. What representation can show the distance the car will travel over time?

B. What expression can show the distance the car will travel over time?

C. Compare the representation and the expression. Which shows the distance traveled over time more clearly? Explain.

Focus on math practices

Be Precise How would the representation or expression change if the speed was converted to miles per minute?

447

VISUAL LEARNING

ASSESS

EXAMPLE 1 **Relate Constant of Proportionality to Slope**

The students in Meg's class are building a fence around the class garden. How can they use the pricing for the different lengths of fencing to determine the cost for 50 feet of fencing?

Look for Relationships What is the relationship between the length of fencing and the cost?

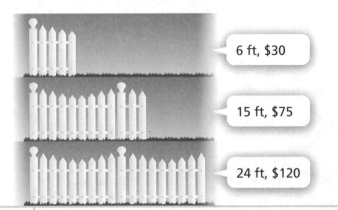

6 ft, $30

15 ft, $75

24 ft, $120

STEP 1 Write the length and cost as an ordered pair. Graph the ordered pairs and find the rise and run using any two ordered pairs.

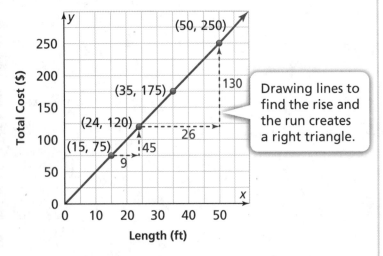

(50, 250)

(35, 175)

130

(24, 120)

26

(15, 75)

45

9

Total Cost ($)

Length (ft)

Drawing lines to find the rise and the run creates a right triangle.

STEP 2 Analyze the two right triangles. Notice that the ratios of the $\frac{rise}{run}$ are equivalent, so the slope of the line is constant.

For any ordered pair (x, y) on the line the slope, m, is constant. That is, $\frac{y}{x} = m$ or $y = mx$.

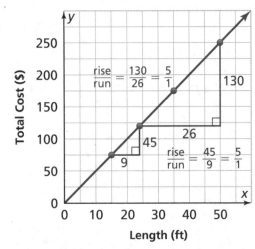

$\frac{rise}{run} = \frac{130}{26} = \frac{5}{1}$

130

26

$\frac{rise}{run} = \frac{45}{9} = \frac{5}{1}$

45

9

Total Cost ($)

Length (ft)

Meg and her classmates can use the equation $y = 5x$ to find the cost.

$5(50) = 250$, so 50 feet of fencing costs $250.

✓ **Try It!**

Write an equation to describe the relationship shown in the graph.

$\frac{rise}{run}: \frac{80 - \boxed{}}{\boxed{} - 3} = \frac{\boxed{}}{\boxed{}}$. The equation of the line is $y = \boxed{}x$.

Distance per Gallon

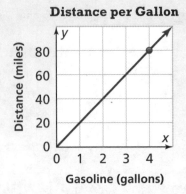

Distance (miles)

Gasoline (gallons)

Convince Me! How do the equations $y = mx$ and $y = kx$ compare?

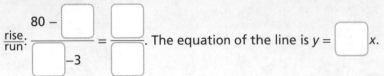

EXAMPLE **2** Write a Linear Equation from Two Points

  ACTIVITY ASSESS

A drone descends into a mining cave. The graph relates its distance below ground to time. Write an equation that describes the relationship.

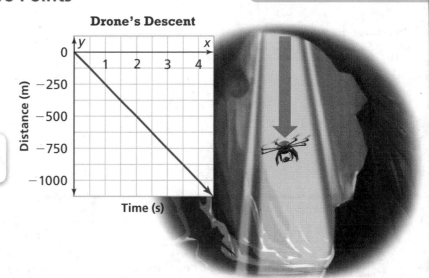

Drone's Descent

STEP 1 Find the slope of the line.

$m = \dfrac{y_2 - y_1}{x_2 - x_1}$

$= \dfrac{-750 - (-500)}{3 - 2}$ ◁ Substitute the coordinates.

$= \dfrac{-250}{1}$

The slope is −250. The drone descends 250 meters per second.

STEP 2 Write the equation of the line.

$y = mx$ ◁ Substitute −250 for *m*.

$y = -250x$

The equation of the line describing the drone's distance over time is $y = -250x$.

Generalize Lines that slant upward from left to right have **positive** slopes. Lines that slant downward from left to right have **negative** slopes.

EXAMPLE **3** Graph an Equation of the Form *y = mx*

A recipe for trail mix calls for 1 cup of raisins for every 2 cups of granola. Write an equation that describes the relationship between raisins and granola. Graph the line.

Trail Mix Recipe

STEP 1 Find the equation of the line.

$y = mx$

$y = \dfrac{1}{2}x$ ◁ Substitute $\dfrac{1}{2}$ for *m*.

STEP 2 Graph the line by plotting the point (0, 0) and using the slope to plot another point.

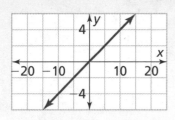 **Try It!**

a. Write the equation of the line.

b. Graph the line $y = -3x$.

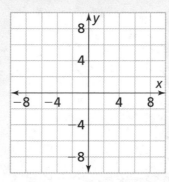

The equation for a proportional relationship is $y = mx$ where m represents the slope of the line.

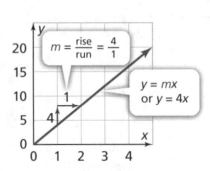

$m = \dfrac{\text{rise}}{\text{run}} = \dfrac{4}{1}$

$y = mx$ or $y = 4x$

Do You Understand?

1. **Essential Question** How does slope relate to the equation for a proportional relationship?

2. **Look for Relationships** What do the graphs of lines in the form $y = mx$ have in common? How might they differ?

3. **Use Structure** The table below shows the distance a train traveled over time. How can you determine the equation that represents this relationship?

Time (s)	Distance (m)
2	25
4	50
6	75
8	100

Do You Know How?

4. The relationship between a hiker's elevation and time is shown in the graph.

Hiking Elevation

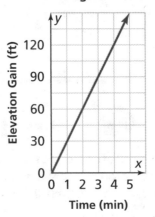

a. Find the constant of proportionality of the line. Then find the slope of the line.

b. Write the equation of the line.

5. Graph the equation $y = -\dfrac{1}{2}x$.

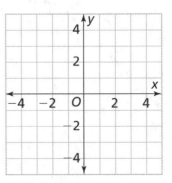

Practice & Problem Solving

6. Leveled Practice Resting heart rate is a measure of how fast the heart beats when a person is not performing physical activity. The graph shows the number of heartbeats over time for a given person.

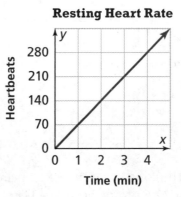

Resting Heart Rate

a. Use two sets of coordinates to write an equation to describe the relationship.

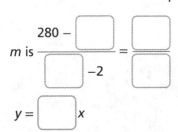

m is $\dfrac{280 - \boxed{}}{\boxed{} - 2} = \dfrac{\boxed{}}{\boxed{}}$

$y = \boxed{}\, x$

b. Interpret the equation in words.

The heart's resting heart rate is $\boxed{}$ beats each minute.

---

7. Model with Math The graph relates the number of gallons of white paint to the number of gallons of red paint Jess used to make the perfect pink. Write an equation that describes the relationship.

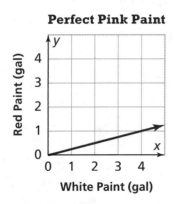

Perfect Pink Paint

8. Critique Reasoning Franco made this graph to show the equation $y = -x$. Is the graph correct? Explain.

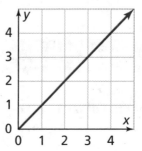

---

9. The graph shows a proportional relationship between the variables x and y.

a. Write an equation to model the relationship.

b. **Reasoning** Explain how you know if an equation or a graph represents a proportional relationship.

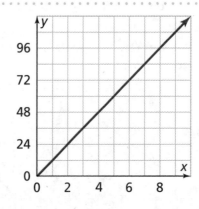

10. Model with Math Graph the equation $y = -5x$ on the coordinate plane.

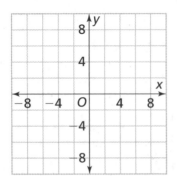

11. Graph the equation $y = \frac{3}{5}x$ on the coordinate plane.

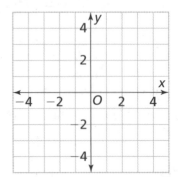

12. Higher Order Thinking A movie theater sends out a coupon for 70% off the price of a ticket.

a. Write an equation for the situation, where y is the price of the ticket with the coupon and x is the original price.

b. Graph the equation and explain why the line should only be in the first quadrant.

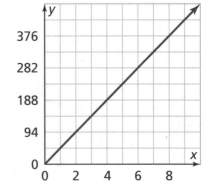

70% OFF
One Regular Movie Ticket

Original Price ($)

Assessment Practice

13. An equation and a graph of proportional relationships are shown. Which has the greater unit rate?

$y = \frac{47}{2}x$

14. Car X travels 186 miles in 3 hours.

PART A Write the equation of the line that describes the relationship between distance and time.

PART B Which graph represents the relationship between distance and time for Car X?

Ⓐ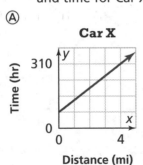

Car X

Ⓑ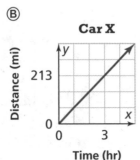

Car X

Ⓒ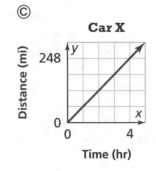

Car X

Ⓓ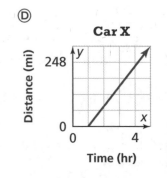

Car X

Solve and Discuss It!

ACTIVITY

Eight year-old Alex is learning to ride a horse. The trainer says that a horse ages 5 years for every 2 human years. The horse is now 50 years old in human years. How can you determine the age of the horse, in human years, when Alex was born?

I can...
find the *y*-intercept of a graph and explain what it means.

Common Core Content Standards
8.EE.B.6

Mathematical Practices
MP.4, MP.7

Focus on math practices

Use Structure A veterinarian says that a cat ages 8 years for every 2 human years. If a cat is now 64 years old in cat years, how old is the cat in human years?

? Essential Question What is the *y*-intercept and what does it indicate?

Scan for
Multimedia

EXAMPLE 1 **Determine the *y*-Intercept of a Relationship**

Mathilde and her friend are going bowling. She can rent shoes at the bowling alley or use her mother's old bowling shoes. How can she determine how much money she will save if she brings her mother's old bowling shoes?

Look for Relationships What pattern can you see in the costs of different numbers of games?

Bowling Prices (includes shoe rental)	
One game	$4.00
Three games	$8.00
Five games	$12.00
Ten Games	$22.00

STEP 1 Write the number of games and the cost as ordered pairs. Graph the ordered pairs and then find the slope to determine the cost of each game.

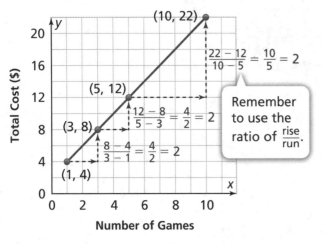

The slope is 2. That means the cost of each game is $2.

STEP 2 Extend the line to show where the line crosses the *y*-axis. The *y*-coordinate of the point where the line crosses the *y*-axis is the y-intercept.

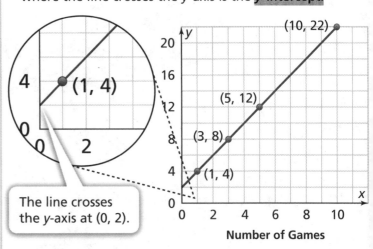

The *y*-intercept is 2. That means that the cost of shoe rental is $2. Mathilde saves $2 if she brings her mother's old bowling shoes.

☑ Try It!

Prices for a different bowling alley are shown in the graph. How much does this bowling alley charge for shoe rental?

The line crosses the *y*-axis as (☐ , ☐).

The *y*-intercept is ☐ .

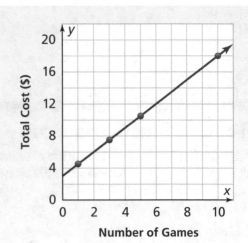

Convince Me! In these examples, why does the *y*-intercept represent the cost to rent bowling shoes?

A robotic assembly line manufactures a set number of parts per minute. Use a graph to verify how many parts the assembly line manufactures when it is first turned on.

STEP 1 Predict the number of parts.

The machine has not made any parts when it is first turned on, so the answer should be 0.

STEP 2 Determine the number of parts manufactured at different intervals.

Parts Manufactured	12	36	60	96
Time (minutes)	1	3	5	8

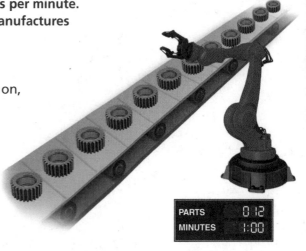

PARTS 0:12
MINUTES 1:00

STEP 3 Plot the points. Then draw a line to connect the points.

The *y*-intercept is 0. That agrees with the prediction. No parts are manufactured when the robotic assembly line is first turned on.

The line passes through the origin (0, 0).

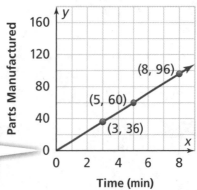

Parts Manufactured

(8, 96)
(5, 60)
(3, 36)

Time (min)

EXAMPLE **3** Identify the *y*-Intercept

What is the *y*-intercept for each of the linear relationships shown?

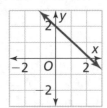

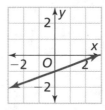

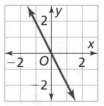

The line crosses the *y*-axis at (0, 2). The *y*-intercept is 2.

The line crosses the *y*-axis at (0, −1). The *y*-intercept is −1.

The line crosses the *y*-axis at (0, 0). The *y*-intercept is 0.

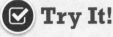 **Try It!**

What is the *y*-intercept of each graph? Explain.

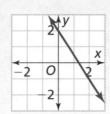

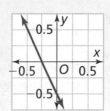

The *y*-intercept is the *y*-coordinate of the point on a graph where the line crosses the *y*-axis.

When the line crosses through the origin, the *y*-intercept is 0.

When the line crosses above the origin, the *y*-intercept is positive.

When the line crosses below the origin, the *y*-intercept is negative.

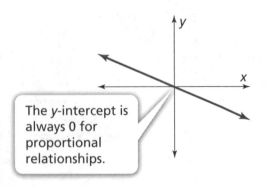

The *y*-intercept is always 0 for proportional relationships.

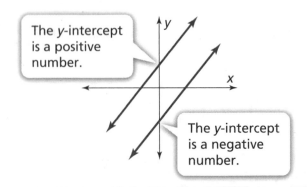

The *y*-intercept is a positive number.

The *y*-intercept is a negative number.

Do You Understand?

1. **? Essential Question** What is the *y*-intercept and what does it indicate?

2. **Look for Relationships** Chelsea graphs a proportional relationship. Bradyn graphs a line that passes through the origin. What do you know about the *y*-intercept of each student's graph? Explain your answer.

3. **Generalize** When the *y*-intercept is positive, where does the line cross the *y*-axis on the graph? When it is negative?

Do You Know How?

4. What is the *y*-intercept shown in the graph?

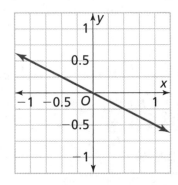

5. The graph shows the relationship between the remaining time of a movie and the amount of time since Kelly hit "play." What is the *y*-intercept of the graph and what does it represent?

Kelly's Movie

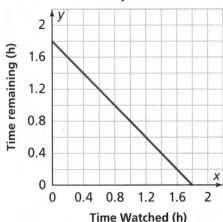

Practice & Problem Solving

Scan for
Multimedia

6. Leveled Practice Find the y-intercept of the line.
The y-intercept is the point where the graph crosses

the ☐ -axis.

The line crosses the y-axis at the point (☐ , ☐).

The y-intercept is ☐ .

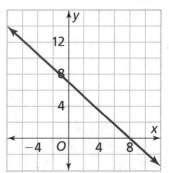

---

7. Find the y-intercept of the graph.

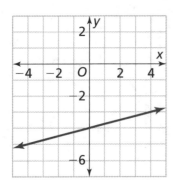

8. Find the y-intercept of the graph.

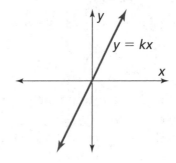

$y = kx$

---

9. The graph represents the height y, in meters, of a hot air
balloon x minutes after beginning to descend. How high
was the balloon when it began its descent?

Height of a Hot Air Balloon

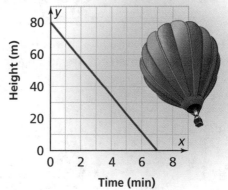

---

10. Model with Math The graph represents the amount of
gasoline in a canister after Joshua begins to fill it at a
gas station pump. What is the y-intercept of the graph
and what does it represent?

Joshua's Gas Canister

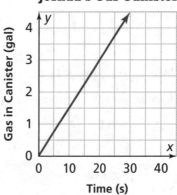

---

11. The line models the temperature on a certain winter day since sunrise.

   a. What is the y-intercept of the line?

   b. What does the y-intercept represent?

Temperature Since Sunrise

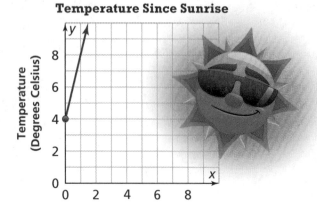

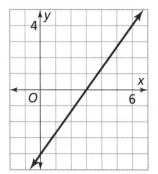

- -

12. Higher Order Thinking Your friend incorrectly makes this graph as an example of a line with a y-intercept of 3.

   a. Explain your friend's possible error.

   b. Draw a line on the graph that does represent a y-intercept of 3.

✓ **Assessment Practice**

13. For each graph, draw a line through the point such that the values of the x-intercept and y-intercept are additive inverses.

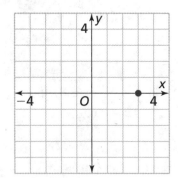

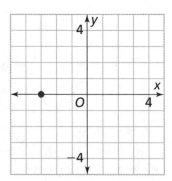

14. Which statements describe the graph of a proportional relationship? Select all that apply.

☐ The y-intercept is always at the point (0, 1).

☐ The line always crosses the y-axis at (0, 0).

☐ The y-intercept is 0.

☐ The y-intercept is 1.

☐ The line does NOT cross the y-axis.

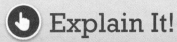 Explain It!

Xiu and Jon take the tram from the base camp to the mountain summit. After about six and a half minutes in the tram, Jon says, "Cool! We are a mile above sea level." Xiu says, "We passed the one-mile mark a couple of minutes ago."

Summit Elevation 9,600 ft

Mountain Tram
800 vertical ft/min

Mountain Lodge Elevation 2,080 ft

Lesson 7-9
Analyze Linear Equations:
$y = mx + b$

Go Online

I can...
derive the equation $y = mx + b$.

© **Common Core Content Standards**
8.EE.B.6

Mathematical Practices
MP.2, MP.6, MP.7, MP.8

A. Construct an argument to defend Xiu's statement.

B. What mistake could Jon have made? Explain.

Focus on math practices

Reasoning Can you use the equation $y = mx$ to represent the path of the tram? Is there a proportional relationship between x and y? Explain.

EXAMPLE 1 Write the Equation of a Line

Scan for Multimedia

The Middle School Student Council is organizing a dance and has $500 to pay for a DJ. DJ Dave will charge $200 for a set-up fee and the first hour, or $425 for a set-up fee and four hours.

How can the Student Council determine whether they can afford to have DJ Dave play for 5 hours?

DJ DAVE

RATES

Set-Up Fee $125
Hourly Rate $75

STEP 1 Plot the total costs for DJ Dave for 1 hour and 4 hours. Find the initial value, or y-intercept, and the rate of change, or slope.

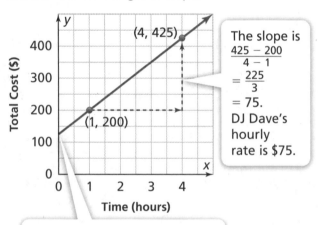

The slope is
$$\frac{425 - 200}{4 - 1}$$
$$= \frac{225}{3}$$
$$= 75.$$
DJ Dave's hourly rate is $75.

The initial value, or y-intercept, is 125. DJ Dave charges a $125 initial fee.

STEP 2 Write an equation to represent the total cost for DJ Dave for any number of hours.

Total Cost	=	Hourly Rate	+	Initial Fee
y	=	$75x$	+	125

This equation is in **slope-intercept form**, $y = mx + b$, where m is the rate of change, or slope, and b is the initial value, or y-intercept.

STEP 3 Evaluate the equation to find the total cost for 5 hours.

$$y = 75x + 125$$
$$y = 75(5) + 125$$
$$= 375 + 125$$
$$= 500$$

The total cost is $500. The student council can afford DJ Dave.

☑ Try It!

Write a linear equation in slope-intercept form for the graph shown.

The y-intercept of the line is ☐.

The slope is $\frac{\Box}{\Box}$. The equation in slope-intercept form is ☐ = ☐ x + ☐.

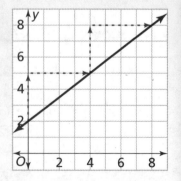

Convince Me! What two values do you need to know to write an equation of a line, and how are they used to represent a line?

EXAMPLE **2**

Write a Linear Equation Given Its Graph

ACTIVITY   ASSESS

A salt water solution is cooled to −6° C. During an experiment, the mixture is heated at a steady rate. Write an equation to represent the temperature, y, after x minutes.

Identify the slope and the y-intercept from the graph.

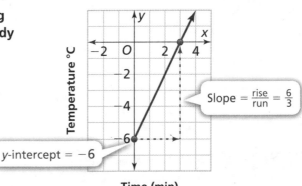

Slope $= \frac{rise}{run} = \frac{6}{3}$

$y = mx + b$

$y = 2x - 6$

The slope $m = \frac{6}{3}$ or 2.

The y-intercept $b = -6$.

y-intercept $= -6$

The equation of the line is $y = 2x - 6$.

EXAMPLE **3** Graph a Given Linear Equation

Graph the equation $y = -4x + 3$.

STEP 2 The slope is −4 or $-\frac{4}{1}$. To locate another point on the line, start at (0, 3) and go down 4 and right 1.

STEP 1 The y-intercept is 3. Plot a point at (0, 3).

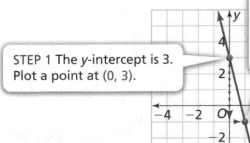

STEP 3 Draw a line through the points.

✅ Try It!

a. What is an equation for the line shown?

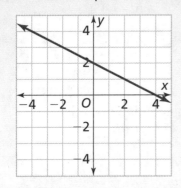

b. Graph the line with equation $y = \frac{1}{3}x - 5$.

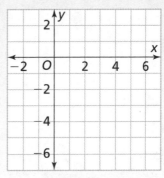

The equation of a line that represents a nonproportional relationship can be written in slope-intercept form, $y = mx + b$, where m is the slope of the line and b is the y-intercept.

Do You Understand?

1. **Essential Question** What is the equation of a line for a nonproportional relationship?

2. **Use Structure** The donations by a restaurant to a certain charity, y, will be two-fifths of its profits, x, plus $50. How can you determine the equation in slope-intercept form that shows the relationship between x and y without graphing the line?

3. **Be Precise** Priya will graph a line with the equation $y = \frac{3}{4}x - 4$. She wants to know what the line will look like before she graphs the line. Describe the line Priya will draw, including the quadrants the line will pass through.

Do You Know How?

4. Chrissie says the equation of the line shown on the graph is $y = \frac{1}{2}x - 5$. George says that the equation of the line is $y = \frac{1}{2}x + 5$. Which student is correct? Explain.

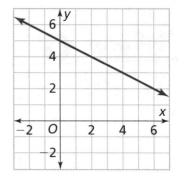

5. Fara wants to rent a tent for an outdoor celebration. The cost of the tent is $500 per hour, plus an additional $100 set-up fee.

   a. Draw a line to show the relationship between the number of hours the tent is rented, x, and the total cost of the tent, y.

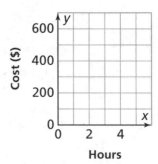

   b. What is the equation of the line in slope-intercept form?

Practice & Problem Solving

6. Leveled Practice What is the graph of the equation $y = 2x + 4$?

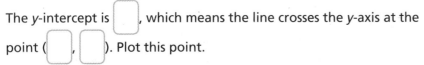

The y-intercept is ☐, which means the line crosses the y-axis at the

point (☐, ☐). Plot this point.

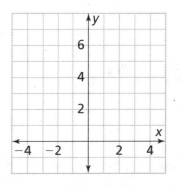

The slope of the line is positive, so it goes ☐ from left to right.

Start at the y-intercept. Move up ☐, and then move right ☐.

You are now at the point (☐, ☐). Plot this point.

Draw a line to connect the two points.

---

7. Write an equation for the line in slope-intercept form.

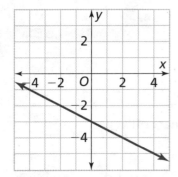

8. Write an equation for the line in slope-intercept form.

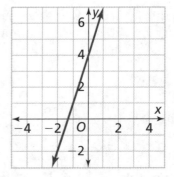

---

9. The line models the cost of renting a kayak. Write an equation in slope-intercept form for the line, where x is the number of hours the kayak is rented and y is the total cost of renting the kayak.

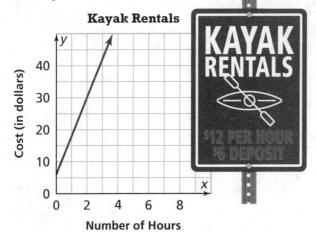

10. Graph the equation $y = 3x - 5$.

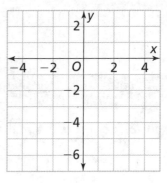

11. Amy began with $25 in her bank account and spent $5 each day. The line shows the amount of money in her bank account. She incorrectly wrote an equation for the line in slope-intercept form as $y = -5x + 5$.

a. What is the correct equation for the line in slope-intercept form?

b. Critique Reasoning What mistake might Amy have made?

Amy's Bank Account

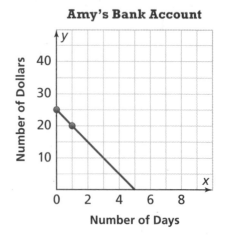

12. Higher Order Thinking The line represents the cost of ordering concert tickets online.

a. Write an equation for the line in slope-intercept form, where x is the number of tickets and y is the total cost.

b. Explain how you can write an equation for this situation without using a graph.

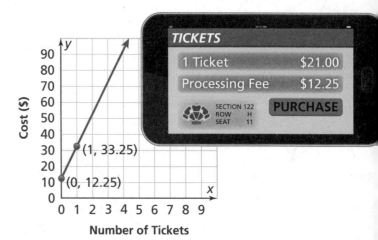

c. Is this graph a good representation of the situation? Explain.

☑ Assessment Practice

13. What should you do first to graph the equation $y = \frac{2}{5}x - 1$?

Ⓐ Plot the point (0, 0).

Ⓑ Plot the point (2, 5).

Ⓒ Plot a point at the x-intercept.

Ⓓ Plot a point at the y-intercept.

14. Write an equation for the line in slope-intercept form.

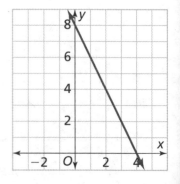

How can you analyze connections between linear equations and use them to solve problems?

Vocabulary Review

Complete each definition and provide an example of each vocabulary word.

Vocabulary   slope of a line   *y*-intercept   slope-intercept form   *x*-intercept

Definition	Example
1. The change in *y* divided by the change in *x* is the _____.	
2. The point on the graph where the line crosses the *y*-axis is the _____ of a line.	
3. The _____ of a line is $y = mx + b$. The variable *m* in the equation stands for the _____. The variable *b* in the equation stands for the _____.	

Use Vocabulary in Writing

Paddle boats rent for a fee of $25, plus an additional $12 per hour. What equation, in $y = mx + b$ form, represents the cost to rent a paddle boat for *x* hours? Explain how you write the equation. Use vocabulary words in your explanation.

Concepts and Skills Review

Combine Like Terms to Solve Equations

Quick Review

You can use variables to represent unknown quantities. To solve an equation, collect like terms to get one variable on one side of the equation. Then use inverse operations and properties of equality to solve the equation.

Example

Solve $5x + 0.45x = 49.05$ for x.

$5x + 0.45x = 49.05$

$5.45x = 49.05$

$\dfrac{5.45x}{5.45} = \dfrac{49.05}{5.45}$

$x = 9$

Practice

Solve each equation for x.

1. $2x + 6x = 1{,}000$

2. $2\frac{1}{4}x + \frac{1}{2}x = 44$

3. $-2.3x - 4.2x = -66.3$

4. Javier bought a microwave for $105. The cost was 30% off the original price. What was the price of the microwave before the sale?

Solve Equations with Variables on Both Sides

Quick Review

If two quantities represent equal amounts and have the same variables, you can set the expressions equal to each other. Collect all the variables on one side of the equation and all the constants on the other side. Then use inverse operations and properties of equality to solve the equation.

Example

Solve $2x + 21 = 7x + 6$ for x.

$2x + 21 = 7x + 6$

$21 = 5x + 6$

$15 = 5x$

$x = 3$

Practice

Solve each equation for x.

1. $3x + 9x = 6x + 42$

2. $\frac{4}{3}x + \frac{2}{3}x = \frac{1}{3}x + 5$

3. $9x - 5x + 18 = 2x + 34$

4. Megan has $50 and saves $5.50 each week. Connor has $18.50 and saves $7.75 each week. After how many weeks will Megan and Connor have saved the same amount?

Solve Multistep Equations

Quick Review

When solving multistep equations, sometimes the Distributive Property is used before you collect like terms. Sometimes like terms are collected, and then you use the Distributive Property.

Example

Solve $8x + 2 = 2x + 4(x + 3)$ for x.

First, distribute the 4. Then, combine like terms. Finally, use properties of equality to solve for x.

$8x + 2 = 2x + 4x + 12$

$8x + 2 = 6x + 12$

$\quad 8x = 6x + 10$

$\quad 2x = 10$

$\quad\ x = 5$

Practice

Solve each equation for x.

1. $4(x + 4) + 2x = 52$

2. $8(2x + 3x + 2) = -4x + 148$

3. Justin bought a calculator and a binder that were both 15% off the original price. The original price of the binder was $6.20. Justin spent a total of $107.27. What was the original price of the calculator?

Equations with No Solutions or Infinitely Many Solutions

Quick Review

When solving an equation results in a statement that is always true, there are infinitely many solutions. When solving an equation produces a false statement, there are no solutions. When solving an equation gives one value for a variable, there is one solution.

Example

How many solutions does the equation $6x + 9 = 2x + 4 + 4x + 5$ have?

First, solve the equation.

$6x + 9 = 2x + 4 + 4x + 5$

$6x + 9 = 6x + 9$

$\quad 9 = 9$

Because $9 = 9$ is alwyas a true statement, the equation has infinitely many solutions.

Practice

How many solutions does each equation have?

1. $x + 5.5 + 8 = 5x - 13.5 - 4x$

2. $4\left(\dfrac{1}{2}x + 3\right) = 3x + 12 - x$

3. $2(6x + 9 - 3x) = 5x + 21$

4. The weight of Abe's dog can be found using the expression $2(x + 3)$, where x is the number of weeks. The weight of Karen's dog can be found using the expression $3(x + 1)$, where x is the number of weeks. Will the dogs ever be the same weight? Explain.

Quick Review

To compare proportional relationships, compare the rate of change or find the unit rate.

Example

The graph shows the rate at which Rob jogs. Emily's jogging rate is represented by the equation $y = 8x$, where x is the number of miles and y is the number of minutes. At these rates, who will finish an 8-mile race first?

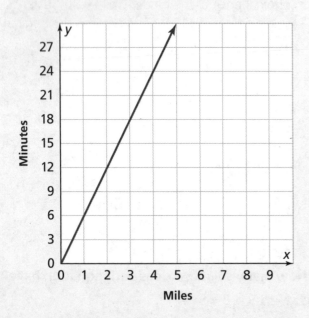

Miles

Emily's unit rate is $y = 8(1) = 8$ minutes per mile.

The point (1, 6) represents Rob's unit rate of 6 minutes per mile.

Rob's unit rate is less than Emily's rate, so Rob will finish an 8-mile race first.

Practice

1. Two trains are traveling at a constant rate. Find the rate of each train. Which train is traveling at the faster rate?

Train A

Time (h)	2	3	4	5	6
Distance (mi)	50	75	100	125	150

Train B

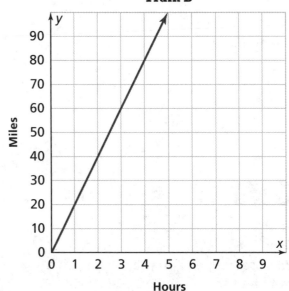

Hours

2. A 16-ounce bottle of water from Store A costs $1.28. The cost in dollars, y, of a bottle of water from Store B is represented by the equation $y = 0.07x$, where x is the number of ounces. What is the cost per ounce of water at each store? Which store's bottle of water costs less per ounce?

Quick Review

The **slope** of a line in a proportional relationship is the same as the unit rate and the constant of proportionality.

Example

The graph shows the number of miles a person walked at a constant speed. Find the slope of the line.

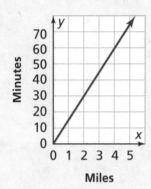

Miles

$$\text{slope} = \frac{y_2 - y_1}{x_2 - x_1} = \frac{60 - 30}{4 - 2} = \frac{30}{2} = 15$$

Practice

1. The graph shows the proportions of blue paint and yellow paint that Briana mixes to make green paint. What is the slope of the line? Tell what it means in the problem situation.

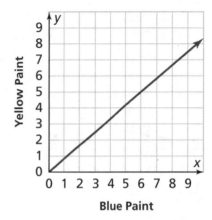

Blue Paint

Quick Review

A proportional relationship can be represented by an equation in the form $y = mx$, where m is the slope.

Example

Graph the line $y = 2x$.

Plot a point at (0, 0). Then use the slope to plot the next point.

Practice

A mixture of nuts contains 1 cup of walnuts for every 3 cups of peanuts.

1. Write a linear equation that represents the relationship between peanuts, x, and walnuts, y.

2. Graph the line.

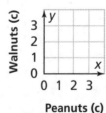

Peanuts (c)

Quick Review

The *y*-intercept is the *y*-coordinate of the point where a line crosses the *y*-axis. The *y*-intercept of a proportional relationship is 0.

Example

What is the *y*-intercept of the line?

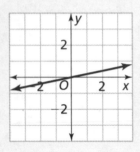

The *y*-intercept is 0.

Practice

The equation $y = 5 + 0.5x$ represents the cost of getting a car wash and using the vacuum for *x* minutes.

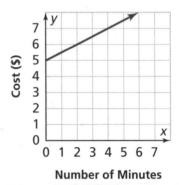

Number of Minutes

1. What is the *y*-intercept?

2. What does the *y*-intercept represent?

LESSON 7-9 ▶ Analyze Linear Equations: $y = mx + b$

Quick Review

An equation in the form $y = mx + b$, where $b \neq 0$, has a slope of *m* and a *y*-intercept of *b*. This form is called the **slope-intercept form**. There is not a proportional relationship between *x* and *y* in these cases.

Example

What is the equation of the line?

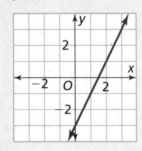

Since $m = 2$ and $b = -3$, the equation is $y = 2x - 3$.

Practice

1. Graph the line with the equation $y = \frac{1}{2}x - 1$.

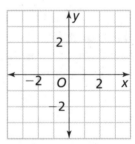

2. What is the equation of the line?

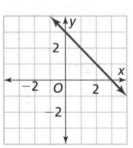

Pathfinder

Each block below shows an equation and a possible solution. Shade a path from START to FINISH. Follow the equations that are solved correctly. You can only move up, down, right, or left.

I can...
solve two-step addition and subtraction equations.
© 8.EE.C.7b

START

$2x + 3 = 7$ $x = 2$	$9y - 1 = -10$ $y = -1$	$5t + 1 = 9$ $t = 2$	$-11x + 12 = 1$ $x = -1$
$6h - 1 = 25$ $h = 4$	$14 + 3m = 35$ $m = 7$	$30 - j = 90$ $j = 60$	$19 - 4p = 9$ $p = -7$
$20t - 1 = 95$ $t = 5$	$20 - q = 17$ $q = 3$	$-4w + 7 = 11$ $w = -1$	$-a + 15 = 13$ $a = 2$
$100 - 4x = 0$ $x = -25$	$-9r - 4 = -85$ $r = -9$	$23 = 1 + 4y$ $y = 6$	$7y + 4 = 32$ $y = 4$
$-6b + 27 = 3$ $b = -4$	$2z + 1 = 0$ $z = \frac{1}{2}$	$47 - 2x = 45$ $x = -1$	$-12 + 9k = 42$ $k = 6$

FINISH

USE SAMPLING TO DRAW INFERENCES ABOUT POPULATIONS

? Topic Essential Question

How can sampling be used to draw inferences about one or more populations?

Topic Overview

8-1 Populations and Samples

8-2 Draw Inferences from Data

8-3 Make Comparative Inferences About Populations

8-4 Make More Comparative Inferences About Populations

3-Act Mathematical Modeling: Raising Money

Topic Vocabulary

- inference
- population
- random sample
- representative sample
- sample
- valid inference

Lesson Digital Resources

INTERACTIVE STUDENT EDITION
Access online or offline.

VISUAL LEARNING ANIMATION
Interact with visual learning animations.

ACTIVITY Use with *Solve & Discuss It, Explore* and *Explain It* activities, and to explore Examp

VIDEOS Watch clips to support *3-Act Mathematical Modeling Lessons* and *STEM Pro*

Go online

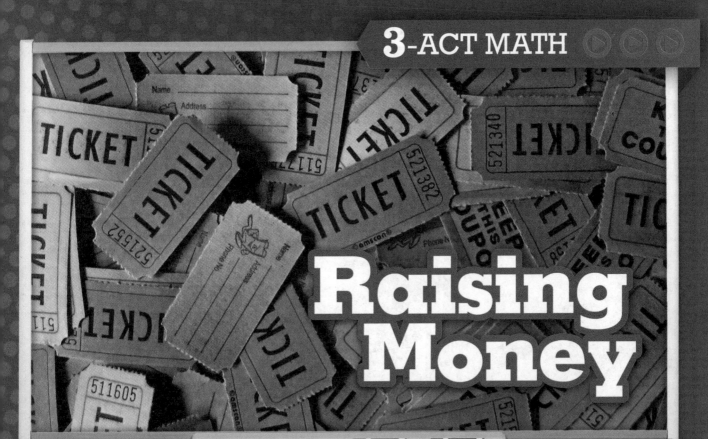

Raising Money

Raising Money

What was the last fundraiser your school hosted? How much money was your school trying to raise? Fundraisers can help your school finance improvements and special events. However, if you have too many fundraisers, people might stop participating.

You can start planning a fundraiser once you know how you will use the money and how much money you will need. Think about this during your 3-Act Mathematical Modeling lesson.

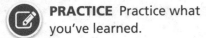 **PRACTICE** Practice what you've learned.

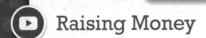 **TUTORIALS** Get help from *Virtual Nerd*, right when you need it.

MATH TOOLS Explore math with digital tools.

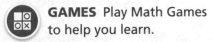 **GAMES** Play Math Games to help you learn.

KEY CONCEPT Review important lesson content.

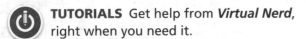 **GLOSSARY** Read and listen to English/Spanish definitions.

 **ASSESSMENT** Show what you've learned.

:enVision® STEM Project

  VIDEO

Did You Know?

Federal and local governments provide their citizens with the basic equipment and structures needed for the region to function properly. This infrastructure includes water, electricity, waste removal, and communication networks.

Roads and public transportation are the most visible elements of infrastructure.

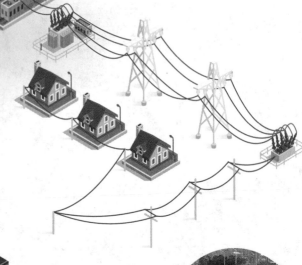

Motorists in cities like Los Angeles, Moscow, and Istanbul experience some of the worst traffic congestion.

UNDERGROUND

London's Metropolitan Railway began operating as the world's first rapid public transportation system in 1863. Boston's Tremont Street Subway, opened in 1897, was the first subway system in the United States.

P

BICYCLE SHARING

Residents of large cities like New York, Amsterdam, and Tel Aviv enjoy a bike-sharing service. City governments provide this infrastructure to reduce traffic congestion and promote fitness.

Your Task: Golden Path ▶

Walking trails and paths and bikeways provide important recreational opportunities and commuting alternatives. They also promote the preservation of green spaces and eco-friendly, energy-efficient transportation. The appropriate design of walking trails and paths and bikeway facilities affects the experience, enjoyment, safety, and comfort of walkers and bicyclists. You and your classmates will develop a survey to understand the needs of walkers and bicyclists and to examine the current and potential uses of existing and planned paths or bikeways.

Review What You Know!

Vocabulary

Choose the best term from the box to complete each definition.

> center
> data distribution
> statistical question
> variability

1. A _____ is how data values are arranged.

2. The part of a data set where the middle values are concentrated is called

the _____ of the data.

3. A _____ anticipates that there will be different
answers when gathering information.

4. _____ is a measure that describes the spread of values in a data set.

Statistical Measures

Use the following data to determine each statistical measure.
9, 9, 14, 7, 12, 8, 11, 19, 15, 11

5. mean

6. median

7. range

8. mode

9. interquartile range (IQR)

10. mean absolute deviation (MAD)

Data Representations

Make each data display using the data from Problems 5–7.

11. Box plot

12. Dot plot

Statistical Questions

13. Which is *NOT* a statistical question that might be used to gather data
from a certain group?

   Ⓐ In what state were you born? Ⓒ What is the capital of the United States?

   Ⓑ How many pets do you have? Ⓓ Do you like strawberry yogurt?

Language Development

Fill in the graphic organizer. Write each definition using your own words. Illustrate or cite supporting examples.

Vocabulary Word	Definition	Illustration or Example
inference		
population		
random sample		
representative sample		
sample		
valid inference		

PROJECT
8A

What types of changes would you like to see in your community?

PROJECT: WRITE TO YOUR REPRESENTATIVE

PROJECT
8B

How could you combine physical activity and a fundraiser?

PROJECT: ANALYZE AN ACTIVITY

PROJECT 8C

If you could study an animal population in depth, which animal would you choose, and why?

PROJECT: SIMULATE A POPULATION STUDY

PROJECT 8D

If you were to design a piece of art that moved, how would you make it move?

PROJECT: BUILD A MOBILE

Solve & Discuss It!  ACTIVITY

The table shows the lunch items sold on one day at the middle school cafeteria. Use the given information to help the cafeteria manager complete his food supply order for next week.

Lunch Item	Number Sold
Turkey Sandwich	43
Hot Dog	51
Veggie Burger	14
Fish Taco	27

Generalize What conclusions can you draw from the lunch data?

I can...
determine if a sample is representative of a population.

 Common Core Content Standards
7. SP.A.1

Mathematical Practices
MP.1, MP.2, MP.3, MP.6, MP.8

Focus on math practices

Construct Arguments Why might it be helpful for the cafeteria manager to look at the items ordered on more than one day?

VISUAL LEARNING ASSESS

EXAMPLE 1 **Understand Populations and Samples**

Scan for Multimedia

The 2,468 registered voters in Morgan's town are voting on whether to build a new stadium. Morgan and her friends really want the town to vote in favor of the new stadium. How can they determine how the voters will vote before the day of the vote?

Model with Math
How can you represent the problem situation?

Morgan and her friends could ask every registered voter, or the entire **population** of voters in town, how they plan to vote.

However, surveying 2,468 people takes a long time. Morgan and her friends may not be able to survey the entire population of voters.

Morgan and her friends could ask a subset, or a **sample**, of the registered voters in town how they plan to vote.

Surveying a sample of voters does not take as long and is more reasonable to do. Morgan and her friends would be able to ask 100 or 200 people.

☑ Try It!

Miguel thinks the science teachers in his school give more homework than the math teachers. He is researching the number of hours middle school students in his school spend doing math and science homework each night.

The ⬚ includes all of the students in Miguel's middle school.

A possible ⬚ is some students from each of the grades in the middle school.

Convince Me! Why is it more efficient to study a sample rather than an entire population?

EXAMPLE **2** Describe a Representative Sample

  ACTIVITY ASSESS

Morgan decides to survey a sample of the town's voting population. How can she know that the survey results from the sample of voters represent the position of the entire town's population?

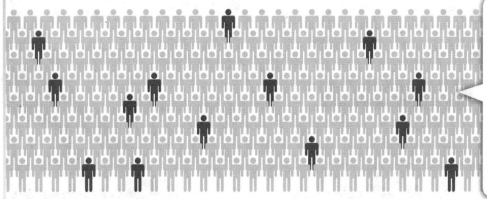

> A **representative sample** accurately reflects the characteristics of the entire population.
>
> In a **random sample**, each member of the population has an equal chance of being included. A random sample tends to be a representative sample.

Morgan can survey a random sample, or a randomly selected group of voters, to make sure her results represent the position of the entire town.

 Try It!

A produce manager is deciding whether there is customer demand for expanding the organic food section of her store. How could she obtain the information she needs?

EXAMPLE **3** Generate a Random Sample

How can Morgan generate a random sample of the town's voting population?

Morgan can follow these steps:

STEP 1 Define the population.
The population consists of the registered voters in the town.

STEP 2 Choose the sample size.
Morgan plans to survey 100 registered voters.

> The larger the sample, the more confident Morgan can be that the results represent the position of the population.

STEP 3 Make or acquire a list of all members of the population.

STEP 4 Assign a number to each member of the population.

STEP 5 Generate a list of random numbers to select sample members.

 Try It!

Ravi is running against two other candidates for student council president. All of the 750 students in Ravi's school will vote for student council president. How can Ravi generate a representative sample that will help him determine whether he will win the election?

EXAMPLE 4   Generate Multiple Random Samples

Morgan and Maddy will each generate a random sample of the 138 students in 7th grade at their school. They each write the numbers from 1 to 138 on small pieces of paper and put them in different hats. Then they draw 20 numbers randomly from their hats. What do you notice about the two random samples taken from the same population? What does this tell you about the sampling technique?

Morgan's Sample			
55	49	28	79
114	(106)	18	130
97	50	83	109
(38)	91	36	46
87	96	15	93

Maddy's Sample			
(38)	(106)	21	102
25	35	94	126
100	119	27	51
135	103	13	72
67	7	74	54

- There are 20 members in each sample.
- The only numbers common to both samples are 38 and 106.
- The numbers are distributed differently in each sample.

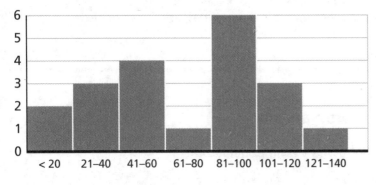

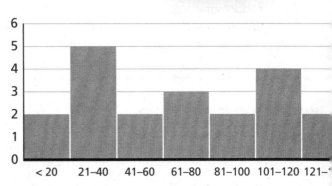

The sampling method produces random samples that have mostly different members, but that are each likely to be representative of the population.

✅ Try It!

The table at the right shows the random sample that Jeremy generated from the same population as Morgan's and Maddy's samples. Compare Jeremy's sample to Morgan's and Maddy's.

Jeremy's Sample			
77	8	32	17
34	95	81	57
125	116	30	126
92	61	22	36
111	68	110	69

 KEY CONCEPT

A *population* is an entire group of objects—people, animals, plants—from which data can be collected. A *sample* is a subset of the population. When you ask a statistical question about a population, it is often more efficient to gather data from a sample of the population.

A *representative sample* of a population has the same characteristics as the population. Generating a *random sample* is one reliable way to produce a representative sample of a population.

You can generate multiple random samples that are different but that are each representative of the population.

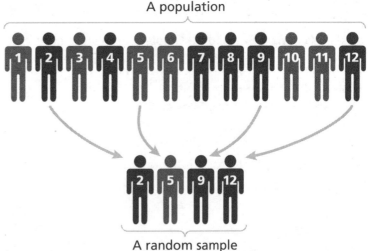

A population

A random sample

Do You Understand?

1. **Essential Question** How can you determine a representative sample of a population?

2. **Construct Arguments** Why does a sample need to be representative of a population?

3. **Be Precise** The quality control manager of a peanut butter manufacturing plant wants to ensure the quality of the peanut butter in the jars coming down the assembly line. Describe a representative sampling method she could use.

Do You Know How?

4. A health club manager wants to determine whether the members would prefer a new sauna or a new steam room. The club surveys 50 of its 600 members. What is the population of this study?

5. A journalism teacher wants to determine whether his students would prefer to attend a national writing convention or tour of a local newspaper press. The journalism teacher has a total of 120 students in 4 different classes. What would be a representative sample in this situation?

6. Garret wants to find out which restaurant people think serves the best beef brisket in town.

   a. What is the population from which Garret should find a sample?

   b. What might be a sample that is not representative of the population?

Practice & Problem Solving

Leveled Practice In **7** and **8**, complete each statement with the correct number.

7. Of a group of 200 workers, 15 are chosen to participate in a survey about the number of miles they drive to work each week.

In this situation, the sample consists of the ☐

workers selected to participate in the survey.

The population consists of ☐ workers.

8. The ticket manager for a minor league baseball team awarded prizes by drawing four numbers corresponding to the ticket stub numbers of four fans in attendance.

In this situation, the sample consists of the ☐

people selected to win a prize. The population

consists of ☐ the spectators who purchased

tickets to attend the game.

9. A supermarket conducts a survey to find the approximate number of its customers who like apple juice. What is the population of the survey?

10. A national appliance store chain is reviewing the performances of its 400 sales associate trainees. How can the store choose a representative sample of the trainees?

11. Of the 652 passengers on a cruise ship, 30 attended the magic show on board.

  a. What is the sample?

  b. What is the population?

12. Make Sense and Persevere The owner of a landscaping company is investigating whether his 120 employees would prefer a water cooler or bottled water. Determine the population and a representative sample for this situation.

13. Higher Order Thinking A bag contains 6 yellow marbles and 18 red marbles. If a representative sample contains 2 yellow marbles, then how many red marbles would you expect it to contain? Explain.

14. Chung wants to determine the favorite hobbies among the teachers at his school. How could he generate a representative sample? Why would it be helpful to generate multiple samples?

15. The table shows the results of a survey conducted to choose a new mascot. Yolanda said that the sample consists of all 237 students at Tichenor Middle School.

a. What was Yolanda's error?

b. What is the sample size? Explain.

Tichenor M.S. Mascot Survey Results

Mascot	Number of Students
Panthers	24
Lions	6
Cyclones	2
Comets	8

16. Reasoning To predict the outcome of the vote for the town budget, the town manager assigned random numbers and selected 125 registered voters. He then called these voters and asked how they planned to vote. Is the town manager's sample representative of the population? Explain.

17. David wants to determine the number of students in his school who like Brussels sprouts. What is the population of David's study?

18. Researchers want to determine the percentage of Americans who have visited The Florida Everglades National Park in Florida. The diagram shows the population of this study, as well as the sample used by the researchers. After their study, the researchers conclude that nearly 75% of Americans have visited the park.

a. What error was likely made by the researchers?

b. Give an example of steps researchers might take to improve their study.

19. An art teacher asks a sample of students if they would be interested in studying art next year. Of the 30 students he surveys, 81% are already enrolled in one of his art classes this year. Only 11% of the school's students are studying art this year. Did the teacher survey a representative sample of the students in the school? Explain.

Are you interested in taking an art class next year?

20. Make Sense and Persevere A supermarket wants to conduct a survey of its customers to find whether they enjoy oatmeal for breakfast. Describe how the supermarket could generate a representative sample for the survey.

21. Critique Reasoning Gwen is the manager of a clothing store. To measure customer satisfaction, she asks each shopper who makes big purchases for a rating of his or her overall shopping experience. Explain why Gwen's sampling method may not generate a representative sample.

☑ Assessment Practice

22. Sheila wants to research the colors of houses on a highly populated street. Which of the following methods could Sheila use to generate a representative sample? Select all that apply.

☐ Assign each house a number and use a random number generator to produce a list of houses for the sample.

☐ Choose every house that has at least 3 trees in the front yard.

☐ Choose only the houses of the people you know.

☐ List the house numbers on slips of paper and draw at least 20% of the numbers out of a box.

☐ Choose all of the houses on the street that have shutters.

23. A national survey of middle school students asks how many hours a day they spend doing homework. Which sample best represents the population?

PART A

Ⓐ A group of 941 students in eighth grade in a certain town

Ⓑ A group of 886 students in sixth grade in a certain county

Ⓒ A group of 795 students in seventh grade in different states

Ⓓ A group of 739 students in different middle school grade levels from various states

PART B

Explain the reasoning for your answer in Part A.

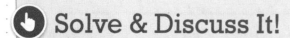 Solve & Discuss It!  ACTIVITY

The students in Ms. Miller's class cast their votes in the school-wide vote for which color to paint the cafeteria walls. Based on the data, what might you conclude about how the rest of the school will vote?

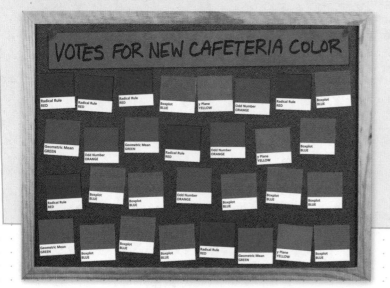

VOTES FOR NEW CAFETERIA COLOR

I can...
make inferences about a population from a sample data set.

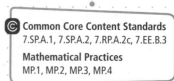

Ⓒ **Common Core Content Standards**
7.SP.A.1, 7.SP.A.2, 7.RP.A.2c, 7.EE.B.3

Mathematical Practices
MP.1, MP.2, MP.3, MP.4

Make Sense and Persevere
How many students are in Ms. Miller's class? How many students voted for each color?

Focus on math practices
Reasoning How can you determine whether a sample is representative of a population?

VISUAL LEARNING ASSES

EXAMPLE 1 **Draw Qualitative Inferences from Data**

Scan for Multimedia

Sasha is trying to convince her mother to change her bedtime on school nights. She gathers data on the average number of hours of sleep that a random sample of seventh-grade students in her school get each night. Will Sasha be able to convince her mother to let her go to bed later?

Model with Math How can you represent the data?

On School Days

My bedtime: **9:00 p.m.**

My wake-up time: **6:30 a.m.**

Hours of sleep: $9\frac{1}{2}$

STEP 1 Sasha displays the data she collected in a dot plot. She describes the data.

About half of the dots are clustered between 9 and $9\frac{1}{2}$ hours.

$9\frac{1}{2}$ hours has the most dots.

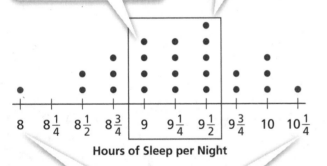

Hours of Sleep per Night

The range is $10\frac{1}{4} - 8 = 2\frac{1}{4}$ hours.

STEP 2 Sasha concludes that about half of the students in her sample get between 9 and $9\frac{1}{2}$ hours of sleep each night, the same number she gets.

You can draw a curve to see the distribution or shape of the data.

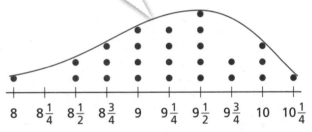

Hours of Sleep per Night

An **inference** is a conclusion made by interpreting data. Sasha infers that about half of the seventh graders in her school get between 9 and $9\frac{1}{2}$ hours of sleep each night. Sasha will probably not be able to convince her mother to let her go to bed later.

✓ **Try It!**

Dash collects data on the hair lengths of a random sample of seventh-grade boys in his school.

The data are clustered between ☐ and ☐ inches and between ☐ and ☐ inches. Dash can infer from the data that seventh-grade boys in his school have both short and long hair.

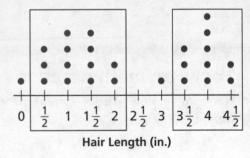

Hair Length (in.)

Convince Me! How does a dot plot help you make inferences from data?

EXAMPLE **2**  Draw Quantitative Inferences from Data

  ACTIVITY ASSESS

Sasha's friend Margo suggests that Sasha calculate the mean and median of the data set to determine whether they support her previous inferences about the population.

Mean: about 9 hours, 16 minutes

Median: $9\frac{1}{4}$ hours (or 9 hours, 15 minutes)

> An inference is valid if it is based on a representative sample, and there are enough data to support it.
>
> A **valid inference** is one that is very likely to be true about the population.

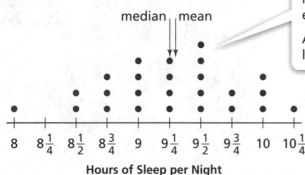

median mean

Hours of Sleep per Night

The mean and median support Sasha's inference that seventh graders get an average of 9 to $9\frac{1}{2}$ hours of sleep each night.

EXAMPLE **3** **Compare Inferences Based on Different Samples**

Margo and Ravi are also trying to get their parents to let them stay up later. They collect data about the number of hours of sleep a random sample of seventh graders get each night. The two box plots show their data. Do Margo's and Ravi's data support Sasha's inference about the number of hours of sleep that seventh graders get?

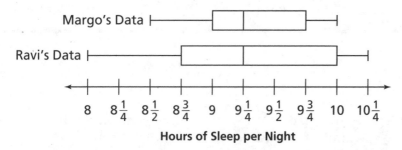

Hours of Sleep per Night

The median time is $9\frac{1}{4}$ hours in each random sample. However, based on the box plots, Margo and Ravi can infer that less than half of seventh graders get between 9 and $9\frac{1}{2}$ hours of sleep each night. So, these data do not support Sasha's inference.

 Try It!

Alexis surveys three different samples of 20 students selected randomly from the population of 492 students in the seventh grade about their choice for class president. In each sample, Elijah receives the fewest votes. Alexis infers that Elijah will not win the election. Is her inference valid? Explain.

EXAMPLE 4 **Make an Estimate from Sample Data**

Derek is writing a report on cell phone usage. He collects data from a random sample of seventh graders in his school, and finds that 16 out of 20 seventh graders have cell phones. If there are 290 seventh graders in his school, estimate the number of seventh graders who have cell phones.

Write and solve a proportion to estimate the number of seventh graders, c, who have cell phones.

$$\frac{\text{7th graders with cell phones in sample}}{\text{number of 7th graders in sample}} = \frac{\text{7th graders with cell phones in school}}{\text{number of 7th graders in school}}$$

$$\frac{16}{20} = \frac{c}{290}$$

$$\frac{16}{20} \cdot 290 = \frac{c}{290} \cdot 290$$

$$232 = c$$

Based on the sample, about 232 seventh graders in Derek's school have cell phones.

 Try It!

For his report, Derek also collects data from a random sample of eighth graders in his school, and finds that 18 out of 20 eighth graders have cell phones. If there are 310 eighth graders in his school, estimate the number of eighth graders who have cell phones.

KEY CONCEPT

You can analyze numerical data from a random sample to draw inferences about the population. Measures of center, like mean and median, and measures of variability, like range, can be used to analyze the data in a sample.

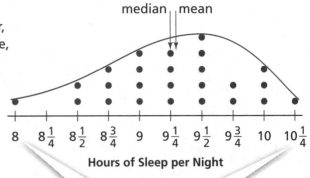

The range is $10\frac{1}{4} - 8 = 2\frac{1}{4}$ hours.

Do You Understand?

1. **? Essential Question** How can inferences be drawn about a population from data gathered from samples?

2. Reasoning Why can you use a random sample to make an inference?

3. Critique Reasoning Darrin surveyed a random sample of 10 students from his science class about their favorite types of TV shows. Five students like detective shows, 4 like comedy shows, and 1 likes game shows. Darrin concluded that the most popular type of TV show among students in his school is likely detective shows. Explain why Darrin's inference is not valid.

4. Reasoning How can you use proportional reasoning to make an estimate about a population using data from a sample?

Do You Know How?

5. In a carnival game, players get 5 chances to throw a basketball through a hoop. The dot plot shows the number of baskets made by 20 different players.

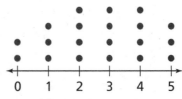

Number of Baskets Made

  a. Make an inference by looking at the shape of the data.

  b. What is the median of the data? What is the mean? Do these measures of center support the inference you made in part (a)?

6. In the dot plot above, 3 of 20 players made all 5 baskets. Based on this data, about how many players out of 300 players will make all 5 baskets?

7. The manager of a box office gathered data from two different ticket windows where tickets to a music concert were being sold. Does the data shown in the box plots below support the inference that most of the tickets sold were about $40? Explain.

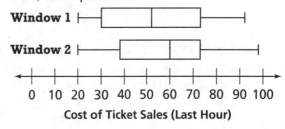

Cost of Ticket Sales (Last Hour)

Practice & Problem Solving

Leveled Practice In 8–10, use the sample data to answer the questions.

Alicia and Thea are in charge of determining the number of T-shirts to order to sell in the school store. Each student collected sample data from the population of 300 students. Alicia surveyed 50 students in the cafeteria. Thea surveyed the first 60 students who arrived at school one morning.

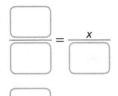

Results of Alicia's Survey	Results of Thea's Survey
$\dfrac{30}{50}$ said they would like a T-shirt.	$\dfrac{51}{60}$ said they would like a T-shirt.

8. Use Alicia's data to estimate the number of T-shirts they should order.

$$\frac{\boxed{}}{\boxed{}} = \frac{x}{\boxed{}}$$

$$\boxed{} = x$$

They should order about $\boxed{}$ T-shirts.

9. Use Thea's data to estimate the number of T-shirts they should order.

$$\frac{\boxed{}}{\boxed{}} = \frac{x}{\boxed{}}$$

$$\boxed{} = x$$

They should order about $\boxed{}$ T-shirts.

10. **Construct Arguments** Can Alicia or Thea make a valid inference? Explain.

11. Three of the five medical doctors surveyed by a biochemist prefer his newly approved Brand X as compared to the leading medicine. The biochemist used these results to write the TV advertisement shown. Is the inference valid? Explain your answer.

12. Aaron conducted a survey of the type of shoes worn by a random sample of students in his school. The results of his survey are shown at the right.

a. Make a valid inference that compares the number of students who are likely to wear gym shoes and those likely to wear boots.

b. Make a valid inference that compares the number of students who are likely to wear boots and those likely to wear sandals.

---

13. Shantel and Syrus are researching the types of novels that people read. Shantel asks every ninth person at the entrance of a mall. She infers that about 26% of the population prefers fantasy novels. Syrus asks every person in only one store. He infers that about 47% of the population prefers fantasy novels.

a. Construct Arguments Whose inference is more likely to be valid? Explain.

b. What mistake might Syrus have made?

14. Higher Order Thinking A national TV news show conducted an online poll to find the nation's favorite comedian. The website showed the pictures of 5 comedians and asked visitors of the site to vote. The news show inferred that the comedian with the most votes was the funniest comedian in the nation.

a. Is the inference valid? Explain.

b. How could you improve the poll? Explain.

In **15** and **16**, use the table of survey results from a random sample of people about the way they prefer to view movies.

15. Lindsay infers that out of 400 people, 300 would prefer to watch movies in a theater. Is her inference valid? Explain.

Preferred Ways to View Movies

Method	Number of People
Theater	30
Streaming	62
DVD	8

16. Which inferences are valid? Select all that apply.

- ☐ Going to a theater is the most popular way to watch a movie.
- ☐ About twice as many people would prefer to stream movies instead of watching in a theater.
- ☐ About 3 times as many people would prefer to watch a movie on DVD instead of watching in a theater.
- ☐ About 8 times as many people would prefer to watch a movie on DVD instead of streaming.
- ☐ Most people would prefer streaming over any other method.

17. Monique collects data from a random sample of seventh graders in her school and finds that 10 out of 25 seventh graders participate in after-school activities. Write and solve a proportion to estimate the number of seventh graders, *n*, who participate in after-school activities if 190 seventh graders attend Monique's school.

18. Each of the 65 participants at a basketball camp attempted 20 free throws. Mitchell collected data for the first 10 participants, most of whom were first-time campers. Lydia collected data for the next 10 participants, most of whom had attended the camp for at least one week.

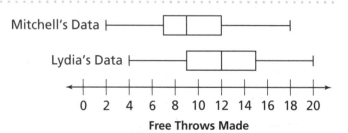

a. Using only his own data, what inference might Mitchell make about the median number of free throws made by the 65 participants?

b. Using only her own data, what inference might Lydia make about the median number of free throws made by the 65 participants?

c. Who made a valid inference? Explain.

✅ Assessment Practice

19. June wants to know how many times most people have their hair cut each year. She asks two of her friends from Redville and Greenburg, respectively, to conduct a random survey. The results of the surveys are shown below.

Redville: 50 people surveyed
Median number of haircuts: 7
Mean number of haircuts: 7.3

Greenburg: 60 people surveyed
Median number of haircuts: 6.5
Mean number of haircuts: 7.6

June infers that most people get 7 haircuts per year. Based on the survey results, is this a valid inference? Explain.

Name: _____

1. **Vocabulary** Krista says that her chickens lay the most eggs of any chickens in the county. To prove her claim, she could survey chicken farms to see how many eggs each of their chickens laid that day. In this scenario, what is the *population* and what is a possible *representative sample*? *Lesson 8-1*

2. Marcy wants to know which type of book is most commonly checked out by visitors of her local public library. She surveys people in the children's reading room between 1:00 and 2:00 on Saturday afternoon. Select all the statements about Marcy's survey that are true. *Lesson 8-1*

☐ Marcy's sample is not representative because not all of the library's visitors go to the children's reading room.

☐ Marcy's sample is a representative sample of the population.

☐ Marcy will get a random sample by surveying as many people in the children's reading room as possible.

☐ The population of Marcy's study consists of all visitors of the public library.

☐ The results of Marcy's survey include a mode, but neither a mean nor a median.

For Problems 3–5, use the data from the table.

3. Michael surveyed a random sample of students in his school about the number of sports they play. There are 300 students in Michael's school. Use the results of the survey to estimate the number of students in Michael's school who play exactly one sport. Explain your answer. *Lesson 8-2*

Number of Sports Students Play

Number of Sports	Number of Students
None	13
Exactly 1	15
More than 1	32

4. What inference can you draw about the number of students who play more than one sport? *Lesson 8-2*

5. Avi says that Michael's sample was not random because he did not survey students from other schools. Is Avi's statement correct? Explain. *Lesson 8-1*

How well did you do on the mid-topic checkpoint? Fill in the stars.

MID-TOPIC PERFORMANCE TASK

Sunil is the ticket manager at a local soccer field. He wants to conduct a survey to determine how many games most spectators attend during the soccer season.

PART A

What is the population for Sunil's survey? Give an example of a way that Sunil could collect a representative sample of this population.

PART B

Sunil conducts the survey and obtains the results shown in the table below. What can Sunil infer from the results of the survey?

Soccer Game Attendance

Number of Games	Number of Spectators
1–2	57
3–4	43
5 or more	50

PART C

Suppose 2,400 spectators attend at least one game this soccer season. Use the survey data to estimate the number of spectators who attended 5 or more games this season. Explain how you made your estimate.

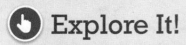

Explore It!

ACTIVITY

Ella surveys a random sample of 20 seventh graders about the number of siblings they have.

Lesson 8-3
Make Comparative Inferences About Populations

Go Online

I can...
draw comparative inferences about two populations using median and interquartile range (IQR).

© **Common Core Content Standards**
7.SP.B.3, 7.SP.B.4

Mathematical Practices
MP.1, MP.2, MP.4, MP.7, MP.8

The table shows the results of her survey.

Student	A	B	C	D	E	F	G	H	I	J	K	L	M	N	O	P	Q	R	S	T
Number of Siblings	1	1	2	0	2	1	3	1	1	6	1	2	3	2	1	3	2	0	2	1

A. Model with Math Draw a model to show how Ella can best display her data.

B. Explain why you chose that model.

Focus on math practices

Reasoning Using your data display, what can you infer about the number of siblings that most seventh graders have? Explain.

VISUAL LEARNING ASSES

EXAMPLE 1 **Use Box Plots to Compare Populations**

Scan for Multimedia

Finn and Jonah attend different middle schools. They compare the number of hours students at each school spend on homework each week. Finn and Jonah each conduct a random sample of 20 students who attend their schools, and then list the data in order from least to greatest. What can Finn notice about the time spent on homework?

Hours That 20 Students Spend on Homework Each Week

Finn's School	1	1	2	3	3	4	4	4	4	5	5	5	5	6	6	7	7	8	9	11
Jonah's School	1	5	5	5	5	6	6	6	6	6	8	8	8	8	8	8	9	9	10	11

STEP 1 Display the two data sets in box plots.

This box is between $3\frac{1}{2}$ and $6\frac{1}{2}$. The median is 5.

This box is between $5\frac{1}{2}$ and 8. The median is 7.

Finn's Data Set

Jonah's Data Set

0 1 2 3 4 5 6 7 8 9 10 11
Hours of Homework per Week

Look for Relationships The median best describes the data because both data sets have outliers.

STEP 2 Use the box plots to compare the two data sets.

Finn's Data Set

Jonah's Data Set

0 1 2 3 4 5 6 7 8 9 10 11
Hours of Homework per Week

The line for the median of Jonah's data set is to the right of the line for the median of Finn's data set. So, Finn can say that the median of Jonah's data set is greater.

The box for Finn's data set is longer than the box for Jonah's data set. So, Finn can say that his data is more spread out, or has greater variability.

☑ **Try It!**

Kono gathers the heights of a random sample of sixth graders and seventh graders and displays the data in box plots. What can he say about the two data sets?

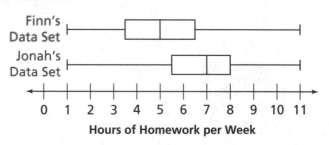

The median of the ⬜ grade sample is greater

than the median of the ⬜ grade sample.

The ⬜ grade sample has greater variability.

6th-Grade Students

7th-Grade Students

52 54 56 58 60 62 64 66 68 70 72 74
Height (in.)

Convince Me! How can you visually compare data from two samples that are displayed in box plots?

EXAMPLE 2 · Draw Inferences Using Median and Interquartile Range

Finn and Jonah analyze the measures of center and variability of the data they collected. Do these measures support Finn's assessment of the two data sets in Example 1?

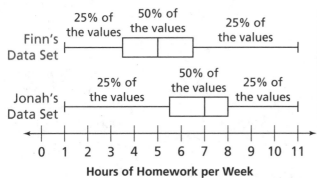

	First Quartile	Median	Third Quartile	Interquartile Range
Finn's Data Set	$3\frac{1}{2}$	5	$6\frac{1}{2}$	3
Jonah's Data Set	$5\frac{1}{2}$	7	8	$2\frac{1}{2}$

The median of Jonah's data set is greater. So the students at Jonah's school generally spend more hours on homework each week than the students at Finn's school.

The interquartile range of Finn's data set is greater. So there is greater variability, or spread, in the number of hours students in Finn's school spend on homework.

EXAMPLE 3 · Draw More Inferences Using Measures of Center and Variability

Mr. Bunsen had students grow the same type of plant in two different rooms to test the growing conditions. The box plots show the heights of all the plants after 3 weeks. How do the two populations compare? What inferences can be drawn?

The median heights are the same.

50% of the plants in 7D are between 8 and 14 inches tall IQR = 6.

50% of the plants in 7G are between 10 and 16 inches tall IQR = 6.

Room 7D

Room 7G

Height (in.)

While the median heights of the plants are the same, the plants in Room 7G are generally taller. You can infer that the growing conditions in Room 7G are more favorable for plant growth than in Room 7D.

☑ Try It!

A local recreation center offers a drop-in exercise class in the morning and in the evening. The attendance data for each class over the first month is shown in the box plots at the right. What can you infer about the class attendance?

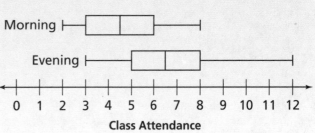

Morning

Evening

Class Attendance

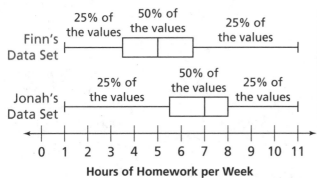

8-3 Make Comparative Inferences About Populations · 499

You can use data displays, such as box plots, to make informal comparative inferences about two populations. You can compare the shapes of the data displays or the measures of center and variability.

The medians of the two data sets appear to be the same.

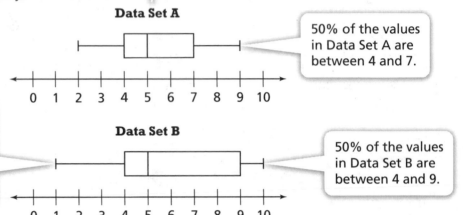

Data Set A

50% of the values in Data Set A are between 4 and 7.

The length of the box, the IQR, for Data Set B is greater than the length of the box, the IQR, for Data Set A. So Data Set B has greater variability.

Data Set B

50% of the values in Data Set B are between 4 and 9.

Do You Understand?

1. **Essential Question** How can data displays be used to compare populations?

2. **Generalize** What measures of variability are used when comparing box plots? What do these measures tell you?

3. **Make Sense and Persevere** Two data sets both have a median value of 12.5. Data Set A has an interquartile range of 4 and Data Set B has an interquartile range of 2. How do the box plots for the two data sets compare?

Do You Know How?

The box plots describe the heights of flowers selected randomly from two gardens. Use the box plots to answer 4 and 5.

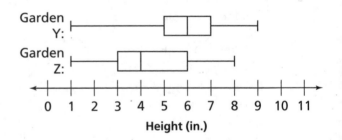

Height (in.)

4. Find the median of each sample.

   Garden Y median = ⬚ inches

   Garden Z median = ⬚ inches

5. Make a comparative inference about the flowers in the two gardens.

Name: _____

Practice & Problem Solving

  PRACTICE   TUTORIAL

Leveled Practice For 6–8, complete each statement.

6. Water boils at lower temperatures as elevation increases. Rob and Ann live in different cities. They both boil the same amount of water in the same size pan and repeat the experiment the same number of times. Each records the water temperature just as the water starts to boil. They use box plots to display their data. Compare the medians of the box plots.

Rob's Temperature Data

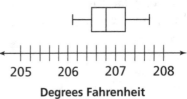

The median of Rob's data is [   ] the median of Ann's data.

This means Rob is at [   ] elevation than Ann.

Ann's Temperature Data

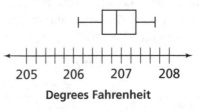

7. Liz is analyzing two data sets that compare the amount of food two animals eat each day for one month.

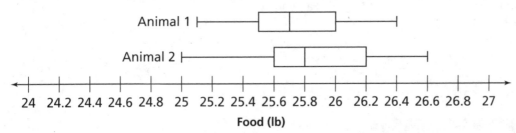

a. The median of Animal 2's data is [   ] than the median of Animal 1's data.

b. Liz can infer that there is [   ] variability in the data for Animal 1 than for Animal 2.

c. Liz can infer that Animal [   ] generally eats more food.

8. The box plots show the heights of a sample of two types of trees.

The median height of Tree [   ] is greater.

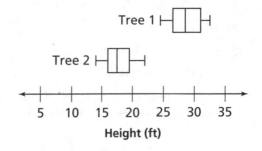

9. **Reasoning** A family is comparing home prices in towns where they would like to live. The family learns that the median home price in Hometown is equal to the median home price in Plainfield and concludes that the homes in Hometown and Plainfield are similarly priced.

What is another statistical measure that the family might consider when deciding where to purchase a home?

10. **Higher Order Thinking** The box plots show the daily average high temperatures of two cities from January to December. Which city should you live in if you want a greater variability in temperature? Explain.

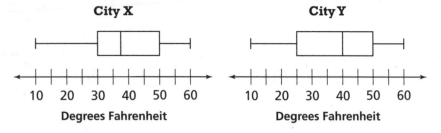

Assessment Practice

11. Paul compares the high temperatures in City 1 and City 2 for one week. In City 1, the range in temperature is 10°F and the IQR is 5°F. In City 2, the range in temperature is 20°F and the IQR is 5°F.

What might you conclude about the weather pattern in each city based on the ranges and interquartile ranges?

Ⓐ The weather pattern in City 1 is more consistent than the weather pattern in City 2.

Ⓑ The weather patterns in City 1 and City 2 are equally consistent.

Ⓒ The weather pattern in City 2 is more consistent than the weather pattern in City 1.

Ⓓ The range and interquartile range do not provide enough information to make a conclusion.

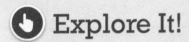 Explore It!

Jackson and his brother Levi watch Jewel Geyser erupt one afternoon. They record the time intervals between eruptions. The dot plot shows their data.

Jackson estimates that the average time between eruptions is 8 minutes. Levi estimates that the average time between eruptions is $8\frac{1}{2}$ minutes.

Jewel Geyser Eruptions

Lesson 8-4
Make More Comparative Inferences About Populations

📶 Go Online

I can...
compare populations using the mean, median, mode, range, interquartile range, and mean absolute deviation.

© **Common Core Content Standards**
7.SP.B.3, 7.SP.B.4

Mathematical Practices
MP.2, MP.3, MP.4, MP.8

A. Construct Arguments Construct an argument to support Jackson's position.

B. Construct Arguments Construct an argument to support Levi's position.

Focus on math practices

Reasoning How can you determine the best measure of center to describe a set of data?

? **Essential Question** How can dot plots and statistical measures be used to compare populations?

   VISUAL LEARNING   ASSESS

EXAMPLE 1 **Use Dot Plots to Compare Populations**

Scan for Multimedia

Quinn collects data from a random sample of 20 seventh-grade students who participate in a youth fitness program. She compares the number of curl-ups each student completed in thirty seconds last year and this year. What can Quinn infer from her comparison of the data sets?

Number of Curl-Ups That 20 Students Completed

Last Year	20	27	21	26	22	25	23	23	26	23	24	24	25	24	22	24	23	24	21	25
This Year	21	30	22	24	29	26	28	26	30	27	27	29	27	28	25	28	25	28	29	23

STEP 1 Display the two data sets in dot plots.

Model with Math Why are dot plots an appropriate representation for the data sets?

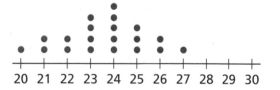

STEP 2 Use the dot plots to compare the two data sets.

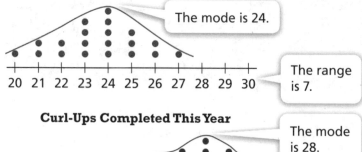

The mode is 24.

The range is 7.

The mode is 28.

The range is 9.

The number of curl-ups completed this year is generally greater than last year. But, based on the shape of the data, not all students made the same progress.

Quinn can infer that most of her classmates were able to do more curl-ups this year.

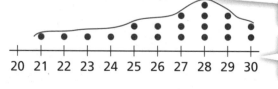 **Try It!**

Quinn also collects data about push-ups. Does it appear that students generally did more push-ups last year or this year? Explain your reasoning.

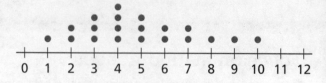

Push-Ups Completed Last Year

Convince Me! How does the range of these data sets affect the shape of the dot plots?

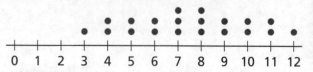

Push-Ups Completed This Year

EXAMPLE 2 Use Measures of Center and Variability to Compare Populations

Quinn computes the mean and mean absolute deviation (MAD) for each data set. How do these measures support Quinn's inference from the data displays?

	Mean	MAD
Curl-Ups Completed Last Year	23.6	1.4
Curl-Ups Completed This Year	26.6	2.1

> The mean can be used to describe the data because the data sets do not have outliers.

The mean number of curl-ups completed this year is greater than the mean number of curl-ups completed last year. This supports Quinn's inference.

The mean absolute deviation is greater for the number of curl-ups completed this year. This suggests that not all students made the same progress.

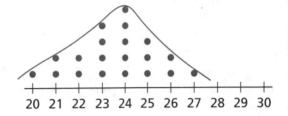

Curl-Ups Completed Last Year

20 21 22 23 24 25 26 27 28 29 30

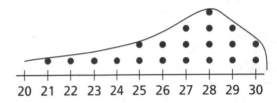

Curl-Ups Completed This Year

20 21 22 23 24 25 26 27 28 29 30

EXAMPLE 3 Use Statistical Measures to Make Predictions

Rafi, one of Quinn's classmates, reported the numbers of curl-ups he completed this year and last year. He did not tell Quinn which number is for which year. Based on the data that Quinn gathered, which number *most likely* represents the curl-ups he completed last year?

Based on the data that Quinn gathered, she inferred that most students could complete more curl-ups this year than last year.

So, Rafi *most likely* completed 19 curl-ups last year and 23 curl-ups this year.

Total curl-ups **19**

Total curl-ups **23**

 Try It!

Peter surveyed a random sample of adults and a random sample of teenagers about the number of hours that they exercise in a typical week. He recorded the data in the table below. What comparative inference can Peter make from the data sets?

Hours of Exercise

	Mean	MAD
Adults	4.4	3.0
Teenagers	7.9	2.8

You can use dot plots to make informal comparative inferences about two populations. You can compare the shapes of the data displays or the measures of center and variability.

	Mean	Mean Absolute Deviation (MAD)
Data Set A	15.04	1.9648
Data Set B	18.56	2.1024

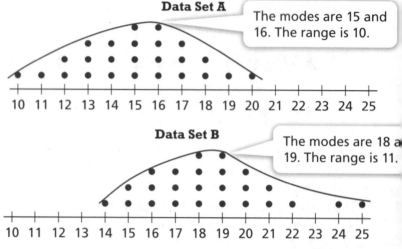

Data Set A

The modes are 15 and 16. The range is 10.

10 11 12 13 14 15 16 17 18 19 20 21 22 23 24 25

Data Set B

The modes are 18 a 19. The range is 11.

10 11 12 13 14 15 16 17 18 19 20 21 22 23 24 25

The modes of Data Set B are greater than the modes of Data Set A.
The mean of Data Set B is greater than the mean of Data Set A.
You can infer that data points are generally greater in Data Set B.

The ranges and the MADs of the data sets are similar. You can infer that the variabilities of the two data sets are about the same.

Do You Understand?

1. **? Essential Question** How can dot plots and statistical measures be used to compare populations?

2. **Reasoning** How can you make predictions using data from samples from two populations?

3. **Construct Arguments** Two data sets have the same mean but one set has a much larger MAD than the other. Explain why you may want to use the median to compare the data sets rather than the mean.

Do You Know How?

For 4 and 5, use the information below.

Coach Fiske recorded the number of shots on goal his first-line hockey players made during two weeks of hockey scrimmage.

	Week 1	Week 2
Day 1	5	8
Day 2	4	7
Day 3	6	9
Day 4	8	5
Day 5	2	5
Day 6	3	7
Day 7	7	8

4. Find the mean number of shots on goal for each week.

5. **a.** Based on the mean for each week, in which week did his first line take more shots on goal?

   b. Based on the comparison of the mean and the range for Week 1 and Week 2, what could the coach infer?

Practice & Problem Solving

Scan for
Multimedia

Leveled Practice In 6 and 7, complete each statement.

6. A study is done to compare the fuel efficiency of cars. Cars in Group 1 generally get about 23 miles per gallon. Cars in Group 2 generally get about 44 miles per gallon. Compare the groups by their means. Then make an inference and give a reason the inference might be true.

The mean for Group ☐ is less than the mean for

Group ☐.

The cars in Group ☐ generally are more fuel-efficient.

The cars in Group ☐ may be smaller.

Group 1

23 miles
per gallon

Group 2

44 miles
per gallon

7. The dot plot shows a random sample of vertical leap heights of basketball players in two different basketball camps. Compare the mean values of the dot plots. Round to the nearest tenth.

Vertical Leap Samples

Camp	Mean
1	$303 \div 11 =$ ☐
2	☐ $\div 11 =$ ☐

The mean values tell you that participants in Camp ☐ jump higher in general.

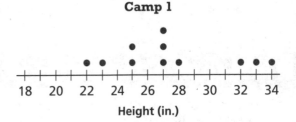

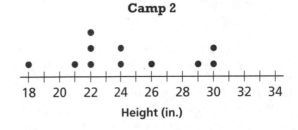

8. A researcher divides some marbles into two data sets. In Data Set 1, the mean mass of the marbles is 13.6 grams. In Data Set 2, the mean mass of the marbles is 14 grams. The MAD of both data sets is 2. What can you infer about the two sets of marbles?

9. **Generalize** Brianna asks 8 classmates how many pencils and erasers they carry in their bags. The mean number of pencils is 11. The mean number of erasers is 4. The MAD of both data sets is 2. What inference could Brianna make using this data?

10. **Higher Order Thinking** Two machines in a factory are supposed to work at the same speed to pass inspection. The number of items built by each machine on five different days is recorded in the table. The inspector believes that the machines should not pass inspection because the mean speed of Machine X is much faster than the mean speed of Machine Y.

Number of Items Built

| Machine X | 20 | 16 | 21 | 18 | 19 |
| Machine Y | 23 | 2 | 18 | 21 | 19 |

a. Which measures of center and variability should be used to compare the performances of each machine? Explain.

b. Is the inspector correct? Explain.

✓ Assessment Practice

11. The dot plots show the weights of a random sample of fish from two lakes.

Which comparative inference about the fish in the two lakes is most likely correct?

Ⓐ There is about the same variation in weight between small and large fish in both lakes.

Ⓑ There is less variation in weight between small and large fish in South Lake than between small and large fish in Round Lake.

Ⓒ There is less variation in weight between small and large fish in Round Lake than between small and large fish in South Lake.

Ⓓ There is greater variability in the weights of fish in Round Lake.

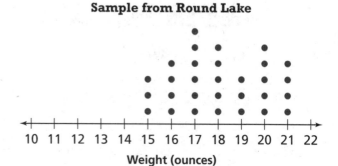

Sample from Round Lake

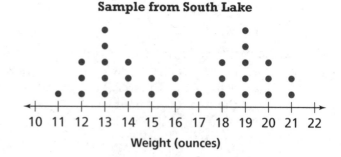

Sample from South Lake

3-ACT MATH

3-Act Mathematical Modeling:
Raising Money

Go Online

© **Common Core Content Standards**
7.SP.A.1, 7.SP.A.2, 7.RP.A.3
Mathematical Practices
MP.4, MP.1, MP.2, MP.3, MP.5, MP.7, MP.8

ACT 1

1. After watching the video, what is the first question that comes to mind?

2. Write the Main Question you will answer.

3. Make a prediction to answer this Main Question.

4. Construct Arguments Explain how you arrived at your prediction.

5. What information in this situation would be helpful to know? How would you use that information?

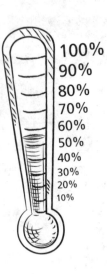

6. Use Appropriate Tools What tools can you use to solve the problem? Explain how you would use them strategically.

7. Model with Math Represent the situation using mathematics. Use your representation to answer the Main Question.

8. What is your answer to the Main Question? Does it differ from your prediction? Explain.

9. Write the answer you saw in the video.

10. Reasoning Does your answer match the answer in the video? If not, what are some reasons that would explain the difference?

11. Make Sense and Persevere Would you change your model now that you know the answer? Explain.

Reflect

12. **Model with Math** Explain how you used a mathematical model to represent the situation. How did the model help you answer the Main Question?

13. **Critique Reasoning** Explain why you agree or disagree with each of the arguments in Act 2.

14. **Use Appropriate Tools** You and your friends are starting a new school club. Design a sampling method that is easy to use to help you estimate how many people will join your club. What tools will you use?

? Topic Essential Question

How can sampling be used to draw inferences about one or more populations?

Vocabulary Review

Complete each definition, and then provide an example of each vocabulary word used.

Vocabulary
inference	population	random sample
representative sample	sample	valid inference

Definition	Example
1. A(n) [_____] is an entire group of objects from which data can be collected.	
2. Making a conclusion by interpreting data is called making a(n) [_____].	
3. A(n) [_____] is one that is true about a population based on a representative sample.	
4. A(n) [_____] accurately reflects the characteristics of an entire population.	

Use Vocabulary in Writing

Do adults or teenagers brush their teeth more? Nelson surveys two groups: 50 seventh-grade students from his school and 50 students at a nearby college of dentistry. Use vocabulary words to explain whether Nelson can draw valid conclusions.

Concepts and Skills Review

Populations and Samples

Quick Review

A population is an entire group of people, items, or events. Most populations must be reduced to a smaller group, or sample, before surveying. A representative sample accurately reflects the characteristics of the population. In a random sample, each member of the population has an equal chance of being included.

Example

Describe the sample and the population.

Honey Bee Florist Customer Survey: Favorite Flowers

Rose	Daisy	Tulip
15	9	16

Sample: 40 customers of Honey Bee Florist

Population: All Honey Bee Florist customers

Practice

1. Anthony opened a new store and wants to conduct a survey to determine the best store hours. Which is the best representative sample?

   Ⓐ A group of randomly selected people who come to the store in one week

   Ⓑ A group of randomly selected people who visit his website on one night

   Ⓒ Every person he meets at his health club one night

   Ⓓ The first 20 people who walk into his store one day

2. Becky wants to know if she should sell cranberry muffins at her bakery. She asks every customer who buys blueberry muffins if they would buy cranberry muffins. Is this a representative sample? Explain.

3. Simon wants to find out which shop has the best frozen fruit drink in town. How could Simon conduct a survey with a sample that is representative of the population?

Quick Review

An inference is a conclusion about a population based on data from a sample or samples. Patterns or trends in data from representative samples can be used to make valid inferences. Estimates can be made about the population based on the sample data.

Example

There are 400 students at Polly's school. She surveyed a random sample of 80 students to find their favorite hobby.

19 said they like to read.

30 said they like to be with friends.

8 said they like to do crafts.

23 said they like to play sports.

Make an inference from the data.

Doing crafts is the least popular hobby at Polly's school.

Practice

1. Refer to the example. Polly surveys two more samples. Do the results from these samples support the inference made from the example?

Random Samples of Students' Favorite Hobbies

Sample 2		Sample 3	
Hobby	Number of Students	Hobby	Number of Students
Read	24	Read	32
Friends	35	Friends	41
Crafts	11	Crafts	16
Sports	30	Sports	31

2. Refer to the example. Yovani estimates that about 200 students in the school favor playing sports as a hobby. Do you agree? Explain.

Quick Review

Box plots and dot plots are common ways to display data gathered from samples of populations. Using these data displays makes it easier to visually compare sets of data and make inferences. Statistical measures such as mean, median, mode, MAD, interquartile range (IQR), and range can also be used to draw inferences when comparing data from samples of two populations.

Example

The box plots show how long it took students in Ms. Huang's two math classes to complete their math homework last night. Use the median time to make an inference.

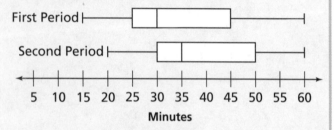

Median for First Period: 30

Median for Second Period: 35

Students in the second-period class tended to take longer to complete their math homework.

Janelle collected data for runs scored for two baseball teams in the first 8 games of the season.

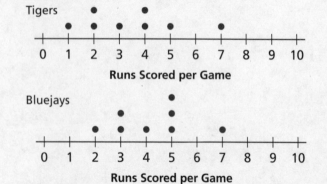

What can Janelle infer from the data sets?

The Bluejays are a higher scoring team. The mode is greater for them than it is for the Tigers.

Practice

1. The two data sets show the number of days that team members trained before a 5K race.

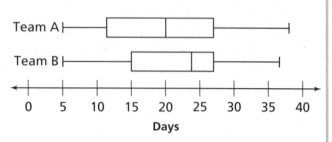

a. What inference can you draw by comparing the medians?

b. What inference can you draw by comparing the interquartile ranges?

2. The dot plots show how long it took students in Mr. Chauncey's two science classes to finish their science homework last night. Find the means to make an inference about the data.

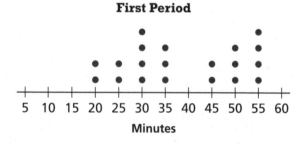

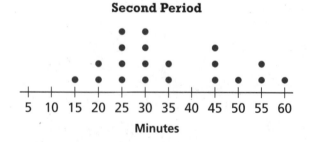

Riddle Rearranging

Find each percent change or percent error. Round to the nearest whole percent as needed. Then arrange the answers in order from least to greatest. The letters will spell out the answer to the riddle below.

I can...
use the percent equation to solve problems. © 7.RP.A.3

V
A young tree is 16 inches tall. One year later, it is 20 inches tall. What is the percent increase in height?

A
A ship weighs 7 tons with no cargo. With cargo, it weighs 10.5 tons. What is the percent increase in the weight?

R
The balance of an account is $500 in April. In May it is $440. What is the percent decrease in the balance?

B
Ben thought an assignment would take 20 minutes to complete. It took 35 minutes. What is the percent error in his estimate of the time?

N
Natalie has $250 in savings. At the end of 6 months, she has $450 in savings. What is the percent increase in the amount of her savings?

I
The water level of a lake is 22 feet. It falls to 18 feet during one month. What is the percent decrease in the water level?

R
Shamar has 215 photos on his cell phone. He deletes some so that only 129 photos remain. What is the percent decrease in the number of photos?

K
Lita estimates she will read 24 books during the summer. She actually reads 9 books. What is the percent error of her estimate?

E
Camden estimates his backpack weighs 9 pounds with his books. It actually weighs 12 pounds. What is the percent error of his estimate?

Where do fish keep their money?

( ) ( ) ( ) ( ) ( )   ( ) ( ) ( ) ( )

? Topic Essential Question

How can you investigate chance processes and develop, use, and evaluate probability models?

Topic Overview

Topic Vocabulary

- compound event
- event
- experimental probability
- outcome
- probability
- probability model
- relative frequency
- sample space
- simulation
- theoretical probability

Lesson Digital Resources

INTERACTIVE STUDENT EDITION
Access online or offline.

INTERACTIVE ANIMATION
Interact with visual learning animations.

ACTIVITY Use with *Solve & Discuss It, Explore* and *Explain It* activities, and to explore Examp

VIDEOS Watch clips to support *3-Act Mathematical Modeling Lessons* and *STEM Pr*

 Go online

3-ACT MATH

Photo Finish

Have you ever watched a race that was so close you couldn't tell who won? That's what a photo finish is for. In shorter races, such as the 100-meter sprint, all the runners could finish within half a second of each other. That's why it's important for athletes to consider every possible way to improve their race times. Think about this during the 3-Act Mathematical Modeling lesson.

PRACTICE Practice what you've learned.

TUTORIALS Get help from *Virtual Nerd*, right when you need it.

MATH TOOLS Explore math with digital tools.

GAMES Play Math Games to help you learn.

KEY CONCEPT Review important lesson content.

GLOSSARY Read and listen to English/Spanish definitions.

ASSESSMENT Show what you've learned.

enVision® STEM Project

Did You Know?

China and India are the two **most populated** nations in the world. More than $\frac{1}{3}$ of all people live in one of these countries.

India
1.252 billion

Chinese and Indian populations compared to rest of World's nations

China
1.357 billion

Rest of the World
4.793 billion

Total Population
7.4 billion

California has a greater **population** than Canada.

Canada
35.16 million

California
38.8 million

Nearly **ten million more** people live in the metropolitan area of Tokyo, Japan, than in the entire State of Texas.

JAPAN

Tokyo

TEXAS

The population of the world has nearly **doubled** in the last 40 years, but is expected to take at least 100 years to double again.

World population

1975: 4.1 billion

2016: 7.4 billion

2125: 15 billion (estimated)

There are more than **100,000 residents per square mile** in Manila, the capital city of the Philippines. There is approximately **1 human** inhabitant per square mile in Alaska.

Your Task: International Trending

Demography is the science of populations. Demographers — scientists who study populations — follow trends in populations, including birth rates and immigration statistics, to learn more about how countries are changing around the world. You and your classmates will use population data like birth rate, age range, and life expectancy to compare and contrast the characteristics of populations.

Review What You Know!

Vocabulary

Choose the best term from the box to complete each definition.

| equivalent |
| frequency |
| diagram |
| ratio |

1. A(n) [ ] is a drawing that can be used to visually represent information.

2. The number of times a specific value occurs is referred to as [ ].

3. A(n) [ ] is a relationship between one quantity and another quantity.

4. Quantities that have the same value are [ ].

Operations with Fractions

Solve for x.

5. $\frac{2}{5} + x = 1$

6. $225 \cdot \frac{1}{3} = x$

7. $1 = \frac{1}{8} + x + \frac{2}{8}$

Ratios

Write each ratio in fraction form. Then write the percent equivalent.

8. 72 out of 96

9. 88 out of 132

10. 39 out of 104

11. 23 out of 69

12. 52 out of 208

13. 25 out of 200

Order Fractions and Decimals

Plot the following fractions and decimals on the number line.

$$0.7, \frac{1}{3}, \frac{7}{8}, 0.4, 0.125, \frac{5}{6}$$

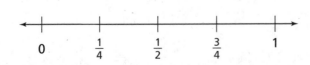

$$0 \qquad \frac{1}{4} \qquad \frac{1}{2} \qquad \frac{3}{4} \qquad 1$$

Language Development

Sort the vocabulary words into categories. Explain your categories.

compound event	event	experimental probability	outcome
probability	probability model	relative frequency	sample space
simulation	theoretical probability		

Category:

Category:

Category:

PROJECT 9A

What makes a carnival game fun and successful?

PROJECT: DEVELOP A GAME OF CHANCE

PROJECT 9B

If you could invent a character for an adventure, what would that character be like?

PROJECT: DESIGN AN ADVENTURE

PROJECT 9C

What is the silliest sentence you can think of? Why is it silly?

PROJECT: GENERATE A FUNNY SENTENCE

PROJECT 9D

How could you teach a math concept through a performance?

PROJECT: PERFORM YOUR KNOWLEDGE

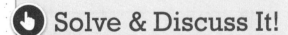

Solve & Discuss It!

 ACTIVITY

For a game show, Jared has to choose 1 of 8 boxes to win a prize. One of the boxes has a big prize, 3 boxes have a medium prize, 3 boxes have smaller prizes, and 1 box is empty. How confident should Jared be that whatever box he chooses, he will win a prize? Support your response with a mathematical argument.

I can...
describe the likelihood that an event will occur.

© **Common Core Content Standards**
7.SP.C.5, 7.EE.B.3

Mathematical Practices
MP.1, MP.2, MP.3, MP.4

Make Sense and Persevere
What are the chances that Jared will choose a box with a prize?

Focus on math practices

Construct Arguments Suppose the empty box is taken out of the game.
How confident should Jared be that he will win a prize? Explain.

VISUAL LEARNING   ASSESS

EXAMPLE 1 **Use Probability to Describe Chance**

Scan for Multimedia

Alisa and Cheri spin the pointer to the right and record the color that it lands on. The table shows their results after 100 spins. How can Alisa and Cheri explain their results?

Color	Frequency
Red	23
Yellow	24
Green	27
Blue	26

There are 4 possible results, or **outcomes**, when Alisa and Cheri spin the pointer:

- The pointer lands on the red section.
- The pointer lands on the yellow section.
- The pointer lands on the green section.
- The pointer lands on the blue section.

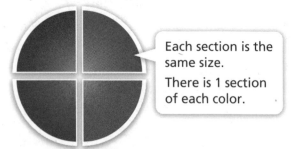

Each section is the same size.

There is 1 section of each color.

Each of the 4 outcomes is equally likely because the pointer has an equal chance of landing on any of the 4 sections.

Each time they spin the pointer, the likelihood, or **probability**, of the pointer landing on red, yellow, green, or blue is the same.

Each of the equal-sized sections is shaded 1 of 4 colors, so the probability of the pointer landing on any given color is 1 out of 4, or $\frac{1}{4}$. Since $\frac{1}{4} = 25\%$, the probability can also be written as 25%.

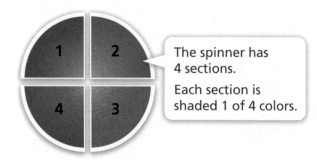

The spinner has 4 sections.

Each section is shaded 1 of 4 colors.

The pointer should land on each color about 1 out of 4 times, or about 25 times out of 100 spins.

☑ Try It!

How might the probability of the pointer landing on a given color change for the spinner shown at the right?

Convince Me! How would the probability of the pointer landing on a given color change if the spinner had six equal-sized sections with each section a different color?

EXAMPLE 2 ACTIVITY ASSESS

EXAMPLE 2 Use Probability and Likelihood to Describe Situations

Carrie will roll a number cube with sides labeled 1 to 6.

a. What is the probability that she will roll a 2?
Only 1 out of 6 total sides is a 2.
So, the probability is 1 out of 6, or $\frac{1}{6}$.

b. What is the probability that she will roll a number less than 7?
All 6 numbers on the cube are less than 7.
So, it is certain that she will roll a number less than 7.
The probability is 6 out of 6, or 1.

c. What is the probability that she will roll a number greater than 6?
None of the 6 numbers on the cube is greater than 6.
So, it is impossible to roll a number greater than 6.
The probability is 0 out of 6, or 0.

Try It!

The game piece shown has 12 sides, labeled 1 to 12.

a. What is the probability of rolling an 11?

b. What is the probability of rolling a number greater than 5?

c. What is the probability of rolling a number greater than 12?

EXAMPLE 3 Use Probability to Examine Fairness

Marisol designed a spinner for a game. The spinner is fair if there is an equal chance for the pointer to land on each letter. Is the spinner a fair spinner?

The probability of the pointer landing on "A" is 2 out of 6, which is equivalent to 1 out of 3, or $\frac{1}{3}$.

> The spinner has 6 equal-sized sections. Two sections are labeled "A."

The probability of the pointer landing on "B" is 1 out of 6, or $\frac{1}{6}$.

Each of the probabilities of the pointer landing on "C", "D", or "E" is also 1 out of 6, or $\frac{1}{6}$.

It is more likely that the pointer will land on "A" than on any other number. So, it is not a fair spinner.

Try It!

Is the spinner shown a fair spinner? If yes, explain why. If not, describe a change that could make the spinner fair.

The probability that something will occur is a value from 0 to 1, which describes its likelihood. You can write probability as a ratio, such as 1 out of 2, or $\frac{1}{2}$, or as a percent, such as 50%.

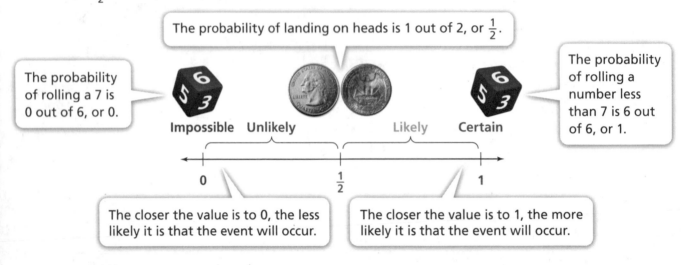

The probability of landing on heads is 1 out of 2, or $\frac{1}{2}$.

The probability of rolling a 7 is 0 out of 6, or 0.

The probability of rolling a number less than 7 is 6 out of 6, or 1.

Impossible Unlikely **Likely** **Certain**

0    $\frac{1}{2}$ 1

The closer the value is to 0, the less likely it is that the event will occur.

The closer the value is to 1, the more likely it is that the event will occur.

Do You Understand?

1. **? Essential Question** What is probability?

2. **Construct Arguments** How can you use probability to draw conclusions about the likelihood that something will occur?

3. **Reasoning** Why is probability limited to numbers between 0 and 1?

Do You Know How?

Allie is going to select a card from the group of cards shown. Complete each statement.

4. The probability that Allie will select a card

   labeled 3 is [　　　] out of 10, or

   [　　　] %.

5. Because the probability that each number will be

   selected is not [　　　], the group of cards
   is not fair.

6. It is [　　　] that Allie will select a card

   labeled with a number less than 6.

7. It is [　　　] that Allie will select a card

   labeled 4.

Practice & Problem Solving

Scan for
Multimedia

Leveled Practice In **8–10**, fill in the boxes to complete each statement.

8. A spinner has 8 equal-sized sections. Six of the sections are green.

    a. What is the probability that the spinner will land on green?

    [　] out of 8, or $\dfrac{[\ ]}{4}$, or [　] %

    b. Use words to describe the probability.

    It is [　] that the spinner will land on green.

9. Marcus is rolling a number cube with sides labeled 1 to 6.

    a. The probability that the number cube will show 10 is [　].

    b. It is [　] that the number cube will show 10.

10. Of the marbles in a bag, 3 are yellow, 2 are red, and 2 are blue. Sandra will randomly choose one marble from the bag.

    a. The probability that Sandra will choose a blue marble from the bag is [　] out of [　], or $\dfrac{[\ ]}{[\ ]}$.

    b. It is [　] that Sandra will choose a blue marble from the bag.

11. Suppose you have a bag with 20 letter tiles in it, and 3 of the tiles are labeled Y. Suppose a second bag has 500 letter tiles in it, and 170 of the tiles are labeled Y. From which bag are you more likely to pick a tile that is labeled Y? Explain.

12. Make Sense and Persevere Suppose you have a bag of 40 marbles, and 20 of them are white. If you choose a marble without looking, the probability that you choose a white marble is $\frac{20}{40}$. Describe the probability.

13. Suppose Nigel has a bag of colored wristbands, and he chooses one without looking. The bag contains a total of 25 wristbands and 6 of the wristbands are blue.

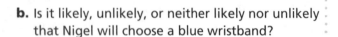

   a. What is the probability that Nigel will choose a blue wristband?

   b. Is it likely, unlikely, or neither likely nor unlikely that Nigel will choose a blue wristband?

14. A box contains four equal-sized cards labeled 1, 3, 5, and 7. Tim will select one card from the box.

   a. What is the probability that Tim will select a card labeled 4?

   b. What is the probability that Tim will select a card labeled with a number less than 6?

   c. What is the probability that Tim will select a card labeled with an odd number?

15. Model with Math Henry is going to color a spinner with 10 equal-sized sections. Three of the sections will be orange and 7 of the sections will be purple. Is this spinner fair? If so, explain why. If not, explain how to make it a fair spinner.

16. Higher Order Thinking Without being able to calculate probability, describe the likelihood that the following event will occur.

All 21 students in a class share the same birthday.

☑ Assessment Practice

17. After many studies, a researcher finds that the probability that a word recognition app correctly interprets a handwritten word is $\frac{9}{10}$. Which statement is true?

   Ⓐ It is impossible that the handwritten word will be correctly interpreted.

   Ⓑ It is unlikely that the handwritten word will be correctly interpreted.

   Ⓒ It is likely that the handwritten word will be correctly interpreted.

   Ⓓ It is certain that the handwritten word will be correctly interpreted.

18. A bag contains 8 letter tiles of the same size. The tiles are labeled either A, B, C, D, E, or F. Three of the tiles are labeled C. If Corey selects 1 tile from the bag without looking, is the selection of letters fair? Explain.

Solve & Discuss It!

Betty and Carl will conduct an experiment. They will flip a coin 100 times and record the result of each flip. What should they expect the results of their experiment to be? Justify your answer.

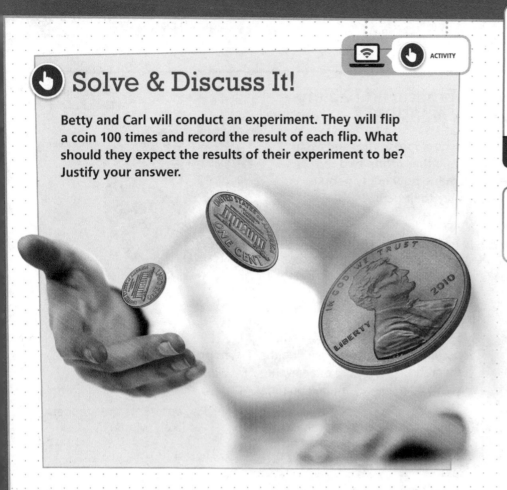

Lesson 9-2
Understand Theoretical Probability

Go Online

I can...
determine the theoretical probability of an event.

© **Common Core Content Standards**
7.SP.C.6, 7.RP.A.2c

Mathematical Practices
MP.1, MP.2, MP.3, MP.4, MP.7

Focus on math practices

Look for Relationships How would their expected results change if Betty and Carl flipped a coin 500 times?

? **Essential Question** How can the probability of an event help make predictions?

 VISUAL LEARNING   ASSESS

EXAMPLE 1 **Use Theoretical Probability to Make Predictions**

Scan for Multimedia

Talia and Yoshi design a game for the school fair. Contestants spin the pointer and win a prize if it lands on either of the two red sections. How can Talia and Yoshi determine how many people are likely to be winners if 500 people play their game?

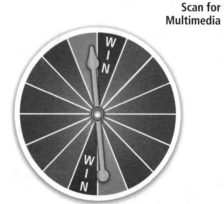

> **Model with Math** How can you use probability to predict the number of winners?

STEP 1 Determine the total number of possible outcomes from one spin of the pointer.

> There are 16 sections that are all the same size. There are 2 sections of each color.

The pointer could land on any of the 16 sections, so there are 16 possible equally likely outcomes.

STEP 2 Because you know all the possible outcomes, you can find the theoretical probability of an event, such as the pointer landing on red.

> *P* represents theoretical probability. An event is a single outcome or group of outcomes.

$$P(\text{event}) = \frac{\text{number of favorable outcomes}}{\text{total number of possible outcomes}}$$

> The event is *landing on red*.

$$P(\text{red}) = \frac{\text{number of red sections}}{\text{total number of sections}}$$
$$= \frac{2}{16} = \frac{1}{8}$$

The theoretical probability that a contestant will win this game is $\frac{1}{8}$ or 12.5%.

STEP 3 Use proportional reasoning to predict the number of likely winners.

> *w* represents the number of likely winners.

$$\frac{1}{8} = \frac{w}{500}$$
$$\frac{1}{8} \cdot 500 = \frac{w}{500} \cdot 500$$
$$62.5 = w$$

Of the 500 contestants, about 62 are likely to be winners.

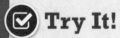 **Try It!**

If Talia and Yoshi redesign their spinner to have 14 sections instead of 16 sections, would they likely have more or fewer winners? Explain why.

Convince Me! If there are always 2 red sections, how does the number of total sections in the spinner relate to the theoretical probability of winning this game?

EXAMPLE 2 ▸ 👆 Determine Theoretical Probability

Archie plays a word board game. He places 98 lettered tiles and 2 blank tiles in a bag. Players will draw tiles from the bag one at a time without looking.

What is the probability that the first tile drawn will be a blank tile? Labeled with a letter? A vowel? A consonant?

$P(\text{blank}) = \frac{2}{100} = \frac{1}{50}$ $P(\text{vowel}) = \frac{42}{100} = \frac{21}{50}$

$P(\text{letter}) = \frac{98}{100} = \frac{49}{50}$ $P(\text{consonant}) = \frac{56}{100} = \frac{28}{50}$

> **Look for Relationships** How are the probabilities related to each other?

A	A	A	A	A	A	A	A	A	E
E	E	E	E	E	E	E	E	E	E
E	I	I	I	I	I	I	I	I	I
O	O	O	O	O	O	O	O	U	U
U	U	B	B	C	C	D	D	D	D
F	F	G	G	G	H	H	J	K	L
L	L	L	M	M	N	N	N	N	N
N	P	P	Q	R	R	R	R	R	R
S	S	S	S	T	T	T	T	T	T
V	V	W	X	Y	Y	Z			

EXAMPLE 3 ▸ 👆 Use Theoretical Probability to Make More Predictions

Joaquin also designs a game for the school fair. Contestants roll two number cubes at the same time. If the sum of the numbers on the two cubes is 7, the player wins. About how many winners should Joaquin expect if 500 contestants play his game?

STEP 1 Find all possible outcomes and all winning outcomes.

2nd number cube

	1	2	3	4	5	6
1	2	3	4	5	6	7
2	3	4	5	6	7	8
3	4	5	6	7	8	9
4	5	6	7	8	9	10
5	6	7	8	9	10	11
6	7	8	9	10	11	12

1st number cube

> There are 6 ways to win out of a total of 36 possible combinations of rolls.

STEP 2 Find the theoretical probability of rolling a sum of 7.

$P(\text{sum of 7}) = \frac{6}{36} = \frac{1}{6}$

STEP 3 Use proportional reasoning to predict the number of winners, w.

$$\frac{1}{6} = \frac{w}{500}$$

$$\frac{1}{6} \cdot 500 = \frac{w}{500} \cdot 500$$

$$83.\overline{3} = w$$

Of 500 contestants, Joaquin should expect about 83 winners.

✅ Try It!

Joaquin wants to reduce the number of winners so he does not have to prepare as many prizes. Choose another sum he could use as a winning sum, and predict the number of winners if 500 people play his game.

You can determine the theoretical probability of an event, *P*(event), if you know all the possible outcomes and they are equally likely.

$$P(\text{event}) = \frac{\text{number of favorable outcomes}}{\text{total number of possible outcomes}}$$

You can use theoretical probability and proportional reasoning to make predictions, such as in a game situation.

$$\frac{\text{number of favorable outcomes}}{\text{total number of possible outcomes}} = \frac{\text{number of winning outcomes}}{\text{total number of possible outcomes}}$$

Do You Understand?

1. **? Essential Question** How can the probability of an event help make predictions?

2. **Construct Arguments** A game board has a spinner with 10 equal-sized sections, of which 4 are green, 3 are blue, 2 are yellow, and 1 is red. What is the sum of the probabilities of the pointer landing in the green, blue, yellow, and red sections? Explain.

3. **Reasoning** What does it mean that there is an equal theoretical probability of each outcome? Explain.

Do You Know How?

In 4–6, Monique rolls a six-sided number cube labeled 1 to 6.

4. Find *P*(rolling a 4).

5. Find *P*(rolling an odd number).

6. If Monique rolls the number cube 12 times, how many times would she expect a number greater than 4 to be rolled?

Practice & Problem Solving

Leveled Practice In 7–9, complete each statement.

7. A spinner has 8 equal-sized sections. To win the game, the pointer must land on a yellow section.

$$P(\text{yellow}) = \frac{\text{favorable outcomes}}{\text{total number of possible outcomes}} = \frac{\boxed{}}{\boxed{}} = \boxed{}$$

8. Natalie is playing a game using a fair coin. Contestants win the game if the fair coin lands tails up.

The theoretical probability that the coin will land tails up is $\boxed{}$.

If 250 contestants play the game, about $\boxed{}$ of them are expected to win.

9. In a different game, the probability of correctly guessing which of 5 boxes contains a tennis ball is $\frac{1}{5}$. About how many winners would be expected if 60 contestants play the game?

$$\frac{1}{5} = \frac{x}{\boxed{}}$$

$x = \boxed{}$ winners

10. Make Sense and Persevere A 12-sided solid has equal-sized faces numbered 1 to 12.

a. Find $P(\text{number greater than 10})$.

b. Find $P(\text{number less than 5})$.

c. If the 12-sided solid is rolled 200 times, how many times would you expect either a 4, 6, or 9 to be rolled?

11. Tamara finds the sum of two number cubes rolled at the same time. The chart below shows all possible sums from the 36 possible combinations when rolling two number cubes. How many times should Tamara expect the sum of the two cubes to be equal to 5 if she rolls the two number cubes 180 times?

Sum	2	3	4	5	6	7	8	9	10	11	12
Possible Combinations	1	2	3	4	5	6	5	4	3	2	1

12. Higher Order Thinking A store is giving every customer who enters the store a scratch-off card labeled with numbers from 1 to 10. It is equally likely that any of the numbers from 1 to 10 will be labeled on a given card. If the card is an even number, the customer gets a 15% discount on a purchase. If the card is an odd number greater than 6, the customer gets a 30% discount. Otherwise, the discount is 20%.

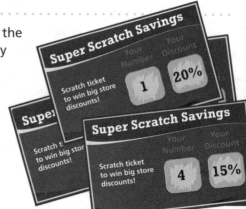

a. What is the probability for each discount?

15% discount: ☐   20% discount: ☐

30% discount: ☐

b. The store manager gives out 300 scratch-off cards. Which discount will the greatest number of customers likely receive? Explain.

✓ Assessment Practice

13. A spinner is divided into 4 equal parts. 1 part is colored red, 2 parts are colored blue, and 1 part is colored yellow. The spinner is spun 1,000 times. Select all of the reasonable possible outcomes.

☐ The spinner lands on blue 445 times.

☐ The spinner lands on red 430 times.

☐ The spinner lands on blue 290 times.

☐ The spinner lands on yellow 200 times.

☐ The spinner lands on red 290 times.

14. One thousand five hundred runners have signed up for a marathon. The probability of a runner finishing the race is $\frac{11}{12}$. Approximately how many runners are expected to finish the race?

 Solve & Discuss It!

Kevin is awarded a penalty shot. He will either score a goal or not score a goal. Are both outcomes equally likely? Explain.

I can...
determine the experimental probability of an event.

© **Common Core Content Standards**
7.SP.C.6, 7.SP.C.7

Mathematical Practices
MP.2, MP.3, MP.7

Look for Relationships
What might affect the outcome?

Focus on math practices

Construct Arguments Lowe Senior High School's soccer team won 12, lost 5, and tied in 3 of their first 20 games this season. Which outcome is most likely for the team's next game? Explain your reasoning.

Scan for Multimedia

EXAMPLE 1 **Compare Theoretical and Experimental Probability**

Talia and Yoshi plan for 1 out of 8, or 12.5%, of the players winning a prize. During the school fair, they kept track of the numbers of total players and winners and recorded the data in the table below. How does the actual number of winners compare to the expected number of winners?

Time Period	Total Players	Winners
10 A.M.–noon	213	22
Noon–2 P.M.	262	36
TOTAL	**475**	**58**

STEP 1 Determine the *relative frequency* of winners during each time period. The relative frequency is the ratio of the number of times an event occurs to the total number of trials.

Ratio of Winners to Total Players

Time Period	Total Players	Winners	Relative Frequency
10 A.M.–noon	213	22	$\frac{22}{213} \approx 10.3\%$
Noon–2 P.M.	262	36	$\frac{36}{262} \approx 13.7\%$
TOTAL	**475**	**58**	$\frac{58}{475} \approx 12.2\%$

STEP 2 The relative frequency of an event can also be called experimental probability. Compare the experimental probability based on the data to the theoretical probability of winning the game.

Theoretical Probability   Experimental Probability

$P(\text{red}) = \frac{1}{8} = 12.5\%$ $\frac{58}{475} \approx 12.2\%$

In the previous lesson, Talia and Yoshi expected about 63 winners for 500 players, based on theoretical probability. Based on the data, there were actually 58 winners out of 475 players.

The experimental probability is slightly lower than the theoretical probability of winning this game. There were slightly fewer winners than expected.

☑ Try It!

During the second day of the school fair, Talia and Yoshi recorded 43 winners out of a total of 324 players. How does the actual number of winners compare to the expected number of winners?

Theoretical Probability

$P(\text{red}) = \frac{1}{8} = 12.5\%$

Experimental Probability

$\dfrac{\boxed{}}{324} \approx \boxed{}\%$

This experimental probability is ☐ than the theoretical probability.

There were ☐ winners than expected.

Convince Me! Will experimental probability always be close to theoretical probability? Explain.

EXAMPLE 2 Use Experimental Probability to Make Predictions

Joaquin also kept track of players and winners for his game during the fair. Based on the results shown in the table, how many winners should he expect if 300 people play his game?

Use proportional reasoning to predict the number of likely winners, w, based on the experimental probability.

$$\frac{71}{416} = \frac{w}{300}$$

$$\frac{71}{416} \cdot 300 = \frac{w}{300} \cdot 300$$

$$51.2 \approx w$$

Time Period	Total Players	Winners	Relative Frequency
10 A.M.–noon	174	28	$\frac{28}{174} \approx 16.1\%$
Noon–2 P.M.	242	43	$\frac{43}{242} \approx 17.8\%$
TOTAL	**416**	**71**	$\frac{71}{416} \approx 17.1\%$

Joaquin should expect about 51 winners out of 300 players.

EXAMPLE 3 Explain Differences Between Theoretical and Experimental Probability

Amir and Marvin each flip a coin 50 times and record the result of each flip. The tables show their results.

Amir's Results

Heads	Tails
26	24

Marvin's Results

Heads	Tails
30	20

A. Based on theoretical probability, what are the expected results of 50 coin flips?

There are two possible outcomes—heads or tails—and both outcomes are equally likely. For each coin flip, the probability of landing heads up (or tails up) is 1 out of 2, or $\frac{1}{2}$.

After 50 flips, the results should be *about* 25 heads and 25 tails.

B. Why might their results be different from the expected results based on theoretical probability?

Theoretical probability can be used to estimate results, but does not guarantee results. The more times they flip their coins, the more likely it is that their results will be closer to the theoretical probability.

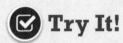 Try It!

Amir and Marvin continue until they each flip a coin 200 times. How do you expect Amir's results and Marvin's results to compare? How will their results compare with expected results based on theoretical probability?

Relative frequency, or experimental probability, is based on the actual results of an experiment, while theoretical probability is based on calculated results from the knowledge of the possible outcomes. Experimental probability and theoretical probability may be close but are rarely exactly the same.

Experimental probability = $\dfrac{\text{number of times an event occurs}}{\text{total number of times the experiment is carried out}}$

This value changes each time an experiment is carried out.

The experimental probability tends to get closer to the theoretical probability of an experiment as more trials are conducted.

Do You Understand?

1. **Essential Question** How is experimental probability similar to and different from theoretical probability?

2. **Construct Arguments** How can experimental probability be used to make predictions?

3. **Reasoning** Is experimental probability always close to theoretical probability? Explain.

Do You Know How?

In 4–6, complete each statement.

Kelly flips a coin 20 times. The results are shown in the table, where "H" represents the coin landing heads up and "T" represents the coin landing tails up.

Flip	1	2	3	4	5
Result	H	T	T	H	H

Flip	6	7	8	9	10
Result	H	H	T	H	T

Flip	11	12	13	14	15
Result	H	T	T	T	H

Flip	16	17	18	19	20
Result	T	H	H	T	H

4. The theoretical probability that the coin will land heads up is ____.

5. Based on the data, the experimental probability that the coin will land heads up is ____.

6. The experimental probability is ____ than the theoretical probability.

Practice & Problem Solving

Leveled Practice In **7** and **8**, complete each statement.

7. The table shows the results of spinning a wheel 80 times. What is the relative frequency of the event "spin a 3"?

Wheel Spins				
Outcomes	1	2	3	4
Frequency	8	22	18	32

The relative frequency of the wheel landing on 3 is

$$\frac{\text{number of times an event occurs}}{\text{total number of trials}} = \frac{\boxed{}}{\boxed{}} = \boxed{}\%$$

8. Liz flips a coin 50 times. The coin lands heads up 20 times and tails up 30 times. Complete each statement.

The theoretical probability of the coin landing

heads up is $\boxed{}$.

Based on Liz's results, the experimental probability

of the coin landing heads up is $\boxed{}$.

The theoretical probability is $\boxed{}$ than

the experimental probability in this experiment.

9. Jess spins a pointer 25 times and finds an experimental probability of the pointer landing on 3 to be $\frac{4}{25}$, or 16%. The theoretical probability of the spinner landing on 3 is $\frac{1}{4}$, or 25%. Why might there be a significant difference between the theoretical and experimental probabilities?

10. The table shows the results of a survey of 100 people randomly selected at an airport. Find the experimental probability that a person is going to City E.

Airport Destinations	
Destination	**Number of Responses**
City A	28
City B	34
City C	16
City D	14
City E	8

11. The theoretical probability of selecting a consonant at random from a list of letters in the alphabet is $\frac{21}{26}$. Wayne opens a book, randomly selects a letter on the page, and records the letter. He repeats the experiment 200 times. He finds P(consonant) = 60%. How does the theoretical probability differ from the experimental probability? What are some possible sources for this discrepancy?

12. **Higher Order Thinking** Seven different names are written onto sticks and placed into a cup. A stick is chosen 100 times, out of which the name Grace is chosen 23 times. How do the theoretical probability and experimental probability compare? Explain why there is a discrepancy between them, if there is any.

13. Each of three friends flips a coin 36 times. Angel records "tails" 20 times. Michael records "tails" 17 times. Fernanda records "tails" 23 times.

   a. Find the relative frequency with which each friend records "tails".

   b. Which friend has a relative frequency that is closest to the theoretical probability of flipping "tails" 36 times? Explain.

14. In a survey, 125 people were asked to choose one card out of five cards labeled 1 to 5. The results are shown in the table. Compare the theoretical probability and experimental probability of choosing a card with the number 1.

Cards Chosen				
Number	1	2	3	4	5
Frequency	15	30	35	20	25

15. A basketball player makes 65% of all free throws in her first 5 seasons. In her 6th season she makes 105 out of 150 free throws. How does the observed frequency of her 6th season compare to the expected frequency? Provide a possible explanation for any similarities or differences in the frequencies.

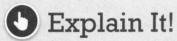 Explain It!

The Chess Club has 8 members. A new captain will be chosen by randomly selecting the name of one of the members. Leah and Luke both want to be captain. Leah says the chance that she will be chosen as captain is $\frac{1}{2}$ because she is either chosen for captain or she is not. Luke says the chance that he is chosen is $\frac{1}{8}$.

Lesson 9-4
Use Probability Models

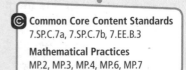 Go Online

I can...
use probability models to find probabilities of events.

© **Common Core Content Standards**
7.SP.C.7a, 7.SP.C.7b, 7.EE.B.3
Mathematical Practices
MP.2, MP.3, MP.4, MP.6, MP.7

A. Construct Arguments Do you agree with Leah's statement? Use a mathematical argument to justify your answer.

B. Construct Arguments Do you agree with Luke's statement? Use a mathematical argument to justify your answer.

Focus on math practices

Look for Relationships How does the probability of Leah being chosen captain compare to the probability of Luke being chosen captain?

VISUAL LEARNING   ASSES

EXAMPLE 1 Develop a Probability Model

Scan for Multimedia

Mr. Campbell has a jar on his desk that contains 10 marbles. At the end of class, each student draws a marble from the jar without looking, notes its color, and then puts it back in the jar. If a student draws the red marble, the student gets a pass on that day's homework. How can the students determine the probability of drawing the red marble?

Model with Math How can you use a model to help you predict what color marble will be drawn?

Develop a *probability model* based on theoretical probability.

A **probability model** consists of:
- the *sample space*, and
- events within the sample space and their probabilities.

A **sample space** is the set of all possible outcomes.

When a marble is drawn, there are 10 possible outcomes.

Sample space, $S = \{R, G, G, G, P, P, P, P, P, P\}$

This is one way to represent the sample space.

R represents a red marble.
G represents a green marble.
P represents a purple marble.

List the three possible events and their probabilities.

– Drawing a ⬤ $P(R) = \frac{1}{10}$

– Drawing a ⬤ $P(G) = \frac{3}{10}$

– Drawing a ⬤ $P(P) = \frac{6}{10}$

The students in Mr. Campbell's class can use a probability model to determine that the probability of drawing the red marble is $\frac{1}{10}$.

✓ Try It!

Mr. Campbell decides that too many students are getting a pass on homework. He adds 10 yellow marbles to the jar. Tell whether each part of the probability model **does** or **does not** change.

The sample space [   ] change. Each event within the sample space [   ] change. The probability of each event [   ] change.

The new probability of drawing a red marble is $P(R) = \dfrac{1}{\boxed{}}$.

Convince Me! How does a probability model help you predict how likely an event is to occur?

EXAMPLE 2 ☝ Use a Probability Model to Evaluate a Situation

Ms. Stillman has a marble jar for the same purpose, but students do not know the number of marbles, or their colors. Each of 30 students draws a marble, notes its color, and then puts it back in the jar. Based on the results shown in the table, what can the students conclude about the probability of drawing a red marble?

Color	Red	Blue	Green
Number of Marbles Drawn	4	11	15

Develop a probability model based on experimental probability.

List the three possible events and their experimental probabilities.

- Drawing a red marble: $\frac{4}{30}$
- Drawing a blue marble: $\frac{11}{30}$
- Drawing a green marble: $\frac{15}{30}$

> The sum of the probabilities of all the possible outcomes in the sample space of a probability model is equal to 1.

Based on this experimental probability, Ms. Stillman's students can conclude that the probability of drawing a red marble is about $13\frac{1}{3}\%$.

EXAMPLE 3 ☝ Use a Probability Model to Make an Estimate

Ms. Stillman tells her students that the jar contains 100 marbles. Based on the table of marble colors after 60 draws, about how many marbles of each color are in the jar?

Color	Red	Blue	Orange	Green
Number of Marbles Drawn	7	20	1	32

Develop a probability model based on experimental probability.

List the four possible events and their experimental probabilities.

- Drawing a red marble: $\frac{7}{60}$
- Drawing a blue marble: $\frac{20}{60}$
- Drawing an orange marble: $\frac{1}{60}$
- Drawing a green marble: $\frac{32}{60}$

> Use proportional reasoning and the probability model to estimate the number of marbles of each color.

The estimated number of marbles in the jar is:

$\frac{7}{60} = \frac{11.\overline{6}}{100}$ or about 12 red marbles

$\frac{20}{60} = \frac{33.\overline{3}}{100}$ or about 33 blue marbles

$\frac{1}{60} = \frac{1.\overline{6}}{100}$ or about 2 orange marbles

$\frac{32}{60} = \frac{53.\overline{3}}{100}$ or about 53 green marbles

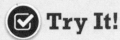 **Try It!**

To reduce the number of homework passes, which color of marble should Ms. Stillman use as the pass on homework? Explain.

KEY CONCEPT

A probability model can help you evaluate a chance process and its outcomes. You can develop a model using theoretical or experimental probability.

A probability model consists of the sample space of an action, events within the sample space, and probabilities associated with each event.

For rolling a number cube labeled from 1 through 6:

Sample space, $S = \{1, 2, 3, 4, 5, 6\}$

$P(1) = \frac{1}{6}$ $P(4) = \frac{1}{6}$

$P(2) = \frac{1}{6}$ $P(5) = \frac{1}{6}$

$P(3) = \frac{1}{6}$ $P(6) = \frac{1}{6}$

Do You Understand?

1. **Essential Question** How can a model be used to find the probability of an event?

2. **Construct Arguments** How can you check the sample space of a probability model?

3. **Reasoning** How does developing a probability model based on experimental probability help you evaluate a situation or make an estimate? Explain.

Do You Know How?

4. Develop a probability model for the spinner shown.

5. Mr. Henry has a basket full of fruit. He does not know how many pieces of fruit are in the basket or the types of fruit. Each of the 20 students in his class selects one piece of fruit from the basket without looking, notes its fruit type, and then puts it back in the basket. Based on the results shown in the table, what can the students conclude about the probability of selecting an apple?

Fruit	Apple	Orange	Pear
Number of Pieces of Fruit	5	2	13

6. The probability model based on experimental probability for randomly selecting a marble from a bag is $P(\text{green}) = \frac{18}{40}$, $P(\text{blue}) = \frac{14}{40}$, and $P(\text{white}) = \frac{8}{40}$. About how many marbles of each color are in the bag if there are 60 total marbles?

Practice & Problem Solving

7. Murray spins the pointer of the spinner shown at the right.

a. What is the sample space for the probability model?

b. What is the probability of each event in the sample space?

8. Rafael spins the pointers of the two spinners shown at the right. Find the probability of each possible sum.

Spinner on Right

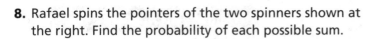

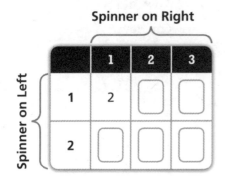

	1	2	3
1	2		
2			

Spinner on Left

$P(\text{sum } 2) = \boxed{}$ $P(\text{sum } 3) = \boxed{}$ $P(\text{sum } 4) = \boxed{}$ $P(\text{sum } 5) = \boxed{}$

9. Be Precise An arts and crafts store has a crate that contains glass, wood, and brass beads. Friends take turns choosing a bead without looking, recording the bead type, and returning the bead to the crate. The table shows the results of 300 selections.

a. Write a probability model for choosing a bead.

Choosing Beads	
Glass	60
Wood	96
Brass	144

b. Based on the frequencies in the table, estimate the number of each type of bead that will be chosen if the friends select a total of 450 beads from the crate.

10. A bag contains 14 green, 12 orange, and 19 purple tennis balls.

   a. Create a probability model for choosing a tennis ball from the bag.

   b. Suppose a tennis ball is randomly selected and then replaced 75 times. How many orange tennis balls do you expect? Explain.

11. Given that $P(\text{red pepper}) = \frac{3}{5}$, write another probability statement to complete the probability model of a random pepper selection from the box below.

12. Higher Order Thinking A survey asked 600 people for their favorite genre of book. The table shows the number of people who preferred four possible genres.

   a. How many people surveyed responded with a genre that is not listed in the table?

   b. Find the probabilities and complete a probability model to describe each response, including "other genre".

Genre	Number of People
Adventure	90
Comedy	102
Mystery	150
Romance	132

✅ Assessment Practice

13. One hundred people buy gum balls from a gum ball machine. 45 of them get a red gum ball, 40 get a blue gum ball and 15 get a yellow gum ball.

PART A

Develop a probability model to predict the color of the next gum ball purchased. Compare the probability of getting a red gum ball to the probability of getting a yellow gum ball.

PART B

Of the next 10 people to buy gum balls, 7 get yellow, 1 gets red and 2 get blue. Explain a possible reason for this outcome.

Name: _____

1. Vocabulary How does the theoretical probability of the event "flip heads" change when a coin is flipped more times in an experiment? *Lesson 9-2*

Ⓐ increases; there are more chances for heads to be flipped

Ⓑ decreases; there are more chances for tails to be flipped

Ⓒ does not change

Ⓓ increases; all values increase

In 2–4, use the information given.

Brianna has a bag of marbles that are all the same size. Of all the marbles in the bag, there are 6 red, 7 white, 3 black, and 4 green marbles.

2. Select all the likelihood statements that are true. *Lesson 9-1*

☐ It is impossible that Brianna will draw a blue marble.

☐ It is more likely that Brianna will draw a black marble than a green marble.

☐ It is certain that Brianna will draw either a red, white, black, or green marble.

☐ It is unlikely that Brianna will draw a black marble.

☐ It is neither likely nor unlikely that Brianna will draw a green marble.

3. Ryan asks 80 people to choose a marble, note the color, and replace the marble in Brianna's bag. The results of the random marble selections in this experiment are: 34 red, 18 white, 9 black, and 19 green marbles. How does the theoretical probability compare with the experimental probability of drawing a white marble? *Lessons 9-2 and 9-3*

Theoretical Probability	Experimental Probability
%	%

4. Write a probability model for this experiment, and use the probability model to predict how many times Brianna would pick a green marble if she chose a marble 50 times. Give the probabilities as simplified fractions. *Lesson 9-4*

Drawing a red marble: _____   Drawing a white marble: _____

Drawing a black marble: _____   Drawing a green marble: _____

Brianna would draw _____ green marbles in 50 tries.

5. Jewel spins the pointer of a spinner. The spinner has 7 equal-sized sections labeled 1 to 7. What is the probability that Jewel will spin a 7? *Lessons 9-2 and 9-4*

How well did you do on the Mid-Topic Checkpoint? Fill in the stars.

MID-TOPIC PERFORMANCE TASK

Viet, Quinn, and Lucy are going to play Bingo, using a standard game set. They make some predictions before the game begins. The table shows how the numbers match with the letters B, I, N, G, and O.

Letter	Numbers
B	1–15
I	16–30
N	31–45
G	46–60
O	61–75

PART A

Viet makes a probability model to describe the probability of each number being called first. Quinn makes a probability model to describe the probability of any particular letter being called first. Compare the probability models.

PART B

Lucy makes a probability model to determine whether the first number drawn will be even or odd. Compare the different probabilities.

PART C

Suppose the game changed to have 90 numbers, instead of 75 numbers, matched with the letters B, I, N, G, and O. How would Viet's, Quinn's, and Lucy's probability models change? Explain.

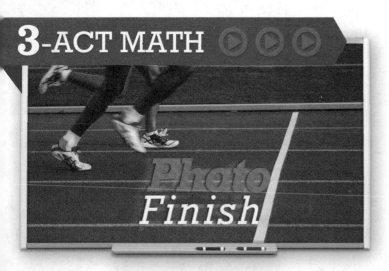

3-Act Mathematical Modeling:
Photo Finish

 Go Online

© Common Core Content Standards
7.SP.C.5, 7.SP.C.6, 7.SP.C.7

Mathematical Practices
MP.4, MP.1, MP.2, MP.3, MP.5, MP.6, MP.7, MP.8

ACT 1

1. After watching the video, what is the first question that comes to mind?

2. Write the Main Question you will answer.

3. Construct Arguments Predict an answer to this Main Question. Explain your prediction.

4. On the number line below, write a number that is too small to be the answer. Write a number that is too large. Plot your prediction on the same number line.

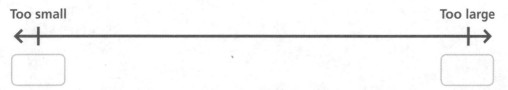

Too small   Too large

5. What information in this situation would be helpful to know? How would you use that information?

6. Use Appropriate Tools What tools can you use to solve the problem? Explain how you would use them strategically.

7. Model with Math Represent the situation using mathematics. Use your representation to answer the Main Question.

8. What is your answer to the Main Question? Is it higher or lower than your prediction? Explain why.

9. Write the answer you saw in the video.

10. Reasoning Does your answer match the answer in the video? If not, what are some reasons that would explain the difference?

11. Make Sense and Persevere Would you change your model now that you know the answer? Explain.

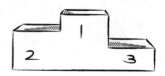

Reflect

12. Model with Math Explain how you used a mathematical model to represent the situation. How did the model help you answer the Main Question?

13. Be Precise What vocabulary have you learned in this topic that helps you communicate the answer to the Main Question?

SEQUEL

14. Generalize How would your answer change if a fifth person joined the race? A sixth person? If *n* people are running in the race?

Solve & Discuss It! 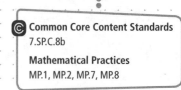 ACTIVITY

Cameron packed two pairs of shorts and three T-shirts for a weekend trip. What are some combinations of shirts and shorts that Cameron can wear while on his trip? How many days will he have a different outfit to wear?

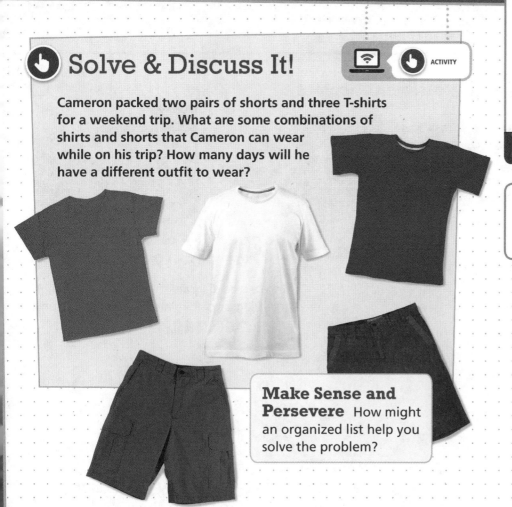

Make Sense and Persevere How might an organized list help you solve the problem?

I can...
find all possible outcomes of a compound event.

© **Common Core Content Standards**
7.SP.C.8b

Mathematical Practices
MP.1, MP.2, MP.7, MP.8

Focus on math practices

Reasoning How would the number of different outfits change if Cameron packed a pair of khaki shorts? Explain.

? **Essential Question** How can all the possible outcomes, or sample space, of a compound event be represented?

EXAMPLE **1** 👁 **Find All Possible Outcomes**

Scan for Multimedia

Hailey has two sisters and no brothers. Josh has two brothers and no sisters. They wonder what the chances are, in a family with three children, that the children will be all boys or all girls. How can they determine all possible combinations of boys and girls in a family with three children?

STEP 1 List the different events.

Child 1 is either a boy or a girl.

Child 2 is either a boy or a girl.

Child 3 is either a boy or a girl.

This is a *compound event*. A **compound event** consists of two or more events. This compound event consists of three events.

STEP 2 Make a tree diagram to represent the sample space. A tree diagram shows all the possible outcomes.

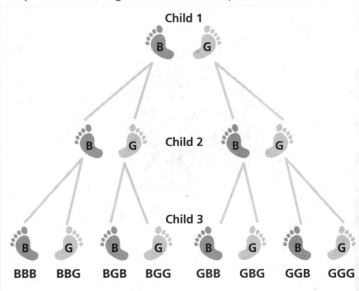

BBB BBG BGB BGG GBB GBG GGB GGG

Hailey and Josh can make a tree diagram to show the sample space of boys and girls in a family with three children.

☑ **Try It!**

Jorge will flip two quarters at the same time. Complete the tree diagram, and then list the sample space of this compound event. Use H for heads and T for tails.

The sample space is: ☐

Convince Me! How does the sample space change when the number of quarters that Jorge flips is increased by 1?

Quarter 1 Quarter 2

```
        H
H <
        ☐

        ☐
☐ <
        T
```

EXAMPLE 2

Use a Table to Represent Sample Spaces

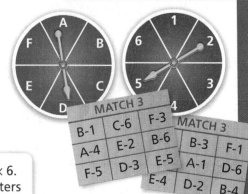

A game is played by spinning the two spinners shown. Players match the results of the spinners to combinations on their game cards. How many different combinations are possible?

Use a table to represent the sample space.

> Remember: The sample space shows all the possible outcomes.

> The table is 6 × 6. There are 6 letters and 6 numbers.

	1	2	3	4	5	6
A	A-1	A-2	A-3	A-4	A-5	A-6
B	B-1	B-2	B-3	B-4	B-5	B-6
C	C-1	C-2	C-3	C-4	C-5	C-6
D	D-1	D-2	D-3	D-4	D-5	D-6
E	E-1	E-2	E-3	E-4	E-5	E-6
F	F-1	F-2	F-3	F-4	F-5	F-6

There are 36 different letter-number combinations.

The sample space consists of 36 possible outcomes.

EXAMPLE 3 Use an Organized List to Represent Sample Spaces

Stan will roll a number cube labeled 1 to 6 and flip a coin.

What are all the possible outcomes?

Use an organized list to represent the sample space.

{(1, H), (1, T),
(2, H), (2, T),
(3, H), (3, T),
(4, H), (4, T),
(5, H), (5, T),
(6, H), (6, T)}

> For each of the 6 possible outcomes of the number cube, there are 2 possible outcomes for the coin.

There are 12 different combinations.

The sample space consists of 12 possible outcomes.

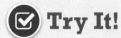 **Try It!**

The bag contains tiles labeled with the letters A, B, and C. The box contains tiles labeled with the numbers 1, 2, and 3. June draws one letter tile and one number tile. Represent the sample space using either a table or an organized list.

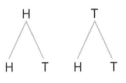

A compound event is a combination of two or more events.

An organized list, table, or tree diagram can be used to represent the sample space of a compound event. The sample space for flipping two coins consists of 4 outcomes.

Organized List

{(H, H), (H, T), (T, H), (T, T)}

Table

	H	T
H	H, H	H, T
T	T, H	T, T

Tree Diagram

H   T

H T   H T

Do You Understand?

1. **? Essential Question** How can all the possible outcomes, or sample space, of a compound event be represented?

2. **Generalize** Will a list, a table, and a tree diagram always give you the same number of outcomes for the same compound event? Explain.

3. **Use Structure** Shari is drawing a tree diagram to represent the sample space of rolling a 12-sided game piece and spinning the pointer of a 4-section spinner. Does it matter if Shari starts the tree diagram with the game piece outcomes or the spinner outcomes? Explain.

Do You Know How?

4. Both Spinner A and Spinner B have equal-sized sections, as shown at the right. Make a table to represent the sample space when both spinners are spun.

Spinner A

Spinner B

5. Tiles labeled with the letters X, Y, and Z are in a bag. Tiles labeled with the numbers 1 and 2 are in a box.

Make a tree diagram to represent the sample space of the compound event of selecting one tile from each container.

Practice & Problem Solving

Scan for
Multimedia

Leveled Practice In 6 and 7, find the number of outcomes for each event.

6. Oliver is playing a game in which he has to choose one of two numbers (2 or 7) and then one of five vowels (a, e, i, o, or u). How many possible outcomes are there?

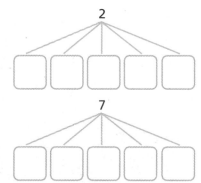

There are ☐ possible outcomes.

7. There are four stores that sell school supplies (S1, S2, S3, and S4) and three stores that sell sporting goods (G1, G2, and G3) nearby. How many possible combinations of stores could you visit to buy a tennis racquet and then a backpack?

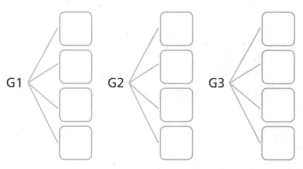

There are ☐ possible combinations.

8. A bakery sells wheat, multigrain, rye, and oat bread. Each type of bread is available as a loaf or as dinner rolls.

a. Complete the table to show all the possible outcomes for the types and styles of bread sold by the bakery.

b. Find the number of possible outcomes.

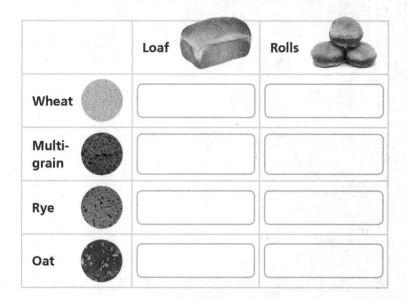

	Loaf	Rolls
Wheat		
Multi-grain		
Rye		
Oat		

9. Generalize How does the number of possible outcomes of a single event help you determine the total number of possible outcomes of a compound event?

10. A new car can be purchased with a choice of four exterior colors (A, B, C, and D) and three interior colors (1, 2, and 3). Make an organized list of all the possible color combinations for the car.

11. Two friends each plan to order a fruit drink at the diner. The available flavors are kiwi (K), lemon (L), and watermelon (W). Make a list to represent all the possible outcomes of the friends' fruit drink order. Write each outcome in the format (Friend 1, Friend 2).

12. Plastic souvenir cups come in three different sizes: small (S), medium (M), and large (L). The available colors are red (R), white (W), and blue (B). Make a list to represent all the possible combinations of the different cups based on size and color. Write each outcome in the format (Size, Color).

13. Higher Order Thinking Heidi's older sister needs to take either Chemistry (C), Geometry (G), or Physics (P) this year. She can take the class during any one of six periods (1 through 6). Is there more than one way to draw a tree diagram to model this situation? Explain.

☑ Assessment Practice

14. A fruit basket has 6 oranges, 4 apples and 2 pears in it. 5 people each select a piece of fruit and eat it. Which of the following outcomes could represent this selection?

☐ All 5 people eat an orange.

☐ 1 person eats an orange, 4 people eat an apple.

☐ 2 people eat an orange, 3 people eat a pear.

☐ 3 people eat an orange, 1 person eats an apple, 1 person eats a pear.

☐ All 5 people eat an apple.

15. Royce has a collection of trading cards. 16 of his cards are baseball cards, 21 are football cards and 13 are basketball cards. He selects half of this collection and gives them to his friend. Which of the following represent possible outcomes of this selection?

☐ He gives his friend 6 baseball cards, 10 football cards and all of his basketball cards.

☐ He gives his friend 4 baseball cards and all of his football cards.

☐ He gives his friend only football cards.

☐ He gives his friend 8 baseball cards, 10 football cards and 7 basketball cards.

☐ He gives his friend all of his baseball and basketball cards.

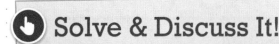 

Solve & Discuss It!

 ACTIVITY

Talia is playing a game in which she must choose Option 1 or Option 2 and then spin the game wheel, flip the coin, and roll the number cube labeled 1 through 6. For her to win a prize, all the conditions listed under the chosen option must occur. Which option should Talia choose? Explain.

SPIN THE WHEEL

SPIN

Option 1	Option 2
• The game wheel lands on S.	• The game wheel lands on Z.
• The coin lands on tails.	• The coin lands on either side.
• An even number is rolled.	• The number 3 is rolled.

Go Online

I can...
find the probability of a compound event.

© **Common Core Content Standards**
7.SP.C.8a

Mathematical Practices
MP.1, MP.4, MP.7, MP.8

Look for Relationships
How can you use what you know about sample spaces to choose the best option?

Focus on math practices

Make Sense and Persevere Suppose an Option 3 was added to the game, with the conditions that the game wheel lands on Q, the coin lands on either side, and an odd number is rolled. Should Talia change her choice to Option 3? Explain.

VISUAL LEARNING   ASSESS

EXAMPLE 1 **Find the Probability of Compound Events Using a Table**

Scan for Multimedia

Sadie has one ticket left at the school fair and she hasn't yet won a prize. She decides between two games. Which game should she play?

Use Structure Does having more possible outcomes make it more likely or less likely that Sadie will win?

STEP 1 Use a table to determine the probability of winning a prize playing *Flip to Win*.

	Heads (H)	Tails (T)
Heads (H)	H, H	H, T
Tails (T)	T, H	T, T

There are 4 possible outcomes.

There is 1 favorable outcome: {H, H}.

$P(H, H) = \frac{1}{4}$, or 25%

STEP 2 Use a table to determine the probability of winning a prize playing *Flip 'n' Spin*.

	Heads (H)	Tails (T)
Red (R)	R, H	R, T
Yellow (Y)	Y, H	Y, T
Blue (B)	B, H	B, T
Green (G)	G, H	G, T

There are 8 possible outcomes.

There is 1 favorable outcome: {B, H}.

$P(B, H) = \frac{1}{8}$, or 12.5%

STEP 3 Compare the probabilities of winning each game.

The probability of winning a prize at *Flip to Win* is 25%.

The probability of winning a prize at *Flip 'n' Spin* is 12.5%.

Sadie is more likely to win a prize playing *Flip to Win*.

So, she should use her last ticket to play *Flip to Win*.

☑ **Try It!**

The designer of *Flip 'n' Spin* creates a new game using a 5-section spinner, as shown. How does the new spinner change the probability of winning a prize?

Using the 5-section spinner, the probability of winning a prize

is [   ].

It is [   ] likely that a player will win a prize when using the 5-section spinner than when using the 4-section spinner.

Convince Me! What generalization can you make about the number of sections on the spinner and the probability of winning a prize while playing the *Flip 'n' Spin* game?

EXAMPLE 2 Find the Probability Using a Tree Diagram

What is the probability that a coin flipped 3 times will land heads up exactly 2 times?

Flip 1

Flip 2

Flip 3

| Outcomes | HHH | HHT | HTH | HTT | THH | THT | TTH | TTT |

> Each of the 8 outcomes is equally likely.
>
> Three of the 8 outcomes are favorable.

P(exactly 2 heads) $= \frac{3}{8}$, or 37.5%

Try It!

Is it more likely that a coin flipped 3 times will land heads up exactly once, or will land heads up exactly 2 twice? Explain using probability.

EXAMPLE 3  Find the Probability Using an Organized List

The names of all middle school students with perfect attendance are entered into a drawing for one of two tickets to a baseball game. This year, Angie, Phil, Marc, Carly, and Josie attended school every day. What is the probability that Marc's name will be drawn to win one of the two tickets?

Make an organized list of possible outcomes for the winners of the two tickets.

If Angie wins the first ticket:
Angie and Phil
Angie and Marc
Angie and Carly
Angie and Josie

If Phil wins the first ticket:
Phil and Angie
Phil and Marc
Phil and Carly
Phil and Josie

If Marc wins the first ticket:
Marc and Angie
Marc and Phil
Marc and Carly
Marc and Josie

If Carly wins the first ticket:
Carly and Angie
Carly and Phil
Carly and Marc
Carly and Josie

If Josie wins the first ticket:
Josie and Angie
Josie and Phil
Josie and Marc
Josie and Carly

There are 20 possible outcomes. Of the 20 outcomes, 8 are favorable.

P(Marc wins one of the tickets) $= \frac{8}{20}$, or 40%

Try It!

Does Marc have a greater chance than Carly of winning the tickets to Carly? Explain using probability.

The probability of a compound event can be represented by a ratio of the number of favorable outcomes to the total number of possible equally likely outcomes. You can use an organized list, a table, or a tree diagram to determine the number of favorable outcomes and the total number of possible outcomes.

Do You Understand?

1. **Essential Question** How can a model help find the probability of a compound event?

2. **Generalize** What do you know about the outcomes of a compound event displayed in an organized list, a table, or a tree diagram?

3. How does finding the probability of a compound event compare with finding the probability of a simple event?

Do You Know How?

4. One of three contestants will be randomly selected to win a prize. One of three different prizes will be randomly awarded to the contestant whose name is selected to win. The tree diagram shows all possible outcomes of this contest.

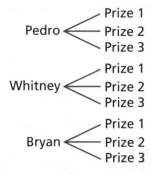

What is the probability that Whitney will win Prize 2?

5. The table shows all the possible outcomes for flipping a coin and spinning the pointer of a spinner with four equal-sized sections labeled 1 through 4.

	1	2	3	4
heads	heads, 1	heads, 2	heads, 3	heads, 4
tails	tails, 1	tails, 2	tails, 3	tails, 4

a. What is the probability that the pointer will stop on 3 and the coin will land on heads?

b. What is the probability that the pointer will stop on an odd number and the coin will land on heads?

Practice & Problem Solving

Scan for
Multimedia

Leveled Practice In 6 and 7, find the probability of each event.

6. A fair coin is tossed twice in succession. The sample space is shown, where H represents heads up and T represents tails up. Find the probability of getting exactly one tail.

(Toss 1, Toss 2)	
(H, H)	(T, H)
(H, T)	(T, T)

There are ☐ outcomes that have exactly

one tail. There are ☐ possible outcomes, which are equally likely.

P(exactly one tail) = ☐ , or ☐ %

7. The tree diagram shows the sample space of two-digit numbers that can be created using the digits 2, 6, 7, and 9. What is the probability of choosing a number from the sample space that contains both 9 and 6?

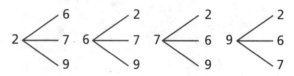

There are ☐ outcomes that include both

9 and 6. There are ☐ possible outcomes, which are equally likely

P(9 and 6) = ☐ , or ☐ %

8. The table shows the possible outcomes of spinning the given spinner and flipping a fair coin. Find the probability of the coin landing heads up and the pointer landing on either 1, 2, or 4.

	1	2	3	4	5
H	H, 1	H, 2	H, 3	H, 4	H, 5
T	T, 1	T, 2	T, 3	T, 4	T, 5

9. The organized list shows all the possible outcomes when three fair coins are flipped. The possible outcomes of each flip are heads (H) and tails (T).

What is the probability that at least 2 fair coins land heads up when 3 are flipped?

Sample Space

HHH

HHT

HTH

HTT

THH

THT

TTH

TTT

10. **Look for Relationships** Gary spins two game wheels at the carnival. He will win a prize if both of the wheels land on any red section. How does the chance of winning change if different game wheels are used with more sections that aren't red?

11. **Model with Math** Each week, a clothing store gives away a shirt to a lucky customer. The shirts vary by sleeve type (Long, Short, No Sleeve) and color (Gray, Blue, Pink). Draw a tree diagram to represent the sample space. What is the probability that the free shirt will have either long or short sleeves and be either pink or blue?

12. **Higher Order Thinking** The table shows the sample space of picking a 2-character password using the letters Y, B, R, O, G, and P. If double letters are not allowed, what is the probability of choosing a password with no Y's? With no O's? Is one probability greater than the other? Explain.

Possible Combinations					
Y, B	B, R	R, O	O, G	G, P	P, Y
Y, R	B, O	R, G	O, P	G, Y	P, B
Y, O	B, G	R, P	O, Y	G, B	P, R
Y, G	B, P	R, Y	O, B	G, R	P, O
Y, P	B, Y	R, B	O, R	G, O	P, G

☑ Assessment Practice

13. A single number cube is rolled twice.

PART A

Determine the number of possible outcomes. Explain how you know you have found all the possible outcomes.

PART B

Find the probability of rolling two numbers that have a sum equal to 10.

Solve & Discuss It! 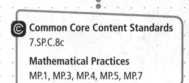 ACTIVITY

Jillian lands the beanbag on the board in about half of her attempts in a beanbag toss game. How can she predict the number of times she will get the beanbag in the hole in her next 5 attempts using a coin toss?

Make Sense and Persevere
How can you use what you know about the theoretical probability of landing heads-up or tails-up?

I can...
simulate a compound event to approximate its probability.

© **Common Core Content Standards**
7.SP.C.8c

Mathematical Practices
MP.1, MP.3, MP.4, MP.5, MP.7

Focus on math practices

Use Appropriate Tools When might it be useful to model a scenario with a coin or other tool?

EXAMPLE 1 Simulate a Probability Situation Using a Spinner

Scan for Multimedia

Nikki is planning a hike for the end of the week. She really does not want to hike if it is raining the whole time, but is okay if it is cloudy. Based on the weather forecast, should she postpone the hike?

Model with Math How can you use a model to represent the situation?

STEP 1 Develop a probability model for rain on a given day.

Sample space, S = {rain, no rain}

List the two possible events and their probabilities.

P (rain) = 40%, or $\frac{4}{10}$

P (no rain) = $1 - \frac{4}{10}$

$\qquad = \frac{6}{10}$

> The sum of the probabilities of the outcomes in a probability model is 1.
> P(rain) + P(no rain) = 1

STEP 2 Design a *simulation* using a spinner. A **simulation** is a model of a real-world situation that can be used to find probabilities. The spinner has outcomes and probabilities that match the real-world situation.

> P(rain) = $\frac{4}{10}$, or $\frac{2}{5}$

STEP 3 Run the simulation.

Spin the spinner 3 times—once for each day—and record the results.

Trial 1: R, N, N

Conduct additional trials.

Trial 2: N, R, N
Trial 3: R, R, N
Trial 4: N, N, N
Trial 5: R, N, N

Based on this simulation, Nikki should expect rain on one day of the three days.

She should not postpone her hike.

✓ Try It!

There is a 50% chance that a volleyball team will win any one of its four remaining games this year. A spinner with 2 equal sections numbered 1 (win) and 2 (loss) is used to simulate the probability that the team will win exactly two of its last four games. The results of the simulation are shown below.

1221   1121   2211   2121   2221   2212   1122   1111   1222   1112

Out of 10 trials, there are ⬚ favorable outcomes. Based on the simulation,

the probability that the team will win exactly 2 of its last 4 games is ⬚ .

Convince Me! Does the probability that the team will win two games change when "exactly" is replaced with "at least"? Explain.

EXAMPLE 2 Simulate a Probability Situation Using a Coin

The Hornets and the Tigers will play a 5-game series, with the winner of 3 games named the state volleyball champion. The two teams are evenly matched. Use a simulation to find the probability that the Hornets will win the 5-game series.

STEP 1 Develop a probability model.

Sample space, S = {Hornets win, Tigers win}

List the events and their probabilities.
P (Hornets win) = 50%
P (Tigers win) = 50%

STEP 2 Design a simulation using a coin. The outcomes and probabilities of flipping a coin can be matched with those of the game.

Heads (H) = Hornets win
Tails (T) = Tigers win

STEP 3 Run the simulation. For each trial, flip the coin 5 times to represent the 5 games.

Trial 1: H, H, T, H, T – The Hornets win.
Trial 2: T, T, H, H, T – The Tigers win.
Trial 3: H, T, H, H, T – The Hornets win.
Trial 4: T, H, T, H, T – The Tigers win.
Trial 5: H, H, T, H, T – The Hornets win.
Trial 6: T, H, T, H, H – The Hornets win.
Trial 7: H, T, T, T, T – The Tigers win.

STEP 4 Find the probability.

Based on 7 trials of the simulation, the probability that the Hornets will win the series is $\frac{4}{7}$.

EXAMPLE 3 Simulate a Probability Situation with a Random Number Generator

An energy bar company is printing equal quantities of 6 different collectible cards. The company will randomly package one card inside the wrapper of each energy bar. What is the probability that all 6 collectible cards will be packaged in a box of 10 energy bars?

Use a random number generator to simulate the situation. The numbers 1 through 6 represent each of the trading cards.

Each trial has 10 numbers to represent the 10 bars.

Trial 1: 4, 4, 6, 3, 5, 6, 1, 6, 6, 1 – Not a full set of cards
Trial 2: 1, 1, 1, 2, 1, 3, 5, 5, 2, 6 – Not a full set of cards
Trial 3: 6, 1, 2, 1, 6, 2, 3, 1, 4, 5 – Full set of cards
Trial 4: 3, 4, 3, 1, 6, 3, 2, 4, 1, 6 – Not a full set of cards
Trial 5: 5, 6, 1, 5, 4, 5, 6, 1, 4, 2 – Not a full set of cards
Trial 6: 2, 1, 3, 2, 5, 5, 2, 4, 3, 4 – Not a full set of cards
Trial 7: 3, 6, 1, 5, 6, 3, 5, 1, 2, 5 – Not a full set of cards
Trial 8: 5, 6, 4, 5, 6, 3, 6, 2, 4, 5 – Not a full set of cards

1 out of 8 trials result in a full set of cards.

Based on 8 trials of the simulation, the probability that all 6 cards will be packaged in a box of 10 energy bars is $\frac{1}{8}$, or 12.5%.

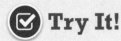 Try It!

In a tennis tournament, 25% of Sarah's serves were aces. Design a simulation to predict how many aces you expect Sarah to serve out of 50 serves.

A simulation is a model of a real-world situation that can be used to predict results or outcomes when the actual event is difficult to perform or record.

A simulation uses a tool, such as a spinner, number cube, coin, or random number generator, for which outcomes have the same probabilities as the actual event.

A greater number of trials will usually give results that are closer to the theoretical probability of the actual event.

Do You Understand?

1. **Essential Question** How can you use simulations to determine the probability of events?

2. **Look for Relationships** What is the connection between the tool used to simulate an event and the probability of the actual event?

3. Why are the results of simulations usually close to the probabilities of their related events?

Do You Know How?

4. Carl hits the target 50% of the time he throws a ball at it. Carl uses a coin to simulate his next three pitches. He assigns H for a hit and T for a miss. The results of 12 trials are shown below.

   HHT   HTH   TTH   HTT   THT   THH

   HHT   HTT   HTH   HTT   TTH   THT

   Based on the results, what is the probability that Carl will hit the target with exactly two of his next three throws?

5. On average, Margo scores a goal for her field hockey team every 2 out of 3 shots. Margo uses a number cube to simulate her next three shots. She assigns 1 to 4 as "goals" and 5 and 6 as "missed shots." Why does this assignment of numbers on the number cube make it a valid simulation?

Practice & Problem Solving

Scan for
Multimedia

Leveled Practice In **6** and **7**, estimate the probability for each event.

6. Molly makes 70% of her free throws. The random numbers below represent 20 trials of a simulation of two free throws, using the numbers 0 through 9.

38	38	21	50	64
71	66	42	47	90
80	92	29	98	27
87	89	89	93	03

Let the numbers from ☐ to ☐ represent a successful free throw.

Let the numbers from ☐ to ☐ represent a missed free throw.

Based on the simulated results, the probability that Molly makes both free throws is

☐ , or ☐ %.

7. Survey results state that 80% of people enjoy going to the beach. The random numbers below represent 10 trials of a simulation of asking two people if they enjoy going to the beach, using the numbers 0 through 9 for their responses.

86	54	22	09	40
53	07	65	56	15

Let the numbers from ☐ to ☐ represent people who enjoy going to the beach.

Let the numbers ☐ to ☐ represent people who do not enjoy going to the beach.

Based on the simulated results, the probability that exactly one of two people enjoys going to the beach is ☐ , or ☐ %.

8. In Stacia's town, 60% of registered people vote regularly. A spinner with equal-sized sections numbered 0 to 9 can be used to represent those who do and do not vote.

a. What numbers can be assigned to represent those who do vote and those who do not vote?

b. Based on the simulated results below, what is the probability that at least one person out of three does not vote?

380	799	331	205	851
182	117	768	715	410

9. Inspection of items at a company shows that an item has a 50% chance of being defective. A spinner with equal-sized sections numbered 0 to 9 can be used to simulate the event that the next 2 items inspected are defective.

a. How would you assign numbers to represent the defective and non-defective items?

b. Based on the simulated results below, what is the probability that the next 2 items are defective?

88	92	87	70	49
44	43	55	32	12

10. Julie used a number cube to simulate a flower seed sprouting, for which the success rate is 50%. She used even numbers to represent success and odd numbers to represent failure. The results of 8 trials that simulate the sprouting of five seeds are shown below.

31534   35635   43631   35633

25143   25643   64133   53113

Based on the simulated results, what is the probability that none of the next five flower seeds will sprout successfully?

11. Construct Arguments How is the difference between the simulated probability and the theoretical probability of an actual event related to the number of simulated trials conducted?

12. Higher Order Thinking Suppose Arun has an 80% chance of winning a game. For a simulation, the numbers 0 to 7 represent winning, and the numbers 8 and 9 represent losing. Write three different trial results that show 5 wins in a row out of 6 games played.

✅ **Assessment Practice**

13. About 50% of the people surveyed in a certain county work for a small business. A random number generator was used to simulate the results of the next four people surveyed.

The numbers 0 to 4 represent people who work for a small business, and the numbers 5 to 9 represent people who do not work for a small business.

6411   0501   7582   0403   3074

7383   5250   2235   0803   3750

7694   9225   7121   4493   7596

8223   1288   8121   7652   3154

PART A

Based on the simulated results shown above, what is the probability that at least one of the next four people surveyed works for a small business?

PART B

How would the design of the simulation change if the percent of people who work for a small business was 70%?

? Topic Essential Question

How can you investigate chance processes and develop, use, and evaluate probability models?

Vocabulary Review

Complete each definition, and then provide an example of each vocabulary word.

Vocabulary

event	outcome	probability
relative frequency	sample space	simulation

Definition	Example
1. The ratio of the number of times an event occurs to the total number of trials is the _____.	
2. The set of all possible outcomes is the _____.	
3. A model of a real-world situation that is used to find probabilities is a(n) _____.	
4. A single outcome or a group of outcomes is a(n) _____.	

Use Vocabulary in Writing

A restaurant serves either skim milk or whole milk in glasses that are either small, medium, or large. Use vocabulary words to explain how you could determine all the possible outcomes of milk choices at the restaurant. Use vocabulary words in your explanation.

Concepts and Skills Review

LESSON 9-1 **Understand Likelihood and Probability**

Quick Review

The probability of an event describes the likelihood an event will occur. The likelihood of an event ranges from impossible to certain, but more common descriptions are likely or unlikely. An event is a single outcome or group of outcomes. An outcome is a possible result of an action. Probability can be represented as a fraction, as a decimal, or as a percent. Something is fair if there is an equal chance for each outcome to occur.

Example

Luke rolls a 10-sided solid with equal-sized faces labeled 1 to 10. What is the probability of rolling a 4?

1 out of 10, or $\frac{1}{10}$. It is unlikely to occur.

Practice

1. Use Luke's 10-sided solid from the example. Describe an event that is certain and one that is impossible using this solid.

2. A spinner with 8 equal-sized sections is used for a game. Based on the descriptions below, is the spinner fair? Explain.
   The probability the pointer will land on yellow is 1 out of 4.
   The probability the pointer will land on blue is 2 out of 8.
   The probabilities that the pointer will land on green or red are both 25%.

LESSON 9-2 **Understand Theoretical Probability**

Quick Review

The theoretical probability of an event can be found if the possible outcomes are known and are all equally likely. Theoretical probability can be used to make predictions.

Example

The numbers from 1 to 5 are written on slips of paper and placed in a bucket. What is the theoretical probability of drawing a 2?

$$P(2) = \frac{\text{number of slips labeled "2"}}{\text{number of possible outcomes}} = \frac{1}{5}$$

Practice

1. Using the example, fifteen people take out a slip of paper from the bucket without looking and record the results before replacing the slip back into the bucket. How many times is a slip labeled "5" expected to be drawn?

Quick Review

The experimental probability or relative frequency is based on actual results from an experiment and may differ from the theoretical probability of an event occurring. This discrepancy decreases as the number of trials of an experiment increases. You can use experimental probability and proportional reasoning to make predictions.

experimental probability =

$$\frac{\text{number of times an event occurs}}{\text{total number of trials}}$$

Example

Four people conduct an experiment to find how often a flipped coin lands heads up. The results are shown in the table below.

Name	Total Flips	Heads
Ashley	55	26
Brent	70	38
Carey	50	22
David	80	41
TOTAL	**255**	

Based on the results from each person's coin flips, find the experimental probability of a flipped coin landing heads up.

The flipped coin landed heads-up in 127 of 255 trials. The experimental probability is about 49.8%.

How does the experimental probability compare to the theoretical probability of a flipped coin landing heads up?

The experimental probability, 49.8%, is very close to the theoretical probability of 50%.

Practice

1. Jaylon and Paula spin the pointer 30 times and get the results shown in the table.

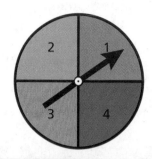

	1	2	3	4
Jaylon	6	8	9	7
Paula	8	5	7	10

What is the theoretical probability of the pointer landing on the number 2?

Based on the results in the table, how does the experimental probability of the pointer landing on 2 compare to the theoretical probability?

2. Based on the results in the table, about how many times should Jaylon and Paula expect the pointer to land on 4 out of a total of 130 spins? Explain your answer.

Quick Review

A probability model consists of a sample space, or all possible outcomes of an action, and a list of events within the sample space with the probability of each. The sum of the probabilities in the model is 1. A probability model can be used to make conclusions about probabilities of events or to make estimates or predictions.

Example

Jenna spins the pointer on her spinner 20 times. Develop a probability model for the situation. What is the sum of the probabilities in the probability model?

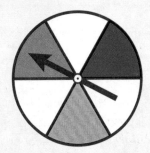

Sample space, $S =$ {white section, blue section, white section, red section, white section, yellow section}

List the events and their probabilities.

$P(\text{white}) = \frac{1}{2}$; $P(\text{blue}) = \frac{1}{6}$;

$P(\text{red}) = \frac{1}{6}$; $P(\text{yellow}) = \frac{1}{6}$

Find the sum of the probabilities.

$$\frac{1}{2} + \frac{1}{6} + \frac{1}{6} + \frac{1}{6} = 1$$

The sum of the probabilities is 1.

Practice

1. Abe has a different spinner. He also wants to develop a probability model.

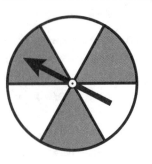

How will his probability model be the same as, and how will it differ from, Jenna's model?

2. Walter has a different spinner.

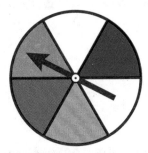

What is the probability that the pointer will land on a color that is not red?

3. What is the sample space of Walter's spinner?

4. Walter will spin the pointer 50 times. About how many times will the pointer land on each color?

Quick Review

A compound event is a combination of two or more events. An organized list, table, or tree diagram can be used to represent the sample space of a compound event.

Example

The student shop sells red and black bags printed with the school logo. Students can choose a backpack, duffel bag, or cinch sack of either color. Make a tree diagram to show all the styles of bags sold at the shop.

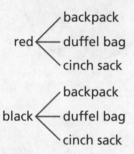

The shop sells 6 different styles of bags.

Practice

1. A basket contains a red, a yellow, and a green apple. A second basket contains an orange, a lemon, and a peach. Use an organized list to show all the outcomes in the sample space.

2. Simon is playing a game with letter tiles. He has 5 tiles remaining and will spell a new word by placing two tiles–first a consonant and then a vowel–in front of a Y already on the board. Complete the table below to describe all combinations of tiles that Simon can use to spell a new word.

	A	O
B		
S		
J		

Quick Review

The probability of a compound event can be represented by a ratio of the favorable outcomes to all possible outcomes. The probability can be calculated using an organized list, a table, or a tree diagram.

Example

If it is equally likely that a soccer team wins or loses any game, what is the probability that the team will win its next two games? Make a tree diagram to list the outcomes.

Only 1 of the 4 outcomes shows the team winning each of its next two games.

P(winning the next two games) $= \frac{1}{4} = 25\%$

Practice

1. One set of cards has a beach, a road, a desert, a mountain, and an island. A second set of cards has a car, a truck, and a van. Complete the table below to find the probability of randomly drawing a mountain card and a truck card.

	Car	Truck	Van
Beach			
Road			
Desert			
Mountain			
Island			

Quick Review

An actual event is sometimes difficult to perform or record. A simulation can be used to model the outcomes of a real-world event. Based on simulated results, you can approximate the probability and predict the future outcomes of an event.

Example

Mr. Jones assigns homework 60% of the days that school is in session. His students use a random number generator to simulate five trials representing Mr. Jones's homework assignments next week. The numbers 0 to 5 represent days on which homework is assigned, and the numbers 6 to 9 represent days without homework. What is the probability that Mr. Jones will assign homework on 3 or more days next week?

14528   62807   53290   24375   40681

Number of weeks simulated: 5

Number of weeks in which homework is assigned on 3 or more days: 4

Based on the simulation, the probability that Mr. Jones will assign homework on 3 or more days next week is $\frac{4}{5}$, or 80%.

Practice

1. Felix's favorite cereal includes 1 of 3 different prizes inside each box. The chance of getting each prize is equally likely. Felix conducts a simulation to see what his chances are of collecting all 3 prizes if he buys 5 boxes over time. Each section of the spinner represents the possible prizes in a single box.

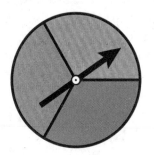

YGGBB   GBGBG   YGGYB   BGGYG

BGBYB   GYBYY   YYGYG   GYYGB

Based on the simulation, what is the probability that Felix will collect all three prizes?

2. Reece is playing a carnival game in which he must guess under which of 2 cups a ball is hidden. To simulate the results of this game, he flips a coin with heads up (H) representing wins and tails up (T) representing losses. Based on the simulation below, what is the probability that Reece will win at least 2 of his next 4 games?

HHTT   HTTT   HTTT   THTH   TTHT
HHHT   TTHH   TTHH   HTTH   HHTH

Hidden Clue

For each ordered pair, one coordinate is given. Find the second coordinate by determining the sale price after the percent markup or markdown. Then locate and label the corresponding point on the graph. Draw line segments to connect the points in alphabetical order. Use the completed picture to help you answer the riddle below.

I can...
use the percent equation
to solve problems.
© 7.RP.A.3

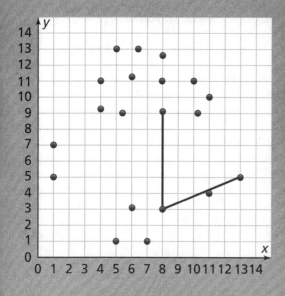

What do you throw out when you want to use it, but take in when you don't want to use it?

A (13, 25% markup on $4)   13, [ ]

B (30% markdown on $10, 1)   [ ], 1

C (20% markdown on $1.25, 5)   [ ], 5

D (6, 40% markdown on $5.10)   6, [ ]

E (35% markup on $4, 9)   [ ], 9

F (4, 50% markdown on $18.50)   4, [ ]

G (60% markup on $2.50, 11)   [ ], 11

H (6, 25% markdown on $15)   6, [ ]

I (60% markup on $4, 13)   [ ], 13

J (8, 30% markdown on $18)   8, [ ]

K (50% markup on $5.30, 11)   [ ], 11

L (10, 45% markdown on $20)   10, [ ]

M (35% markup on $7.60, 9)   [ ], 9

N (8, 30% markdown on $13)   8, [ ]

TOPIC 10

SOLVE PROBLEMS INVOLVING GEOMETRY

? Topic Essential Question

How can geometry be used to solve problems?

Topic Overview

10-1 Solve Problems Involving Scale Drawings

10-2 Draw Geometric Figures

10-3 Draw Triangles with Given Conditions

10-4 Solve Problems Using Angle Relationships

10-5 Solve Problems Involving Circumference of a Circle

10-6 Solve Problems Involving Area of a Circle

3-Act Mathematical Modeling: Whole Lotta Dough

10-7 Describe Cross Sections

10-8 Solve Problems Involving Surface Area

10-9 Solve Problems Involving Volume

Topic Vocabulary

- adjacent angles
- circumference
- complementary angles
- composite figure
- cross section
- scale drawing
- supplementary angles
- vertical angles

Lesson Digital Resources

 INTERACTIVE STUDENT EDITION
Access online or offline.

 VISUAL LEARNING ANIMATION
Interact with visual learning animations.

 ACTIVITY Use with *Solve & Discuss It, Explore*
and *Explain It* activities, and to explore Examp

 VIDEOS Watch clips to support *3-Act Mathematical Modeling Lessons* and *STEM Pr*

 Go online

Whole Lotta Dough

In 2012, a team of Italian chefs baked a pizza that was 131 feet across and weighed more than 50,000 pounds! Imagine how many people it would take to eat one slice of that pizza, assuming you can find a tool big enough to cut it. Think about this during the 3-Act Mathematical Modeling lesson.

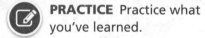 **PRACTICE** Practice what you've learned.

 TUTORIALS Get help from *Virtual Nerd*, right when you need it.

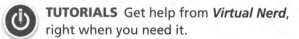 **MATH TOOLS** Explore math with digital tools.

 **GAMES** Play Math Games to help you learn.

 KEY CONCEPT Review important lesson content.

 GLOSSARY Read and listen to English/Spanish definitions.

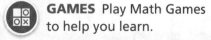 **ASSESSMENT** Show what you've learned.

Did You Know?

The Rail-Trail Hall of Fame includes these exemplary rail-trails.

The High Line in NYC allows New Yorkers to float over busy streets in an innovative park. A decaying urban eyesore for decades, this 30-foot high freight line carried goods in and out of Manhattan's industrial district from 1934 to 1980.

The Fred Marquis Pinellas Trail in FL was built along a railroad right of way which was abandoned in the mid 1980's. Designed with safety in mind, the trail allows users to travel easily between numerous parks and provides a variety of beautiful scenic vistas.

The Paul Bunyan State Trail in MN is built on a former Burlington Northern corridor dating back to 1893. Towns along this 115-mile trail come in 10 to 15-mile intervals—a byproduct of the railroading era.

France has experimented with paying people to bike to work. They hope to reduce air pollution and cut fossil fuel consumption while at the same time boosting people's health.

Copenhagen is the most bike-friendly city in the world.

41%
of residents bike to school or work

55%
bike every day

Your Task:
Upscale Design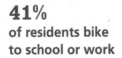

Review your survey results on the needs of walkers and bicyclists in your area. Choose an existing path or bikeway and make a scale drawing of the route. Add improvements or extensions to your drawing that enhance the trails and better meet the needs of users. If your area lacks a trail, choose a possible route and make a scale drawing that proposes a new path. How will your proposal enhance the quality of life and provide solutions for potential users?

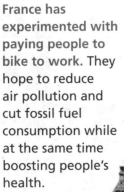

Review What You Know!

Vocabulary

Choose the best term from the box to complete each definition.

| area |
| base |
| diameter |
| height |
| radius |
| volume |

1. The number of square units that a figure covers is its _____ .

2. The _____ of a triangle is the length of the perpendicular line segment from a vertex to the opposite side.

3. The _____ of a solid figure is the number of cubic units needed to fill it.

4. Any line segment that connects the center of a circle to a point on the circle is called a _____ .

Area and Volume

Find each measure.

5. Area of a triangle with a base 6 feet and height 9 feet

6. Volume of a rectangular prism with length 4 inches, width 2 inches, and height 2 inches

Measure Angles

Use a protractor to find the measure of each angle.

7.

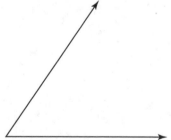

8.

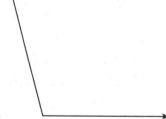

Describe Characteristics of Shapes

Describe this figure using as many geometry terms as you can.

9.

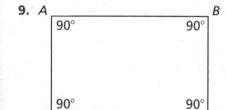

Language Development

Fill in the word web to connect key words you learn in this topic. A sample key word and its connections are given.

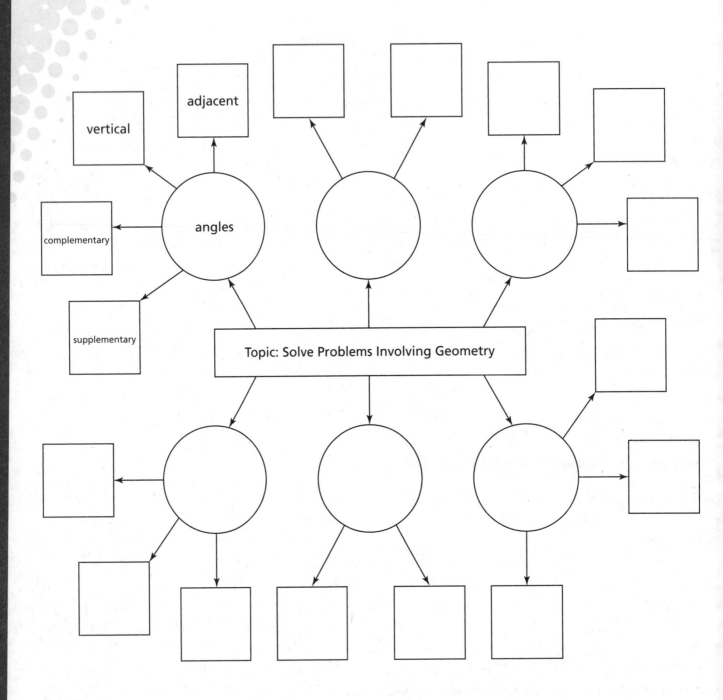

**PROJECT
10A**

If you built a sculpture, what materials would you use?

PROJECT: CONSTRUCT A THREE-DIMENSIONAL SCULPTURE

**PROJECT
10B**

If you made a pizza, what kind of pizza would it be?

PROJECT: ANALYZE A PEPPERONI PIZZA

PROJECT 10C

What places have you visited where being a tour guide would be fun?

PROJECT: PLAN A GUIDED TOUR

PROJECT 10D

How could you determine which is larger—a tall building or a wide building?

PROJECT: BUILD A SCALE MODEL

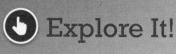

Go Online

Calvin made a scale model of the plane shown.

15 in.

I can...
use the key in a scale drawing to find missing measures.

 Common Core Content Standards
7.G.A.1

Mathematical Practices
MP.2, MP.7, MP.8

A. How can you represent the relationship between the model of the plane and the actual plane?

B. What do you notice about the relationship between the model of the plane and the actual plane?

Focus on math practices

Look for Relationships If the model and the actual plane are to scale, what do you know about the relationship between all the other parts of the model and the actual plane, aside from the total length?

? Essential Question How do scale drawings and actual measurements represent proportional relationships?

EXAMPLE 1 ◉ **Find Actual Lengths Using a Scale Drawing**

The island in the blueprint is 6 inches long. What is the actual length of the island in the kitchen?

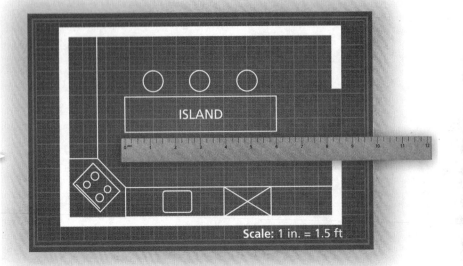

ISLAND

Scale: 1 in. = 1.5 ft

A **scale drawing** is an enlarged or reduced drawing of an object that is proportional to the actual object.

Use a double number line to represent the scale drawing length and the actual length.

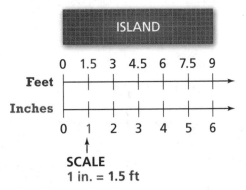

ISLAND

Feet 0 1.5 3 4.5 6 7.5 9

Inches 0 1 2 3 4 5 6

↑ SCALE
1 in. = 1.5 ft

Use a proportion to find the actual length, x, of the island.

$$\frac{1.5}{1} = \frac{x}{6}$$

Use the scale $\frac{1.5\text{ ft}}{1\text{ in.}}$ to write the proportion.

$$\frac{1.5}{1} \cdot 6 = \frac{x}{6} \cdot 6$$

$$9 = x$$

Look for Relationships The ratio $\frac{1.5\text{ ft}}{1\text{ in.}}$ will be the constant scale factor for all lengths in the drawing relative to the actual lengths.

The actual length of the island is 9 feet.

☑ **Try It!**

What is the actual width, w, of the island if the width in the drawing is 2.5 inches?

$$\frac{1.5\text{ ft}}{\boxed{}\text{ in.}} = \frac{w\text{ ft}}{\boxed{}\text{ in.}}$$

Convince Me! How would the proportion for Example 1 change if the scale changed?

$$\frac{1.5}{\boxed{}} \cdot \boxed{} = \frac{w}{\boxed{}} \cdot \boxed{}$$

$$\boxed{} = w$$

The actual width of the island is $\boxed{}$ feet.

EXAMPLE 2 — Use Scale Factors to Solve Area Problems

What is the area, in square yards, of the deck represented by the scale drawing?

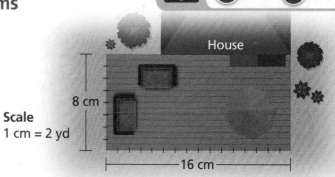

House

8 cm

Scale
1 cm = 2 yd

16 cm

Use Structure You can use an equation in the form $y = kx$ to represent the proportional relationship between lengths in the scale drawing, x, and actual lengths, y. The constant of proportionality, k, is the scale factor.

STEP 1 Find the actual length, L, of the deck using the length, ℓ, in the scale drawing.

$L = k\ell$

$= 2 \cdot 16$ — Use the scale factor of $\frac{2\ yd}{1\ cm}$ for k.

$= 32$

The actual length is 32 yards.

STEP 2 Find the actual width, W, of the deck using the width, w, in the scale drawing.

$W = kw$

$= 2 \cdot 8$

$= 16$

The actual width is 16 yards.

STEP 3 Calculate the actual area of the deck.

Area = Length × Width

$= 32 \times 16$

$= 512$

The actual area of the deck is 512 square yards.

EXAMPLE 3 — Reproduce a Scale Drawing at a Different Scale

Students are recreating the landscape drawing shown at the right for a mural. They want the length of the drawing on the mural to be 80 inches. What will be the new scale and the height of the drawing on the mural?

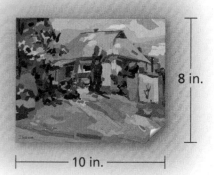

8 in.

Scale
1 in. = 4 ft

10 in.

Look for Relationships What is the scale factor, k, that relates the actual lengths to the lengths in the scale drawing?

STEP 1 Find the actual length, L, and actual height, H, of the landscape.

$L = k \cdot 10 \qquad H = k \cdot 8$

$= 4 \cdot 10 \qquad = 4 \cdot 8$

$= 40 \qquad = 32$

The actual dimensions of the landscape are 40 feet by 32 feet.

STEP 2 Find the new scale for the mural to the actual landscape.

÷ 80

$\dfrac{40\ ft}{80\ in.} = \dfrac{?\ ft}{1\ in.} \qquad ? = 0.5$

÷ 80

The new scale of 1 in. = 0.5 ft means 1 inch on the mural represents 0.5 feet in the actual landscape.

STEP 3 Find the height, h, of the drawing on the mural using the new scale.

$H = kh$

$32 = 0.5 \cdot h$

$64 = h$

The dimensions of the drawing on the mural are 80 inches by 64 inches.

✓ Try It!

The scale drawing shown represents an existing barn. The shortest side of the barn measures 150 meters. If a new barn that is $\frac{2}{3}$ its size replaces the existing barn, what will be the scale of this drawing to the new barn?

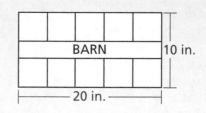

BARN 10 in.

20 in.

The scale factor of a scale drawing is the ratio of an actual length, y, to the corresponding length, x, in the drawing. The ratio is the constant of proportionality, k, that relates the actual figure to the scale drawing. You can use a proportion or use an equation of the form $y = kx$ to solve problems involving scale drawings.

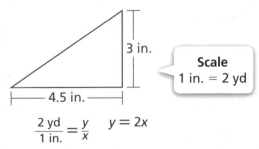

$$\frac{2 \text{ yd}}{1 \text{ in.}} = \frac{y}{x} \qquad y = 2x$$

Do You Understand?

1. **Essential Question** How do scale drawings and actual measurements represent proportional relationships?

2. **Generalize** Describe the ratio of corresponding measures in scale drawings and the actual measures they represent.

3. **Reasoning** Mikayla is determining the actual distance between Harrisville and Lake Town using a map. The scale on her map reads.

1 inch = 50 miles. She measures the distance to be 4.5 inches and writes the following proportion:

$$\frac{1 \text{ in.}}{4.5 \text{ in.}} = \frac{50 \text{ mi}}{x \text{ mi}}$$

Explain why her proportion is equivalent to $\frac{50 \text{ mi}}{1 \text{ in.}} = \frac{x \text{ mi}}{4.5 \text{ in.}}$.

Do You Know How?

4. What is the actual base length of the triangle depicted in the scale drawing?

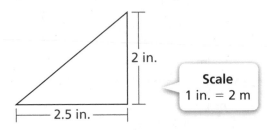

5. What is the area of the actual square window shown in the scale drawing?

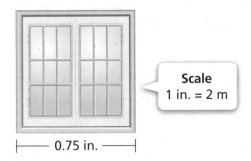

6. A distance of 30 miles on a map is represented by a 2-inch line. If the map is enlarged to 3 times its size, what will be the scale of the enlarged map?

Practice & Problem Solving

Scan for
Multimedia

Leveled Practice For **7** and **8**, fill in the boxes to find the actual measures.

7. On a map, 1 inch equals 5 miles. Two cities are 8 inches apart on the map.

What is the actual distance between the cities?

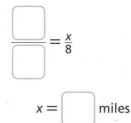

$$\frac{\Box}{\Box} = \frac{x}{8}$$

$x = \boxed{}$ miles

8. Ryan makes a scale drawing of a banner for a school dance. He uses a scale of 1 inch = 3 feet, and the width of the drawing is 5 inches.

What is the actual width, w, of the banner?

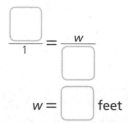

$$\frac{\Box}{1} = \frac{w}{\Box}$$

$w = \boxed{}$ feet

9. On a map, 1 inch equals 7.2 miles. Two houses are 1.5 inches apart on the map. What is the actual distance between the houses?

10. The original blueprint for the Morenos' living room has a scale of 2 inches = 5 feet. The family wants to use a new blueprint that shows the length of the living room to be 15 inches. If the width of the living room on the original blueprint is 6 inches and the length is 9.6 inches, what are the scale and the width of the new blueprint?

11. The scale for a drawing of the tennis court is 1 centimeter = 2 meters. What is the area of the actual tennis court?

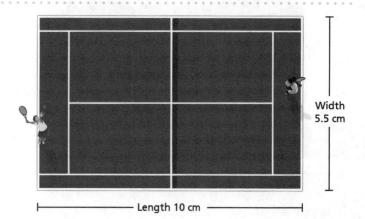

Width
5.5 cm

Length 10 cm

12. The scale for the drawing of a rectangular playing field is 2 inches = 5 feet.

a. Write an equation you can use to find the dimensions of the actual field, where x is a dimension of the scale drawing (in inches) and y is the corresponding dimension of the actual field (in feet).

b. What is the area of the field?

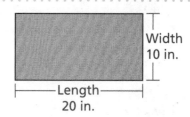

Width
10 in.

Length
20 in.

13. How many square feet of flooring are needed to cover the entire floor of Bedroom 1?

Bedroom 1

Scale: 1 in. = 4 ft
The gridlines are spaced 1 inch apart.

14. The actual distance between Point A and Point B is 200 meters. A length of 1.9 feet represents this distance on a certain wall map. Point C and Point D are 3.8 feet apart on this map. What is the actual distance between Point C and Point D?

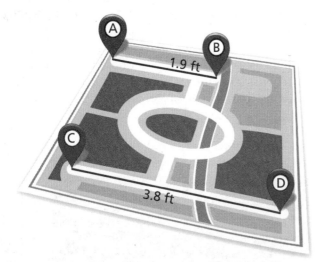

15. Higher Order Thinking A map of a highway has a scale of 2 inches equals 33 miles. The length of the highway on the map is 6 inches. There are 11 rest stops equally spaced on the highway, including one at each end. You are making a new map with a scale of 1 inch equals 30 miles. How far apart are the rest stops on the new map?

 Assessment Practice

16. The original blueprint of a concrete patio has a scale of 2 inches = 3 feet.

Victoria wants to make a new blueprint of the patio with a length of 16.8 inches.

PART A
What is the scale for the new blueprint?

1 inch = ☐ feet

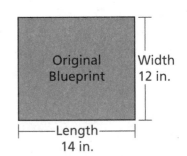

Original Blueprint

Width
12 in.

Length
14 in.

PART B
What is the width, in inches, of the blueprint with the new scale?

☐

 Solve & Discuss It! ACTIVITY

Students in the Art Club are designing a flag with the school's mascot and emblem. The flag has four sides, with two sides that are twice as long as the other two sides. What shape could the flag be, and what dimensions could it have? Make and label a scale drawing as part of your answer.

I can...
draw figures with given conditions.

© **Common Core Content Standards**
7.G.A.2

Mathematical Practices
MP.1, MP.2, MP.3, MP.5

Make Sense and Persevere Is there more than one shape that could represent the flag?

Focus on math practices

Reasoning How did you decide what lengths to use for the four sides of the flag you drew? What lengths could the actual flag be, based on your drawing?

VISUAL LEARNING ASSESS

EXAMPLE 1   Draw a Quadrilateral with Given Conditions

Scan for Multimedia

The school's landscaping club is designing a 4-sided patio and garden. The patio has 2 perpendicular sides that each measure 4 yards, and a third side that is perpendicular to one of the equal sides but twice as long. One angle of the patio measures 135°. Make a scale drawing of the patio using a scale of 1 cm = 1 yd.

Use Appropriate Tools You can use rulers and protractors to construct precise drawings.

STEP 1 Use a ruler to draw three sides that meet the given conditions.

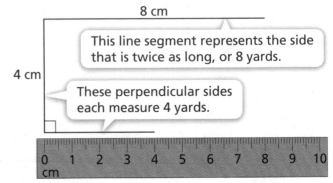

8 cm

This line segment represents the side that is twice as long, or 8 yards.

4 cm

These perpendicular sides each measure 4 yards.

STEP 2 Use a protractor to draw a 135° angle that connects and completes the shape.

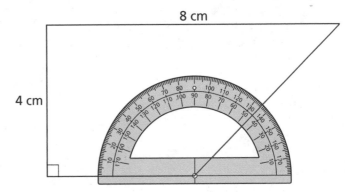

8 cm

4 cm

The scale drawing shows that the patio is the shape of a trapezoid.

☑ Try It!

Use a ruler and protractor to draw a quadrilateral with two equal sides that meet at a right angle, and two nonadjacent angles of the same measure. What is the name of the quadrilateral you drew?

The quadrilateral I drew is a _____.

Convince Me!
Could you have drawn more than one shape that fits the given conditions? Explain.

EXAMPLE **2** **Draw a Figure to Solve a Problem**

 ACTIVITY   ASSESS

Mr. Miller's classroom has desks shaped like equilateral triangles. He is planning to arrange the desks for a lunch for 10 people. If one person can sit at each edge of each desk, make a sketch to show how many desks he needs.

> **Use Appropriate Tools** Why is a freehand drawing precise enough for the table arrangement?

ONE WAY Mr. Miller can arrange the desks in one row to make a long lunch table.

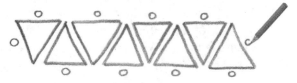

He will need 8 desks to make this arrangement.

ANOTHER WAY Mr. Miller can arrange the desks in two rows to make a wider lunch table.

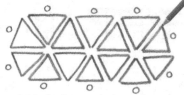

He will need 14 desks to make this arrangement.

EXAMPLE **3** **Draw a Figure Using Technology**

An engineer makes a scale drawing of the floor of a building. The floor has two pairs of parallel sides that are 50 feet and 80 feet. Two of the four angles measure 60°. Use geometry software to make a scale drawing. What is the name of the floor's shape?

> **Use Appropriate Tools** Why would the engineer use technology, rather than a freehand sketch?

STEP 1 Draw two line segments at a 60° angle. Using a scale of 1 unit = 10 feet, the segments should be 5 units and 8 units long.

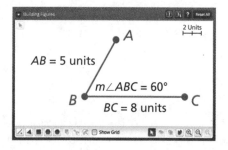

STEP 2 Duplicate each line segment to create pairs of parallel sides, and move them to construct a closed figure.

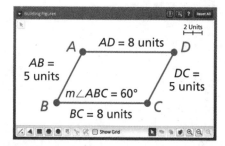

The floor shape of the building is a parallelogram.

✅ **Try It!**

a. Make a sketch to show another way Mr. Miller can arrange the desks to seat 10 people for lunch.

b. Use geometry software to make a rhombus with a side length of 6 units and two angles that measure 45°.

You can draw shapes that meet given conditions freehand, with a ruler and protractor, or with technology. The given conditions may include properties of geometric figures and relationships between parts of the figures.

> **Use Appropriate Tools** Deciding how precise the drawing of the shape should be will help you choose the method you use to draw the shape.

Do You Understand?

1. **? Essential Question** How can a shape that meets given conditions be drawn?

2. **Use Appropriate Tools** How can you decide whether to draw a shape freehand, with a ruler and protractor, or using technology?

3. **Construct Arguments** Why can you draw more than one quadrilateral using four right angles?

Do You Know How?

4. Draw, freehand, a quadrilateral with exactly one pair of parallel sides and at least one angle measuring 45°.

5. Use a ruler and protractor to draw a quadrilateral with four right angles, two side lengths each measuring 3 inches, and two side lengths each measuring 4 inches. What is the most descriptive name of the figure you drew?

6. Use geometry software to draw a quadrilateral with two angles measuring 80° and two angles measuring 100°. What is the name of the figure you drew?

Practice & Problem Solving

7. What quadrilaterals can you draw that have exactly four right angles?

8. A four-sided sandbox has more than two right angles, two side lengths of 2 feet, and two side lengths of 5 feet. What geometric shape best describes the shape of the sandbox?

9. What quadrilateral can you draw that has exactly one pair of parallel sides?

10. A friend is building a 4-sided garden with two side lengths of 19 feet and exactly one right angle. What quadrilaterals could describe the garden?

11. What quadrilaterals can you draw that have two side lengths of 9 centimeters and two side lengths of 4 centimeters?

12. A park has a pond shaped like a quadrilateral with side lengths of 17 feet and no right angles. What other geometric shapes could describe the shape of the pond?

13. Draw a quadrilateral that has one angle measure of 20° and exactly one side length of 4 units.

14. Which of the following shapes are trapezoids that have side lengths of 7 inches and 5 inches and a right angle? Select all that apply.

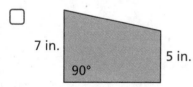

7 in. 90° 5 in.

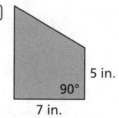

5 in. 90° 7 in.

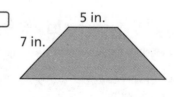

5 in. 7 in.

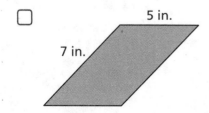

5 in. 7 in.

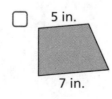

5 in. 7 in.

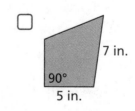

7 in. 90° 5 in.

15. Using computer software, draw a quadrilateral with two sets of parallel sides and two angles measuring 135 degrees.

16. Higher Order Thinking Draw a rhombus with side lengths of 6 units and angle measures of 100°, 80°, 100°, and 80°.

☑ Assessment Practice

17. Thomas is painting a geometry mural. He is painting quadrilaterals that have at least 1 line of symmetry.

PART A

Which could be a quadrilateral that Thomas painted? Select all that apply.

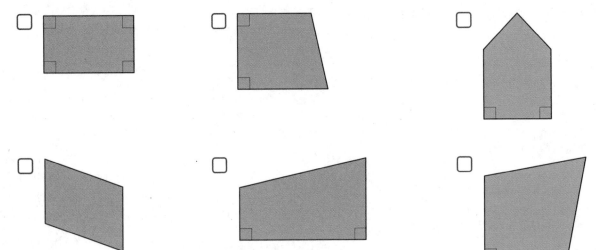

PART B

Which of the following figures can he also include in his painting?

Ⓐ A quadrilateral with no equal sides

Ⓑ A quadrilateral with only 2 equal sides that are perpendicular to each other

Ⓒ A quadrilateral with 2 pairs of equal sides and 1 right angle

Ⓓ A quadrilateral with 2 pairs of parallel equal sides, with no right angles

Solve & Discuss It!

 ACTIVITY

Kane has 4 pieces of wood available to build a triangle-shaped garden. Which pieces of wood can he use?

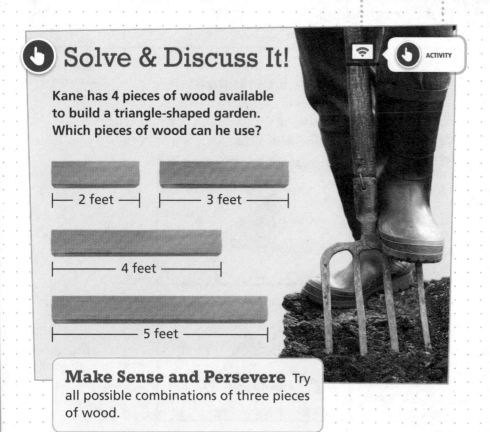

├── 2 feet ──┤   ├──── 3 feet ────┤

├──── 4 feet ────┤

├──── 5 feet ────┤

Make Sense and Persevere Try all possible combinations of three pieces of wood.

I can...
draw triangles when given information about their side lengths and angle measures.

© **Common Core Content Standards**
7.G.A.2

Mathematical Practices
MP.1, MP.7, MP.8

Focus on math practices

Use Structure Are there any combinations of three pieces of wood that will not create a triangle? Explain.

VISUAL LEARNING ASSESS

EXAMPLE 1 Draw Triangles with Given Side Lengths

Scan for Multimedia

Students in woodshop class are measuring and cutting out a triangular base for a corner shelf, with sides measuring 6 inches, 8 inches, and 10 inches. How can you determine if all the students will cut out the same triangle? Explain.

> **Look for Relationships** Does the orientation of a triangle change its shape?

Use geometry software to draw and compare triangles with the given side lengths.

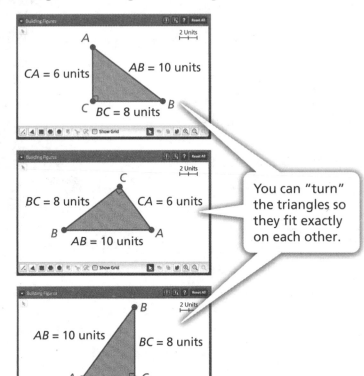

You can "turn" the triangles so they fit exactly on each other.

Triangles with the same side lengths are the same shape and size, no matter how they are positioned.

So, all the students will cut out the same triangle.

✓ Try It!

How many unique triangles can be drawn with given side lengths of 8 inches, 10.3 inches, and 13 inches?

[ ] unique triangle(s) can be drawn with the given side lengths.

Convince Me! When two sides of a triangle are switched, why is it still considered the same triangle?

EXAMPLE **2** 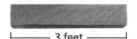 Determine Possible Side Lengths of Triangles

  ACTIVITY ASSESS

Steve gathers three pieces of wood from the scrap pile in woodshop class.

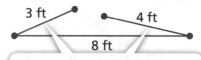 3 feet

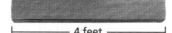 4 feet

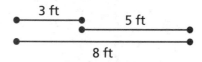 8 feet

a. Can Steve make a triangle with these three wood pieces? Explain.

3 ft
4 ft
8 ft

No. The 3-ft and 4-ft wood pieces are not long enough to form a triangle. $3 + 4 < 8$

b. Generalize What can you conclude about the lengths that make a triangle possible?

3 ft
5 ft
8 ft

The sum of the lengths of the two shortest sides must be greater than the length of the third side in order to form a triangle.

EXAMPLE **3** Draw a Triangle with a Combination of Given Side Lengths and Angle Measures

Can more than one triangle be drawn with the following conditions?

a. side lengths of 5 inches and 6 inches which make an angle of 45°

Draw a 45° angle with line segments of 5 inches and 6 inches.

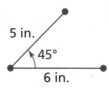

5 in.
45°
6 in.

Connect the sides by drawing the third side.

5 in.
45°
6 in.

Generalize Is there more than one way to connect the two ends of the given sides?

Only one triangle can be drawn with the given measures.

b. a side length of 6 inches with angles at each end measuring 40° and 60°

Draw a 6-inch line segment and rays that form the 40° and 60° angles.

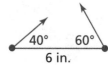

40°   60°
6 in.

Extend the rays until they intersect.

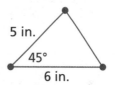

40°   60°
6 in.

Generalize Is there more than one way to draw the two other sides?

Only one triangle can be drawn with the given measures.

✓ **Try It!**

a. Write three side lengths that will form a triangle. Write three side lengths that will NOT form a triangle.

b. Can a triangle be drawn with a side length of 3 inches and angles at each end measuring 90° and 89°? Explain.

EXAMPLE 4 Draw a Triangle with Two Given Side Lengths and a Nonincluded Angle Measure

Can more than one triangle be drawn using two side lengths of 6 units and 9 units, and a 40° angle that is not formed by their intersection?

Draw △ABC with side lengths 6 units and 9 units, and a nonincluded angle of 40°.

Swing side AB left to create an obtuse triangle, keeping m∠C at 40°.

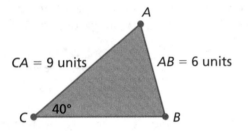

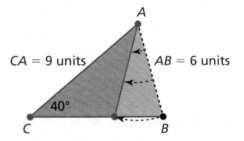

The new triangle still has the given side lengths and angle measure, but it is a different triangle.

So, more than one triangle can be made with the given measures.

EXAMPLE 5 Draw a Triangle with Three Given Angle Measures

Is there a unique triangle with angle measures of 30°, 60°, and 90°?

Draw a triangle with the given angle measures. Notice that side lengths are not required.

Enlarge and reduce your drawing, keeping the angle measures the same but changing the side lengths to proportional measurements.

> **Generalize** Is there more than one way to draw a triangle with three given angles?
>
> Many different triangles can be drawn with the given angle measures.

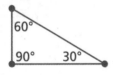

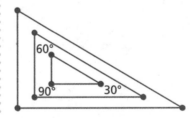

So, there is not one unique triangle with angle measures of 30°, 60°, and 90°.

☑ Try It!

Can more than one triangle be drawn with two side lengths of 6 inches and a nonincluded angle of 60°? Explain.

You can analyze given conditions of side lengths and angle measures to determine whether one unique triangle, more than one unique triangle, or no triangle can be drawn.

There is more than one possible triangle given these cases: all three angles, or two sides and a nonincluded angle.

There is one unique triangle given these cases: all three sides, two sides and an included angle, or two angles and an included side.

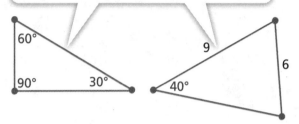

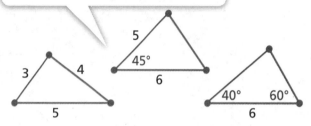

Do You Understand?

1. **Essential Question** How can you determine when it is possible to draw a triangle given certain conditions?

2. Look for Relationships What is the relationship between all triangles that can be drawn given the same three angle measures?

3. Why can there be only one way to draw a triangle if two sides and an included angle are given?

Do You Know How?

4. How many triangles can be drawn with side lengths 4 centimeters, 4.5 centimeters, and 9 centimeters? Explain.

5. Can more than one triangle be drawn with side lengths of 5 inches and 7 inches and an included angle with a measure of 50°? Explain.

6. Sketch two different triangles that have angle measures of 45°, 45°, and 90°.

Practice & Problem Solving

Scan for
Multimedia

7. Draw two different triangles with angle measurements 90°, 35°, and 55°.

8. If you form a triangle from three given side lengths, will you always get one triangle or more than one triangle?

9. How can you make different-looking triangles given two of the angle measures and the included side lengths?

10. If you form a triangle from two given angle measures and the length of the included side, will you always get one triangle or will you get more than one triangle?

11. How can you make different triangles with the same angle measures?

12. Given two side lengths of 15 units and 9.5 units, with a nonincluded angle of 75°, can you draw no triangles, only one triangle, or more than one triangle?

13. A student was asked to form different triangles with angle measures of 90°, 30°, and 60°. She incorrectly said this triangle is the only triangle with angle measures of 90°, 30°, and 60°. What mistake might she have made?

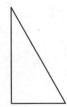

14. In triangle *QRS*, m∠*QSR* = 100°, m∠*SQR* = 45°, and *QR* = 4 units. In triangle *XYZ*, m∠*XYZ* = 100°, m∠*ZXY* = 45°, and *XY* = 4 units. Are triangles *QRS* and *XYZ* the same? Explain.

15. You are asked to make a triangular sign using the given information about triangle *WXY*. In triangle *WXY*, m∠*WXY* = 45°, m∠*YWX* = 90°, and *WX* = 5 feet.

a. Which triangle is correct? Each square on the grid is equal to 1 square foot.

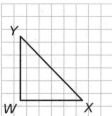 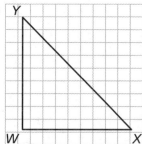 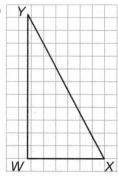

b. Explain why only one triangle can be formed with these three pieces of information.

16. Look for Relationships Two different triangles have side lengths of 13 and 16 units and a nonincluded angle of 50°. Explain how the triangles are different.

17. Higher Order Thinking Two triangles have side lengths of 12 units and 15 units and the non-included angle of 45°. Draw two different triangles with these conditions.

18. For triangle RST, RS is 12 centimeters, ST is 16 centimeters, and RT is 19 centimeters. How many triangles can be drawn with the given side lengths?

19. A triangle has two side lengths of 8.5 centimeters and 9.5 centimeters. What is a possible length for the third side? Explain why this is a possible length.

20. Can a triangle be formed with side lengths of 4, 5, and 7 units?

21. Which of the following combinations of side lengths would form a triangle? Select all that apply.

☐ 7 in., 10 in., 2.5 in.

☐ 4.5 ft, 8 ft, 5 ft

☐ 5 yd, 11 yd, 5 yd

☐ 12 in., 5 in., 9.5 in.

☐ 7 m, 7 m, 9 m

☐ 6 ft, 16 ft, 9 ft

22. Which of the following combinations of side lengths would NOT form a triangle?

Ⓐ 7 cm, 10 cm, 13 cm

Ⓑ 10 ft, 13 ft, 15 ft

Ⓒ 10 yd, 11 yd, 13 yd

Ⓓ 10 in., 13 in., 23 in.

23. Draw a triangle that has exactly one line of symmetry.

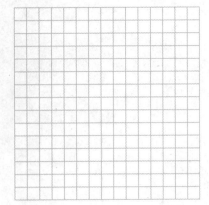

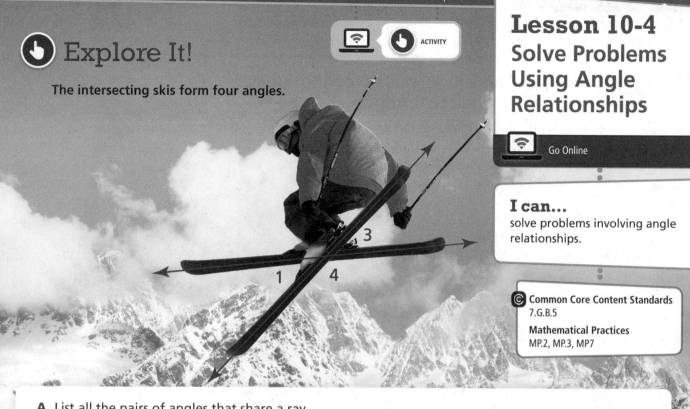

Explore It!

The intersecting skis form four angles.

Lesson 10-4
Solve Problems Using Angle Relationships

Go Online

I can...
solve problems involving angle relationships.

© **Common Core Content Standards**
7.G.B.5

Mathematical Practices
MP.2, MP.3, MP7

A. List all the pairs of angles that share a ray.

B. Suppose the measure of ∠1 increases. What happens to the size of ∠2? ∠3?

C. How does the sum of the measures of ∠1 and ∠2 change when one ski moves? Explain.

Focus on math practices

Construct Arguments Why does the sum of all four angle measures stay the same when one of the skis moves?

? Essential Question How are angles formed by intersecting lines related?

  VISUAL LEARNING   ASSESS

EXAMPLE 1 ◉ **Solve Problems Involving Adjacent and Vertical Angles**

 Scan for Multimedia

A skewed intersection has two roads that intersect at more than 20 degrees away from 90°. Determine whether the road intersection shown is skewed by finding the measures of ∠ABC and ∠DBE.

> **Look for Relationships** What angle measures would a skewed intersection have?

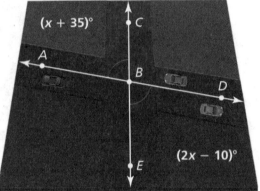

Examine how the angles are related.

> Angles opposite each other are called **vertical angles**. Vertical angles have equal measures. ∠ABC and ∠DBE are vertical angles.

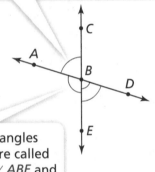

> Non-overlapping angles that share a ray are called **adjacent angles**. ∠ABE and ∠EBD are adjacent angles, sharing ray BE.

Write and solve an equation to find the value of x.

> Read "m" as "the measure of" the named angle.

$$m\angle ABC = m\angle DBE$$
$$x + 35 = 2x - 10$$
$$x + 35 + 10 = 2x - 10 + 10$$
$$x + 45 = 2x$$
$$x - x + 45 = 2x - x$$
$$45 = x$$

Find the measure of an angle in the intersection.

$$m\angle ABC = (x + 35)°$$
$$= (45 + 35)°$$
$$= 80°$$

> ∠ABC and ∠DBE both measure 80°.

Since 80° is within 20° of 90°, the road intersection is not skewed.

☑ **Try It!**

∠MNQ and ∠PNR are vertical angles. What is the value of x?

Vertical angles are [   ], so the equation [   ] can be used to find x. The value of x is [   ].

$(3x - 6)°$
$114°$

Convince Me! Why can you use an equation when solving for x in the diagram?

EXAMPLE **2**

 Solve Problems Involving Complementary and Supplementary Angles

 ACTIVITY   ASSESS

a. Ray *EG* splits right angle *DEF* into two angles, ∠*DEG* and ∠*GEF*. Find the value of *x*.

b. The two angles shown are *supplementary angles*. Find the value of *x*.

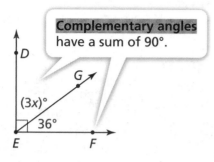

Complementary angles have a sum of 90°.

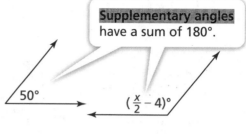

Supplementary angles have a sum of 180°.

$m\angle DEG + m\angle GEF = 90$

$3x + 36 = 90$

$3x + 36 - 36 = 90 - 36$

$3x = 54$

$\dfrac{3x}{3} = \dfrac{54}{3}$

$x = 18$

$\left(\dfrac{x}{2} - 4\right) + 50 = 180$

$\dfrac{x}{2} + 46 = 180$

$\dfrac{x}{2} + 46 - 46 = 180 - 46$

$\dfrac{x}{2} = 134$

$2 \cdot \dfrac{x}{2} = 2 \cdot 134$

$x = 268$

EXAMPLE **3**   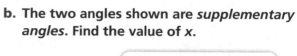 Find the Measure of an Unknown Angle

Find the measure of ∠*PAR*.

STEP 1 Use vertical angles to find the value of *x*.

$m\angle UAG = m\angle KAR$

$6x = 2x + 16$

$6x - 2x = 2x - 2x + 16$

$4x = 16$

$\dfrac{4x}{4} = \dfrac{16}{4}$

$x = 4$

$m\angle UAG = (6x)°$
$= (6 \cdot 4)° = 24°$
So $m\angle KAR = 24°$.

STEP 2 Use complementary angles to find the measure of ∠*PAR*.

$m\angle KAR + m\angle PAR = 90°$

$24° + m\angle PAR = 90°$

$m\angle PAR = 66°$

 **Try It!**

$m\angle 1$ is 4 times $m\angle 2$. ∠1 and ∠2 are complementary. ∠1 and ∠3 are vertical angles. ∠3 and ∠4 are supplementary. What are the measures of the four angles?

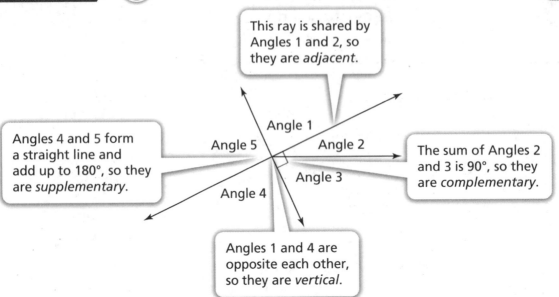

This ray is shared by Angles 1 and 2, so they are *adjacent*.

Angles 4 and 5 form a straight line and add up to 180°, so they are *supplementary*.

The sum of Angles 2 and 3 is 90°, so they are *complementary*.

Angles 1 and 4 are opposite each other, so they are *vertical*.

Do You Understand?

1. 🔑 **Essential Question** How are angles formed by intersecting lines related?

2. **Use Structure** Can vertical angles also be adjacent angles? Explain.

3. **Reasoning** Do complementary and supplementary angles also have to be adjacent angles? Explain.

Do You Know How?

Use the diagram below for 4–6.

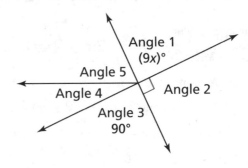

4. List two pairs of adjacent angles.

5. List all pairs of vertical angles.

6. If ∠1 and ∠3 are the same measure, what is the value of x?

Practice & Problem Solving

7. List each angle adjacent to ∠w.

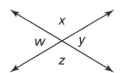

8. List two pairs of adjacent angles.

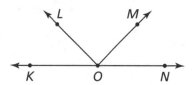

9. Find the value of x.

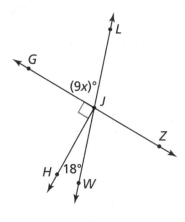

10. Find the value of x.

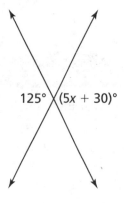

125° (5x + 30)°

11. ∠1 and ∠2 are complementary angles. The measure of ∠1 is 42°. The measure of ∠2 is (3x)°. Find the value of x.

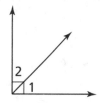

12. Two streets form an intersection. ∠C and ∠D are supplementary angles. If the measure of ∠C is 128° and the measure of ∠D is two times the value of x, what is the value of x?

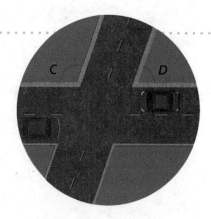

13. If ∠A and ∠B are supplementary angles and ∠A is three times as large as ∠B, find the measures of ∠A and ∠B.

14. **Higher Order Thinking** The measure of ∠DBE is $(0.1x - 22)°$ and the measure of ∠CBE is $(0.3x - 54)°$. Find the value of x.

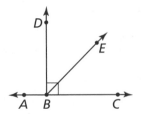

15. **Reasoning** ∠1 and an angle that measures 50° are supplementary. Another angle that measures 50° and ∠3 are supplementary. Show that m∠1 and m∠3 are equal.

16. Using the diagram at the right, Martin incorrectly writes $m∠b = 125°$.

What mistake did Martin likely make? Find the correct measure of ∠b.

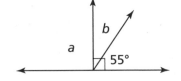

17. What is the measure, in degrees, of angle x?

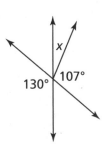

18. What is the measure, in degrees, of the highlighted angle?

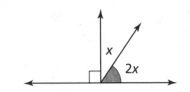

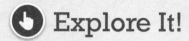 Explore It!

   ACTIVITY

The distance around a circle and the distance across a circle are related.

   Go Online

I can...
solve problems involving radius, diameter, and circumference of circles.

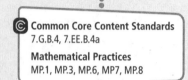

© **Common Core Content Standards**
7.G.B.4, 7.EE.B.4a

Mathematical Practices
MP.1, MP.3, MP.6, MP.7, MP.8

A. Use string to measure the distance across each circle. How many of these lengths does it take to go completely around the circle?

B. Use the string and a ruler to measure the distance across the circle and the distance around the circle. Complete the table. Round each measurement to the nearest quarter inch.

	Button	Disk	Dartboard
Distance Around the Circle			
Distance Across the Circle			

C. What do you notice about the ratio of the distance around the circle to the distance across the circle for each circle?

Focus on math practices

Look for Relationships How can you estimate the distance around any circle when given the distance across the circle?

VISUAL LEARNING   ASSES

EXAMPLE 1 **Describe Parts of a Circle and Find Circumference to Solve Problems**

Scan for Multimedia

Mark recently replaced his front bicycle wheel. How far does the bike travel with each revolution of his new front wheel?

Look for Relationships
How is one revolution of the wheel related to linear distance?

Diameter = 26 inches

Relate the given information to the parts of a circle.

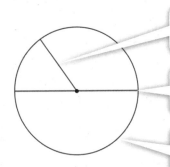

The *radius* is the distance from the outside of the circle to the center.

The *diameter* is the distance across the circle through the center.

The **circumference** is the distance around the circle.

$\frac{C}{d} = \pi$

$C = \pi d$

π is the ratio of the circumference, C, of a circle to its diameter, d.

π is a decimal that never repeats or terminates. $\pi = 3.14159\ldots$

Use the circumference formula to calculate the distance around the wheel.

$C = \pi d$

$C = \pi(26)$

The diameter of the wheel is 26 inches.

$C = 26\pi$

The circumference is exactly 26π.

$C \approx 26(3.14)$

$= 81.64$

To approximate the distance, use 3.14 for π.

The distance around the wheel is about 81.64 inches. So the bike travels about 81.64 inches with each revolution of the wheel.

✓ **Try It!**

What is the circumference of the rim of a basketball hoop with a radius of 9 inches?

First, multiply the radius by [ ] to get the diameter, [ ] inches.

Then, multiply the diameter by 3.14 (an approximation for π) to get

a circumference of about [ ] inches.

Convince Me! If the diameter is doubled, what happens to the circumference? Explain.

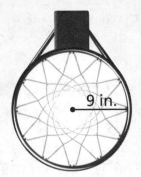

9 in.

EXAMPLE 2 Find the Diameter Using the Circumference

Kayla and Theo got on the Ferris wheel shown. About how high will they be at the top of the Ferris wheel?

Use the circumference formula to find the diameter of the Ferris wheel.

Circumference: 220 ft

ONE WAY Use 3.14 as an approximation for π.

$C = \pi d$

$220 \approx (3.14)d$ ← Substitute 3.14 for π.

$\dfrac{220}{3.14} = \dfrac{3.14d}{3.14}$

$70 \approx d$

ANOTHER WAY Use $\frac{22}{7}$ as an approximation for π.

$C = \pi d$

$220 \approx \left(\dfrac{22}{7}\right)d$ ← Substitute $\frac{22}{7}$ for π.

$\dfrac{7}{22} \cdot 220 = \dfrac{7}{22} \cdot \dfrac{22}{7}d$

$70 = d$

Kayla and Theo will be about 70 feet above the ground when at the top of the Ferris wheel.

EXAMPLE 3 Use Circumference to Solve a Problem

The larger gear turns twice per second. It causes the smaller gear to turn. How fast does the smaller gear turn per second?

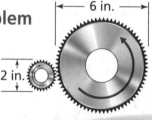

6 in.

2 in.

STEP 1 Use the circumference formula to find the circumferences of the larger gear and the smaller gear.

Larger gear	Smaller gear
$C = \pi d$	$C = \pi d$
$C \approx (3.14)(6)$	$C \approx (3.14)(2)$
$C = 18.84$	$C = 6.28$

STEP 2 Divide to find the number of full turns the smaller gear makes when the larger gear makes one full turn.

$\dfrac{18.84}{6.28} = 3$

The smaller gear makes three full turns for every full turn of the larger gear.

STEP 3 Multiply to find the number of full turns the smaller gear makes in one second.

$3 \times 2 = 6$

The larger gear turns two times per second.

The smaller gear makes 6 full turns per second.

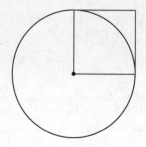 Try It!

The circle has a circumference of 9.42 units. What is the area of the square? Use 3.14 for π. Explain how you found the answer.

The parts of a circle and their relationships are summarized in the diagram below.

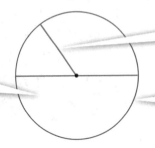

The radius of a circle is half the length of its diameter.

The ratio of the circumference of a circle to its diameter is π. The value of π is approximately 3.14 or $\frac{22}{7}$.

Circumference is the distance around a circle. It can be calculated using the formula $C = \pi d$ or equivalently $C = 2\pi r$.

Do You Understand?

1. **Essential Question** How is the circumference of a circle related to the length of its diameter?

2. **Construct Arguments** Are there any circles for which the relationship between the diameter and circumference cannot be represented by π? Explain.

3. **Be Precise** Can you find the exact circumference of a circle when you multiply the diameter by $\frac{22}{7}$? Explain.

Do You Know How?

4. What is the circumference of a circle with a radius of 5 inches?

5. What is the diameter of a circle with a circumference of 10.99 feet?

6. How many full revolutions does a car tire with a diameter of 25 inches make when the car travels one mile?

←— 25 in.

Practice & Problem Solving

7. Find the circumference of the circle. Use π as part of the answer.

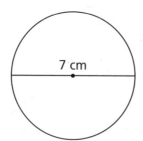

7 cm

8. Find the circumference of the circle. Use 3.14 for π. Round to the nearest hundredth.

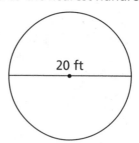

20 ft

9. Find the circumference of the circle. Use π as part of the answer.

12 mi

10. Find the circumference of the circle. Use 3.14 for π. Round to the nearest hundredth.

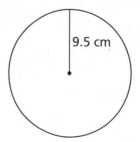

9.5 cm

11. Find the diameter of a circle with a circumference of 27 centimeters. Use 3.14 for π. Round to the nearest tenth.

12. The distance around a meteor crater is 9,687 feet. Find the diameter of the crater. Use $\frac{22}{7}$ for π. Round to the nearest tenth.

13. Make Sense and Persevere The circumference of the inner circle is 44 feet. The distance between the inner circle and the outer circle is 3 feet. By how many feet is the circumference of the outer circle greater than the circumference of the inner circle? Use $\frac{22}{7}$ for π. Round to the nearest hundredth of a foot.

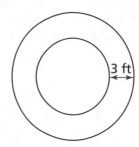

3 ft

14. Generalize What is the ratio of the radius to the circumference of any circle, using 3.14 for π?

15. What is the radius of a circle with a circumference of 26.69 centimeters?

16. Higher Order Thinking A unicycle wheel makes five rotations. The unicycle travels 37.94 feet. Find the diameter of the wheel in inches. Use 3.14 for π. Round to the nearest tenth of an inch.

5 rotations

☑ Assessment Practice

17. Camille drew the figure shown at the right.

Which of the following is the best estimate of the perimeter of the figure?

Ⓐ 36 feet

Ⓑ 81 feet

Ⓒ 45 feet

Ⓓ 50 feet

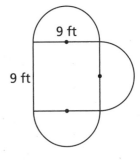

9 ft

9 ft

18. A cabin on a ferris wheel has traveled one fourth of the circumference of the wheel, a distance of 117.75 feet. What is the radius, in feet, of the ferris wheel? Use 3.14 for π.

19. The diagram shows a track composed of a rectangle with a semicircle on each end. The area of the rectangle is 7,200 square meters. What is the perimeter, in meters, of the track? Use 3.14 for π.

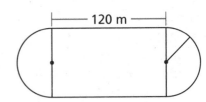

120 m

1. Vocabulary How are *adjacent angles* and *vertical angles* alike? How are they different? *Lesson 10-4*

2. On a map, 1 inch equals 150 miles. The border between two states is 5.5 inches long on the map. What is the actual length of the border? *Lesson 10-1*

In 3 and 4, use the figure to the right.

3. What is the measure of ∠BZD? *Lesson 10-4*

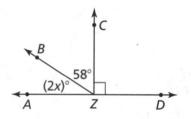

  Ⓐ 58°   Ⓑ 148°

  Ⓒ 32°   Ⓓ 90°

4. Find the value of x. *Lesson 10-4*

5. Pierce draws a circle with a radius of 3 centimeters. Gianna draws a circle with a radius that is twice as long as the radius of Pierce's circle. How will the circumference of Gianna's circle compare with the circumference of Pierce's circle? *Lesson 10-5*

The circumference of Gianna's circle is _____ times the circumference of Pierce's circle.

6. Draw a triangle with one side length of 5 units and another side length of 7 units. What additional piece of information will guarantee that only one triangle can be drawn? *Lessons 10-2 and 10-3*

How well did you do on the mid-topic checkpoint? Fill in the stars.

MID-TOPIC
PERFORMANCE TASK

Mrs. Thomas has two rolls of garden edging that are each 96 inches long. She wants to make two new flower beds in her back yard. Each flower bed will be bordered by one roll of the edging. One flower bed will be in the shape of a quadrilateral. The other will be in the shape of a triangle.

PART A

Mrs. Thomas decides to make a scale drawing of each flower bed using a scale of 1 centimeter = 5 inches. What will be the total length of each roll of edging in her scale drawings?

PART B

Mrs. Thomas wants the quadrilateral flower bed to have at least two 90° angles. Draw a possible plan for this flower bed using the scale from Part A. Make sure to use a complete roll of edging in the border. Label your drawing with all the angle measures and with the scaled length of each side. Name the shape of the flower bed you drew. What will be its actual dimensions?

PART C

Mrs. Thomas began to make a drawing for the triangular flower bed. In her drawing, the length of one side of the triangle is 4.8 centimeters, the length of a second side is 6.4 centimeters, and the included angle is a right angle. Use these measures and the scale from Part A to make a completed scale drawing. Label your drawing with all the angle measures to the nearest whole degree and with the scale length of each side. What will be the actual dimensions of this flower bed?

Explore It!

ACTIVITY

Latoya cut a circle into 8 equal sections and arranged the pieces to form a shape resembling a parallelogram.

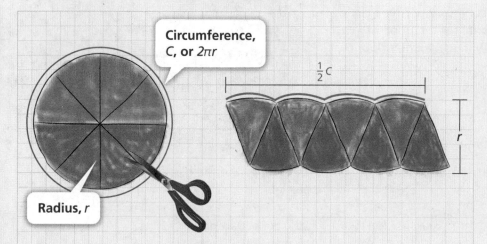

I can...
solve problems involving the area of a circle.

© **Common Core Content Standards**
7.G.B.4, 7.EE.B.3, 7.EE.B.4a

Mathematical Practices
MP.2, MP.6, MP.7

A. How is the base length of the new shape related to the circumference of the circle?

B. How is the height of the new shape related to the radius of the circle?

C. Since this new shape was made from a circle, use the information from the diagram and the formula for the area of the parallelogram, $A = bh$, to discover the formula for the area of a circle.

Focus on math practices

Look for Relationships The formula $A = bh$ can be used to find a good estimate for the area of the cut-out diagram. What would happen to this estimate if the circle were cut into 100 sections? 1,000 sections?

VISUAL LEARNING ASSESS

EXAMPLE 1 Solve Problems Involving the Area of a Circle

Scan for Multimedia

The floor of a new butterfly conservatory will be a circle with an 18-foot radius. The material for the floor will cost $3.95 per square foot. About how much will the floor cost?

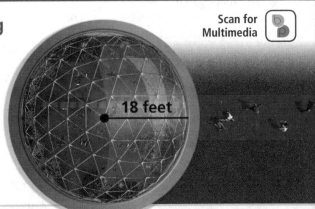

18 feet

STEP 1 Use the formula for the area of a circle to find the area of the floor.

An approximation for π is 3.14.

$A = \pi r^2$

$A \approx (3.14)(18)^2$

$A = (3.14)(324)$

$A = 1,017.36$

18 ft
r

The area of the floor of the new conservatory is about 1,018 square feet.

Reasoning Why round the area to the next whole foot?

STEP 2 Calculate the cost of the necessary floor material.

Cost per square foot

$3.95 \times 1,018 = 4,021.10$

Total square feet of floor

Total cost of the floor

The total cost of the floor will be about $4,021.

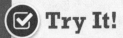 **Try It!**

At a school play, there is a spotlight above the center of the floor that covers a lighted area with a radius of 7 feet. What is the area covered by the spotlight?

$A = \pi r^2$

$A \approx \left(\frac{22}{7}\right) \cdot \boxed{}^2$

An approximation for π is $\frac{22}{7}$.

$A = \frac{22}{7} \cdot \boxed{}$

$A = \boxed{}$

The area covered by the spotlight is about $\boxed{}$ square feet.

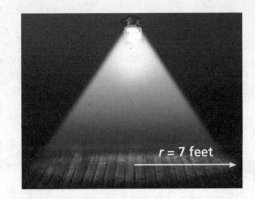

r = 7 feet

Convince Me! If the diameter of a circle is given, how would you find the area?

EXAMPLE 2 — Use Area to Find the Radius and Diameter

The athletic department wants to paint the school's mascot logo on the gym locker room wall. They start by painting a solid blue circle on the wall. What is the maximum diameter of the logo if only one quart of blue paint is used?

$A = \pi r^2$

> The radius is the unknown in the equation.

$78.5 \approx (3.14) \cdot r^2$

> An approximation for π is 3.14.

$\dfrac{78.5}{3.14} = \dfrac{(3.14) \cdot r^2}{3.14}$

$25 = r^2$

> What number times itself is equal to 25?

$5 = r$

> 1 quart of blue paint covers 78.5 ft².

The radius is 5 feet, so the diameter of the school's mascot logo can be up to 10 feet.

EXAMPLE 3 — Use Circumference to Find the Area of a Circle

Ellie needs new grass in the circular pen for her chickens. What is the area of the pen?

Look for Relationships How can you use the circumference to find the information needed to calculate the area?

> 176 feet of fencing

STEP 1 Find the radius, r, of the circular pen.

$C = 2\pi r$

$176 \approx 2 \cdot \left(\dfrac{22}{7}\right) \cdot r$

> An approximation for π is $\dfrac{22}{7}$.

$176 = \dfrac{44}{7} \cdot r$

$\dfrac{7}{44} \cdot 176 = \dfrac{7}{44} \cdot \left(\dfrac{44}{7}\right) \cdot r$

$28 = r$

The radius of the circular pen is about 28 feet.

STEP 2 Use the radius to find the area of the circular pen.

$A = \pi r^2$

$A \approx \dfrac{22}{7}(28)^2$

$A = 2{,}464$

The area of the circular pen is about 2,464 square feet.

Try It!

a. How far away can a person live from a radio station and hear its broadcast if the signal covers a circular area of 40,000 square miles? Write your answer as a whole number.

b. What circular area is covered by the signal if the circumference is 754 miles?

You can find the area, **A**, of a circle using the formula $A = \pi r^2$, where **r** is the radius.

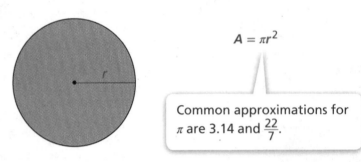

$$A = \pi r^2$$

Common approximations for π are 3.14 and $\frac{22}{7}$.

Do You Understand?

1. **? Essential Question** How can the area formula for a circle be used to solve problems?

2. **Be Precise** Is an area calculation exact when you use 3.14 or $\frac{22}{7}$ as a value for π? Explain.

3. **Use Structure** If you know the diameter of a circle, how can you find the area?

Do You Know How?

For 4–7, use 3.14 for π.

4. What is the area of a circle with a radius of 8 inches?

5. What is the radius of a circle with an area of 28.26 square feet?

6. What is the area of a circle with a circumference of 25.12 meters?

7. The diameter of a pizza is 12 inches. What is its area?

|← ———— 12 in. ———— →|

Practice & Problem Solving

8. Find the area of the circle. Use 3.14 for π.

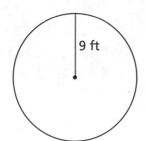

9 ft

9. Find the area of the circle. Use 3.14 for π.

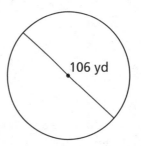

106 yd

10. Jaylon created this stained-glass window. The upper two corners are quarter circles, each with a radius of 4 inches. Find the area of the window. Use 3.14 for π.

4 in.   4 in.

26 in.

12 in.

11. The circumference of a circle is 50.24 meters. What is the area of the circle? Use 3.14 for π.

12. Higher Order Thinking A circular flower bed is 20 meters in diameter and has a circular sidewalk around it that is 3 meters wide. Find the area of the sidewalk in square meters. Use 3.14 for π. Round to the nearest whole number.

13. A circular plate has a circumference of 16.3 inches. What is the area of this plate? Use 3.14 for π. Round to the nearest whole number.

14. A water sprinkler sends water out in a circular pattern. How many feet away from the sprinkler can it spread water if the area formed by the watering pattern is 379.94 square feet?

15. The circumference of a circular rug is 24.8 meters. What is the area of the rug? Use 3.1 for π. Round your answer to the nearest tenth.

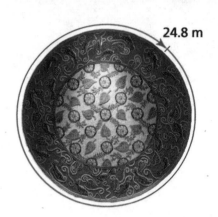

24.8 m

16. Frank wants to find the area enclosed by the figure at the right. The figure has semicircles on each side of a 40-meter-by-40-meter square. Find the area enclosed by the figure. Use 3.14 for π.

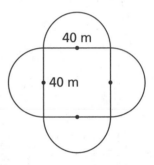

40 m

40 m

✓ Assessment Practice

17. Julia's bedroom is 10 feet by 10 feet. She wants to place a circular rug in the corner of her room.

PART A

She places a rug with a radius of 2 feet in her room. How much of her bedroom floor, in square feet, is not covered by the rug? Use 3.14 for π. Round to the nearest tenth.

PART B

Julia decides she wants a rug that covers about 50% of her floor. Which rug should she buy?

Ⓐ A rug with a radius of 5 feet

Ⓑ A rug with a diameter of 5 feet

Ⓒ A rug with a radius of 4 feet

Ⓓ A rug with a diameter of 4 feet

18. The circumference of a hubcap of a tire is 81.58 centimeters. Find the area, in square centimeters, of this hubcap. Use 3.14 as an approximation for π. Round your answer to the nearest whole centimeter.

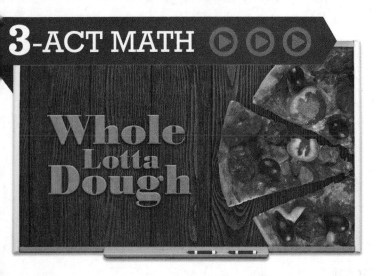

3-Act Mathematical Modeling:
Whole Lotta Dough

 Go Online

ⓒ Common Core Content Standards
7.G.B.4

Mathematical Practices
MP.4, MP.1, MP.2, MP.3, MP.3, MP.5, MP.7, MP.8

ACT 1

1. After watching the video, what is the first question that comes to mind?

2. Write the Main Question you will answer.

3. Construct Arguments Predict an answer to this Main Question. Explain your prediction.

4. On the number line below, write a number that is too small to be the answer. Write a number that is too large.

Too small   Too large

5. Plot your prediction on the same number line.

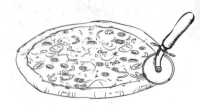

6. What information in this situation would be helpful to know?
How would you use that information?

7. Use Appropriate Tools What tools can you use to solve the problem?
Explain how you would use them strategically.

8. Model with Math Represent the situation using mathematics.
Use your representation to answer the Main Question.

9. What is your answer to the Main Question? Is it higher or lower than
your prediction? Explain why.

10. Write the answer you saw in the video.

11. Reasoning Does your answer match the answer in the video? If not, what are some reasons that would explain the difference?

12. Make Sense and Persevere Would you change your model now that you know the answer? Explain.

13. Model with Math Explain how you used a mathematical model to represent the situation. How did the model help you answer the Main Question?

14. Reasoning Explain why your answer to the Main Question does *not* involve the symbol π.

SEQUEL

15. Use Structure If the regular pizza costs $8.99, how much do you think the big pizza costs?

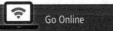

Solve & Discuss It!

 ACTIVITY

How could Mrs. Mendoza divide the ream of paper equally between two art classes? She has a paper cutter to slice the paper, if needed. What will the dimensions for each sheet of paper be once she has divided the ream? How many sheets will each class receive?

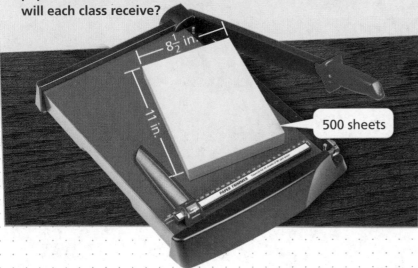

$8\frac{1}{2}$ in.

11 in.

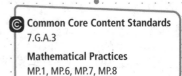 500 sheets

I can...
determine what the cross section looks like when a 3D figure is sliced.

© **Common Core Content Standards**
7.G.A.3

Mathematical Practices
MP.1, MP.6, MP.7, MP.8

Focus on math practices

Use Structure How would the number of sheets of paper each class receives change if Mrs. Mendoza started with 300 sheets?

? Essential Question How do the faces of a three-dimensional figure determine the two-dimensional shapes created by slicing the figure?

  VISUAL LEARNING ASSES

EXAMPLE 1 Describe Cross Sections of Right Rectangular Prisms

Scan for Multimedia

Rachel and Francesca went to a restaurant that serves rectangular bread rolls. Each sliced her roll in a different way. What do the *cross sections* look like?

> **Use Structure** What faces are parallel to the slice?

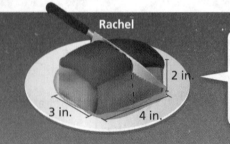

Rachel

A **cross section** is the two-dimensional shape that is exposed when a slice is made through a three-dimensional object.

2 in.

3 in.   4 in.

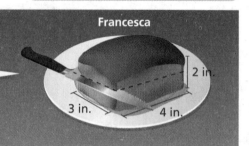

Francesca

2 in.

3 in.   4 in.

Rachel made a vertical slice that was parallel to the front and back faces of the roll.

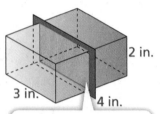

2 in.

3 in.   4 in.

The cross section is parallel to the front and back faces, so it is the same shape as those faces.

3 in.

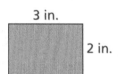

2 in.

The cross section is a rectangle that is 3 inches by 2 inches.

Francesca made a horizontal slice that was perpendicular to the front and back faces of the roll.

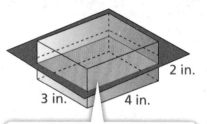

2 in.

3 in.   4 in.

The cross section is parallel to the top and bottom faces, so it is the same shape as those faces.

4 in.

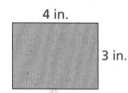

3 in.

The cross section is a rectangle that is 4 inches by 3 inches.

Try It!

Zachary made a vertical slice that was parallel to the left and right faces of a bread roll. What shape is the cross section, and what are its dimensions?

The shape of the cross section is a [ ]

that is [ ] inches by [ ] inches.

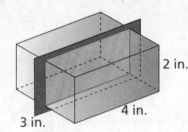

2 in.

4 in.

3 in.

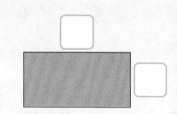

Convince Me! What are the shapes of horizontal and vertical cross sections of a rectangular prism, and how can you determine the dimensions of the cross sections?

EXAMPLE 2 — Describe Cross Sections of Right Rectangular Pyramids

Kenya made a sand castle in the shape of a right rectangular pyramid with a height of 0.9 feet.

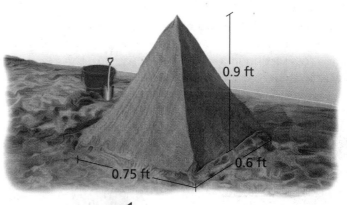

0.9 ft
0.6 ft
0.75 ft

a. If Kenya sliced the castle horizontally, parallel to the base, what would the cross section look like?

Horizontal cross sections are rectangles that are smaller than the base of the pyramid.

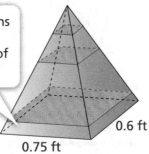

0.6 ft
0.75 ft

b. If Kenya sliced the castle vertically, through the top vertex, perpendicular to the base, and intersecting the 0.75-foot edges, what would the cross section look like?

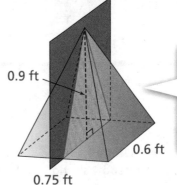

0.9 ft
0.6 ft
0.75 ft

The cross section would be an isosceles triangle with a height of 0.9 feet and a base length of 0.6 foot.

EXAMPLE 3 — Solve Problems Involving Cross Sections

A truck needs a metal divider that separates the refrigerated part of the truck from the dry goods. What should the divider look like, and how many square feet will the metal divider be?

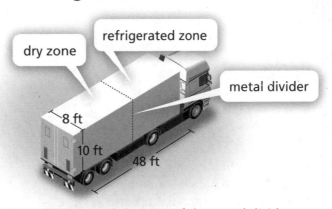

dry zone
refrigerated zone
metal divider
8 ft
10 ft
48 ft

STEP 1 Draw a picture of the cross section.

10 ft
8 ft

STEP 2 Find the area of the metal divider.

$A = \ell \times w$

$= 10(8) = 80 \text{ ft}^2$

The metal divider will be 80 square feet.

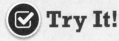 **Try It!**

Draw the cross section that is created when a vertical plane intersects the top vertex and the shorter edge of the base of the pyramid shown. What is the area of the cross section?

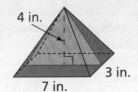

4 in.
3 in.
7 in.

A cross section is the two-dimensional shape exposed when a three-dimensional figure is sliced. The shape and dimensions of a cross section in a rectangular prism are the same as the faces that are parallel to the slice.

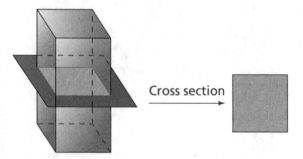

Cross section

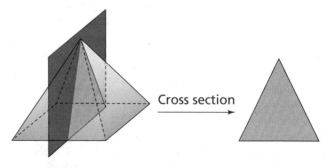

Cross section

Do You Understand?

1. **Essential Question** How do the faces of a three-dimensional figure determine the two-dimensional shapes created by slicing the figure?

2. **Generalize** What are the shapes of the cross sections that are parallel or perpendicular to the bases of a right rectangular prism?

3. **Generalize** What are the shapes of the horizontal cross sections of a right rectangular pyramid? What are the shapes of vertical cross sections through the vertex opposite the base?

Do You Know How?

4. The divider in a desk drawer is a cross section that is parallel to the front of the drawer. What is its shape, and what are its dimensions?

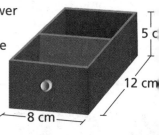

5 c

12 cm

8 cm

5. Use the diagram to answer the questions.

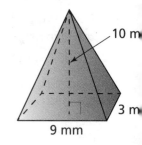

10 m

3 m

9 mm

a. Draw the cross section that is formed when the pyramid is sliced vertically through its vertex and its right face, perpendicular to its base.

b. What is the area of this cross section?

Name: _____

Practice & Problem Solving

PRACTICE   TUTORIAL

Scan for
Multimedia

6. What are the dimensions of the vertical cross section shown on this right rectangular prism?

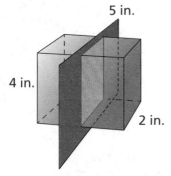

5 in.

4 in.

2 in.

7. Be Precise Describe the cross section that is formed by a vertical plane, perpendicular to the base of the pyramid, that intersects the 9-in. edge and the top vertex of the pyramid shown.

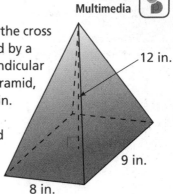

12 in.

9 in.

8 in.

8. Mason is slicing butter for the meal he is preparing. Describe the vertical cross section when the knife slices through the butter, parallel to its sides.

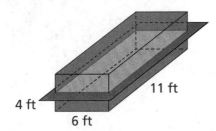

5 in.   3 in.

2.5 in.

9. a. Look for Relationships What are the dimensions of the vertical cross section?

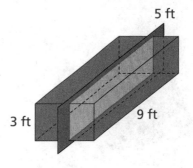

5 ft

3 ft

9 ft

b. What would be the dimensions of a horizontal cross section?

10. Use the figure to the right.

a. Describe the cross section shown.

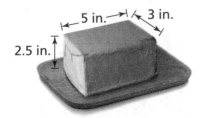

11 ft

4 ft

6 ft

b. Is it possible to have a horizontal cross section with different dimensions if you had the plane intersect the prism at another height? Explain.

11. Make Sense and Persevere The base of a right rectangular pyramid has a length of 12 centimeters, a width of 6 centimeters, and a height of 14 centimeters. Describe the cross section formed by a horizontal plane that intersects the faces of the pyramid above the base.

10-7 Describe Cross Sections   **635**

12. Higher Order Thinking Luis makes blocks from a painted piece of wood with dimensions of 27 inches × 24 inches × 1.5 inches. To make 72 blocks, the wood is cut into 3-inch squares.

Draw two pictures showing the horizontal cross section and the vertical cross section of each block.

13. Make Sense and Persevere
The area of the cross section shown is 52 square yards. What is the length of the unknown side of the base of the pyramid?

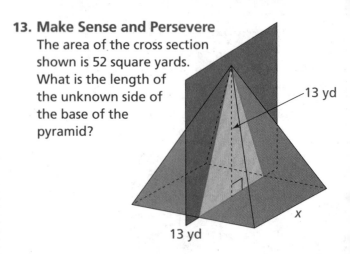

13 yd

13 yd

x

14. A waiter slices a cake shaped like a square pyramid vertically through the top point.

    a. Make Sense and Persevere Draw the cross section that is made by slicing the cake in this way.

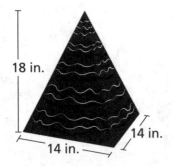

18 in.

14 in.

14 in.

    b. What is the area of this cross section?

15. Miranda says that the triangle below represents the cross section of the rectangular pyramid shown.

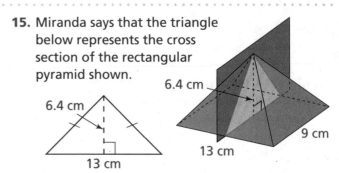

6.4 cm

6.4 cm

9 cm

13 cm

13 cm

What mistake might Miranda have made?

![Assessment Practice]

16. Estimate, to the nearest whole number, the number of vertical cross sections needed to equal the area of the base of the figure to the right. Explain how you made your estimate, and decide whether your estimate is higher or lower than the actual number.

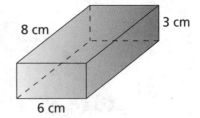

8 cm

3 cm

6 cm

Solve & Discuss It!

Alaya will paint the outside of a box with three different colors. Decide how she could paint the box. What is the total area that each color will cover?

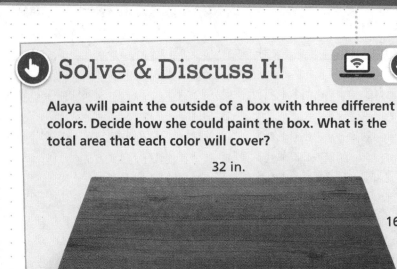

32 in.

16 in.

14 in.

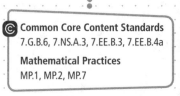

Make Sense and Persevere
What do you know about the faces of a rectangular prism?

I can...
find the area and surface area of 2-dimensional composite shapes and 3-dimensional prisms.

© **Common Core Content Standards**
7.G.B.6, 7.NS.A.3, 7.EE.B.3, 7.EE.B.4a
Mathematical Practices
MP.1, MP.2, MP.7

Focus on math practices

Reasoning Trista paints each pair of opposite sides of the box with the same color. How many different areas does she need to find to determine the total area covered by each color? Explain.

Scan for
Multimedia

EXAMPLE 1 👁 Find the Area of Composite Figures

A city planner wants all neighborhood parks to have more green space than non-green space. Does this park meet the requirements? Explain.

> **Look for Relationships**
> How are the areas of the green and non-green spaces related to the total area of the park?

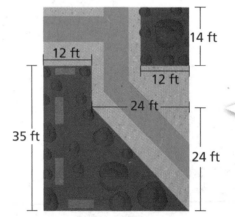

14 ft

12 ft

12 ft

24 ft

35 ft

24 ft

> The shape of the non-green space is a *composite figure*. A **composite figure** is the combination of two or more geometric shapes.

Divide the park into familiar shapes. Use the information given to find the dimensions.

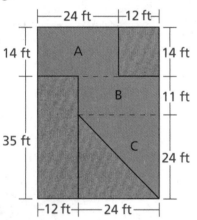

├── 24 ft ──┼─12 ft─┤

14 ft   A   14 ft

B   11 ft

35 ft   C   24 ft

├─12 ft─┼── 24 ft ──┤

Add the areas of the non-green shapes.

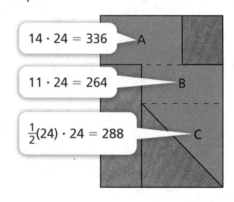

$14 \cdot 24 = 336$ A

$11 \cdot 24 = 264$ B

$\frac{1}{2}(24) \cdot 24 = 288$ C

$336 + 264 + 288 = 888 \text{ ft}^2$
The total non-green area is 888 ft².

Find the area of the green space.

> Area of
> entire park

> Non-green
> area

$(49 \bullet 36) - 888$

$= 1{,}764 - 888$

$= 876 \text{ ft}^2$

The park does not meet the requirements since the non-green area, 888 ft², is greater than the green area, 876 ft².

☑ Try It!

This diagram shows the area of a room to be carpeted. What will be the area of the new carpet?

A = [   ] = [   ] ft² B = [   ] = [   ] ft²

Total area = [   ] + [   ]

The area of the new carpet is [   ] square feet.

├── 5 ft ──┤

6 ft   A

B

├──── 9 ft ────┤

Convince Me! How does knowing the area of familiar shapes help find the total area of a composite shape?

EXAMPLE **2** Solve Surface Area Problems

Gavin constructed a model building and wants to cover the outside with paper. How much paper will he need to cover the entire model?

STEP 1 Find the area of each face of the model.

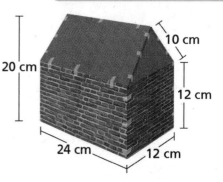

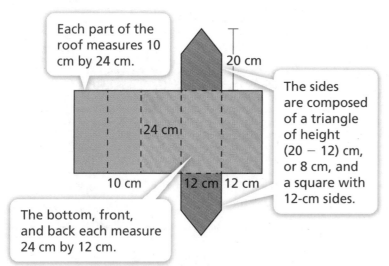

Each part of the roof measures 10 cm by 24 cm.

20 cm

24 cm

10 cm   12 cm 12 cm

The sides are composed of a triangle of height (20 − 12) cm, or 8 cm, and a square with 12-cm sides.

The bottom, front, and back each measure 24 cm by 12 cm.

STEP 2 Find the total surface area of the model.

$(240 \cdot 2) + (288 \cdot 3) + (144 \cdot 2) + (48 \cdot 2) = 1{,}728$ cm^2

EXAMPLE **3** **Solve Mathematical Problems Involving Surface Area**

What is the surface area of the composite figure shown?

4 in.

6 in.

6 in.   6 in.

STEP 1 Find the surface area of the bottom of the composite figure.

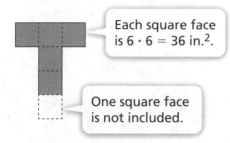

Each square face is $6 \cdot 6 = 36$ in.^{2}.

One square face is not included.

5 faces $\bullet$ 36 in.^{2} = 180 in.^{2}

STEP 2 Find the surface area of the top of the composite figure.

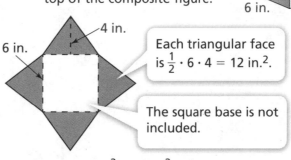

6 in.

4 in.

Each triangular face is $\frac{1}{2} \cdot 6 \cdot 4 = 12$ in.^{2}.

The square base is not included.

4 faces $\bullet$ 12 in.^{2} = 48 in.^{2}

The total surface area of the composite figure is $180 + 48 = 228$ in.^{2}.

☑ **Try It!**

Hiromi is painting the front and back of a barn. Each can of paint covers 32 square feet. How many cans of paint does Hiromi need to cover the entire front and back of the barn?

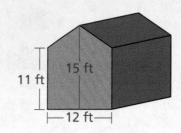

15 ft

11 ft

12 ft

The area of a two-dimensional composite figure is the sum of the areas of all the shapes that compose it. The surface area of a three-dimensional composite figure is the sum of the areas of all its faces.

Two-dimensional composite figure

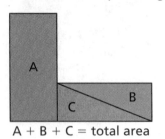

A + B + C = total area

Three-dimensional composite figure

Add the areas of each face of the rectangular prism, but not the face that is shared with Figure B.

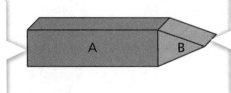

Add the areas o each face of the triangular prism but not the face that is shared with Figure A.

Surface area of shape A **+** Surface area of shape B

= Surface area of composite shape

Do You Understand?

1. **? Essential Question** How is finding the area of composite two-dimensional figures similar to finding the surface area of three-dimensional figures?

2. **Make Sense and Persevere** Laine wants to determine the amount of fabric needed to cover a triangular prism-shaped box. She begins by measuring the dimensions of the box. Explain her next steps.

3. **Use Structure** Explain how you would find the surface area of the figure below.

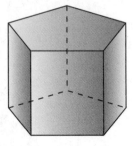

Do You Know How?

4. Paula is painting a henhouse. If a can of paint will cover 24 square feet, how many cans of paint does she need to buy? Explain the steps she might take to solve this problem.

5. Find the area of the composite figure. The two triangles have the same dimensions.

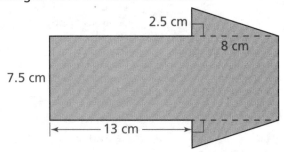

6. A stage block is being covered in carpet. The dimensions of the block are 2 feet by 3 feet by 6 feet. Every surface will need covering except for the surface touching the floor, which is 3 feet by 6 feet. How would you calculate the surface area that needs covering?

Practice & Problem Solving

Scan for
Multimedia

Leveled Practice In **7**, fill in the boxes to solve.

7. Jacob is putting tiles on the sections of his yard labeled A, B, and C. What is the area of the parts that need tiles?

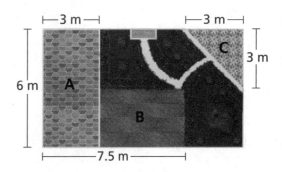

Part A = ☐ · ☐ = ☐ m²

Part B = ☐ · ☐ = ☐ m²

Part C = $\frac{1}{2}$ · ☐ · ☐ = ☐ m²

Total area = ☐ + ☐ + ☐ = ☐ m²

---

8. What is the total area of the figure?

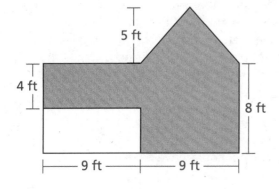

9. Find the surface area of the prism.

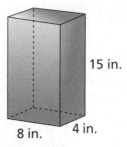

---

10. Find the surface area of the triangular prism. The base of the prism is an isosceles triangle.

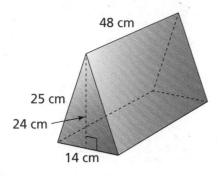

11. A block of wood has the shape of a triangular prism. The bases are right triangles. Find its surface area.

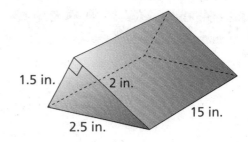

12. A box has the shape of a rectangular prism. How much wrapping paper do you need to cover the box?

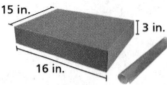

15 in.
3 in.
16 in.

13. Higher Order Thinking Find the surface area of the rectangular hexagonal prism. Show your work.

5 cm
14 cm
4.3 cm

14. A box has the shape of a rectangular prism with a height of 29 centimeters. If the height is increased by 0.7 centimeter, by how much does the surface area of the box increase?

29 cm
12 cm   6.3 cm

15. The base of a prism is an equilateral triangle with an area of 73.2 square centimeters. The area of each lateral face is 104 square centimeters. Riley incorrectly claims that the surface area is 250.4 square centimeters.

a. What is the correct surface area?

b. What could have been Riley's error?

✓ Assessment Practice

16. The bottom part of this block is a rectangular prism. The top part is a square pyramid. How much paper, in square centimeters, is needed to cover the block completely?

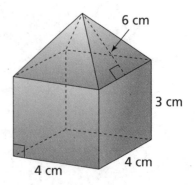

6 cm
3 cm
4 cm
4 cm

Solve & Discuss It!

ACTIVITY

Volunteers at a food pantry pack boxes of soup into crates. How many boxes of soup will fill each crate? Show your work.

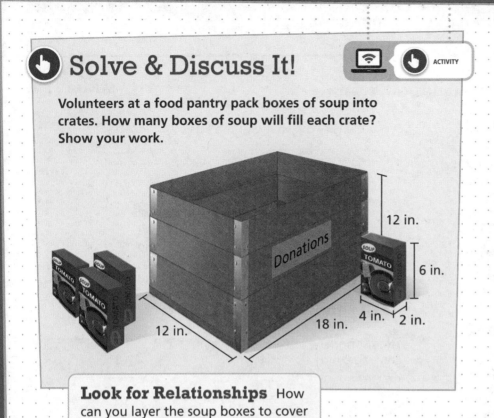

12 in.

6 in.

18 in.   4 in.   2 in.

12 in.

Look for Relationships How can you layer the soup boxes to cover the bottom of the crate?

I can...
use the area of the base of a three-dimensional figure to find its volume.

© **Common Core Content Standards**
7.G.B.6, 7.NS.A.3, 7.EE.B.3, 7.EE.B.4a

Mathematical Practices
MP.1, MP.2, MP.4, MP.7

Focus on math practices

Reasoning A supplier donated crates to the food pantry that are 15 inches long, instead of 18 inches long. All other dimensions are the same. What is the greatest number of boxes of soup that will fit in the donated crates? How will the volume of the soup vary from the total volume of the crate?

? **Essential Question** How does the formula for volume of a prism help you understand what volume of a prism means?

VISUAL LEARNING   ASSESS

EXAMPLE 1 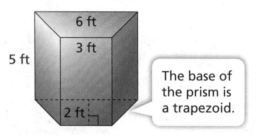 **Find Volumes of Prisms**

Scan for Multimedia

Cora has an aquarium with exotic fish. The tank is the size and shape of a trapezoidal prism. The distance from the front glass to the back is 2 feet. What is the volume of the aquarium tank?

STEP 1 Identify the shape of the base.

6 ft
3 ft
5 ft
2 ft

The base of the prism is a trapezoid.

STEP 2 Find the area of the base, B, of the prism.

Area formula for trapezoid

$A = \frac{1}{2}(b_1 + b_2)h$

$= \frac{1}{2}(3 + 6)2$

$= \frac{1}{2}(9)(2)$

$= 9$ ft^2

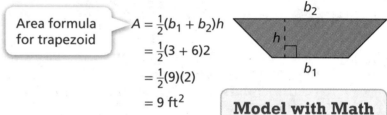

The area of the base is 9 ft^2.

Model with Math
Why does this formula work?

STEP 3 Find the volume of the prism.

Volume = Area of base of prism ✕ height of the prism

$V = Bh$

$= 9(5)$

$= 45$ ft^3

Volume is measured in cubic units.

The volume of the aquarium tank is 45 ft^3.

☑ Try It!

What is the volume of the triangular prism?

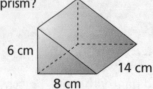

6 cm
14 cm
8 cm

$V = B \cdot h$

$V = \left(\frac{1}{2} \cdot \boxed{} \cdot \boxed{}\right) \cdot h$

$V = \left(\boxed{}\right) \cdot \boxed{}$

$V = \boxed{}$

The volume of the prism is $\boxed{}$ cubic centimeters.

Convince Me! What is the shape of the base of the figure? What are its dimensions? Explain.

EXAMPLE 2 Solve Problems Involving Volume

Students are selling a souvenir basketball. Will the basketball fit inside the gift box that has a regular hexagonal base so that the lid fits on top?

STEP 1 Find the area of the hexagonal base.

Area of base = 6 • (area of one triangle in base)

$$A = 6 \cdot \left(\frac{1}{2}b \cdot h\right)$$

$$\approx 6 \cdot \frac{1}{2}(4) \cdot (3.5)$$

$$= 6 \cdot \frac{1}{2}(14)$$

$$= 42$$

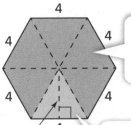

You can decompose a regular hexagon into 6 equal triangles.

The area of the base is about 42 square inches.

The height of each triangle in the base is about 3.5 inches.

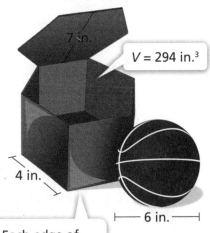

$V = 294$ in.³

Each edge of the hexagon base is 4 inches.

STEP 2 Use the volume formula to find the height.

$$V = Bh$$
$$294 = (42)h$$
$$\frac{294}{42} = \frac{42h}{42}$$
$$7 = h$$

The width of the box is given at 7 inches. The height of the box is 7 inches. Both the height and width are greater than the diameter of the basketball, so the basketball will fit with the lid on top of the box.

Look for Relationships
If you find the base area and the volume is given, can you find the height of the box?

EXAMPLE 3 **Find Volumes of Composite Figures**

Sequan has a shed for his athletic equipment. What is the total volume of the shed?

STEP 1 Find the volume of the **bottom** section.

$$V = Bh$$
$$= (18)(18) \cdot 18$$
$$= 324(18)$$
$$= 5,832$$

The volume of the bottom section is 5,832 cubic feet.

STEP 2 Find the volume of the **top** section.

$$V = Bh$$
$$= \frac{1}{2}(18)(10) \cdot 18$$
$$= 90(18)$$
$$= 1,620$$

The volume of the top section is 1,620 cubic feet.

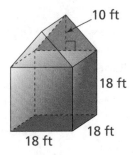

STEP 3 Add the volumes together.

$$5,832 + 1,620 = 7,452$$

The total volume of the shed is 7,452 cubic feet.

✓ **Try It!**

Amber built a custom terrarium for her plants. What is the volume of the terrarium?

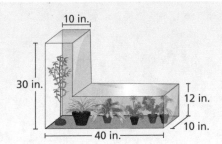

You can use formulas to solve problems involving the volume of three-dimensional figures.

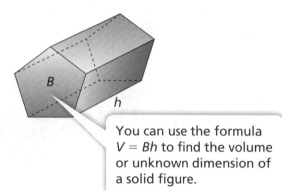

B

h

You can use the formula $V = Bh$ to find the volume or unknown dimension of a solid figure.

Find the volume of a composite figure by finding the sum of the volumes of each solid figure.

Do You Understand?

1. **Essential Question** How does the formula for volume of a prism help you understand what volume of a prism means?

2. **Look for Relationships** If you know the volume of a three-dimensional figure, how can you find a missing dimension of the figure?

3. **Make Sense and Persevere** How do you find the volume of a three-dimensional figure that can be decomposed into prisms?

Do You Know How?

4. An aquarium has a regular hexagonal base with side lengths of 15 centimeters. When the hexagon is divided into six equal triangles, the height of each triangle is about 13 centimeters. If the aquarium is 50 centimeters tall, what is its volume?

5. A cheese box is shaped like a right triangular prism. The box is 6 inches long, 4 inches tall, and has a volume of 24 cubic inches. Can a cube of cheese that is 2.5 inches on each side fit inside the box? Explain.

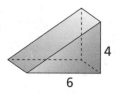

4

6

6. Ray made a toolbox with the dimensions shown to store garden tools. What is the volume of the toolbox?

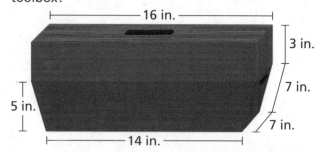

16 in.

3 in.

7 in.

5 in.

7 in.

14 in.

Practice & Problem Solving

Leveled Practice In 7–8, find the volume of each prism.

7.

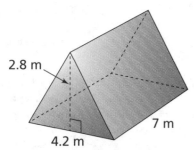

2.8 m

7 m

4.2 m

$V = Bh$

$= (0.5 \cdot \boxed{} \cdot \boxed{}) \cdot 7$

$= \boxed{} \text{ m}^3$

8.

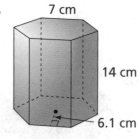

7 cm

14 cm

6.1 cm

$V = Bh$

$= (0.5 \cdot \boxed{} \cdot 7 \cdot 6) \cdot \boxed{}$

$= 128.1 \cdot \boxed{}$

$= \boxed{} \text{ cm}^3$

---

9. A tunnel for an amusement park ride has the shape of a regular hexagonal prism with dimensions shown. The prism has a volume of 3,572.1 cubic meters. Can two 8-meter cars connected by a 3-meter connector pass through the tunnel at the same time? Explain.

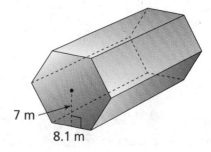

7 m

8.1 m

---

10. A volume of 185.5 cubic feet of concrete was used to make the section of a skateboard ramp shown. How long is the ramp?

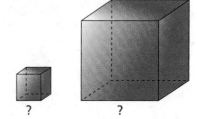

4 ft

7 ft

?

11. Make Sense and Persevere A small cube has a volume of 64 cubic feet. A larger cube has sides that are three times as long as the small cube. How long are the sides of each cube?

?   ?

12. What is the volume of the regular hexagonal prism, to the nearest cubic centimeter?

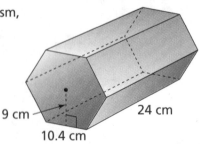

9 cm

24 cm

10.4 cm

13. A mailbox has the dimensions shown. What is the volume of the mailbox?

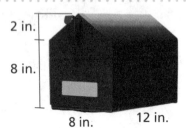

2 in.

8 in.

8 in.

12 in.

14. Use Structure A glass bead has the shape of a prism with a rectangular prism removed. What is the volume of the glass that forms the bead?

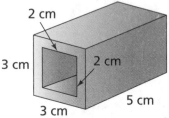

2 cm

3 cm

2 cm

3 cm

5 cm

15. Higher Order Thinking A cake has two layers. Each layer is a regular hexagonal prism. A slice removes one face of each prism, as shown.

a. What is the volume of the slice?

b. What is the volume of the remaining cake?

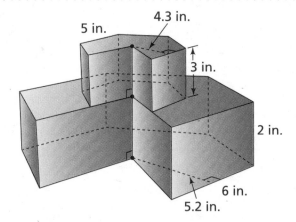

4.3 in.

5 in.

3 in.

2 in.

6 in.

5.2 in.

16. The area of the top of the box shown is 60 square centimeters. What is the volume, in cubic centimeters, of the box?

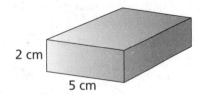

2 cm

5 cm

17. Which of the following freezers is the best buy in terms of dollars per cubic foot?

Ⓐ Freezer A has an interior of 1 foot by 1 foot by 5 feet and sells for $499.99.

Ⓑ Freezer B has two sections of 3 cubic feet each and sells for $629.99.

Ⓒ Freezer C has interior dimensions of 1.5 feet by 1.5 feet by 4 feet and sells for $849.99.

Ⓓ Freezer D has 3 sections of 1.5 cubic feet each and sells for $444.99.

? Topic Essential Question

How can geometry be used to solve problems?

Vocabulary Review

Complete each definition, and then provide an example of each vocabulary word.

Vocabulary
adjacent angles   circumference   complementary angles
composite figure   cross section   scale drawing
supplementary angles   vertical angles

Definition	Example
1. The distance around a circle is the _____.	
2. _____ have a sum of 180 degrees.	
3. A(n) _____ is the combination of two or more geometric shapes.	
4. A(n) _____ is the two-dimensional shape that is exposed when a slice is made through a three-dimensional object.	

Use Vocabulary in Writing

Shawna drew this picture of three intersecting lines. Use vocabulary terms to explain how she could determine the value of x.

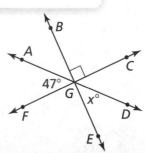

Concepts and Skills Review

LESSON 10-1 · Solve Problems Involving Scale Drawings

Quick Review

In a scale drawing, the scale is a ratio that relates each drawing length to the actual length it represents. To find unknown lengths, you can use the scale to write a proportion.

Example

A blueprint of a room is drawn to a scale of 2 inches = 7 feet. The actual length of one wall is 56 feet. What is the length of this wall on the blueprint?

Use the scale to write a proportion.

$\frac{2 \text{ in.}}{7 \text{ ft}} = \frac{x \text{ in.}}{56 \text{ ft}}$

56 feet = 7 feet × 8, so multiply 2 inches by 8

$x = 2 \text{ inches} \times 8 = 16 \text{ inches}$

The length in the blueprint is 16 inches.

Practice

Use the scale drawing to answer the questions.

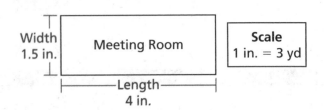

1. What is the actual area of the meeting room in square yards?

2. John decides to make a new scale drawing of the meeting room. He wants the length of the room in the new drawing to be 8 inches. What is the new scale for the drawing?

LESSON 10-2 · Draw Geometric Figures

Quick Review

You can classify a quadrilateral as a trapezoid, a rectangle, a square, or a parallelogram based on its side lengths, side relationships, and angle measures.

Example

Draw a quadrilateral with exactly two perpendicular sides and one angle measuring 120°. What is the name of the figure you drew?

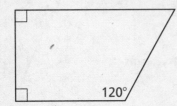

The figure has exactly one pair of parallel sides, so it is a trapezoid.

Practice

1. Draw a quadrilateral with two pairs of parallel sides, with one side measuring 5 centimeters, one side measuring 3 centimeters, and one angle measuring 45°. What is the name of the figure you drew?

2. What quadrilaterals can you draw that have two angles measuring 115° and two angles measuring 65°?

Quick Review

When you are given certain conditions for a triangle, it may be possible to draw one triangle, more than one triangle, or no triangle.

Example

How many triangles can be drawn with side lengths of 3 inches, 5 inches, and 6 inches?

No matter how you position the sides, the triangle has the same shape and size. There is only one way to draw a triangle with these side lengths.

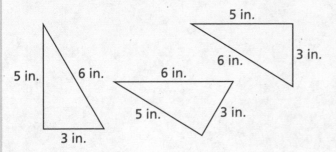

Practice

1. Can more than one triangle be drawn with side lengths of 4 centimeters and 2 centimeters and an included angle of 50°? Explain.

2. When given angle measures of 25°, 65°, and 90°, is it impossible to draw a triangle, possible to draw only one triangle, or possible to draw more than one triangle? Explain.

Quick Review

Angles that have a common vertex and a common side but no common interior points are adjacent angles. Supplementary angles are angles with a sum of 180°. Complementary angles are angles with a sum of 90°. When two lines intersect, the angles that have no side in common are called vertical angles. Vertical angles are equal.

Example

List all pairs of vertical angles in this figure.

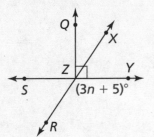

There are two pairs of vertical angles:

- ∠SZR and ∠XZY
- ∠SZX and ∠RZY

Practice

Use the figure from the example.

1. Name a pair of complementary angles.

2. The measure of ∠XZY is 55°. Which other angle has a measure of 55°? Explain.

3. Use the information from Problem 2. Find the value of n.

Quick Review

The distance around a circle is called its circumference. The number π (pi) is the ratio of the circumference of any circle to its diameter. So when you know the diameter, *d*, of a circle, or its radius, *r*, you can determine its circumference, *C*, with the formula **C = πd** or **C = 2πr.**

Example

What is the circumference of a circle with a radius of 6 meters? Use 3.14 for π.

$C = 2\pi r$

$C = 2\pi(6)$

$C \approx 2(3.14)(6)$

$C = 37.68$

The circumference is about 37.68 meters.

Practice

1. The length of the minute hand of a clock is 14 inches. What is the length of the path traced by the outer tip of the minute hand in one hour? Use $\frac{22}{7}$ for π.

2. The circumference of a bicycle tire is 126.5 centimeters. What is the diameter of the tire? Use 3.14 for π. Round to the nearest tenth as needed.

Quick Review

The area, *A*, of a circle can be found using the formula $A = \pi r^2$, where *r* is the radius. You can use 3.14 or $\frac{22}{7}$ as an approximation for π.

Example

The diameter of the logo at the center of a basketball court is 10 feet. What is the area of the logo? Use 3.14 for π.

The radius of a circle is half the diameter. So the radius of the logo is half of 10 feet, or 5 feet. Substitute the radius into the circle area formula.

$A = \pi r^2$

$A = \pi(5)^2$

$A \approx 3.14(25)$

$A = 78.5$

The area of the logo is about 78.5 square feet.

Practice

1. Jessie wants to paint the top of the table shown. What is the approximate area that she will paint? Use 3.14 for π. Round to the nearest whole number of inches.

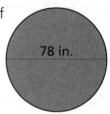

78 in.

2. What is the diameter of a circle with an area of 113.04 square centimeters. Use 3.14 for π.

3. The distance around a circular park is 88 yards. What is the area of the park? Use $\frac{22}{7}$ for π.

Quick Review

A **cross section** is the two-dimensional shape exposed when a three-dimensional figure is sliced. Recognizing the shape of a cross section can help in solving some problems.

Example

Muffins are packed in two layers in a box with a piece of cardboard placed between. What shape is the cardboard and what are its dimensions?

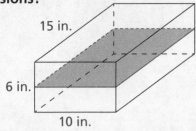

The cardboard lies on a cross section shaped like a rectangle that is 15 inches long and 10 inches wide.

Practice

1. The figure shows a vertical cross section of a right rectangular pyramid. What shape is the cross section and what is its area?

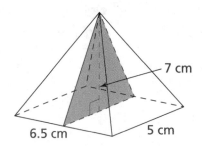

2. Zach wants to slice the pyramid along a horizontal plane that intersects the pyramid above its base. Describe the cross section that would be formed.

Quick Review

A **composite figure** is the combination of two or more geometric shapes. The surface area of a two- and a three-dimensional composite figure will be the sum of the areas of all the shapes, or faces.

Example

The figure shows the plan for a kitchen countertop. What is the area of the countertop?

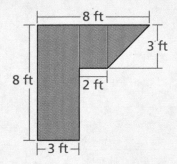

$(3 \cdot 8) + (3 \cdot 2) + \frac{1}{2}(3 \cdot 3) = 24 + 6 + 4.5 = 34.5$

The area of the countertop is 34.5 ft².

Practice

1. Kara wants to paint the four outside walls of her dog's house. She will not paint the roof or the door on the front of the house. What is the area of the surface that Kara needs to paint?

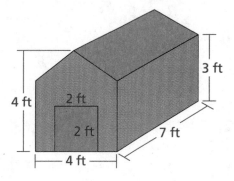

Quick Review

You can find the volume, *V*, of a prism using the formula *V = Bh*. In this formula, *B* represents the area of the base of the prism and *h* represents the height of the prism. Volume is measured in cubic units.

If the volume of a prism is known, you may be able to use this formula to find an unknown dimension of the prism. You also can use this formula to solve problems involving volumes of composite figures that are made up of two or more prisms.

Example

Rhonda received a package in a box shaped like a rectangular prism. What is the volume of the box?

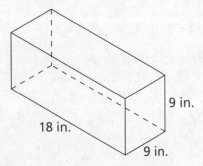

18 in.   9 in.   9 in.

Find the area of the rectangular base.

$A = 9(18) = 162$ in.^{2}

Find the volume of the prism.

$V = Bh$

$V = 162(9)$

$V = 1{,}458$ in.^{3}

Practice

1. Holly has a gift box that is shaped like a regular hexagonal prism. What is the volume of the box?

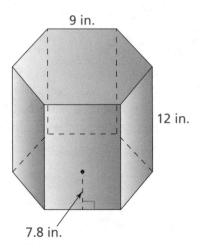

9 in.

12 in.

7.8 in.

2. A designer is planning a trail mix box that is shaped like a rectangular prism. The front of the box must have the width and height shown. The volume of the box must be 162 cubic inches. What must be the depth, *d*, of the box?

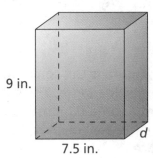

9 in.

7.5 in.   *d*

3. A building that is used for storage has the dimensions shown. What is the volume of the building?

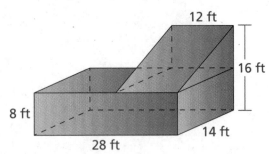

12 ft

16 ft

8 ft

28 ft

14 ft

Pathfinder

Shade a path from START to FINISH. Follow the answers to the problems so that each answer is greater than the one before. You can only move up, down, right, or left.

I can...
use the percent equation to solve problems. © 7.RP.A.3

START

Amy deposits $360 in an account that pays 1.2% simple annual interest. How much interest will she earn in 6 years?	Nat opened an account that earns 1.4% simple annual interest. He will earn $21 total interest after 3 years. How much did he deposit when he opened the account?	An account is opened with an initial balance of $950 and a simple annual interest rate of 1.6%. What is the balance after 5 years?
Ilsa withdraws $300 from an account that had a balance of $1,000. How much interest will she earn on the remaining balance at a simple annual interest rate of 1.8% over 3 years?	Jacey gets a $500 loan at a simple annual interest rate of 5%. She will pay back the loan in equal monthly payments over one year. How much is each payment?	Travis has $1,500 in a savings account. He deposits $75. How much interest will he earn after 2 years at a simple annual interest rate of 1.3%?
Pablo saves $85 per month for 6 months. Then he deposits the money in an account that earns 2.1% simple annual interest. How much interest will he earn over 4 years?	Cam borrows $1,000 from her bank. She will pay back the loan at a simple annual interest rate of 4% over 4 years. How much will she pay back altogether?	Hank deposits money in an account that pays 1.5% simple annual interest. He earns $50.25 interest in the first year. How much money did he deposit?

FINISH

TOPIC 11

CONGRUENCE AND SIMILARITY

? Topic Essential Question

How can you show that two figures are either congruent or similar to one another?

Topic Overview

11-1 Analyze Translations

11-2 Analyze Reflections

11-3 Analyze Rotations

11-4 Compose Transformations

3-Act Mathematical Modeling: Tricks of the Trade

11-5 Understand Congruent Figures

11-6 Describe Dilations

11-7 Understand Similar Figures

11-8 Angles, Lines, and Transversals

11-9 Interior and Exterior Angles of Triangles

11-10 Angle-Angle Triangle Similarity

Topic Vocabulary

- alternate interior angles
- angle of rotation
- center of rotation
- congruent
- corresponding angles
- dilation
- enlargement
- exterior angle of a triangle
- image
- line of reflection
- reduction
- reflection
- remote interior angles
- rotation
- same-side interior angles
- scale factor
- similar
- transformation
- translation
- transversal

Lesson Digital Resources

 INTERACTIVE STUDENT EDITION
Access online or offline.

 VISUAL LEARNING ANIMATION
Interact with visual learning animations.

 ACTIVITY Use with *Solve & Discuss It, Explore* and *Explain It* activities, and to explore Examp

VIDEOS Watch clips to support *3-Act Mathematical Modeling Lessons* and *STEM Pr*

 Go online

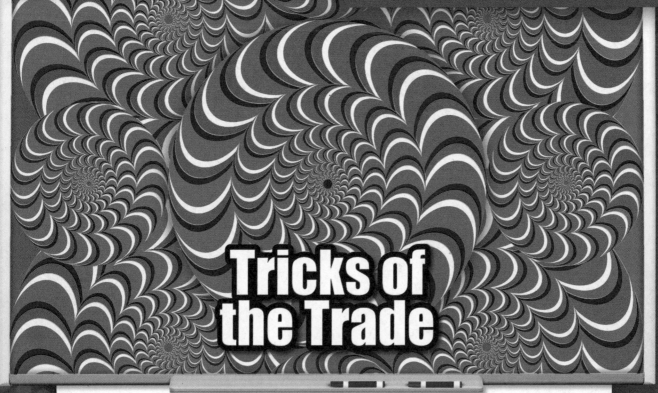
Tricks of the Trade

Tricks of the Trade

All kinds of objects in nature have symmetry: beehives, pine cones, butterflies, and snowflakes, to name a few. If you look closely, you will start to see patterns left and right. Think about this during the 3-Act Mathematical Modeling lesson.

PRACTICE Practice what you've learned.

TUTORIALS Get help from *Virtual Nerd*, right when you need it.

MATH TOOLS Explore math with digital tools.

GAMES Play Math Games to help you learn.

KEY CONCEPT Review important lesson content.

GLOSSARY Read and listen to English/Spanish definitions.

ASSESSMENT Show what you've learned.

enVision® STEM Project

Did You Know?

Trees provide **wood for cooking** and **heating** for half of the world's population.

As trees grow, **carbon dioxide** is removed from the atmosphere for **photosynthesis**. Forests are called "carbon sinks" because one acre of forest absorbs six tons of carbon dioxide and puts out four tons of **oxygen**.

Carbon Dioxide

Oxygen

Sunlight

In addition to providing oxygen and improving air quality, trees conserve water and soil and preserve wildlife.

Trees provide **lumber for buildings**, tools, and furniture. Other products include rubber, sponges, cork, paper, **chocolate**, nuts, and fruit.

About **30%** of land is covered by forests.

Forests are now being **managed** to preserve wildlife and old growth forests, protect biodiversity, safeguard watersheds, and develop **recreation**, as well as extract timber.

Forests also need managed to prevent raging **wildfires**, **invasive species**, overgrazing, and disease.

Your Task: Forest Health

The proper management of forests is a growing science. You and your classmates will learn about forest health indicators and use what you know about similar triangles and ratios to gather and interpret data in order to assess the health of a forest.

Review What You Know!

Vocabulary

Choose the best term from the box to complete each definition.

adjacent angles
complementary angles
supplementary angles
vertical angles

1. _____ have a sum of 90°.

2. _____ share the same ray.

3. _____ are pairs of opposite angles made by intersecting lines.

4. _____ have a sum of 180°.

Multiplying Real Numbers

Simplify the expression.

5. $5 \times 2 =$ ☐

6. $6 \times \frac{1}{2} =$ ☐

7. $12 \times \frac{1}{3} =$ ☐

Identifying Points on a Coordinate Plane

Name the location of the point.

8. point *W*

9. point *X*

10. point *Y*

11. point *Z*

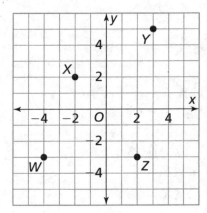

Supplementary Angles

The angles are supplementary. Find the missing angle measure.

12.

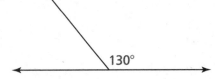

130°

13.

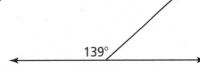

139°

Language Development

Complete the graphic organizer with an illustration for each transformation.
Write either *congruent* or *similar* to make the given statement true.

Reflection

Illustration

The *image* is [   ]
to the *preimage*.

Translation

Illustration

The *image* is [   ]
to the *preimage*.

What transformation?
Congruent or similar?

Rotation (90°)

Illustration

The *image* is [   ]
to the *preimage*.

Dilation

Illustration

The *image* is [   ]
to the *preimage*.

How might an artist use mathematics?

PROJECT: WRITE A BIOGRAPHY

PROJECT 11B

What geometric shapes do you see around you?

PROJECT: RECORD A VIDEO ABOUT SIMILAR FIGURES

What different types of bridges have you crossed?

PROJECT: BUILD A MODEL OF A TRUSS BRIDGE

PROJECT
11D

What shapes tessellate?

PROJECT: DESIGN A TESSELLATION

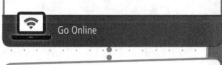
Solve & Discuss It!

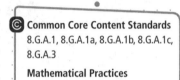
ACTIVITY

Ashanti draws a trapezoid on the coordinate plane and labels it Figure 1. Then she draws Figure 2. How can she determine whether the figures have the same side lengths and the same angle measures?

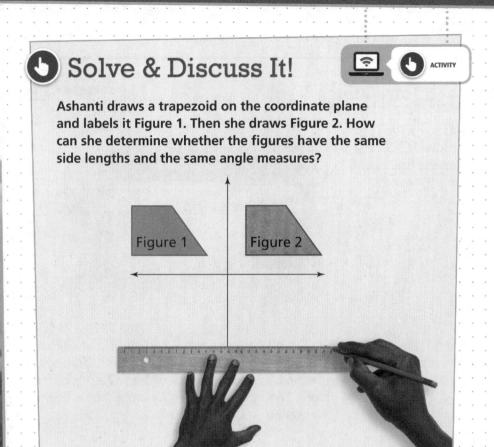

Go Online

I can...
translate two-dimensional figures.

© **Common Core Content Standards**
8.G.A.1, 8.G.A.1a, 8.G.A.1b, 8.G.A.1c, 8.G.A.3

Mathematical Practices
MP.3, MP.4, MP.6, MP.7, MP.8

Focus on math practices

Be Precise How do you know that the method you described shows whether the side lengths and angle measures are equal? Explain.

VISUAL LEARNING · ASSES

EXAMPLE 1 Understand Translations

Scan for Multimedia

A landscape architect shows a plan for a new patio to a client. The client wants the fire pit moved 6 feet to the right and 3 feet farther from the house. Where should the architect place the fire pit? How will the client's request change the fire pit?

> **Model with Math** How can you represent the problem situation?

The architect translates, or slides, the fire pit 6 feet to the right and 3 feet away from the house.

> A **transformation** is a change in the position, shape, or size of a figure.
>
> A **translation** is a transformation that moves every point of a figure the same distance and the same direction.

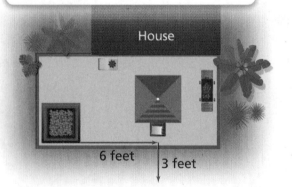

The fire pit has been translated. Each part of the pit has been moved an equal number of feet to the right and an equal number of feet away from the house. The fire pit still has the same shape, size, and orientation.

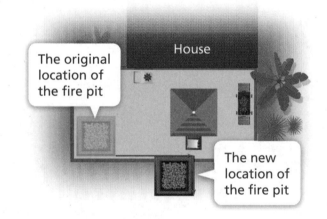

☑ Try It!

The clients also want the small table below the window moved 5 feet to the right. Where should the architect place the small table? Draw the new location of the table on the plan.

Convince Me! An equilateral triangle with side lengths 5 inches is translated 3 units down and 2 units right. Describe the shape and dimensions of the translated figure.

EXAMPLE 2 — Translate a Figure on a Coordinate Plane

Polygon *ABCD* has vertices *A*(−1, 6), *B*(4, 5), *C*(2, 2), and *D*(−2, 0). Graph and label the vertices of *ABCD'* and , *A' B' C' D'* its image after a translation of 8 units down and 3 units left.

STEP 1 Graph polygon *ABCD*.

STEP 2 Translate each vertex 8 units down and 3 units left.

STEP 3 Draw and label the vertices of polygon *A' B' C' D'*.

> In a transformation, the original figure is the preimage. The resulting figure is the **image**. The image of point A is point *A'*, read "A prime."

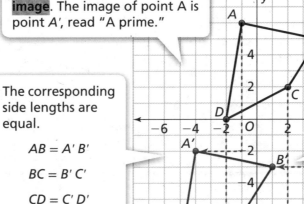

> The corresponding side lengths are equal.
>
> $AB = A'B'$
>
> $BC = B'C'$
>
> $CD = C'D'$
>
> $AD = A'D'$

> A translation maps angles to angles with the same measure.
>
> $m\angle A = m\angle A'$
>
> $m\angle B = m\angle B'$
>
> $m\angle C = m\angle C'$
>
> $m\angle D = m\angle D'$

EXAMPLE 3 — Describe a Translation

What is a rule that describes the translation that maps trapezoid *PQRS* onto trapezoid *P' Q' R' S'*?

The translation maps every point of *PQRS* to its corresponding point of *P' Q' R' S'*.

> **Use Structure** How do you know which vertex of the trapezoid to use to determine the rule?

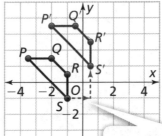

> Each vertex of trapezoid *PQRS* is translated 1.5 units to the right and 2 units up.

Try It!

Triangle *ABC* is translated 5 units right and 1 unit down. Graph and label the image *A' B' C'*. If $m\angle A = 30°$, what is $m\angle A'$?

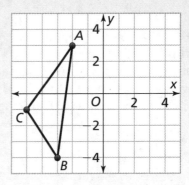

A *translation*, or slide, is a *transformation* that moves every point of a figure the same distance and the same direction.

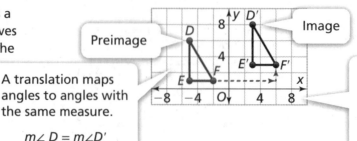

Preimage

Image

A translation maps angles to angles with the same measure.

$m\angle D = m\angle D'$

$m\angle E = m\angle E'$

$m\angle F = m\angle F'$

A translation maps line segments to line segments of the same length.

$DE = D'E'$

$DF = D'F'$

$EF = E'F'$

Do You Understand?

1. **? Essential Question** How does a translation affect the properties of a two-dimensional figure?

2. **Construct Arguments** Triangle $L'M'N'$ is the image of triangle LMN after a translation. How are the side lengths and angle measures of the triangles related? Explain.

3. **Generalize** Sanjay determined that one vertex of a figure was mapped to its image by translating the point 2 units left and 7 units down. What is the rule that maps the other vertices of the figure to their images?

Do You Know How?

In 4–6, use the coordinate plane.

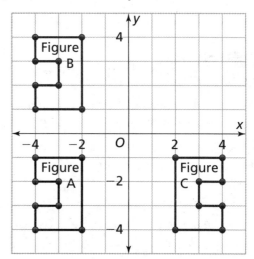

4. Which figure is a translation of Figure A? Explain.

5. Graph the translation of Figure A 3 units right and 4 units up.

6. Describe the translation needed to move Figure B to the same position as the image from Item 5.

Practice & Problem Solving

Scan for
Multimedia

7. Graph *G′ R′ A′ M′*, the image of *GRAM* after a translation 11 units right and 2 units up.

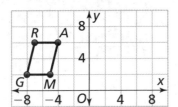

8. △*A′ B′ C′* is a translation of △*ABC*. Describe the translation.

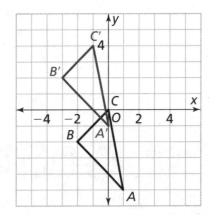

9. Which triangle is the image of △*DEF* after a translation? Describe the translation.

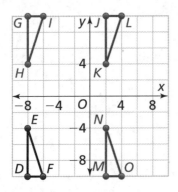

10. The vertices of figure *QRST* are translated 3 units left and 11 units down to form figure *Q′ R′ S′ T′*. Explain the similarities and differences between the two figures.

11. Graph the image of the given triangle after a translation 3 units right and 2 units up.

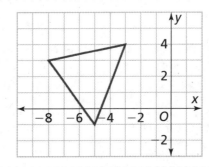

12. Quadrilateral *P′ Q′ R′ S′* is the image of quadrilateral *PQRS* after a translation.

   a. If the length of side *PQ* is about 2.8 units, what is the length of side *P′ Q′*?

   b. If *m∠R* = 75°, what is *m∠R′*?

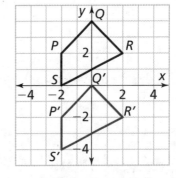

13. **Higher Order Thinking** A farmer has a plot of land shaped like the figure in the graph. There is another identical plot of land 120 yards east and 100 yards north of the original plot.

   a. Draw the image after the given translation.

   b. Find the combined area of the 2 plots in square yards.

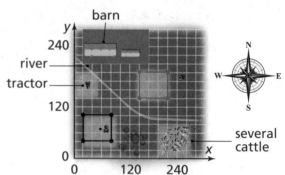

Assessment Practice

14. What is true about the preimage of a figure and its image created by a translation? Select all that apply.

☐ Each point in the image moves the same distance and direction from the preimage.

☐ Each point in the image has the same x-coordinate as the corresponding point in the preimage.

☐ Each point in the image has the same y-coordinate as the corresponding point in the preimage.

☐ The preimage and the image are the same size.

☐ The preimage and the image are the same shape.

15. The vertices of parallelogram *QUAD* are Q(−7, −7), U(−6, −4), A(−2, −4), and D(−3, −7).

   PART A

   Graph and label the image of QUAD after a translation 11 units right and 9 units up.

   PART B

   If $m\angle U = 110°$, what is $m\angle U'$?

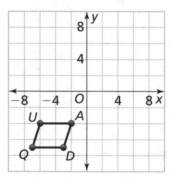

   PART C

   If the length of side *UA* is 4 units, what is the length of side *U′A′*?

Solve & Discuss It!

ACTIVITY

Dale draws a triangle on grid paper and labels it Figure 1. Then using his pencil as a guide, he draws another triangle directly on the opposite side of the pencil so that the vertical side is now one square to the right of the pencil instead of one square to the left of the pencil. He labels this triangle Figure 2. How are the figures the same? How are they different?

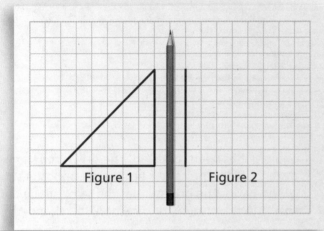

Figure 1   Figure 2

I can...
reflect two-dimensional figures.

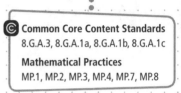
Ⓒ **Common Core Content Standards**
8.G.A.3, 8.G.A.1a, 8.G.A.1b, 8.G.A.1c
Mathematical Practices
MP.1, MP.2, MP.3, MP.4, MP.7, MP.8

Look for Relationships
What do you notice about the size, shape, and direction of the two figures?

Focus on math practices

Reasoning Dale draws a line in place of his pencil and folds the grid paper along the line. How do the triangles align when the grid paper is folded? Explain.

? Essential Question How does a reflection affect the properties of a two-dimensional figure?

EXAMPLE 1 👁 Understand Reflections

Scan for Multimedia

The client also wants the architect to flip the placement of the grill, putting it on the other side of the patio. Where does the client want the grill to be placed?

> **Model with Math** Can a picture or an object be used to represent the problem situation?

The architect flips the placement of the grill over the vertical line segment dividing the patio.

> A **reflection**, or flip, is a transformation that flips a figure over a *line of reflection*. Reflected figures are the same distance from the line of reflection but on opposite sides.

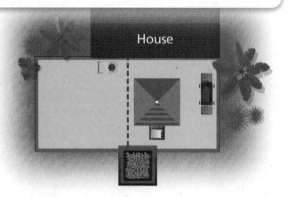

The grill has been reflected. The grill is the same distance from the center but on the opposite side of the patio. The grill still has the same shape and size. The orientation, or direction, has changed.

> The new location of the grill.

> The original location of the grill.

> A **line of reflection** is a line over which a figure is reflected. The original location and the new location of the grill are the same distance from the line of reflection.

☑ Try It!

While updating the design, the architect accidentally clicked on the chair and reflected it across the center line. Draw the new location of the chair on the plan.

Convince Me! How do the preimage and image compare after a reflection?

EXAMPLE 2 — Reflect a Figure on a Coordinate Plane

Polygon *ABCDE* has vertices *A*(−5, 2), *B*(−5, 4), *C*(−4, 5), *D*(−3, 5) and *E*(−3, 2). Graph and label the vertices of *ABCDE* and its image, *A′ BC′ D′ E*, after a reflection across the *x*-axis.

STEP 1 Graph polygon *ABCDE*.

STEP 2 Show how each vertex of *ABCDE* maps to its image after a reflection across the *x*-axis.

STEP 3 Draw and label the vertices of polygon *A′ B′ C′ D′ E*.

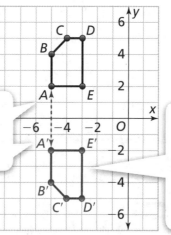

Since point *A* is 2 units above the *x*-axis, point *A′* will be 2 units below the *x*-axis.

The corresponding side lengths and angle measures remain the same but their positions and orientations are different.

Try It!

Quadrilateral *KLMN* has vertices at *K*(2, 6), *L*(3, 8), *M*(5, 4), and *N*(3, 2). It is reflected across the *y*-axis, resulting in quadrilateral *K′ L′ M′ N′*. What are the coordinates of point *N′*?

EXAMPLE 3 — Describe a Reflection

What is a rule that describes the reflection that maps parallelogram *ABCD* onto parallelogram *A′B′C′D′*?

A reflection maps every point of *ABCD* to the corresponding point of *A′ B′ C′ D′*.

Parallelogram *A′B′C′D′* is the image of parallelogram *ABCD* after a reflection across the *y*-axis.

Generalize When reflecting across the *y*-axis, the *y*-coordinate of the vertex of the image remains the same and the *x*-coordinate is the opposite. $(x, y) \rightarrow (-x, y)$

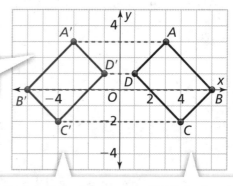

Each point of preimage *ABCD* is the same distance from the line of reflection as the corresponding point of image *A′ B′ C′ D′*.

Try It!

Polygon *ABCDE* is reflected across the line *x* = −2. Graph and label the image *A′B′C′D′E′*. Is *m∠A* = *m∠A′*? Explain.

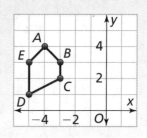

A **reflection**, or flip, is a transformation that flips a figure across a line of reflection. The preimage and image are the same distance from the line of reflection but on opposite sides. They have the same size and shape but different orientations.

Do You Understand?

1. **? Essential Question** How does a reflection affect the properties of a two-dimensional figure?

2. **Generalize** What do you notice about the corresponding coordinates of the preimage and image after a reflection across the *x*-axis?

3. **Construct Arguments** Jorge said the *y*-values would stay the same when you reflect a preimage across the line $y = 5$ since the *y*-values stay the same when you reflect a preimage across the *y*-axis. Is Jorge correct? Explain.

Do You Know How?

4. Is △*X′ Y′ Z′* a reflection of △*XYZ* across line *g*?

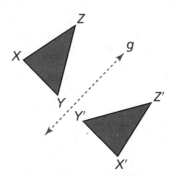

Use the coordinate grid below for 5 and 6.

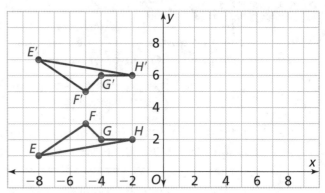

5. Describe the reflection of figure *EFGH*.

6. Draw the image that would result from a reflection of figure *EFGH* across the line $x = -1$.

Practice & Problem Solving

7. Leveled Practice Trapezoid *ABCD* is shown.
Draw the reflection of trapezoid *ABCD* across the *y*-axis.

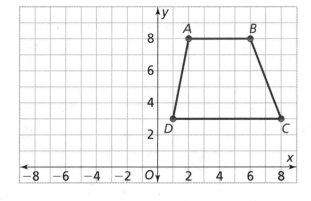

Identify the points
of the preimage.

Identify the points
of the image.

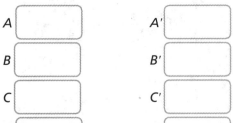

A [ ]   A' [ ]

B [ ]   B' [ ]

C [ ]   C' [ ]

D [ ]   D' [ ]

Plot the points and draw trapezoid *A′ B′ C′ D′*.

8. Reasoning Is triangle *A′ B′ C′* a reflection of
triangle *ABC* across the line? Explain.

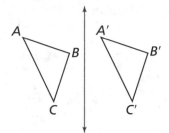

9. Your friend gives you the graph of quadrilateral
ABCD and its image, quadrilateral *A′ B′ C′ D′*.
What reflection produces this image?

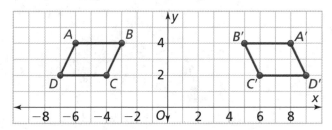

10. Construct Arguments Your friend incorrectly says that the reflection
of △*EFG* to its image △*E′ F′ G′* is a reflection across the *x*-axis.

a. What is your friend's mistake?

b. What is the correct description of the reflection?

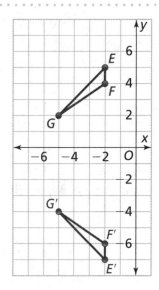

11. **Make Sense and Persevere** The vertices of △ABC are A(−5, 5), B(−2, 5), and C(−2, 3). If △ABC is reflected across the line y = −1, find the coordinates of the vertex C'

12. **Higher Order Thinking** What reflection of the parallelogram ABCD results in image A' B' C' D'?

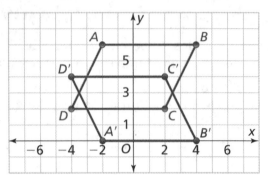

 Assessment Practice

13. △JAR has vertices J(4, 5), A(6, 4), and R(5, 2). What graph shows △JAR and its image after a reflection across the line x = 1?

PART A

Ⓐ
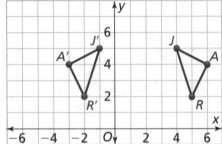

Ⓒ
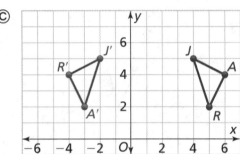

Ⓑ
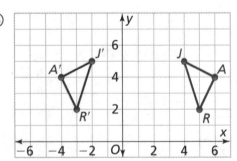

Ⓓ
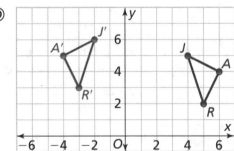

PART B

The measure of ∠A = 90°. What is m∠A'?

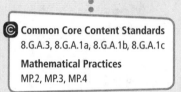
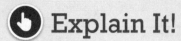
Explain It!

Maria boards a car at the bottom of the Ferris wheel. She rides to the top, where the car stops. Maria tells her friend that she completed $\frac{1}{4}$ turn before the car stopped.

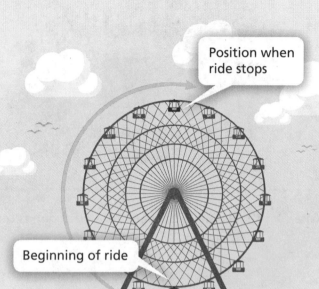

Position when ride stops

Beginning of ride

I can...
rotate a two-dimensional figure.

© **Common Core Content Standards**
8.G.A.3, 8.G.A.1a, 8.G.A.1b, 8.G.A.1c

Mathematical Practices
MP.2, MP.3, MP.4

A. Do you agree with Maria? Explain.

B. How could you use angle measures to describe the change in position of the car?

Focus on math practices

Construct Arguments How can you describe Maria's change in position when her car returns to the position at which she began the ride?

VISUAL LEARNING ASSESS

EXAMPLE 1 **Understand Rotations**

Scan for Multimedia

One feature of the new patio plan is a rectangular umbrella that can easily rotate so that clients can enjoy either the sun or the shade. Where should the architect move the umbrella to highlight this feature for his clients?

> **Model with Math** How can you describe the rotation of the umbrella?

The architect rotates the umbrella 90° counterclockwise.

> A **rotation** is a transformation that turns a figure around a fixed point, called the center of rotation.

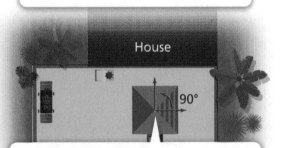

> The **angle of rotation** is the number of degrees the figure rotates. A positive angle of rotation turns the figure counterclockwise.

The umbrella has been rotated about its center. The umbrella has the same size, shape, and orientation.

✓ **Try It!**

The architect continues to rotate the umbrella in a counterclockwise direction until it is in its original position. What is the angle of this rotation?

Convince Me! How does an image compare to its preimage after a −45° rotation?

EXAMPLE 2 Complete a Rotation

What are the coordinates of the image of trapezoid *ABCD* after a 90° rotation about the origin?

STEP 1 Draw a ray from the origin to point *D*. Then use a protractor to draw a 90° angle in the counterclockwise direction.

STEP 2 Plot point *D'* the same distance from the origin as point *D*.

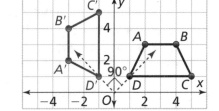

STEP 3 Use the same method to map each vertex of trapezoid *ABCD* to its image. Draw trapezoid *A' B' C' D'*.

$A(2, 3) \rightarrow A'(-3, 2)$

$B(4, 3) \rightarrow B'(-3, 4)$

$C(5, 1) \rightarrow C'(-1, 5)$

$D(1, 1) \rightarrow D'(-1, 1)$

Generalize The *x*- and *y*-coordinates of a point change as shown in the table below when rotated in a counterclockwise direction about the origin.

Angle of Rotation	Rule
90°	$(x, y) \rightarrow (-y, x)$
180°	$(x, y) \rightarrow (-x, -y)$
270°	$(x, y) \rightarrow (y, -x)$

✅ Try It!

The coordinates of the vertices of quadrilateral *HIJK* are *H*(1, 4), *I*(3, 2), *J*(−1, −4), and *K*(−3, −2). If quadrilateral *HIJK* is rotated 270° about the origin, what are the vertices of the resulting image, quadrilateral *H' I' J' K*?

EXAMPLE 3 Describe a Rotation

Describe the rotation that maps parallelogram *ABCD* to parallelogram *A' B' C' D'*.

STEP 1 Draw rays from the origin through point *A* and point *A'*.

STEP 2 Measure the angle formed by the rays.

A 270° rotation about the origin maps parallelogram *ABCD* to parallelogram *A' B' C' D'*.

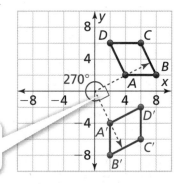

> This rotation could also be described as a −90°, or 90° clockwise, rotation.

✅ Try It!

Describe the rotation that maps △*FGH* to △*F' G' H'*.

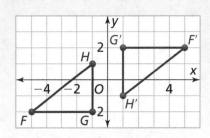

A rotation is a transformation that turns a figure about a fixed point called the center of rotation. The angle of rotation is the number of degrees the figure is rotated. The x- and y-coordinates change in predictable ways when rotated.

Counterclockwise Rotations about the Origin

Angle of Rotation	Transformation
90°	$(x, y) \rightarrow (-y, x)$
180°	$(x, y) \rightarrow (-x, -y)$
270°	$(x, y) \rightarrow (y, -x)$

Do You Understand?

1. **Essential Question** How does a rotation affect the properties of a two-dimensional figure?

2. **Reasoning** If a preimage is rotated 360 degrees about the origin how can you describe its image?

3. **Construct Arguments** In Example 3, side *AB* is parallel to side *DC*. How are side *A′B′* and side *D′C′* related? Explain.

Do You Know How?

4. The coordinates of the vertices of rectangle *ABCD* are *A*(3, −2), *B*(3, 2), *C*(−3, 2), and *D*(−3, −2).

   a. Rectangle *ABCD* is rotated 90° about the origin. What are the coordinates of the vertices of rectangle *A′B′C′D′*?

   b. What are the measures of the angles of A′B′C′D′?

5. Describe the counterclockwise rotation that maps △*QRS* to △*Q′R′S′*.

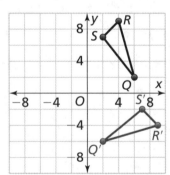

Practice & Problem Solving

Scan for
Multimedia

6. What is the angle of rotation about the origin that maps △PQR to △P′ Q′ R′ ?

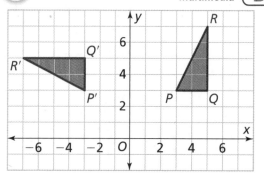

7. Is △X′ Y′ Z′ a rotation of △XYZ? Explain.

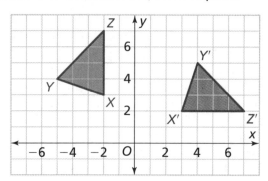

8. △PQR is rotated 270° about the origin. Graph and label the coordinates of P′, Q′, and R′.

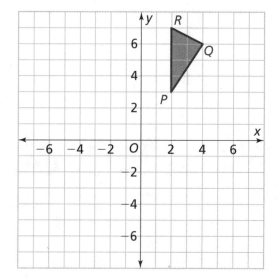

9. Is △P′ Q′ R′ a 270° rotation of △PQR about the origin? Explain.

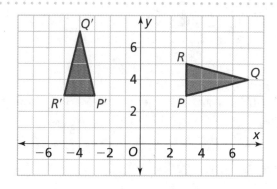

10. Reasoning Explain why any rotation can be described by an angle between 0° and 360°.

11. Rotate rectangle *KLMN* 270° about the origin.

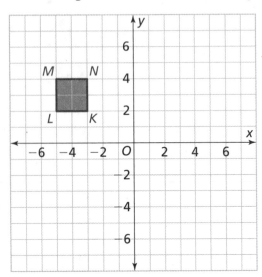

12. Higher Order Thinking An architect is designing a new windmill with four sails. In her sketch, the sails' center of rotation is the origin, (0, 0), and the tip of one of the sails, point *Q*, has coordinates (2, −3). She wants to make another sketch that shows the windmill after the sails have rotated 270° about their center of rotation. What would be the coordinates of ?

☑ Assessment Practice

13. A rotation about the origin maps △*TRI* to △*T' R' I'*.

PART A Which graph shows an angle you could measure to find the angle of rotation about the origin?

Ⓐ 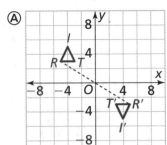 Ⓑ 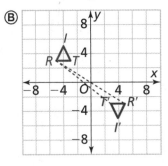 Ⓒ 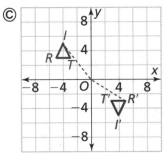 Ⓓ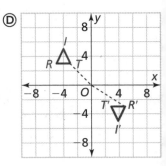

PART B What is the angle of rotation about the origin?

Ⓐ 90°　　　　　Ⓑ 180°　　　　　Ⓒ 270°　　　　　Ⓓ 360°

Solve & Discuss It! 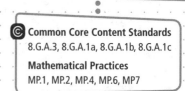 ACTIVITY

How can you map Figure A onto Figure B?

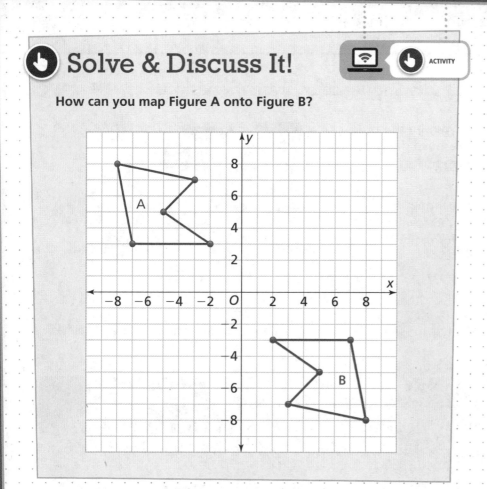

I can...
describe and perform a sequence of transformations.

© **Common Core Content Standards**
8.G.A.3, 8.G.A.1a, 8.G.A.1b, 8.G.A.1c

Mathematical Practices
MP.1, MP.2, MP.4, MP.6, MP7

Focus on math practices

Look for Relationships Is there another transformation or sequence of transformations that will map Figure A to Figure B?

Essential Question How can you use a sequence of transformations to map a preimage to its image?

     VISUAL LEARNING   ASSESS

EXAMPLE 1 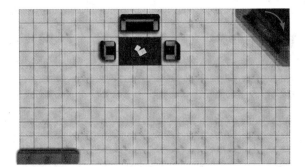 Understand a Sequence of Transformations

Scan for Multimedia

Ava is using interior design software to design the layout of her family room. How can she move the corner fireplace to the top right corner of the room?

Be Precise You can compose transformations by applying a sequence of two or more transformations. How can you use a sequence of transformations to represent the problem?

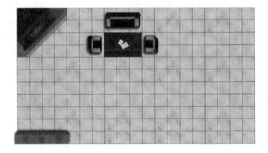

STEP 1 Ava translates the fireplace 15 units to the right.

15 Units

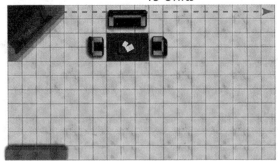

STEP 2 Then Ava rotates the fireplace 90° clockwise about the its center.

 **Try It!**

Ava decided to move the cabinet to the opposite wall. What sequence of transformations moves the cabinet to its new position?

Convince Me! Ava decides that she would like the chairs to be placed directly across from the couch. What is a sequence of transformations that she can use to move the chairs to their new positions?

EXAMPLE **2**

Complete a Sequence of Transformations on a Coordinate Plane

ACTIVITY   ASSESS

Translate quadrilateral *MNPQ* 7 units left, and then reflect it across the line $x = -3$.

This is called a *glide reflection*, because it is a sequence of a translation and a reflection.

> **Be Precise** The image of point N' is N'' (read "N double prime").

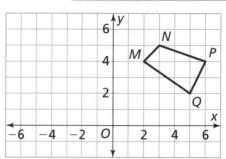

STEP 1 Translate quadrilateral *MNPQ* 7 units left.

Each point moves 7 units left.

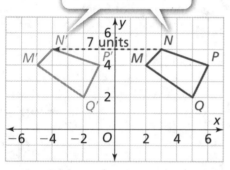

STEP 2 Reflect quadrilateral $M'\,N'\,P'\,Q'$ across the line $x = -3$.

Reflect each point across the line of reflection.

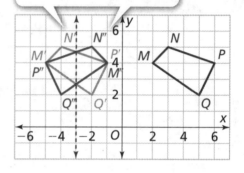

EXAMPLE **3**

 Describe a Sequence of Transformations

What is a sequence of transformations that maps $\triangle ABC$ onto $\triangle A''\,B''\,C''$?

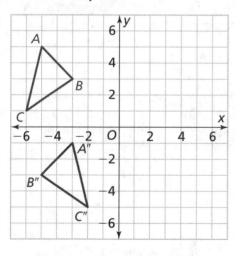

STEP 1 Translate $\triangle ABC$ 8 units right and 6 units down to map it onto $\triangle A'\,B'\,C'$.

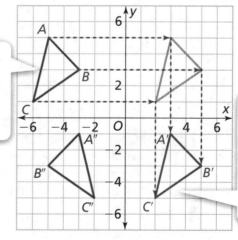

STEP 2 Reflect $\triangle A'\,B'\,C'$ across the y-axis to map it onto $\triangle A''\,B''\,C''$.

 Try It!

What is another sequence of transformations that maps $\triangle ABC$ onto $\triangle A''\,B''\,C''$?

You can use a sequence of two or more transformations to map a preimage to its image.

You can map △ABC onto △A″ B″ C″ by a translation 3 units right followed by a 90° clockwise rotation about the origin.

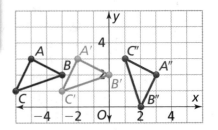

Do You Understand?

1. **? Essential Question** How can you use a sequence of transformations to map a preimage to its image?

2. **Make Sense and Persevere** A preimage is rotated 180° about the origin and then rotated 180° about the origin again. Compare the preimage and image.

3. **Reasoning** A figure ABC, with vertices A(2, 1), B(7, 4), and C(2, 7), is rotated 90° clockwise about the origin, and then reflected across the y-axis. Describe another sequence that would result in the same image.

Do You Know How?

In 4–6, use the diagram below.

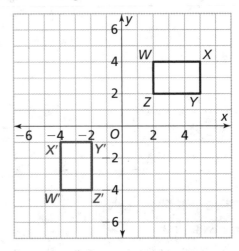

4. Describe a sequence of transformations that maps rectangle WXYZ onto rectangle W′ X′ Y′ Z′.

5. Describe another way that you could map rectangle WXYZ onto W′ X′ Y′ Z′.

6. Draw the image of rectangle WXYZ after a reflection across the line y = 1 and a translation 1 unit right. Label the image W″ X″ Y″ Z″.

Practice & Problem Solving

7. Leveled Practice Describe a sequence of transformations that maps △QRS onto △TUV.

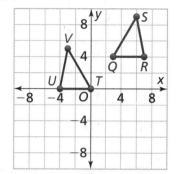

A translation ☐ units left and ☐ units down,

followed by a ☐ across the ☐.

---

8. Model with Math A family moves a table, shown as rectangle *EFGH*, by translating it 3 units left and 3 units down followed by a 90° rotation about the origin. Graph *E′ F′ G′ H′* to show the new location of the table.

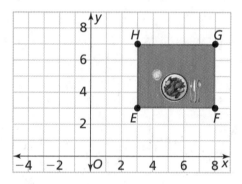

9. Describe a sequence of transformations that maps quadrilateral *ABCD* to quadrilateral *HIJK*.

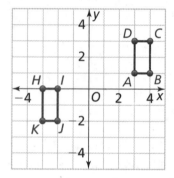

---

10. Map △QRS to △Q′ R′ S′ with a reflection across the *y*-axis followed by a translation 6 units down.

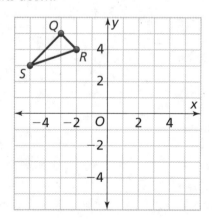

11. Higher Order Thinking A student says that he was rearranging furniture at home and he used a glide reflection to move a table with legs from one side of the room to the other. Will a glide reflection result in a functioning table? Explain.

☑ Assessment Practice

12. PART A Which sequence of transformations maps rectangle *ABCD* onto rectangle *A′ B′ C′ D′*?

Ⓐ translation 6 units down, reflection across the *x*-axis

Ⓑ reflection across the *x*-axis, translation 6 units right

Ⓒ reflection across the *x*-axis, translation 6 units left

Ⓓ translation 6 units left, reflection across the *y*-axis

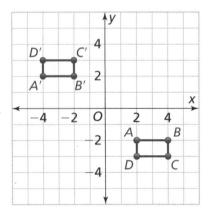

PART B Describe a sequence of transformations that maps *A′ B′ C′ D′* onto *ABCD*.

13. PART A Which figure is the image of Figure A after a reflection across the *x*-axis and a translation 4 units right?

Ⓐ Figure B

Ⓑ Figure C

Ⓒ Figure D

Ⓓ Figure E

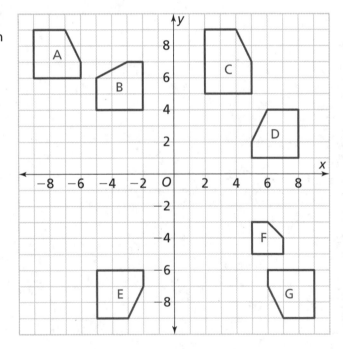

PART B Which figure can be transformed into Figure G after a rotation 90° about the origin, then a translation 13 units right and 4 units down?

Ⓐ Figure B

Ⓑ Figure D

Ⓒ Figure E

Ⓓ Figure F

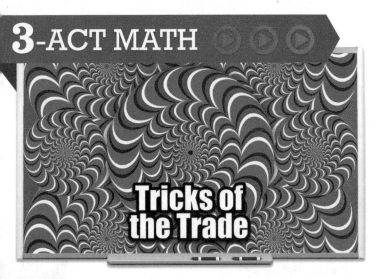

Tricks of
the Trade

3-Act Mathematical Modeling:
Tricks of the Trade

 Go Online

© **Common Core Content Standards**
8.G.A.2, 8.G.A.1
Mathematical Practices
MP.4, MP.1, MP.2, MP.3, MP.7, MP.8

ACT 1

1. After watching the video, what is the first question that comes to mind?

2. Write the Main Question you will answer.

3. Make a prediction to answer this Main Question.

4. Construct Arguments Explain how you arrived at your prediction.

5. What information in this situation would be helpful to know? How would you use that information?

6. Use Appropriate Tools What tools can you use to solve the problem? Explain how you would use them strategically.

7. Model with Math Represent the situation using mathematics. Use your representation to answer the Main Question.

8. What is your answer to the Main Question? Does it differ from your prediction? Explain.

9. Write the answer you saw in the video.

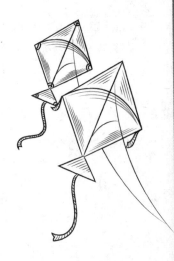

10. Reasoning Does your answer match the answer in the video? If not, what are some reasons that would explain the difference?

11. Make Sense and Persevere Would you change your model now that you know the answer? Explain.

Reflect

12. Model with Math Explain how you used a mathematical model to represent the situation. How did the model help you answer the Main Question?

13. Make Sense and Persevere When did you struggle most while solving the problem? How did you overcome that obstacle?

SEQUEL

14. Be Precise Find another optical illusion online involving shapes that look different but are the same. Explain how you know the shapes are the same.

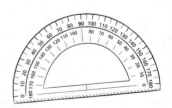

Solve & Discuss It!

 ACTIVITY

Simone plays a video game in which she moves shapes into empty spaces. After several rounds, her next move must fit the blue piece into the dashed space. How can Simone move the blue piece to fit in the space?

I can...
use a sequence of translations, reflections, and rotations to show that figures are congruent.

Common Core Content Standards
8.G.A.3, 8.G.A.2

Mathematical Practices
MP.2, MP.3, MP.7

Reasoning How can you use what you know about sequences of transformations to move the piece?

Focus on math practices

Construct Arguments How do you know that the piece that fits into the space is the same as the original blue shape? Explain.

VISUAL LEARNING ASSE

EXAMPLE 1 Understand Congruence

Scan for Multimedia

Ava wants to place a flame-resistant hearth rug in front of the fireplace that is the same size and shape as the rug in front of the sofa. How can she determine whether the rugs are the same size and shape?

> **Reasoning** How does translating, reflecting, and rotating a figure change its shape and size?

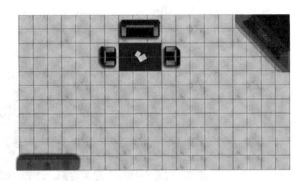

If a sequence of translations, reflections, and rotations maps one rug onto the other then the rugs are the same size and shape.

> *Congruent figures* have the same size and shape. Two-dimensional figure are congruent (≅) if the second figure can be obtained from the first by a sequence of rotations, reflections, and translations.

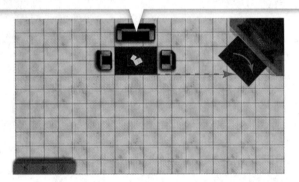

Ava uses a translation followed by a rotation to map the living room rug onto the hearth rug.

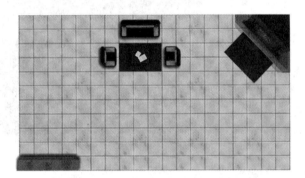

Since the two rugs are the same size and the same shape, they are congruent figures.

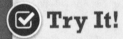 Try It!

How can you determine whether the orange and blue rectangles are congruent?

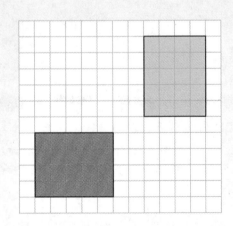

Convince Me! Quadrilateral *PQRS* is congruent to quadrilateral *P′ Q′ R′ S′*. What do you know about how these figures relate?

EXAMPLE **2** Identify Congruent Figures ACTIVITY ASSESS

A. Is quadrilateral ABCD congruent to quadrilateral QRST?

Look for Relationships Is there a sequence of transformations that will map one of the figures onto the other?

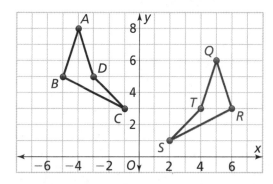

STEP 1 Reflect quadrilateral ABCD across the line x = −1.

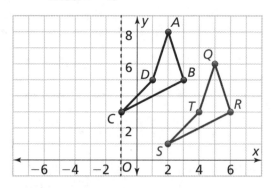

STEP 2 Translate quadrilateral ABCD 3 units right and 2 units down.

There is a sequence of transformations that maps ABCD onto QRST.

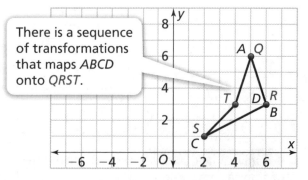

Since quadrilateral ABCD maps onto quadrilateral QRST, quadrilateral ABCD ≅ quadrilateral QRST.

B. Is △ABC ≅ △JKL?

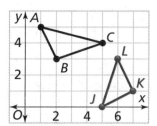

You can start by mapping one vertex to its corresponding vertex.

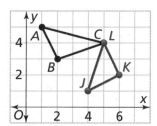

Translate point L 1 unit left and 1 unit up to map it to point C.

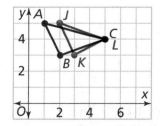

Rotate △JKL about point L so that side LK aligns with side CB.

There is no sequence of transformations that maps △JKL directly onto △ABC, so △ABC is NOT congruent to △JKL.

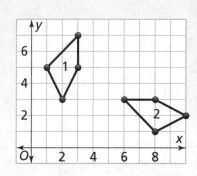

✅ Try It!

Are the figures congruent? Explain.

Two-dimensional figures are congruent if there is a sequence of translations, reflections, and rotations that maps one figure onto the other.

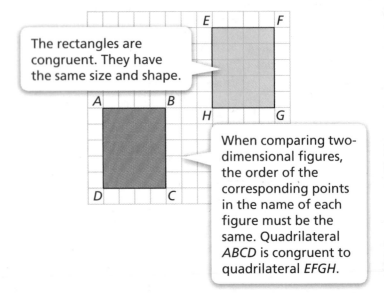

The rectangles are congruent. They have the same size and shape.

When comparing two-dimensional figures, the order of the corresponding points in the name of each figure must be the same. Quadrilateral *ABCD* is congruent to quadrilateral *EFGH*.

Do You Understand?

1. **? Essential Question** How does a sequence of translations, reflections, and rotations result in congruent figures?

2. **Reasoning** Does a sequence of transformations have to include a translation, a reflection, and a rotation to result in congruent figures? Explain.

3. **Construct Arguments** Is there a sequence of reflections, rotations, and translations that makes the preimage and image not only congruent, but identical in orientation? Explain.

Do You Know How?

4. A rectangle with an area of 25 square centimeters is rotated and reflected in the coordinate plane. What will be the area of the resulting image? Explain.

In 5 and 6, use the coordinate grid below.

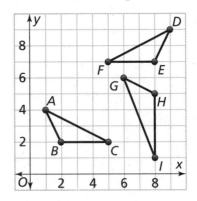

5. Is △*ABC* ≅ △*DEF*? Explain.

6. Is △*ABC* ≅ △*GHI*? Explain.

Practice & Problem Solving

7. △Q′ R′ S′ is the image of △QRS after a reflection across the y-axis and a translation 6 units down. Is the image the same size and shape as the preimage?

△QRS and △Q′ R′S′ [____] the same size and shape.

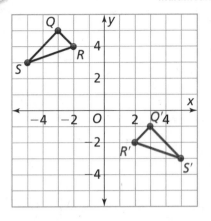

8. Is △DEF ≅ △D′ E′ F′? Explain.1

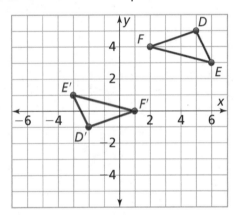

9. **Construct Arguments** Describe a way to show that quadrilateral ABCD is congruent to quadrilateral A′ B′ C′ D′.

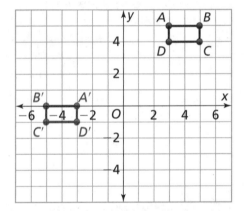

10. You are making two triangular flags for a project and need the flags to be the same shape and size. △XYZ and △X′ Y′ Z′ are the flags you have drawn. Are the flags the same shape and size? Explain.

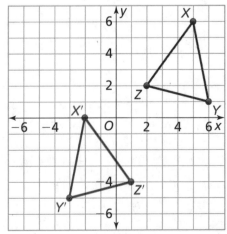

11. Which two triangles are congruent? Describe the sequence of transformations that maps one figure onto the other.

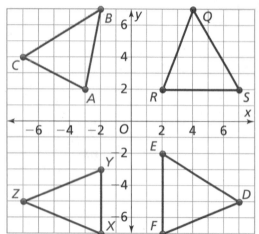

12. Is △LMN ≅ △XYZ? Explain.

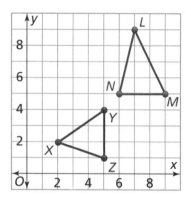

13. Higher Order Thinking A student was asked to describe a sequence of transformations that maps △DEF onto △D′ E′ F′, given that △DEF ≅ △D′ E′ F′. She incorrectly said the sequence of transformations that maps △DEF onto △D′ E′ F′ is a reflection across the x-axis, followed by a translation 6 units right and 4 units up.

What mistake did the student likely make?

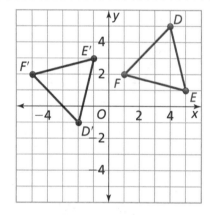

✓ Assessment Practice

14. PART A

How can you determine whether △DEF ≅ △D′ E′ F′?

Ⓐ Determine whether a sequence of rotations maps △DEF onto △D′ E′ F′.

Ⓑ Determine whether a sequence of transformations maps △DEF onto △D′ E′ F′.

Ⓒ Determine whether a sequence of translations maps △DEF onto △D′ E′ F′.

Ⓓ Determine whether a sequence of reflections maps △DEF onto △D′ E′ F′.

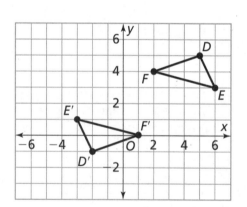

PART B

Is △DEF ≅ △D′ E′ F′? Explain.

1. **Vocabulary** Describe three transformations where the image and preimage have the same size and shape. *Lesson 11-1, Lesson 11-2, and Lesson 11-3*

For 2–6, use the figures below.

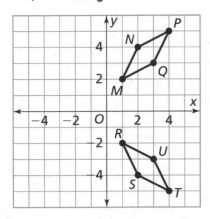

2. What are the coordinates of each point after quadrilateral *RSTU* is rotated 90° about the origin? *Lesson 11-3*

3. What are the coordinates of each point after quadrilateral *MNPQ* is translated 2 units right and 5 units down? *Lesson 11-1*

4. What are the coordinates of each point after quadrilateral *MNPQ* is reflected across the *x*-axis and then translated 3 units left? *Lessons 11-2 and 11-4*

5. Which series of transformations maps quadrilateral *MNPQ* onto quadrilateral *RSTU*? *Lesson 11-4*

   Ⓐ reflection across the *x*-axis, translation 4 units down

   Ⓑ reflection across the *y*-axis, translation 4 units down

   Ⓒ rotation 180° about the origin, and then reflection across the *x*-axis

   Ⓓ rotation 180° about the origin, and then reflection across the *y*-axis

6. Is quadrilateral *MNPQ* congruent to quadrilateral *RSTU*? Explain. *Lesson 11-5*

How well did you do on the mid-topic checkpoint? Fill in the stars.

MID-TOPIC
PERFORMANCE TASK

A tessellation is a design in a plane that uses one or more congruent figures, with no overlaps and no gaps, to cover the entire plane. A tessellation of an equilateral triangle is shown.

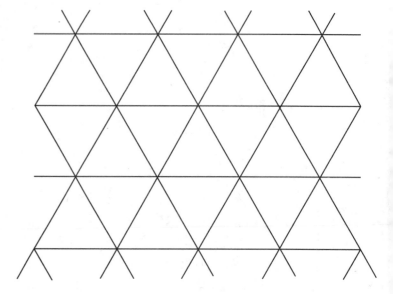

PART A

Explain how the tessellation of an equilateral triangle is formed using reflections.

PART B

Explain how the tessellation of an equilateral triangle is formed using rotations.

PART C

Which of the regular polygon(s) below can be tessellated using a series of transformations?

square   pentagon   hexagon

Solve & Discuss It!

ACTIVITY

A landscape architect designs a small splash pad represented by △ABC. Then she decides to make the splash pad larger as shown by △ADE. How are the splash pad designs alike? How are they different?

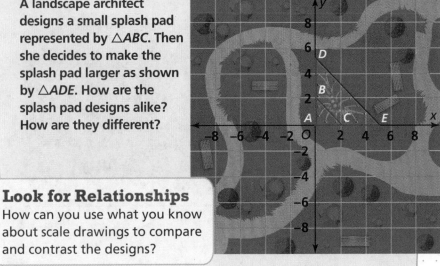

I can...
dilate two-dimensional figures

Common Core Content Standards
8.G.A.4, 8.G.A.3

Mathematical Practices
MP.2, MP.3, MP.7, MP.8

Look for Relationships
How can you use what you know about scale drawings to compare and contrast the designs?

Focus on math practices

Reasoning Paul wants to make two square picnic tables. One table will have side lengths that are $\frac{1}{2}$ the lengths of the second table. How do the tables compare? Explain.

? **Essential Question** What is the relationship between a preimage and its image after a dilation?

 VISUAL LEARNING   ASSES

EXAMPLE 1 👁 Understand Dilations

Scan for Multimedia

The landscape architect designs two open green spaces for another area of the park. She designs the larger space so that the length of each side is three times the length of its corresponding side in the smaller green space. Where should the architect draw the larger green space?

Look for Relationships How can you use what you know about scale drawings to determine the space?

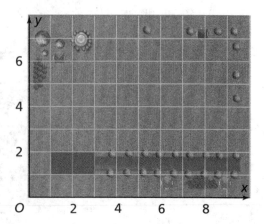

The architect dilates the smaller space by a scale factor of 3. A **dilation** is a transformation that moves each point along the ray through the point, starting from a fixed center, and multiplies distances from the center by a common scale factor.

The **scale factor**, r, is the ratio of a length in the image to the corresponding length in the preimage.

The image of a dilation has the same shape, angle measures, and orientation, but different side lengths.

The fixed center of this dilation is the origin O. A dilation with fixed center O and scale factor r maps any point P to P' such that $OP' = rOP$.

$$OA' = rOA$$
$$OB' = rOB$$
$$OC' = rOC$$
$$OD' = rOD$$

☑ Try It!

$F'G'H'I'$ is the image of $FGHI$ after a dilation with center at the origin. What is the scale factor?

The ratio of a side length in $FGHI$ to a corresponding side length in $F'G'H'I'$ is: $\dfrac{\boxed{}}{\boxed{}}$

The scale factor is $\boxed{}$.

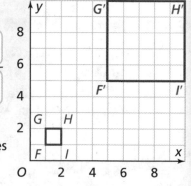

Convince Me! Quadrilateral $WXYZ$ is the image of quadrilateral $FGHI$ after a dilation with center at the origin and a scale factor of 3.5. What are the coordinates of the vertices of quadrilateral $WXYZ$?

What are the coordinates of the image of *ABCD* after a dilation with center (0, 0) and a scale factor of 2?

STEP 1 Identify the coordinates of each vertex of the preimage.

A(2, −2), *B*(2, 1), *C*(4, 0), *D*(4, −1)

STEP 2 Dilate to find the coordinates of the vertices of *A′ B′ C′ D′*.

You can find the image points of a dilation in the coordinate plane with center at the origin by multiplying the coordinates of the preimage by the scale factor.

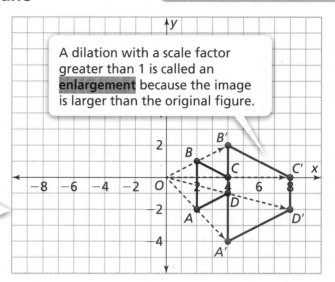

A dilation with a scale factor greater than 1 is called an **enlargement** because the image is larger than the original figure.

A(2, −2) → *A′* (4, −4)

B(2, 1) → *B′* (4, 2)

C(4, 0) → *C′* (8, 0)

D(4, −1) → *D′* (8, −2)

STEP 3 Graph *A′ B′ C′ D*.

EXAMPLE **3** **Dilate to Reduce a Figure**

What are the coordinates of the image of *PQRS* after a dilation with center (0, 0) and a scale factor of $\frac{1}{2}$?

STEP 1 Identify the coordinates of each vertex of the preimage.

P(6, 10), *Q*(10, 10), *R*(10, 6), *S*(6, 6)

STEP 2 Dilate to find the coordinates of the vertices of *P′ Q′ R′ S′*.

P(6, 10) → *P′*(3, 5)

Q(10, 10) → *Q′*(5, 5)

R(10, 6) → *R′*(5, 3)

S(6, 6) → *S′*(3, 3)

Multiply the coordinates by the scale factor $\frac{1}{2}$.

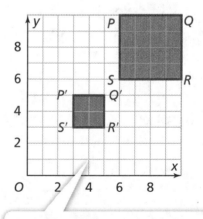

A dilation with a scale factor between 0 and 1 is called a **reduction** because the image is smaller than the original figure.

STEP 3 Graph *P′ Q′ R′ S′*.

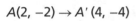 **Try It!**

A dilation maps point *L*(3, 6) to its image *L′* (2, 4). Complete the dilation of figure *LMN* and label the image *L′ M′ N′*. What is the scale factor? What is the length of side *M′ N′*?

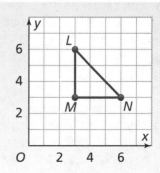

A dilation is a transformation that results in an image with the same shape, angle measures, and orientation as the preimage, but different side lengths.

When the scale factor is greater than 1, the dilation is an enlargement.

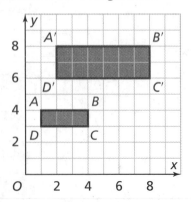

When the scale factor is between 0 and 1, the dilation is a reduction.

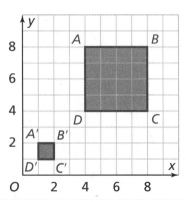

Do You Understand?

1. **Essential Question** What is the relationship between a preimage and its image after a dilation?

2. **Generalize** When will a dilation be a reduction? When will it be an enlargement?

3. **Reasoning** Flora draws a rectangle with points at (12, 12), (15, 12), (15, 9) and (12, 9). She dilates the figure with center at the origin and a scale factor of $\frac{3}{4}$. What is the measure of each angle in the image? Explain.

Do You Know How?

In 4–6, use the coordinate grid below.

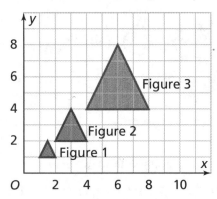

4. Figure 3 is the image of Figure 1 after a dilation with center at the origin. What is the scale factor? Explain.

5. What are the coordinates of the image of Figure 2 after a dilation with center at the origin and a scale factor of 3?

6. Which figures represent a dilation with a scale factor of $\frac{1}{2}$?

Name: _____

Practice & Problem Solving

7. Leveled Practice Draw the image of △DEF after a dilation with center (0, 0) and scale factor of 2.

Find the coordinates of each point in the original figure.

D(☐, (☐) E(☐, (☐) F(☐, (☐)

Multiply each coordinate by ☐.

Find the coordinates of each point in the image:

D'(☐, (☐) E'(☐, (☐) F'(☐, (☐)

Graph the image.

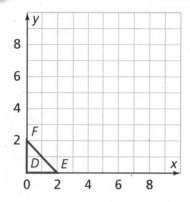

8. Find the scale factor for the dilation shown.

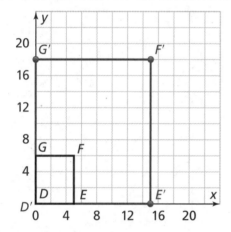

9. Critique Reasoning For the dilation with center (0, 0) shown on the graph, your friend says the scale factor is $\frac{5}{2}$. What is the correct scale factor? What mistake did your friend likely make?

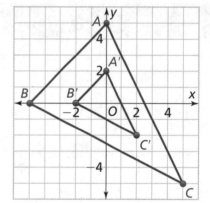

10. The smaller figure is the image of a dilation of the larger figure. The origin is the center of dilation. Tell whether the dilation is an enlargement or a reduction. Then find the scale factor of the dilation.

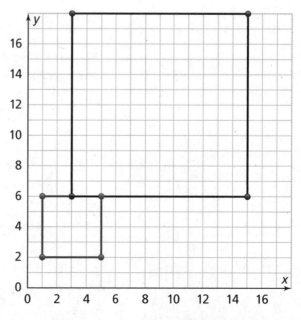

11. **Higher Order Thinking** *Q' R' S' T'* is the image of *QRST* after a dilation with center at the origin.

   a. Find the scale factor.

   b. Find the area of each parallelogram. What is the relationship between the areas?

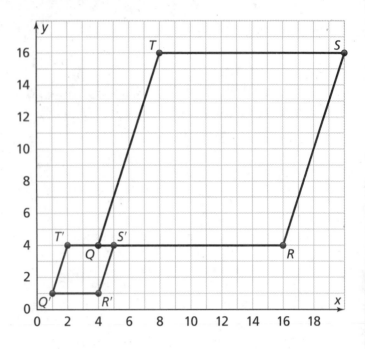

✓ Assessment Practice

12. Triangle *PQR* is the image of △*JKL* after a dilation. Is the dilation an enlargement or a reduction? Explain.

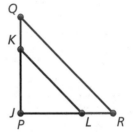

   Ⓐ An enlargement, because the image is larger than the original figure

   Ⓑ An enlargement, because the image is smaller than the original figure

   Ⓒ A reduction, because the image is smaller than the original figure

   Ⓓ A reduction, because the image is larger than the original figure

13. Rectangle *QUAD* has coordinates *Q*(0, 0), *U*(0, 3), *A*(6, 3), and *D*(6, 0). *Q' U' A' D'* is the image of *QUAD* after a dilation with center (0, 0) and a scale factor of 6. What are the coordinates of point *D'*? Explain.

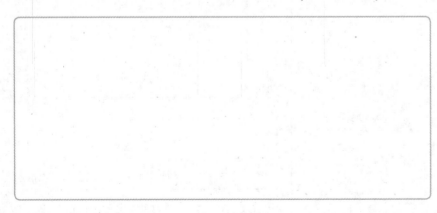

Solve & Discuss It! ACTIVITY

Andrew draws the two figures shown on a coordinate plane. How are the two figures alike? How are they different? How do you know?

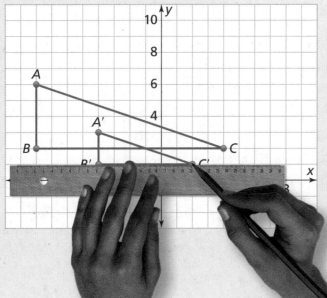

I can...
use a sequence of transformations, including dilations, to show that figures are similar.

Common Core Content Standards
8.G.A.4, 8.G.A.3

Mathematical Practices
MP.2, MP.3, MP.6, MP.7, MP.8

Look for Relationships
Is △ABC a preimage of △A′B′C′? How do you know?

Focus on math practices

Reasoning How can you use the coordinates of the vertices of the triangles to identify the transformation that maps △ABC to △A′B′C′? Explain.

VISUAL LEARNING ASSES

EXAMPLE 1 Understand Similarity

Scan for Multimedia

Albert graphed trapezoid *ABCD* and trapezoid *GHJK*. How can he tell whether the parallelograms are similar?

> Two-dimensional figures are **similar** (∽) if you can map one figure to the other by a sequence of rotations, reflections, translations, and dilations.

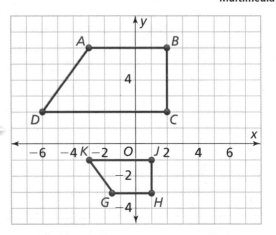

Determine whether there is a sequence of transformations, including a dilation that maps *ABCD* to *GHJK*.

> The trapezoids have opposite orientations, so the sequence must include a reflection. Reflect *ABCD* across the *x*-axis.

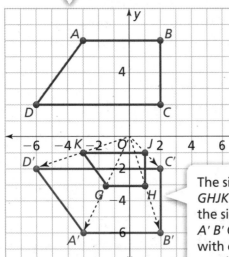

> The side lengths of trapezoid *GHJK* are half the length of the sides of trapezoid *A' B' C' D'*. Dilate *A' B' C' D'* with center at the origin and a scale factor of $\frac{1}{2}$.

A sequence of a reflection across the *x*-axis followed by a dilation of scale factor $\frac{1}{2}$ centered at the origin maps trapezoid *ABCD* to trapezoid *GHJK*.

$$ABCD \backsim GHJK$$

> **Generalize** Similar figures have the same shape and congruent angles. The corresponding side lengths are in proportion.

✓ Try It!

Is △*ABC* similar to △*A' B' C*?

The triangles ☐ similar.

Convince Me! What sequence of transformations shows that △*ABC* is similar to △*A' B' C'*?

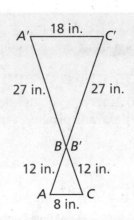

EXAMPLE **2** **Complete a Similarity Transformation**

   ACTIVITY ASSESS

Quadrilateral *JKLM* has coordinates *J*(2, −1), *K*(1, −2), *L*(1, −3), and *M*(3, −2). Graph *J″ K″ L″ M″*, the image of *JKLM* by a dilation with center (0, 0) and scale factor 3 and a reflection across the *y*-axis.

STEP 1 Graph the dilation.

Find the coordinates of the dilated image, *J′ K′ L′ M′*.

J(2, −1) → *J′* (6, −3)

K(1, −2) → *K′* (3, −6)

L(1, −3) → *L′* (3, −9)

M(3, −2) → *M′* (9, −6)

Multiply each coordinate by the scale factor, 3.

STEP 2 Graph the reflection.

Find the coordinates of the reflected image, *J″K″L″M″*.

J′ (6, −3) → *J″* (−6, −3)

K′ (3, −6) → *K″* (−3, −6)

L′ (3, −9) → *L″* (−3, −9)

M′ (9, −6) → *M″* (−9, −6)

To reflect across the *y*-axis, (*x*, *y*) becomes (−*x*, *y*).

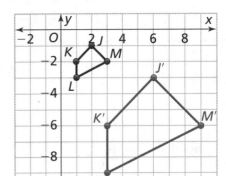

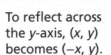

EXAMPLE **3** **Identify Similar Figures**

Is *ABCD* similar to *EFGH*? Explain.

Compare corresponding coordinates.

A(4, 4) → *E*(−2, −2)

B(8, 4) → *F*(−4, −2)

C(10, −2) → *G*(−5, 1)

D(2, −2) → *H*(−1, 1)

(*x*, *y*) → (−0.5*x*, −0.5*y*)

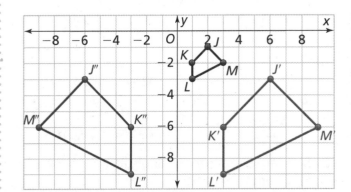

Yes, *ABCD* ~ *EFGH* because a rotation of 180° about the origin and a dilation with a scale factor of 0.5 about the origin maps *ABCD* to *EFGH*.

☑ **Try It!**

a. Graph the image of *JKL* after a reflection across the line *x* = 1 followed by a dilation with a scale factor of $\frac{1}{2}$ and center of dilation point *J′*.

b. Is △*JKL* similar to △*PQR*?

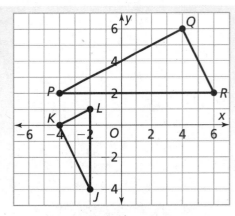

Two-dimensional figures are similar if there is a sequence of rotations, reflections, translations, and dilations that maps one figure onto the other.

Do You Understand?

1. **? Essential Question** How are similar figures related by a sequence of transformations?

2. **Be Precise** How do the angle measures and side lengths compare in similar figures?

3. **Generalize** Does a given translation, reflection, or rotation, followed by a given dilation, always map a figure to the same image as that same dilation followed by that same translation, reflection, or rotation? Explain.

Do You Know How?

4. Is trapezoid *ABCD* ~ trapezoid *EFGH*? Explain.

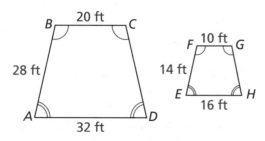

Use the graph for 5 and 6.

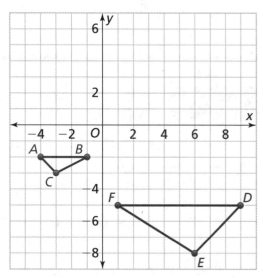

5. △*ABC* is dilated by a factor of 2 with a center of dilation at point *C*, reflected across the x-axis, and translated 3 units up. Graph the resulting similar figure.

6. Is △*ABC* similar to △*DEF*? Explain.

PRACTICE TUTORIAL

Practice & Problem Solving

Scan for
Multimedia

7. Leveled Practice *RSTU* and *VXYZ* are quadrilaterals. Given *RSTU* ∽ *VXYZ*, describe a sequence of transformations that maps *RSTU* to *VXYZ*.

- reflection across the ☐

- translation ☐ unit(s) left and ☐ unit(s) down

- dilation with center (0,0) and a scale factor of ☐

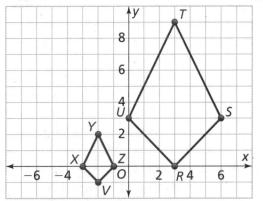

8. Reasoning Is △*MNO* similar to △*PQO*? Explain.

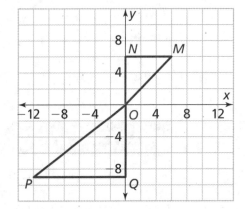

9. △*PQR* is dilated by a scale factor of 2 with center of dilation (0, 0) and rotated 180° about the origin. Graph the resulting similar △*XYZ*.

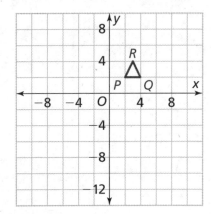

10. Describe a sequence of transformations that shows that quadrilateral *RSTU* is similar to quadrilateral *VXYZ*.

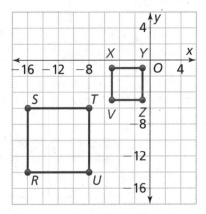

11. Construct Arguments Is △PQR similar to △XYZ? Explain.

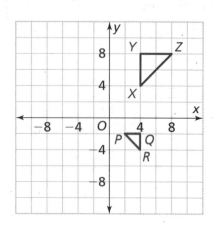

12. Higher Order Thinking Given △JKL ∼ △XYZ, find two possible coordinates for missing point Y. For each coordinate chosen, describe a sequence of transformations, including a dilation, that will map △JKL to △XYZ.

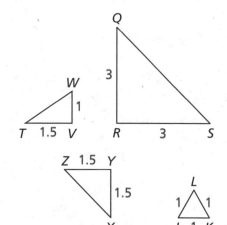

✓ Assessment Practice

13. Rajesh is making pennants in preparation for a school soccer game. He wants the pennants to be similar triangles. Which of these triangles could he use for the pennants?

Ⓐ △QRS and △TVW

Ⓑ △QRS and △XYZ

Ⓒ △TVW and △JKL

Ⓓ △TVW and △XYZ

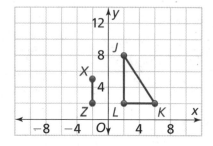

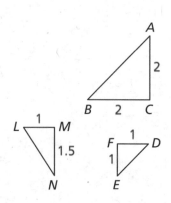

14. Determine whether the following pairs of triangles are similar or not similar.

	Similar	Not Similar
△ABC and △DEF	☐	☐
△ABC and △LMN	☐	☐
△LMN and △DEF	☐	☐

Solve & Discuss It!

 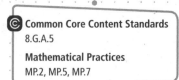 ACTIVITY

Draw two parallel lines.

Then draw a line that intersects both lines. Which angles have equal measures?

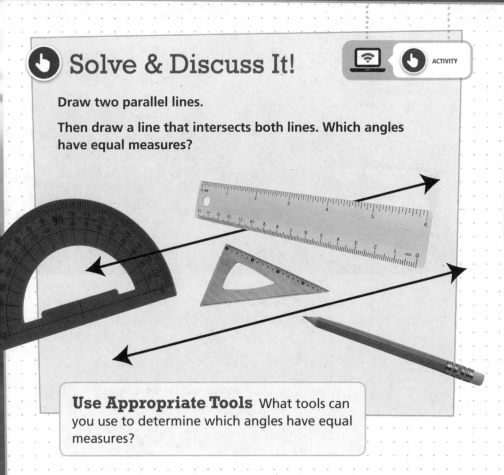

Use Appropriate Tools What tools can you use to determine which angles have equal measures?

Go Online

I can...
identify and find the measures of angles formed by parallel lines and a transversal.

ⓒ **Common Core Content Standards**
8.G.A.5

Mathematical Practices
MP.2, MP.5, MP.7

Focus on math practices

Reasoning What properties or definitions can you use to describe which angles have equal measures?

VISUAL LEARNING ASSESS

EXAMPLE 1 Identify Angles Created by Parallel Lines Cut by a Transversal

Scan for Multimedia

Sarah is building a handrail for a ramp. According to the design plan, the posts must be parallel. How can Sarah determine how the angles formed by the posts and the ramp are related?

Draw parallel lines r and s to represent the posts and an intersecting line t to represent the ramp.

A **transversal** is a line that intersects two or more lines at different points.

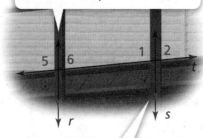

The red arrows indicate that line r is parallel to line s.

Translate line r to the same position as line s.

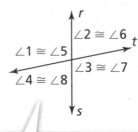

$\angle 2 \cong \angle 6$
$\angle 1 \cong \angle 5$
$\angle 3 \cong \angle 7$
$\angle 4 \cong \angle 8$

Corresponding angles are congruent.

You can use what you know about vertical angles and supplementary angles to determine other angle pair relationships.

Alternate interior angles are congruent.
$m\angle 4 = m\angle 6$ $m\angle 1 = m\angle 7$

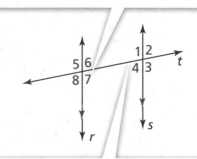

Same-side interior angles are supplement
$m\angle 1 + m\angle 6 = 180°$ $m\angle 4 + m\angle 7 = 180$

Try It!

Which angles are congruent to ∠8?

Which angles are supplementary to ∠8?

Convince Me! Use what you know about other angle relationships to explain why ∠4 and ∠5 are supplementary angles.

EXAMPLE 2 Find Unknown Angle Measures

In the figure, $a \parallel b$. What are the measures of $\angle 4$ and $\angle 5$? Explain.

Use what you know about the angles created when parallel lines are cut by a transversal.

$m\angle 4 = 99°$ — The 99° angle and $\angle 5$ are corresponding angles.

$m\angle 4 + m\angle 5 = 180°$

$\angle 4$ and $\angle 5$ are supplementary angles.

$m\angle 5 = 180° - 99°$

$m\angle 5 = 81°$

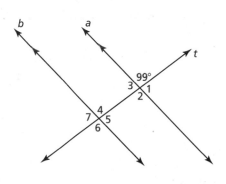

Try It!

What are the measures of $\angle 7$ and $\angle 2$? Explain.

EXAMPLE 3 Use Algebra to Find Unknown Angle Measures

In the figure, a, b, and c are parallel lines. What is the value of x?

Write an equation that relates the angle measures and solve.

$(x + 25) + 75 = 180$

$x + 100 = 180$

$x + 100 - 100 = 180 - 100$

$x = 80$

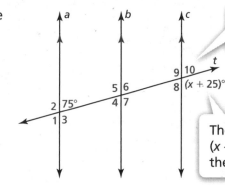

∠10 and the 75° angle are corresponding angles.

The angle that measures $(x + 25)°$ is supplementary to the angle that measures 75°.

Look for Relationships
What is another way to use the angle relationships to find the value of x?

Try It!

In the figure, $a \parallel b$. What is the value of x?

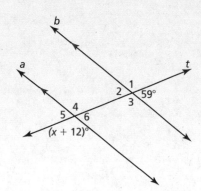

EXAMPLE 4 **Reason about Parallel Lines**

What must _x_ equal if lines _c_ and _d_ are parallel? Explain.

The 60° angle and the angle that measures $2x + 10$ are corresponding angles. For lines _c_ and _d_ to be parallel, the corresponding angles must be congruent.

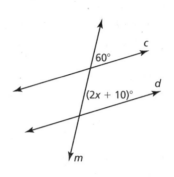

$$2x + 10 = 60$$

$$2x + 10 - 10 = 60 - 10$$

$$2x = 50$$

$$x = 25$$

If $x = 25$, then lines _c_ and _d_ are parallel lines.

> **Look for Relationships** Two lines are parallel if
> - the corresponding angles formed by the lines and a transversal are congruent, or
> - the alternate interior angles formed by the lines and a transversal are congruent, or
> - the same-side interior angles formed by the lines and a transversal are supplementary.

☑ Try It!

a. What must _x_ equal if _a_ ‖ _b_? Explain.

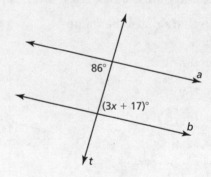

b. What must _x_ equal if _g_ ‖ _h_? Explain.

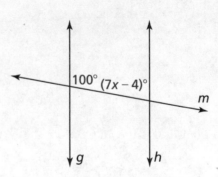

If parallel lines are intersected by a transversal, then

- Corresponding angles are congruent.
- Alternate interior angles are congruent.
- Same-side interior angles are supplementary.

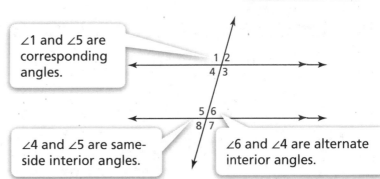

∠1 and ∠5 are corresponding angles.

∠4 and ∠5 are same-side interior angles.

∠6 and ∠4 are alternate interior angles.

Do You Understand?

1. **❓ Essential Question** What are the relationships among angles that are created when a line intersects two parallel lines?

2. When parallel lines are cut by a transversal, how can you use a translation to describe how angles are related?

3. How many angles are created when two parallel lines are cut by a transversal? How many different angle measures are there?

4. **Use Structure** How can you use angle measures to tell whether two lines are parallel?

Do You Know How?

In 5–7, use the figure below.

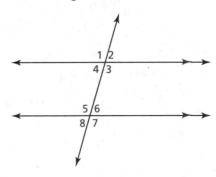

5. Which angles are congruent to ∠8?

6. If $m\angle 4 = 70°$, what is $m\angle 6$? Explain.

7. If $m\angle 1 = 95°$, write an equation that could be used to find the measure of ∠8. Find $m\angle 8$.

8. What must x equal if line a is parallel to line b?

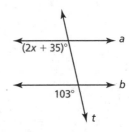

$(2x + 35)°$ a

$103°$ b

t

Practice & Problem Solving

Scan for
Multimedia

9. If $p \parallel q$, what is the value of u?

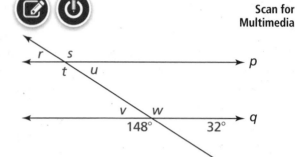

10. Are $\angle K$ and $\angle B$ corresponding angles? Explain.

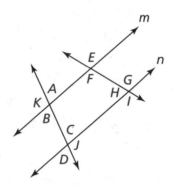

11. Streets A and B run parallel to each other. The measure of $\angle 6$ is 155°. What is the measure of $\angle 4$?

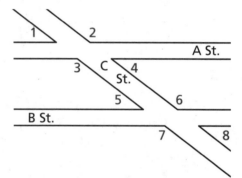

12. Reasoning The figure shows the design of a rectangular windowpane. The four horizontal lines are parallel. The measure of $\angle 6$ is 53°. What is the measure of $\angle 12$? Write and solve an equation to find the answer.

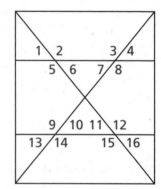

13. In the figure, $m \parallel n$. If $m\angle 8$ is $(4x + 7)°$ and $m\angle 2$ is $107°$, what is the value of x? Explain.

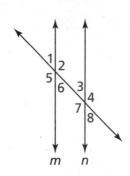

14. For the given figure, can you conclude $m \parallel n$? Explain.

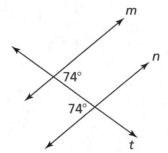

15. Line m is parallel to line n. Find the value of x and each missing angle measure.

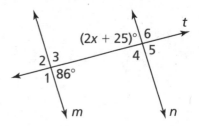

16. Higher Order Thinking

  a. Find the value of x given that $r \parallel s$.

    $m\angle 1 = (63 - x)°$

    $m\angle 2 = (72 - 2x)°$

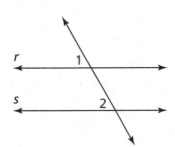

  b. Find $m\angle 1$ and $m\angle 2$.

17. Find the measures of ∠b and ∠d given that m ∥ n.

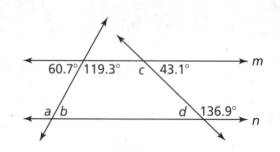

✅ Assessment Practice

18. In the figure, g ∥ p. Which angles are alternate interior angles? Select all that apply.

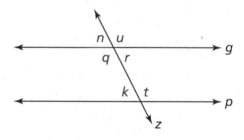

☐ ∠q and ∠r

☐ ∠q and ∠t

☐ ∠q and ∠k

☐ ∠r and ∠t

☐ ∠r and ∠k

☐ ∠u and ∠q

19. In the figure, p ∥ q. On a recent math test, Jacob incorrectly listed the value of w as 101.

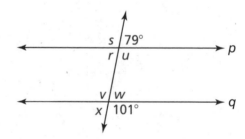

PART A

Find the value of w.

PART B

What mistake did Jacob likely make?

👆 Solve & Discuss It!

Nell cuts tile to make a decorative strip for a kitchen backsplash. She must cut the tiles precisely to be congruent triangles. She plans to place the tiles between two pieces of molding, as shown. What is $m\angle 1$? Explain.

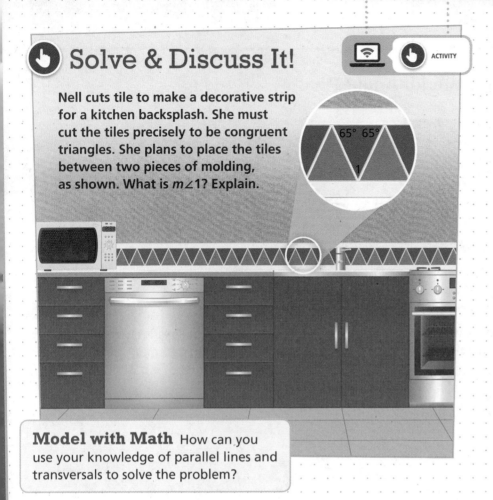

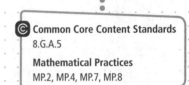

I can...
find the interior and exterior angle measures of a triangle.

© **Common Core Content Standards**
8.G.A.5

Mathematical Practices
MP.2, MP.4, MP.7, MP.8

Model with Math How can you use your knowledge of parallel lines and transversals to solve the problem?

Focus on math practices

Reasoning What assumption(s) did you need to make to find $m\angle 1$? Explain why your assumption(s) is reasonable.

Scan for Multimedia

EXAMPLE 1 Relate Interior Angle Measures in Triangles

How can you describe the relationship between the three interior angles of each triangular tile in the backsplash?

You can rotate and place the congruent tiles side-by-side to form the alternating pattern.

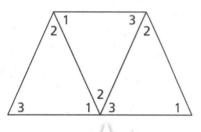

∠1, ∠2, and ∠3 appear to fit together to form a line.

Use what you know about lines, transversals, and angle pair relationships to determine a relationship between the interior angles of a triangle.

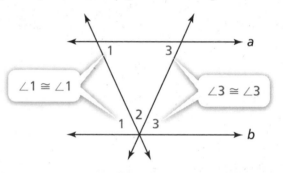

∠1 ≅ ∠1

∠3 ≅ ∠3

Alternate interior angles are congruent, so a ∥ b. Since ∠1, ∠2, and ∠3 form line b, a straight angle, $m\angle 1 + m\angle 2 + m\angle 3 = 180°$.

Generalize The sum of the measures of the interior angles of a triangle is 180°.

☑ Try It!

Find the unknown angle measure in the triangle at the right.

Convince Me! Could a triangle have interior angle measures of 23°, 71°, and 96°? Explain.

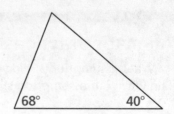

68°   40°

EXAMPLE **2** Find Exterior Angle Measures

In the diagram, $m\angle 2$ is 68° and $m\angle 3$ is 42°. What is $m\angle 4$?

∠1 and ∠4 form a straight angle and are supplementary.

∠1, ∠2, and ∠3 are the interior angles of a triangle.

$$m\angle 1 + m\angle 4 = 180°$$

$$m\angle 1 + m\angle 2 + m\angle 3 = 180°$$

$$m\angle 4 = m\angle 2 + m\angle 3$$

$$m\angle 4 = m\angle 2 + m\angle 3$$
$$= 68° + 42°$$
$$m\angle 4 = 110°$$

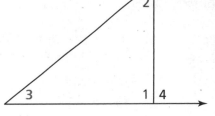

> For each exterior angle of a triangle, the two nonadjacent interior angles are its **remote interior angles**.

> An **exterior angle of a triangle** is an angle formed by a side and an extension of an adjacent side.

> **Generalize** The measure of an exterior angle of a triangle is equal to the sum of the measures of its remote interior angles.

EXAMPLE **3** Use Algebra to Find Unknown Angle Measures

In the diagram, $m\angle 4$ is $(7x + 7)°$, $m\angle 2$ is $(4x + 4)°$, and $m\angle 3$ is $(4x - 9)°$. What are $m\angle 4$ and $m\angle 1$?

Look for Relationships How could you write an algebraic expression to represent $m\angle 1$?

STEP 1 Find the value of x.

$$m\angle 4 = m\angle 2 + m\angle 3$$
$$(7x + 7)° = (4x + 4)° + (4x - 9)°$$
$$7x + 7 = 8x - 5$$
$$7x + 7 - 7x = 8x - 5 - 7x$$
$$7 = x - 5$$
$$12 = x$$

STEP 2 Find $m\angle 4$.

$$m\angle 4 = (7x + 7)°$$
$$= 7(12) + 7$$
$$= 84 + 7$$
$$m\angle 4 = 91°$$

STEP 3 Find $m\angle 1$.

$$m\angle 4 + m\angle 1 = 180°$$
$$91° + m\angle 1 = 180°$$
$$91 + m\angle 1 - 91° = 180° - 91°$$
$$m\angle 1 = 89°$$

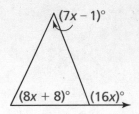 Try It!

What is the measure of the exterior angle shown?

$(7x - 1)°$

$(8x + 8)°$ $(16x)°$

The sum of the measures of the interior angles of a triangle is 180°.

$$m\angle 1 + m\angle 2 + m\angle 3 = 180°$$

The measure of an exterior angle of a triangle is equal to the sum of the measures of its remote interior angles.

$$m\angle 2 + m\angle 3 = m\angle 4$$

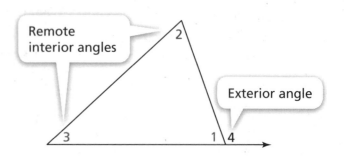

Remote interior angles

Exterior angle

Do You Understand?

1. **? Essential Question** How are the interior and exterior angles of a triangle related?

2. **Reasoning** Maggie draws a triangle with a right angle. The other two angles have equal measures. What are the possible values of the exterior angles for Maggie's triangle? Explain.

3. Brian draws a triangle with interior angles of 32° and 87°, and one exterior angle of 93°. Draw the triangle. Label all of the interior angles and the exterior angle.

Do You Know How?

Use the diagram below for 4 and 5. Assume that a ∥ b.

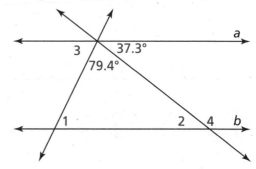

4. What are the measures of ∠1 and ∠2? Explain.

5. What are the measures of ∠3 and ∠4? Explain.

6. In △ABC, $m\angle A = x°$, $m\angle B = (2x)°$, and $m\angle C = (6x + 18)°$. What is the measure of each angle?

Practice & Problem Solving

Scan for
Multimedia

7. Leveled Practice For the figure shown, find $m\angle 1$.

Angle 1 is an [_____] angle of the triangle.

$m\angle 1$ is equal to the sum of its [_____].

$m\angle 1 = \boxed{}^\circ + \boxed{}^\circ$

$m\angle 1 = \boxed{}^\circ$

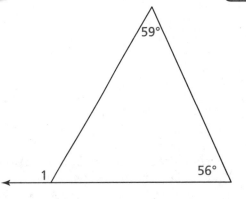

---

8. Find $m\angle 1$ and $m\angle 2$.

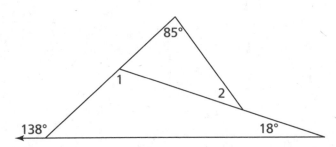

9. In $\triangle ABC$, what is $m\angle C$?

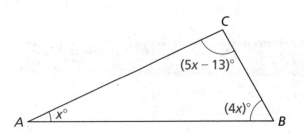

---

10. In the figure, $m\angle 1 = (8x + 7)°$, $m\angle 2 = (4x + 14)°$, and $m\angle 4 = (13x + 12)$. Your friend incorrectly says that $m\angle 4 = 51$. What is $m\angle 4$? What mistake might your friend have made?

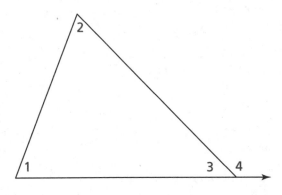

11. What is $m\angle 1$?

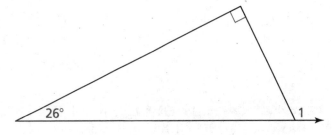

12. Higher Order Thinking Given that $m\angle 1 = (16x)°$, $m\angle 2 = (8x + 21)°$, and $m\angle 4 = (25x + 19)°$, what is an expression for $m\angle 3$? What is $m\angle 3$?

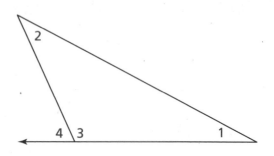

13. A ramp attached to a building is being built to help with deliveries. The angle that the bottom of the ramp makes with the ground is 37.2°. Find the measure of the other acute angle.

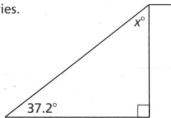

14. The measure of $\angle F$ is 110°. The measure of $\angle E$ is 100°. What is the measure of $\angle D$?

Ⓐ 150°

Ⓑ 80°

Ⓒ 70°

Ⓓ 30°

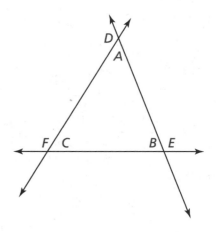

15. In the figure, $m\angle 1 = (3x + 12)°$, $m\angle 2 = (3x + 18)°$ and $m\angle 3 = (7x + 10)°$. What is $m\angle 3$ in degrees?

Lesson 11-10
Angle-Angle Triangle Similarity

Go Online

I can...
use angle measures to determine whether two triangles are similar.

© **Common Core Content Standards**
8.G.A.5
Mathematical Practices
MP.2, MP.3

Explore It!

Justin made two flags for his model sailboat.

46°

5 in.

67°

4 in.

67°

A. Draw and label triangles to represent each flag.

B. How are the side lengths of the triangles related?

C. How are the angle measurements of the triangles related?

Focus on math practices

Reasoning Justin makes a third flag that has sides that are shorter than the sides of the small flag. Two of the angles for each flag measure the same. Are the third angles for each flag the same measure? Explain.

VISUAL LEARNING ASSESS

EXAMPLE 1 Determine Whether Triangles are Similar

Scan for Multimedia

Justin designs another pair of flags for another model sailboat. The larger flag is 1.5 times the size of the smaller flag. How can Justin determine whether the triangles that represent the flags are similar?

Remember, figures are similar if a sequence of rotations, reflections, translations, and dilations maps one figure onto the other.

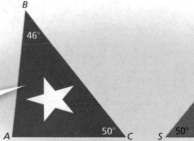
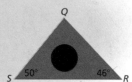

Draw and label triangles to represent the flags.

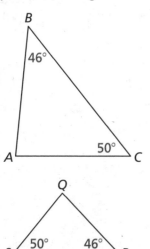

Find a sequence of transformations that maps one pair of congruent angles to each other.

A rotation and translation map ∠S to ∠C.

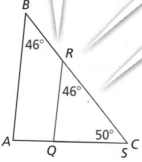

∠R and ∠B are corresponding angles. Because ∠B ≅ ∠B, $\overline{AB}$ is parallel to $\overline{QR}$.

BC = 1.5 · RS so a dilation from center C with scale factor 1.5 maps △ABC to △QRS.

Generalize If two angles of a triangle are congruent to the corresponding angles of another triangle, then the triangles are similar. This is called the Angle-Angle (AA) Criterion.

There is a sequence of translations, rotations, and dilations that maps △ABC to △QRS.

So △ABC ∽ △QRS

☑ **Try It!**

Is △XYZ ∽ △LMN?

m∠X = [ ]

m∠N = [ ]

The triangles [ ] similar.

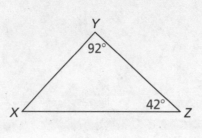
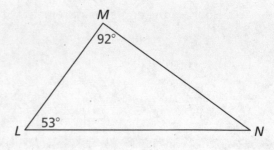

Convince Me! Use what you know about transformations and parallel lines to explain why the Angle-Angle Criterion is true for all triangles.

EXAMPLE 2 · Determine Whether Triangles are Similar

Are the triangles similar? Explain.

a.

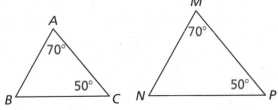

Because $\angle M \cong \angle A$ and $\angle P \cong \angle C$, $\triangle MNP \backsim \triangle ABC$.

b.

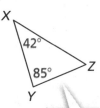

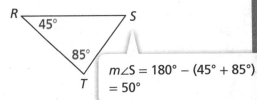

$m\angle S = 180° - (45° + 85°)$
$= 50°$

$m\angle Z = 180° - (42 + 85)° = 53°$

$\triangle XYZ$ is not similar to $\triangle RST$.

 Try It!

If $QR \parallel YZ$, is $\triangle XYZ \backsim \triangle XRQ$? Explain.

EXAMPLE 3 · Solve Problems Involving Similar Triangles

If $\triangle ABC \backsim \triangle EDC$, what are the values of x and y?

STEP 1 Find the value of x.

$2x + x = 180$

$3x = 180$

$x = 60$

Vertical angles are congruent, so $m\angle BCA = x°$.

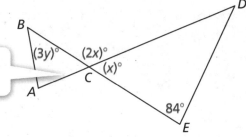

STEP 2 Find the value of y.

$m\angle A = 84°$

$m\angle A + m\angle B + m\angle ACB = 180°$

$84 + 3y + 60 = 180$

$3y = 36$

$y = 12$

The triangles are similar, so corresponding angles are congruent.

Try It!

Find the value of x if the two triangles are similar. Explain.

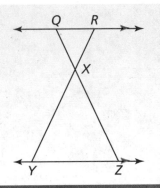

The Angle-Angle (AA) Criterion states that if two angles in one triangle are congruent to two angles in another triangle, the two triangles are similar triangles.

∠A ≅ ∠D and ∠B ≅ ∠E, so △ABC ∽ △DEF.

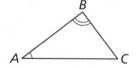

Do You Understand?

1. **?** **Essential Question** How can you use angle measures to determine whether two triangles are similar?

2. **Construct Arguments** Claire says that the AA Criterion should be called the AAA Criterion. Explain why Claire might say this. Do you agree? Explain.

3. **Reasoning** Which triangle pairs below are always similar? Explain.

   Two right triangles
   Two isosceles right triangles
   Two equilateral triangles

Do You Know How?

4. Are the two triangles similar? Explain.

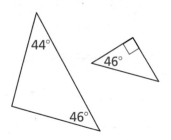

5. Is △QRS ∽ △QLM? Explain.

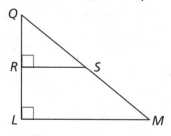

6. Are the triangles similar? What is the value of x?

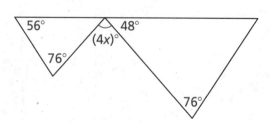

Practice & Problem Solving

Scan for
Multimedia

7. Is △XYZ ~ △XTU?

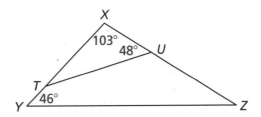

8. For what value of x are △RST and △NSP similar? Explain.

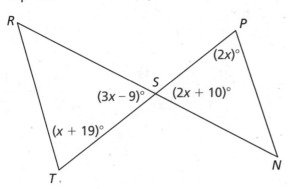

9. Is △FGH ~ △JIH? Explain.

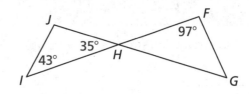

10. Are △RST and △NSP similar? Explain.

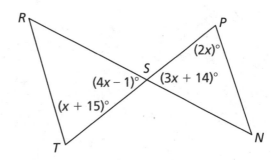

11. Contruct Arguments Describe how to use angle relationships to decide whether any two triangles are similar.

12. Higher Order Thinking Are the triangles shown below similar? Explain.

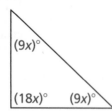 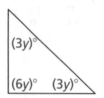

13. Which of the following statements are true? Select all that apply.

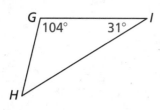 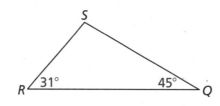 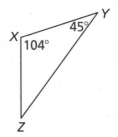

☐ △XYZ ~ △SQR

☐ △XYZ ~ △QSR

☐ △XYZ ~ △GHI

☐ △GIH ~ △SRQ

☐ △ZXY ~ △GIH

☐ △GHI ~ △SRQ

14. Is △GHI ~ △QRS? Explain your reasoning.

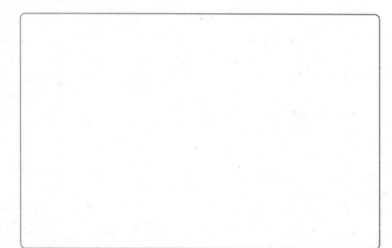 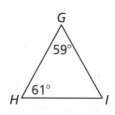 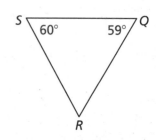

? Topic Essential Question

How can you show that two figures are either congruent or similar to one another?

Vocabulary Review

Complete each sentence by matching each vocabulary word to its definition.
Assume pairs of lines are parallel.

Vocabulary Term	Definition
1. Alternate interior angles	lie on the same side of the transversal and in corresponding positions.
2. Same-side interior angles	lie within a pair of lines and on opposite sides of a transversal.
3. Corresponding angles	are two adjacent interior angles corresponding to each exterior angle of a triangle.
4. An exterior angle of a triangle	is formed by a side and an extension of an adjacent side of a triangle.
5. Remote interior angles of a triangle	lie within a pair of lines and on the same side of a transversal.

Use Vocabulary in Writing

Describe a way to show that $\triangle ABC$ is congruent to $\triangle DEF$.
Use vocabulary terms from this Topic in your description.

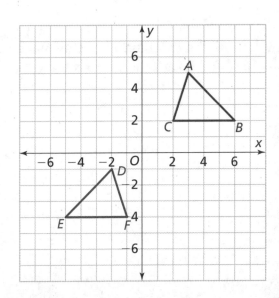

Concepts and Skills Review

Analyze Translations

Quick Review

A translation is a transformation that maps each point of the preimage the same distance and in the same direction.

Example

Translate △XYZ 5 units right and 3 units up.

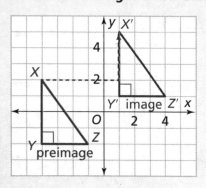

Practice

1. Draw the image after a translation 3 units left and 2 units up.

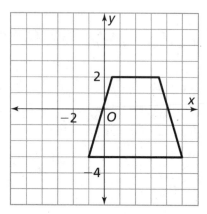

Analyze Reflections

Quick Review

Reflected figures are the same distance from the line of reflection but on opposite sides.

Example

What are the coordinates of the image of △ABC after a reflection across the y-axis?

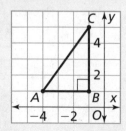

Use the rule $(x, y) \rightarrow (-x, y)$.

$A(-4, 1) \rightarrow A'(4, 1)$

$B(-1, 1) \rightarrow B'(1, 1)$

$C(-1, 5) \rightarrow C'(1, 5)$

Practice

Use the figure.

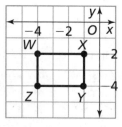

1. What are the coordinates of the image of rectangle WXYZ after a reflection across the x-axis?

2. What are the coordinates of the image of WXYZ after a reflection across the y-axis?

Quick Review

A rotation turns a figure about a fixed point, called the *center of rotation*. The angle of rotation is the number of degrees the figure is rotated.

Example

What are the coordinates of the image of △*ABC* after a 90° rotation about the origin?

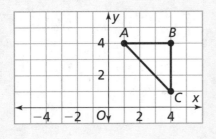

Use the rule $(x, y) \rightarrow (-y, x)$.

$A(1, 4) \rightarrow A'(-4, 1)$

$B(4, 4) \rightarrow B'(-4, 4)$

$C(4, 1) \rightarrow C'(-1, 4)$

Practice

Use the figure.

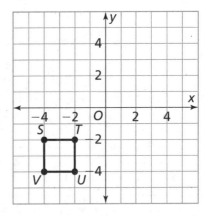

1. What are the coordinates of the image of quadrilateral *STUV* after a 180° rotation about the origin?

2. What are the coordinates of the image of quadrilateral *STUV* after a 270° rotation about the origin?

ESSON 11-4 **Compose Transformations**

Quick Review

To compose a sequence of transformations, perform one transformation, and then use the resulting image to perform the next transformation.

Example

How can you use a sequence of transformations to map Figure A onto Figure B?

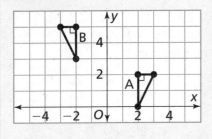

Translate Figure A 3 units up, and then reflect Figure A across the y-axis.

Practice

1. Translate rectangle *ABCD* 5 units down, and then reflect it across the *y*-axis.

Quick Review

Two figures are congruent if a sequence of transformations maps one figure onto the other.

Example

How can you determine if Figure A is congruent to Figure B?

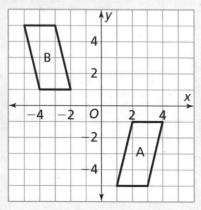

Reflect Figure A across the y-axis, and then translate Figure A 6 units up and 1 unit left.

Practice

1. Is quadrilateral A congruent to quadrilateral B? Explain.

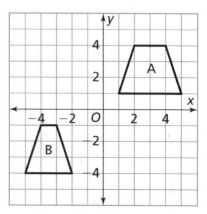

Quick Review

A dilation results in an image that is the same shape but not the same size as the preimage.

Example

What dilation maps *WXYZ* to *W'X'Y'Z'*?

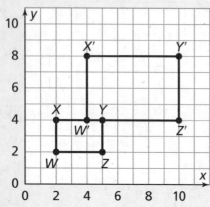

A dilation with center at the origin and a scale factor of 2 maps *WXYZ* to *W'X'Y'Z'*.

Practice

Use the figure.

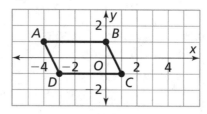

1. What are the coordinates of the image of parallelogram *ABCD* after a dilation with center (0, 0) and a scale factor of 3?

2. What are the coordinates of the image of parallelogram *ABCD* after a dilation with center (0, 0) and a scale factor of $\frac{1}{2}$?

Quick Review

Two-dimensional figures are similar if there is a sequence of translations, reflections, rotations, and dilations that maps one figure onto the other figure. Similar figures have the same shape, congruent angles, and proportional side lengths.

Example

Is rectangle *ABCD* ∽ rectangle *A′ B′ C′ D*?

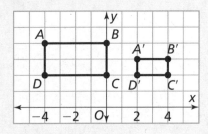

All the angles are right angles.

$$\frac{AB}{A'B'} = \frac{BC}{B'C'} = \frac{CD}{C'D'} = \frac{AD}{A'D'} = \frac{2}{1} = 2$$

The figures have congruent angle measures and proportional side lengths, so they are similar.

Practice

Use the figure.

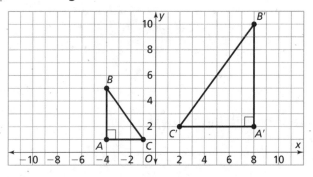

1. Is △*ABC* similar to △*A′ B′ C* ? Explain.

2. What sequence of transformations shows that △*ABC* is similar to △*A′ B′ C* ?

Quick Review

When parallel lines are intersected by a transversal, corresponding angles are congruent, alternate interior angles are congruent, and same-side interior angles are supplementary.

Example

If *m* ∥ *n*, what is the value of *x*?

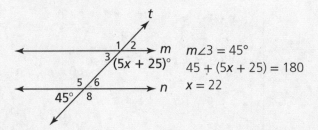

$m\angle 3 = 45°$

$45 + (5x + 25) = 180$

$x = 22$

Practice

In the figure, *a* ∥ *b*. What is the value of *x*?

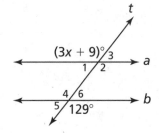

Quick Review

The sum of the measures of the interior angles of a triangle is 180°. The measure of an exterior angle of a triangle is equal to the sum of the measures of its remote interior angles.

Example

Find the missing angle measure.

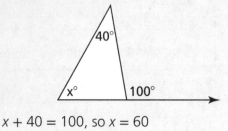

$x + 40 = 100$, so $x = 60$

Practice

1. Find the missing angle measure.

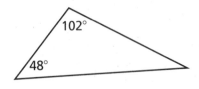

2. Find the value of x.

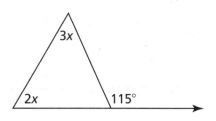

Quick Review

By the AA Criterion, if two angles in one triangle are congruent to two angles in another triangle, then the triangles are similar.

Example

Is △ABC ~ △DEF? Explain.

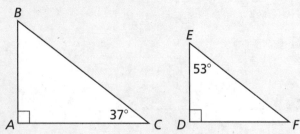

$m\angle B = 180° - 90° - 37° = 53°$

$m\angle A = m\angle D = 90°$ and $m\angle B = m\angle E = 53°$

Because two angles of the triangles are congruent, the triangles are similar by the AA Criterion.

Practice

1. $AB \parallel XY$. Is △ABC ~ △XYC? Explain.

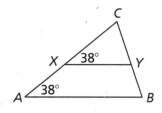

2. Find the values of x and y given that △ABC is similar to △MNC.

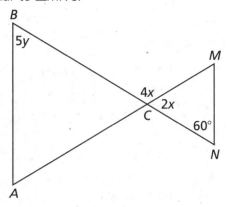

Crisscrossed

Solve each equation. Write your answers in the cross-number puzzle below. Each digit, negative sign, and decimal point of your answer goes in its own box.

I can...
solve multistep equations. © 8.EE.C.7b

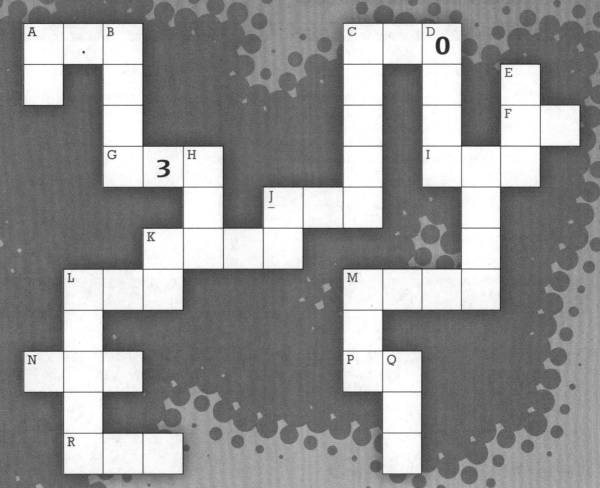

ACROSS

A $9n + 13 = 3n + 62.2$

C $\frac{1}{5}x + 13 = x - 107$

F $\frac{3}{4}k + 7 = \frac{1}{8}k + 27$

G $\frac{1}{3}t = t - 154$

I $g + 43 = 3g - 975$

J $\frac{1}{2}c + 13 = 3c + 48$

K $0.2m = -13(m + 330)$

L $-12 - r = -17.2$

M $4{,}500 - b = -3b + 4{,}098$

N $\frac{1}{4}w = 2(w - 87.5)$

P $\frac{1}{8}y + 17 = 2y - 118$

R $4p = 2(p + 7.1)$

DOWN

A $5q + 1 = 6q - 79$

B $5(z - 0.52) = 8$

C $2(a - 5) = a + 2.54$

D $8(n + 2) = 22$

E $5(t + 40) = -t - 34$

H $4h + 18 = 2(h + 10.3)$

K $4y - 1 = 3(-5 - y)$

L $d - 15.6 = 2d - 556.3$

M $3.5q - 145.5 = 5q$

Q $4(x + 2) = 5(x - 38.4)$

TOPIC 12

UNDERSTAND AND APPLY THE PYTHAGOREAN THEOREM

? Topic Essential Question

How can you use the Pythagorean Theorem to solve problems?

Topic Overview

3-Act Mathematical Modeling: Go with the Flow

12-1 Understand the Pythagorean Theorem

12-2 Understand the Converse of the Pythagorean Theorem

12-3 Apply the Pythagorean Theorem to Solve Problems

12-4 Find Distance in the Coordinate Plane

Topic Vocabulary

- Converse of the Pythagorean Theorem
- hypotenuse
- leg
- proof
- Pythagorean Theorem

Lesson Digital Resources

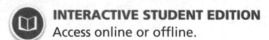
INTERACTIVE STUDENT EDITION
Access online or offline.

VISUAL LEARNING ANIMATION
Interact with visual learning animations.

ACTIVITY Use with *Solve & Discuss It, Explor* and *Explain It* activities, and to explore Examp

VIDEOS Watch clips to support *3-Act Mathematical Modeling Lessons* and *STEM Pr*

 Go online

▶ ▶ ▶

Go with *the* Flow

▶ ## Go with the Flow

You may have noticed that when you double the base and the height of a triangle, the area is more than doubled. The same is true for doubling the sides of a square or the radius of a circle. So what is the relationship? Think about this during the 3-Act Mathematical Modeling lesson.

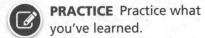 **PRACTICE** Practice what you've learned.

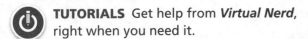 **TUTORIALS** Get help from *Virtual Nerd*, right when you need it.

 **MATH TOOLS** Explore math with digital tools.

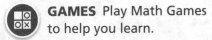 **GAMES** Play Math Games to help you learn.

 **KEY CONCEPT** Review important lesson content.

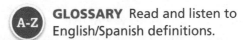 **GLOSSARY** Read and listen to English/Spanish definitions.

 **ASSESSMENT** Show what you've learned.

⚙enVision® STEM Project

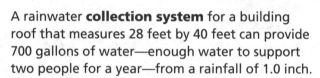

Did You Know?

Over **two billion** people will face **water shortages** by 2050 according to a 2015 United Nations Environment Program report.

Using **water wisely** saves money on water and energy bills and extends the life of supply and wastewater facilities.

Rainwater can be **collected** and stored for use in irrigation, industrial uses, flushing toilets, washing clothes and cars, or it can be purified for use as everyday drinking water.

This **alternative water source** reduces the use of fresh water from reservoirs and wells.

Roofs of buildings or large tarps are used to collect rainwater.

A rainwater **collection system** for a building roof that measures 28 feet by 40 feet can provide 700 gallons of water—enough water to support two people for a year—from a rainfall of 1.0 inch.

Even a **5 foot by 7 foot tarp** can collect **2 gallons** of water from a rainfall total of only 0.1 in.

The **rainwater harvesting** market is expected to **grow 5%** from 2016 to 2020.

Your Task: Rainy Days

Rainwater collection is an inexpensive way to save water in areas where it is scarce. One inch of rain falling on a square roof with an area of 100 ft² collects 62 gallons of water that weighs over 500 pounds. You and your classmates will research the necessary components of a rainwater collection system. Then you will use what you know about right triangles to design a slanted roof system that will be used to collect rainwater.

Review What You Know!

Vocabulary

Choose the best term from the box to complete each definition.

cube root

diagonal

isosceles triangle

perimeter

right triangle

square root

1. The _____ of a number is a factor that when multiplied by itself gives the number.

2. A _____ is a line segment that connects two vertices of a polygon and is not a side.

3. The _____ of a figure is the distance around it.

4. A _____ is a triangle with one right angle.

Simplify Expressions with Exponents

Simplify the expression.

5. $3^2 + 4^2$

6. $2^2 + 5^2$

7. $10^2 - 8^2$

Square Roots

Determine the square root.

8. $\sqrt{81}$

9. $\sqrt{144}$

10. $\sqrt{225}$

Distance on a Coordinate Plane

Determine the distance between the two points.

11.

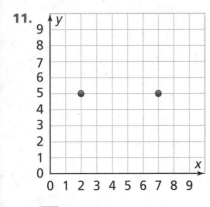

 units

12.

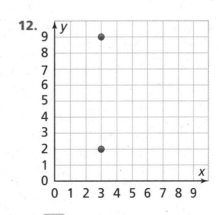

 units

Language Development

Complete the word map using key terms, examples, or illustrations related to the Pythagorean Theorem and its Converse.

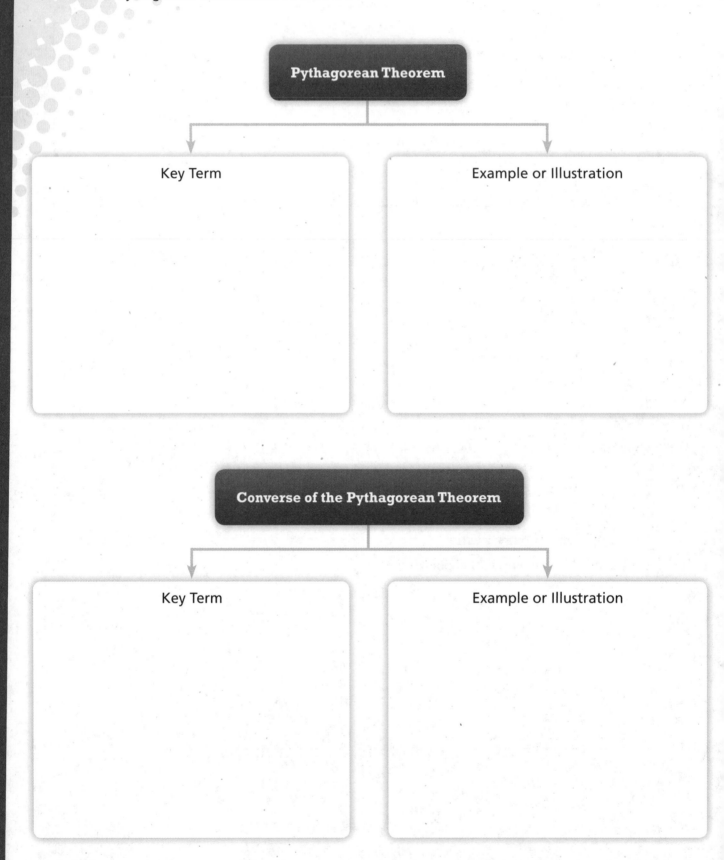

Pythagorean Theorem

Key Term

Example or Illustration

Converse of the Pythagorean Theorem

Key Term

Example or Illustration

PROJECT 12A

Where would you like to bike ride in your neighborhood?

PROJECT: PLAN A METRIC CENTURY RIDE

PROJECT 12B

What designs have you seen on kites?

PROJECT: BUILD A KITE

PROJECT 12C

What buildings in your community have unusual shapes as part of their structure or design?

PROJECT: MAKE A SCRAPBOOK

PROJECT 12D

What geometric designs have you noticed on your clothes?

PROJECT: DESIGN A FABRIC TEMPLATE

3-ACT MATH

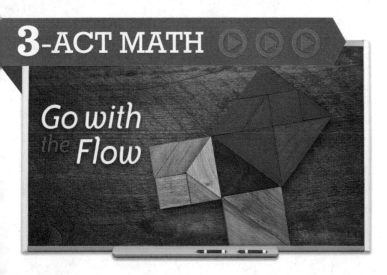

Go with the Flow

3-Act Mathematical Modeling:
Go with the Flow

Go Online

© **Common Core Content Standards**
8.G.B.6

Mathematical Practices
MP.4, MP.1, MP.2, MP.3, MP.7, MP.8

ACT 1

1. After watching the video, what is the first question that comes to mind?

2. Write the Main Question you will answer.

3. Make a prediction to answer this Main Question.

% will fit in the third square.

4. Construct Arguments Explain how you arrived at your prediction.

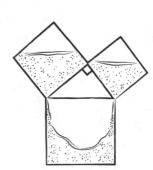

5. What information in this situation would be helpful to know? How would you use that information?

6. **Use Appropriate Tools** What tools can you use to solve the problem? Explain how you would use them strategically.

7. **Model With Math** Represent the situation using mathematics. Use your representation to answer the Main Question.

8. What is your answer to the Main Question? Does it differ from your prediction? Explain.

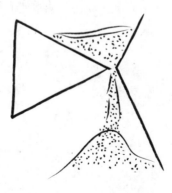

9. Write the answer you saw in the video.

10. Reasoning Does your answer match the answer in the video? If not, what are some reasons that would explain the difference?

11. Make Sense and Persevere Would you change your model now that you know the answer? Explain.

Reflect

12. Model with Math Explain how you used a mathematical model to represent the situation. How did the model help you answer the Main Question?

13. Reason Abstractly How did you represent the situation using symbols? How did you use those symbols to solve the problem?

14. Construct Arguments Explain why you can use an area formula when the problem involves comparing volumes.

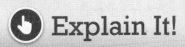

Explain It!

 ACTIVITY

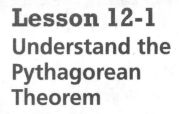

Lesson 12-1
Understand the Pythagorean Theorem

Kelly drew a right triangle on graph paper. Kelly says that the sum of the areas of squares with side lengths *a* and *b* is the same as the area of a square with side length *c*.

Go Online

I can...
use the Pythagorean Theorem to find unknown sides of triangles.

 Common Core Content Standards
8.G.B.6, 8.G.B.7

Mathematical Practices
MP.3, MP.7, MP.8

A. Do you agree with Kelly? Explain.

B. Sam drew a different right triangle with side lengths *a* = 5, *b* = 12, and *c* = 13. Is the relationship Kelly described true for Sam's right triangle? Explain.

Focus on math practices

Generalize Kelly draws another right triangle. What would you expect to be the relationship between the areas of the squares drawn on each side of the triangle? Explain.

VISUAL LEARNING ASSES

Scan for Multimedia

EXAMPLE 1 **Understand the Pythagorean Theorem**

△ABC is a right triangle with side lengths *a*, *b*, and *c*. Construct a logical argument to show that $a^2 + b^2 = c^2$.

Construct Arguments When you think logically and use definitions, properties, and given facts to construct an argument, you are developing a mathematical proof.

The **hypotenuse**, *c*, is the longest side of the right triangle.

The **legs**, *a* and *b*, are the shorter sides of the right triangle.

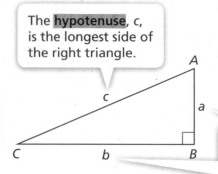

Compose a square using four copies of the right triangle. Write an expression to represent the area of the large square.

$A = \frac{1}{2}bh$ or $\frac{1}{2}ab$

$A = c^2$

The total area of the large square is $A = 4(\frac{1}{2}ab) + c^2$.

Rearrange the triangles inside the same square and write an expression to represent the area of the large square.

$A = ab$ $A = a^2$

$A = b^2$

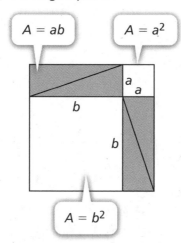

The total area of the large square is
$A = ab + ab + a2 + b^2$

Because both large squares are exactly the same size, the areas are equal.

$4(\frac{1}{2}ab) + c^2 = ab + ab + a^2 + b^2$

$2ab + c^2 = 2ab + a^2 + b^2$

$c^2 = a^2 + b^2$

Combine like terms. Apply the Subtraction Property of Equality.

If △ABC is a right triangle, then $a^2 + b^2 = c^2$. This is a proof of the **Pythagorean Theorem**.

A logical mathematical argument in which every statement of fact is supported by a reason is called a **proof**.

✓ Try It!

A right triangle has side lengths 15 centimeters, 25 centimeters, and 20 centimeters. How can you use the Pythagorean Theorem to write an equation that describes how the side lengths are related?

$a^2 + b^2 = c^2$

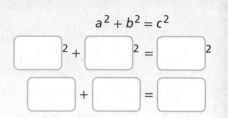

Convince Me! How do you know that the geometric proof of the Pythagorean Theorem shown above can be applied to all right triangles?

EXAMPLE 2 — Use the Pythagorean Theorem to Find the Length of the Hypotenuse

What is the length of the hypotenuse of the right triangle?

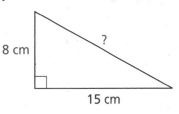

Use the Pythagorean Theorem.

$(\text{leg})^2 + (\text{leg})^2 = (\text{hypotenuse})^2$

$a^2 + b^2 = c^2$

$8^2 + 15^2 = c^2$

$64 + 225 = c^2$

$289 = c^2$

$\sqrt{289} = \sqrt{c^2}$

$17 = c$

The length of the hypotenuse is 17 centimeters.

EXAMPLE 3 — Use the Pythagorean Theorem to Find the Length of a Leg

Mara is repairing the trim on one side of a display case sketched at the right. She has a piece of trim that is 20 inches long. Does Mara have enough trim to repair the display case?

The display case is in the shape of a right triangle. Use the Pythagorean Theorem to find the missing side length.

$a^2 + b^2 = c^2$

$20^2 + b^2 = 29^2$ — Substitute the given information.

$400 + b^2 = 841$

$400 + b^2 - 400 = 841 - 400$

$b^2 = 441$

$\sqrt{b^2} = \sqrt{441}$

$b = 21$

Mara needs a 21-inch piece of trim, so she does not have enough trim to repair the display case.

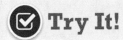 Try It!

A right triangle has a hypotenuse length of 32 meters. It has one leg with a length of 18 meters. What is the length of the other leg? Express your answer as a square root.

The Pythagorean Theorem is an equation that relates the side lengths of a right triangle, $a^2 + b^2 = c^2$, where a and b are the legs of a right triangle and c is the hypotenuse.

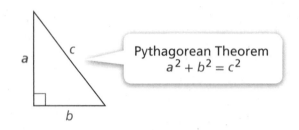

Pythagorean Theorem
$$a^2 + b^2 = c^2$$

Do You Understand?

1. **? Essential Question** How does the Pythagorean Theorem relate the side lengths of a right triangle?

2. **Use Structure** A side of each of the three squares forms a side of a right triangle.

   Would any three squares form the sides of a right triangle? Explain.

   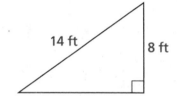

3. **Construct Arguments** Xavier said the missing length is about 18.5 units. Without calculating, how can you tell that Xavier solved incorrectly?

   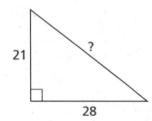

Do You Know How?

4. A right triangle has leg lengths of 4 inches and 5 inches. What is the length of the hypotenuse? Write the answer as a square root and round to the nearest tenth of an inch.

5. Find the missing side length to the nearest tenth of a foot.

   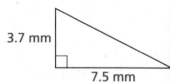

   14 ft   8 ft

6. Find the missing side length to the nearest tenth of a millimeter.

   3.7 mm

   7.5 mm

Practice & Problem Solving

Leveled Practice In 7 and 8, find the missing side length of each triangle.

7.

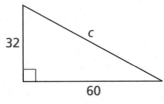

$$\boxed{}^2 + 60\boxed{} = c^2$$

$$\boxed{} + \boxed{} = c^2$$

$$\boxed{} = c^2$$

$$\sqrt{\boxed{}} = \sqrt{\boxed{}}$$

$$c = \boxed{}$$

The length of the hypotenuse is $\boxed{}$ units.

8.

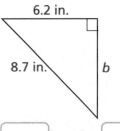

$$\boxed{}^2 + b^2 = \boxed{}^2$$

$$\boxed{} + b^2 = \boxed{}$$

$$b^2 = \boxed{}$$

$$\sqrt{\boxed{}} = \sqrt{\boxed{}}$$

$$b \approx \boxed{}$$

The length of leg b is about $\boxed{}$ inches.

---

9. What is the length of the hypotenuse of the triangle when $x = 15$? Round your answer to the nearest tenth of a unit.

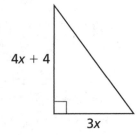

10. What is the length of side a rounded to the nearest tenth of a centimeter?

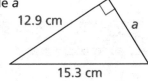

---

11. Use the Pythagorean Theorem to find the unknown side length of the right triangle.

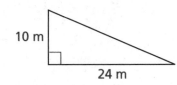

12. What is the length of the unknown leg of the right triangle rounded to the nearest tenth of a foot?

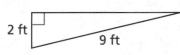

13. A student is asked to find the length of the hypotenuse of a right triangle. The length of one leg is 32 centimeters, and the length of the other leg is 26 centimeters. The student incorrectly says that the length of the hypotenuse is 7.6 centimeters.

  a. Find the length of the hypotenuse of the right triangle to the nearest tenth of a centimeter.

  b. What mistake might the student have made?

14. Find the length of the unknown leg of the right triangle.

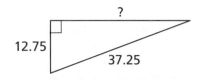

15. Higher Order Thinking A right triangle has side lengths 12 centimeters and 14 centimeters. Name two possible side lengths for the third side, and explain how you solved for each.

✓ Assessment Practice

16. Which right triangle has a hypotenuse that is about 39 feet long?

Ⓐ
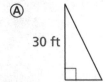
30 ft
15 ft

Ⓑ
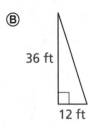
36 ft
12 ft

Ⓒ
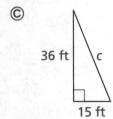
36 ft c
15 ft

Ⓓ
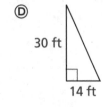
30 ft
14 ft

17. Which right triangle does NOT have an unknown leg length of about 33 cm?

Ⓐ
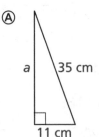
a   35 cm
11 cm

Ⓑ
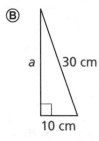
a   30 cm
10 cm

Ⓒ
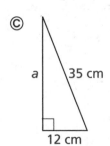
a   35 cm
12 cm

Ⓓ
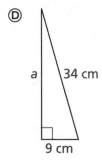
a   34 cm
9 cm

Solve & Discuss It!

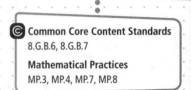 ACTIVITY

Kayla has some straws that she will use for an art project. She wants to glue three of the straws onto a sheet of paper, without overlapping, to make the outline of a right triangle.

Which three straws could Kayla use to make a right triangle? Explain.

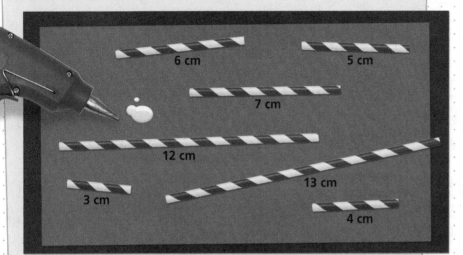

6 cm

5 cm

7 cm

12 cm

3 cm

13 cm

4 cm

I can...
use the Converse of the Pythagorean Theorem to identify right triangles.

© **Common Core Content Standards**
8.G.B.6, 8.G.B.7

Mathematical Practices
MP.3, MP.4, MP.7, MP.8

Look for Relationships How could you use the Pythagorean Theorem to determine whether the lengths form a right triangle?

Focus on math practices

Use Structure Could Kayla use the straws that form a right triangle to make a triangle that is not a right triangle? Explain.

VISUAL LEARNING

ASSES

EXAMPLE 1 Understand the Converse of the Pythagorean Theorem

Scan for Multimedia

$\triangle ABC$ has side lengths a, b, and c such that $a^2 + b^2 = c^2$. Construct a logical argument to show that $\triangle ABC$ is a right triangle.

> You have to show that $\angle B$ is a right angle to prove that $\triangle ABC$ is a right triangle.

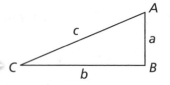

Draw right triangle DEF with leg lengths a and b and hypotenuse length x.

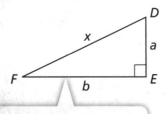

> By the Pythagorean Theorem, $a^2 + b^2 = x^2$.

Use substitution to show that $c = x$.

You are given that $a^2 + b^2 = c^2$.

You know that $a^2 + b^2 = x^2$.

By substitution, $x^2 = c^2$.

$$x^2 = c^2$$
$$\sqrt{x^2} = \sqrt{c^2}$$
$$x = c$$

The three sides of $\triangle DEF$ are congruent to the three sides of $\triangle ABC$, so there is a sequence of transformations that maps $\triangle DEF$ to $\triangle ABC$.

$$\triangle ABC \cong \triangle DEF$$
$$\angle B \cong \angle E$$

$\angle B$ is a right angle, so $\triangle ABC$ is a right triangle.

This is a proof of the **Converse of the Pythagorean Theorem**.

> **Generalize** If $a^2 + b^2 = c^2$, then $\triangle ABC$ is a right triangle.

☑ Try It!

A triangle has side lengths 4 inches, 5 inches, and 7 inches. Is the triangle a right triangle?

$$a^2 + b^2 \stackrel{?}{=} c^2$$

$$\boxed{}^2 + \boxed{}^2 \stackrel{?}{=} \boxed{}^2$$

$$\boxed{} + \boxed{} \stackrel{?}{=} \boxed{}$$

Is $a^2 + b^2$ equal to c^2? $\boxed{}$

Is the triangle a right triangle? $\boxed{}$

Convince Me! Explain the proof of the Converse of the Pythagorean Theorem in your own words.

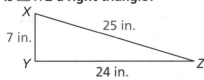

EXAMPLE 2 · Apply the Converse of the Pythagorean Theorem to Identify Right Triangles

A. Is △XYZ a right triangle?

Apply the Converse of the Pythagorean Theorem.

$a^2 + b^2 \stackrel{?}{=} c^2$

$7^2 + 24^2 \stackrel{?}{=} 25^2$

$49 + 576 \stackrel{?}{=} 625$

$625 = 625$

△XYZ is a right triangle.

B. The side lengths of a triangle are 6 inches, 4.5 inches, and 3.75 inches. Is this triangle a right triangle?

Apply the Converse of the Pythagorean Theorem.

$a^2 + b^2 \stackrel{?}{=} c^2$

$4.5^2 + 3.75^2 \stackrel{?}{=} 6^2$

$20.25 + 14.0625 \stackrel{?}{=} 36$

> How do you know which side lengths are a, b, and c?

$34.3125 \neq 36$

This triangle is not a right triangle.

 **Try It!**

A triangle has side lengths 10 feet, $\sqrt{205}$ feet, and $\sqrt{105}$ feet. Is this a right triangle? Explain.

EXAMPLE 3 · Use the Converse of the Pythagorean Theorem to Analyze Shapes

Rey drew the isosceles triangle *LMN* and the segment *LP*. How can Rey tell whether the segment drawn is the height of the triangle?

Use the Converse of the Pythagorean Theorem to determine whether △*LPN* is a right triangle.

$a^2 + b^2 \stackrel{?}{=} c^2$

$1.3^2 + 3.5^2 \stackrel{?}{=} 3.7^2$

$1.69 + 12.25 \stackrel{?}{=} 13.69$

$13.94 \neq 13.69$

> Remember, the corresponding base and height of a triangle are perpendicular. If segment *LP* is the height of △*LMN*, then △*LPN* is a right triangle.

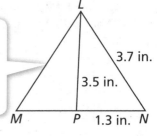

Segment *LP* is not the height of △*LMN*.

 Try It!

A triangle is inside a trapezoid. Is the triangle a right triangle? Explain.

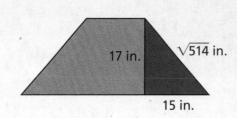

The Converse of the Pythagorean Theorem states that if the sum of the squares of the lengths of two sides of a triangle is equal to the square of the length of the third side, the triangle is a right triangle.

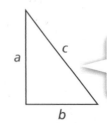

Converse of Pythagorean Theorem
If $a^2 + b^2 = c^2$, then a triangle is a right triangle.

Do You Understand?

1. **? Essential Question** How can you determine whether a triangle is a right triangle?

2. **Construct Arguments** A triangle has side lengths of 3 centimeters, 5 centimeters, and 4 centimeters. Abe used the Converse of the Pythagorean Theorem to determine whether it is a right triangle.

$$3^2 + 5^2 \overset{?}{=} 4^2$$

$$9 + 25 \overset{?}{=} 16$$

$$34 \neq 16$$

Abe concluded that it is not a right triangle. Is Abe correct? Explain.

3. **Use Structure** When you are given three side lengths for a triangle, how do you know which length to substitute for a, b, or c in the Pythagorean Theorem?

Do You Know How?

4. Is the triangle a right triangle? Explain.

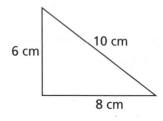

6 cm   10 cm

8 cm

5. Is the triangle a right triangle? Explain.

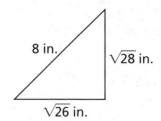

8 in. $\sqrt{28}$ in.

$\sqrt{26}$ in.

6. Is the purple triangle a right triangle? Explain.

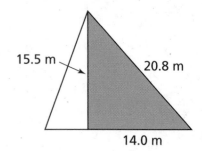

15.5 m   20.8 m

14.0 m

Practice & Problem Solving

Scan for
Multimedia

Leveled Practice In **7** and **8**, determine whether each triangle is a right triangle.

7.

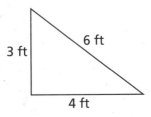

3 ft
6 ft
4 ft

$a^2 + b^2 = c^2$

$$\boxed{}^2 + \boxed{}^2 \overset{?}{=} \boxed{}^2$$

$$\boxed{} + \boxed{} \overset{?}{=} \boxed{}$$

$$\boxed{}\ \bigcirc\ \boxed{}$$

Is the triangle a right triangle? $\boxed{}$

8.

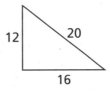

12
20
16

$a^2 + b^2 = c^2$

$$\boxed{}^2 + \boxed{}^2 \overset{?}{=} \boxed{}^2$$

$$\boxed{} + \boxed{} \overset{?}{=} \boxed{}$$

$$\boxed{}\ \bigcirc\ \boxed{}$$

Is the triangle a right triangle? $\boxed{}$

9. Can the sides of a right triangle have lengths 5, 15, and $\sqrt{250}$? Explain.

10. Is $\triangle PQR$ a right triangle? Explain.

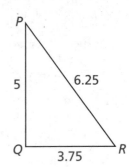

P
5
6.25
Q
3.75
R

11. The green triangle is set inside a rectangle. Is the green triangle a right triangle? Explain.

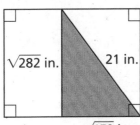

$\sqrt{282}$ in.
21 in.
$\sqrt{159}$ in.

12. The side lengths of three triangles are shown. Which of the triangles are right triangles?

Triangle	Side Lengths		
1	$\frac{3}{7}$	$\frac{4}{7}$	$\frac{5}{7}$
2	8	8	15
3	$\frac{5}{17}$	$\frac{12}{17}$	$\frac{13}{17}$

13. **Construct Arguments** Three students draw triangles with the side lengths shown. All three say that their triangle is a right triangle. Which students are incorrect? What mistake might they have made?

Student 1: 22, 33, 55

Student 2: 44, 33, 77

Student 3: 33, 44, 55

14. **Model with Math** $\triangle JKL$ is an isosceles triangle. Is $\overline{KM}$ the height of $\triangle JKL$? Explain.

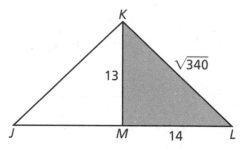

15. **Higher Order Thinking** The side lengths of three triangles are given.

Triangle 1: $\sqrt{229}$ units, $\sqrt{225}$ units, 22 units
Triangle 2: $\sqrt{11\frac{1}{3}}$ units, $\sqrt{13\frac{2}{3}}$ units, 5 units
Triangle 3: 16 units, 17 units, $\sqrt{545}$ units

a. Which lengths represent the side lengths of a right triangle?

b. For any triangles that are not right triangles, use two of the sides to make a right triangle.

Assessment Practice

16. Which shaded triangle is a right triangle? Explain.

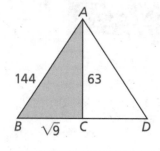
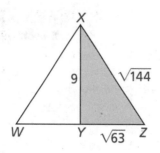

17. Which triangle is a right triangle?

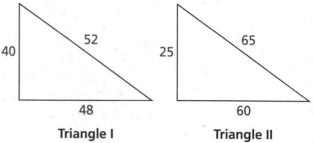

Ⓐ Triangle I only

Ⓑ Triangle II only

Ⓒ Triangle I and Triangle II

Ⓓ Neither Triangle I nor Triangle II

1. Vocabulary How are the hypotenuse and the legs of a right triangle related? *Lesson 12-1*

2. Given that △*PQR* has side lengths of 12.5 centimeters, 30 centimeters, and 32.5 centimeters, prove △*PQR* is a right triangle. *Lesson 12-2*

3. Ella said that if she knows the lengths of just two sides of any triangle, then she can find the length of the third side by using the Pythagorean Theorem. Is Ella correct? Explain. *Lesson 12-1*

4. Find the unknown side length. Round to the nearest tenth. *Lesson 12-1*

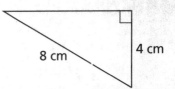

8 cm   4 cm

5. The height of a shed is 6 m. A ladder leans against the shed with its base 4.5 m away, and its top just reaching the roof. What is the length of the ladder? *Lesson 12-1*

6. Select all the sets of lengths that could represent the sides of a right triangle. *Lesson 12-2*

☐ 5 cm, 10 cm, 15 cm

☐ 7 in., 14 in., 25 in.

☐ 13 m, 84 m, 85 m

☐ 5 ft, 11 ft, 12 ft

☐ 6 ft, 9 ft, $\sqrt{117}$ ft

How well did you do on the mid-topic checkpoint? Fill in the stars.

MID-TOPIC PERFORMANCE TASK

Javier is standing near a palm tree. He holds an electronic tape measure near his eyes and finds the three distances shown.

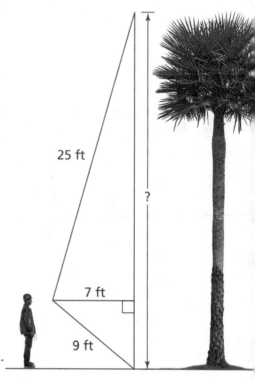

25 ft

?

7 ft

9 ft

PART A

Javier says that he can now use the Pythagorean Theorem to find the height of the tree. Explain. Use vocabulary terms in your explanation.

PART B

Find the height of the tree. Round to the nearest tenth. Show your work.

PART C

Javier moves backward so that his horizontal distance from the palm tree is 3 feet greater. Will the distance from his eyes to the top of the tree also be 3 feet greater? Explain.

PART D

Could Javier change his horizontal distance from the tree so that the distance from his eyes to the top of the tree is only 20 feet? Explain.

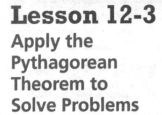
Solve & Discuss It!

 ACTIVITY

Carlos is giving his friend in another state a new umbrella as a gift. He wants to ship the umbrella in a box he already has. Which box can Carlos use to ship the umbrella? Explain.

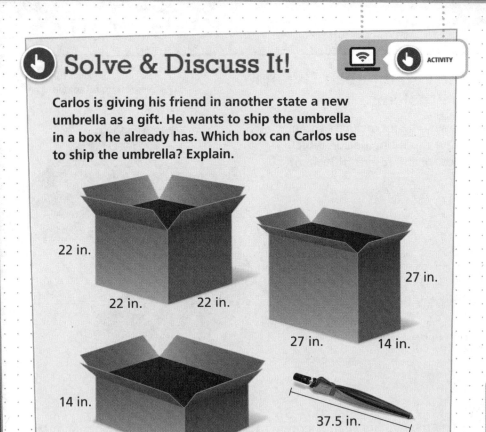

22 in.

22 in.   22 in.

27 in.

27 in.   14 in.

14 in.

27 in.   22 in.

37.5 in.

I can...
use the Pythagorean Theorem to solve problems.

© Common Core Content Standards
8.G.B.7

Mathematical Practices
MP.1, MP.2, MP.3, MP.7, MP.8

Make Sense and Persevere How will the umbrella fit inside any of the boxes?

Focus on math practices

Construct Arguments Tim says that the diagonal of any of the boxes will always be longer than the sides. Is Tim correct? Explain.

VISUAL LEARNING ASSESS

EXAMPLE 1 ◉ **Apply the Pythagorean Theorem to Solve Problems**

Scan for Multimedia

Kiana is using a kit to build the kite shown. The kit includes three different lengths of wooden dowels. How can Kiana decide which pieces of wood to use as diagonal braces for the top or bottom of the kite?

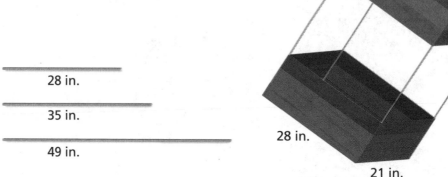

28 in.

35 in.

49 in.

28 in.

21 in.

Draw a diagram. Use a rectangle to represent the top and bottom of the kite.

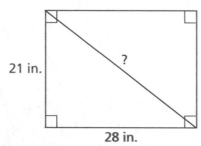

21 in.

?

28 in.

Use the Pythagorean Theorem to find the length of the diagonal.

$$a^2 + b^2 = c^2$$
$$21^2 + 28^2 = c^2$$
$$441 + 784 = c^2$$
$$1,225 = c^2$$
$$\sqrt{1,225} = c$$
$$35 = c$$

The length of the diagonal of the rectangle is 35 inches.

So Kiana could use the 35-inch dowel as a brace for the top or bottom of the kite.

Generalize You can use the Pythagorean Theorem to solve problems with squares and rectangles since the corners are always right angles.

☑ **Try It!**

What is the length of the diagonal, d, of a rectangle with length 19 feet and width 17 feet?

$leg^2 + leg^2 = hypotenuse^2$

$\boxed{}^2 + \boxed{}^2 = d^2$

$\boxed{} + \boxed{} = d^2$

$\boxed{} = d^2$

$\boxed{} \approx d$

Convince Me! If the rectangle were a square, would the process of finding the length of the diagonal change? Explain.

EXAMPLE 2  Apply the Pythagorean Theorem to Triangles in Three Dimensions

Alex has a column aquarium with a rectangular base that has a height of 66 inches, a length of 10 inches, and a width of 14.5 inches. What is the longest piece of choya wood that Alex can buy to fit in his tank?

STEP 1 Draw and label a diagram to represent the aquarium.

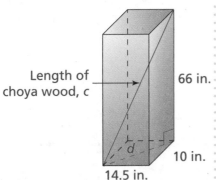

Length of choya wood, c — 66 in.
d
14.5 in.   10 in.

STEP 2 Find the length of the diagonal, d, of the bottom of the tank.

$$10^2 + 14.5^2 = d^2$$
$$100 + 210.25 = d^2$$
$$310.25 = d^2$$
$$17.6 \approx d$$

STEP 3 Use the Pythagorean Theorem to find the length of the choya wood.

$$66^2 + 17.6^2 = c^2$$
$$4{,}356 + 310.25 = c^2$$
$$4{,}666.25 = c^2$$
$$68.3 \approx c$$

A piece of choya wood that is about 68.3 inches long is the longest piece of choya wood Alex can buy.

EXAMPLE 3 Apply the Converse of the Pythagorean Theorem to Solve Problems

Sandra bought a triangular shelf to hang in the corner of her room. Will this shelf fit in the 90° corner? Explain.

Use the Converse of the Pythagorean Theorem to determine if the triangle is a right triangle.

$$a^2 + b^2 \stackrel{?}{=} c^2$$
$$18^2 + 24 \stackrel{?}{=} 30^2$$
$$324 + 576 \stackrel{?}{=} 900$$
$$900 = 900$$

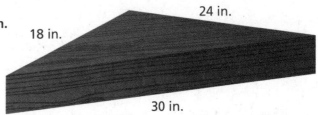

24 in.
18 in.
30 in.

The shelf is in the shape of a right triangle. It will fit in the corner.

 **Try It!**

A company wants to rent a tent that has a height of at least 10 feet for an outdoor show. Should they rent the tent shown at the right? Explain.

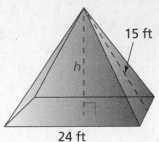

15 ft
h
24 ft

You can use the Pythagorean Theorem and its converse to solve problems involving right triangles.

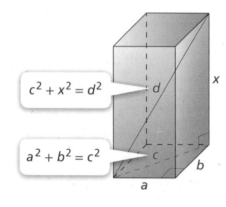

$c^2 + x^2 = d^2$

d

x

$a^2 + b^2 = c^2$

c

b

a

Do You Understand?

1. **? Essential Question** What types of problems can be solved using the Pythagorean Theorem?

2. **Look for Structure** How is using the Pythagorean Theorem in a rectangular prism similar to using it in a rectangle?

3. **Construct Arguments** Glen found the length of the hypotenuse of a right triangle using $\sqrt{a^2 + b^2}$. Gigi used $\sqrt{(a + b)^2}$. Who is correct? Explain.

Do You Know How?

4. You are painting the roof of a boathouse. You are going to place the base of a ladder 12 feet from the boathouse. How long does the ladder need to be to reach the roof of the boathouse?

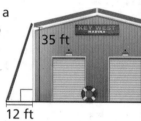

35 ft

12 ft

5. A box shaped like a right rectangular prism measures 5 centimeters by 3 centimeters by 2 centimeters. What is the length of the interior diagonal of the prism to the nearest hundredth?

6. A wall 12 feet long makes a corner with a wall that is 14 feet long. The other ends of the walls are about 18.44 feet apart. Do the walls form a right angle? Explain.

Practice & Problem Solving

Scan for
Multimedia

Leveled Practice In **7** and **8**, use the Pythagorean Theorem to solve.

7. You are going to use an inclined plane to lift a heavy object to the top of a shelving unit with a height of 6 feet. The base of the inclined plane is 16 feet from the shelving unit. What is the length of the inclined plane? Round to the nearest tenth of a foot.

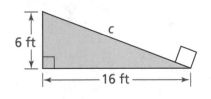

6 ft   c

16 ft

$$a^2 + b^2 = c^2$$

$\boxed{}^2 + \boxed{}^2 = \boxed{}^2$

$\boxed{} + \boxed{} = \boxed{}$

$\boxed{} = \boxed{}$

$\boxed{} \approx \boxed{}$

The length of the inclined plane is about $\boxed{}$ feet.

8. Find the missing lengths in the rectangular prism.

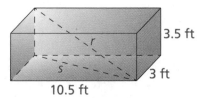

3.5 ft
3 ft
10.5 ft

$$a^2 + b^2 = c^2$$

$\boxed{}^2 + \boxed{}^2 = \boxed{}^2$

$\boxed{} + \boxed{} = \boxed{}$

$\boxed{} = \boxed{}$

$\boxed{} \approx \boxed{}$

$$a^2 + b^2 = c^2$$

$\boxed{}^2 + \boxed{}^2 = \boxed{}^2$

$\boxed{} + \boxed{} = \boxed{}$

$\boxed{} = \boxed{}$

$\boxed{} \approx \boxed{}$

9. A stainless steel patio heater is shaped like a square pyramid. The length of one side of the base is 19.8 inches. The slant height is 92.8 inches. What is the height of the heater? Round to the nearest tenth of an inch.

10. Reasoning What is the measurement of the longest line segment in a right rectangular prism that is 16 centimeters long, 9 centimeters wide, and 7 centimeters tall? Round to the nearest tenth of a centimeter.

11. Felipe is making triangles for a stained glass window. He made the design shown, but wants to change it. Felipe wants to move the purple triangle to the corner. The purple piece has side lengths of 4.5 inches, 6 inches, and 7 inches. Can the purple piece be moved to the corner? Explain.

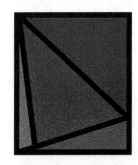

12. **a.** What is the longest poster you could fit in the box? Express your answer to the nearest tenth of an inch.

   b. Explain why you can fit only one maximum-length poster in the box, but you can fit multiple 21.5-inch posters in the same box.

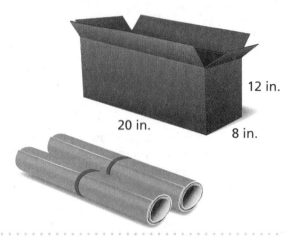

12 in.

20 in.

8 in.

13. The corner of a room where two walls meet the floor should be a right angle. Jeff makes a mark along each wall. One mark is 3 inches from the corner. The other is 4 inches from the corner. How can Jeff use the Pythagorean Theorem to see if the walls form a right angle?

14. **Higher Order Thinking** It is recommended that a ramp have at least 6 feet of horizontal distance for every 1 foot of vertical rise along an incline. The ramp shown has a vertical rise of 2 feet. Does the ramp shown match the recommended specifications? Explain.

21 ft

☑ Assessment Practice

15. A machine in a factory cuts out triangular sheets of metal. Which of the triangles are right triangles? Select all that apply.

   ☐ Triangle 1

   ☐ Triangle 2

   ☐ Triangle 3

   ☐ Triangle 4

Triangle Side Lengths

Triangle	Side Lengths (in.)		
1	12	19	$\sqrt{505}$
2	16	19	$\sqrt{467}$
3	14	20	$\sqrt{596}$
4	11	23	$\sqrt{421}$

16. What is the length b, in feet, of the rectangular plot of land shown?

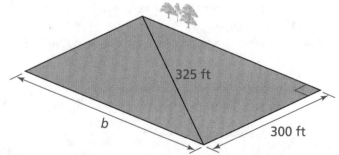

325 ft

b

300 ft

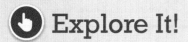 **Explore It!**  ACTIVITY

Thomas and Jim are outside the haunted castle ride and
want to get to the clown tent in time for the next show.

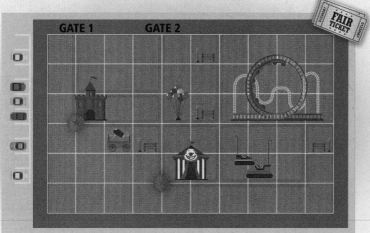

1 grid square = 1 cm by 1 cm
1 cm = 500 feet

Lesson 12-4
Find Distance in the Coordinate Plane

Go Online

I can...
use the Pythagorean Theorem to
find the distance between two
points in the coordinate plane.

© **Common Core Content Standards**
8.G.B.8

Mathematical Practices
MP.3, MP.4, MP.7, MP.8

A. How can you represent the starred locations on a coordinate plane?

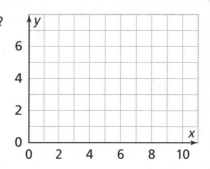

B. Jim says that the marked yellow paths show the shortest path to the
tent. Write an expression to represent this and find the distance Jim
walks from the haunted mansion to the clown tent.

Focus on math practices

Construct Arguments Why is the distance between two nonhorizontal and
nonvertical points always greater than the horizontal or vertical distance?

VISUAL LEARNING ASSESS

EXAMPLE 1 **Apply the Pythagorean Theorem to Find the Distance Between Two Points**

Scan for Multimedia

Thomas says that walking along a straight path from the haunted mansion to the clown tent is the shorter path. How can you use the Pythagorean Theorem to determine whether he is correct?

Model with Math How can you use a coordinate plane and the Pythagorean Theorem to represent and find the distance Thomas will walk?

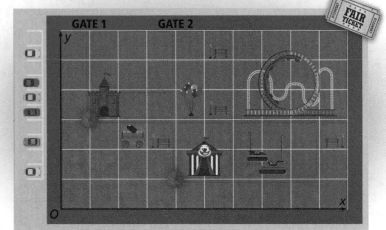

1 grid square = 1 cm by 1 cm
1 cm = 500 feet

Plot and label the locations of the stars on a coordinate plane. Use the stars as two vertices and draw a right triangle.

Remember, you can use absolute values to find the vertical distance.
$|1| + |1| = 2$

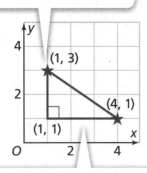

The horizontal distance is $|4| - |1| = 3$.

Use the Pythagorean Theorem to find the distance between the two points.

$$a^2 + b^2 = c^2$$

$$2^2 + 3^2 = c^2$$ Substitute the known lengths.

$$13 = c^2$$

$$\sqrt{13} = c$$

$$3.61 \approx c$$

Use the map scale to find the actual distance.

$$\frac{1\text{ cm}}{500\text{ ft}} = \frac{3.61\text{ cm}}{x\text{ ft}}$$

$$x = 1,805$$

Tom walks about 1,805 feet, which is shorter than the 2,500 feet that Jim walks.

✓ **Try It!**

What is the distance between points A and B?

The distance between point A and point B is about ☐ units.

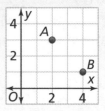

Convince Me! Why do you need to use the Pythagorean Theorem to find the distance between points A and B.

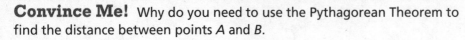

EXAMPLE **2** ● **Find the Perimeter of a Figure on a Coordinate Plane**

Find the perimeter of △*ABC*.

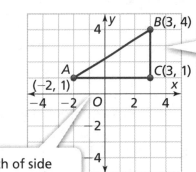

STEP 1 Use absolute value to find the lengths of side *AC* and side *BC*.

The length of side *BC* = |4| − |1| = 3.

STEP 2 Find the length of the hypotenuse *AB*.

$$c^2 = 5^2 + 3^2$$

$$c^2 = 25 + 9$$

Substitute the known side lengths into the Pythagorean Theorem.

$$c^2 = 34$$

$$\sqrt{c^2} = \sqrt{34}$$

$$c \approx 5.83$$

The length of side *AC* = |−2| + |−3| = 5.

The distance between point *A* and point *B* is about 5.83 units.

STEP 3 Add the lengths of all three sides to find the perimeter.

$$5 + 3 + 5.83 = 13.83$$

The perimeter of △*ABC* is about 13.83 units.

✓ **Try It!**

Find the perimeter of △*ABC* with vertices (2, 5), (5, −1), and (2, −1).

EXAMPLE **3** ● **Use the Pythagorean Theorem to Solve Problems on the Coordinate Plane**

Li draws one side of an equilateral triangle with vertices (−1, 1) and (3, 1) on the coordinate plane. The third vertex is in the first quadrant. What are the coordinates of the third vertex of Li's triangle?

STEP 1 Find the length of the side drawn.

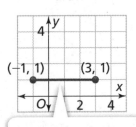

|−1| + |3| = 4 units

STEP 2 Use the Pythagorean Theorem to find the height of Li's triangle to the nearest tenth.

$$a^2 + b^2 = c^2$$

$$a^2 + 2^2 = 4^2$$

$$a^2 + 4 = 16$$

$$a^2 = 12$$

$$a = \sqrt{12} \approx 3.5$$

STEP 3 Complete the triangle by drawing the height to locate and label the third vertex.

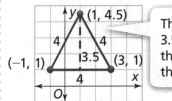

The vertex is 3.5 units above the midpoint of the side drawn.

The coordinates of the third vertex of Li's triangle are (1, 4.5).

✓ **Try It!**

What are the coordinates, to the nearest tenth, of the third vertex in an isosceles triangle that has one side length of 2 and two side lengths of 5, with vertices at (1, 0) and (1, 2)? The third vertex is in the first quadrant.

You can use the Pythagorean Theorem to find the distance between any two points, *P* and *Q*, on the coordinate plane.

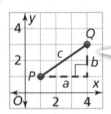

Draw a right triangle with side *PQ* as its hypotenuse.

Do You Understand?

1. **Essential Question** How can you use the Pythagorean Theorem to find the distance between two points?

2. **Model with Math** Can you use a right triangle to represent the distance between any two points on the coordinate plane? Explain.

3. **Generalize** How does the fact that the points are on opposite sides of the *y*-axis affect the process of finding the distance between the two points?

Do You Know How?

In 4–6, use the coordinate plane below.

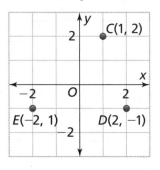

4. Find the distance between points *C* and *D*. Round to the nearest hundredth.

5. Find the perimeter of △*CDE*.

6. Point *B* is plotted on the coordinate plane above the *x*-axis. △*BDE* is equilateral. What are the coordinates of point *B* to the nearest hundredth?

Practice & Problem Solving

Scan for
Multimedia

7. Leveled Practice Use the Pythagorean Theorem
to find the distance between points *P* and *Q*.

Label the length, in units, of each leg of the right triangle.

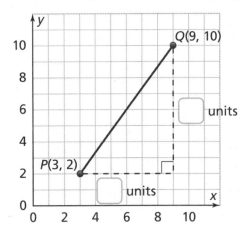

$c^2 = \boxed{}^2 + \boxed{}^2$

$c = \sqrt{\boxed{}}$

The distance between point *P* and point *Q* is

$\boxed{}$ units.

8. Find the perimeter of triangle *PQR*. Round
to the nearest hundredth.

9. Determine whether the triangle is equilateral,
isosceles, or scalene.

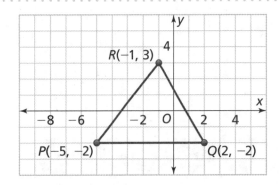

10. You walk along the outside of a park starting at point *P*.
Then you take a shortcut represented by $\overline{PQ}$ on the graph.

a. What is the length of the shortcut in meters?
Round to the nearest tenth of a meter.

b. What is the total length of your walk in the park?
Round to the nearest tenth of a meter.

Walking Through the Park

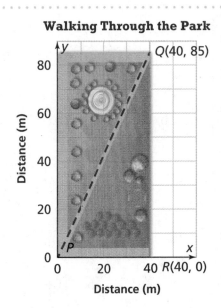

11. Suppose a park is located 3.6 miles east of your home. The library is 4.8 miles north of the park. What is the shortest distance between your home and the library?

12. **Use Structure** Point *B* has coordinates (2, 1). The *x*-coordinate of point *A* is −10. The distance between point *A* and point *B* is 15 units. What are the possible coordinates of point *A*?

13. **Higher Order Thinking** △*EFG* and △*HIJ* have the same perimeter and side lengths. The coordinates are *E*(6, 2), *F*(9, 2), *G*(8, 7), *H*(0, 0), and *I*(0, 3).

   a. What are possible coordinates of point *J*?

   b. Explain why there can be different possibilities for the coordinates for point *J*.

Assessment Practice

14. Find the distance, in units, between *P* and *R*. Round to the nearest tenth.

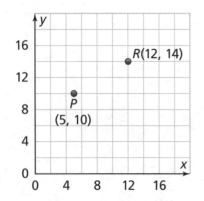

15. Find the distance, in units, between *A*(1, 5) and *B*(5.5, 9.25). Round to the nearest tenth.

? Topic Essential Question

How can you use the Pythagorean Theorem to solve problems?

Vocabulary Review

Complete each definition and then provide an example of each vocabulary word.

> **Vocabulary** Converse of the Pythagorean Theorem
> hypotenuse   leg   proof   Pythagorean Theorem

Definition	Example
1. A [ ] is a logical argument in which every statement of fact is supported by a reason.	
2. The [ ] states that if $a^2 + b^2 = c^2$ for side lengths a, b, and c of a triangle, then the triangle is a right triangle.	
3. The [ ] states that in a right triangle the sum of the squares of the lengths of the legs is equal to the square of the length of the hypotenuse.	

Use Vocabulary in Writing

All faces of the figure are rectangles. Explain how to find the length of d. Use vocabulary terms in your description.

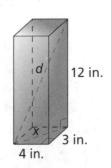

12 in.

3 in.

4 in.

Concepts and Skills Review

LESSON 12-1 Understand the Pythagorean Theorem

Quick Review

The **Pythagorean Theorem** states that, in a right triangle, the sum of the squares of the lengths of the legs, *a* and *b*, is equal to the square of the length of the hypotenuse, *c*. So, $a^2 + b^2 = c^2$.

Example

Find the length of the hypotenuse of a triangle with legs of 7 meters and 24 meters.

Substitute 7 for *a* and 24 for *b*. Then solve for *c*.

$$a^2 + b^2 = c^2$$
$$49 + 576 = c^2$$
$$\sqrt{625} = c$$

The length of the hypotenuse is 25 meters.

Practice

1. Find the length of the hypotenuse.

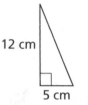

12 cm

5 cm

2. Find the unknown side length. Round to the nearest tenth.

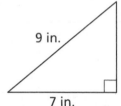

9 in.

7 in.

LESSON 12-2 Understand the Converse of the Pythagorean Theorem

Quick Review

For a triangle with side lengths *a*, *b*, and *c*, if $a^2 + b^2 = c^2$, then the triangle is a right triangle by the **Converse of the Pythagorean Theorem.**

Example

Is a triangle with side lengths of 8 m, 15 m, and 17 m a right triangle? Explain.

Substitute 8 for *a*, 15 for *b*, and 17 for *c*.

$$a^2 + b^2 \stackrel{?}{=} c^2$$
$$8^2 + 15^2 \stackrel{?}{=} 17^2$$
$$289 = 289 \ ✔$$

Because $a^2 + b^2 = c^2$, the triangle is a right triangle.

Practice

1. Is the triangle a right triangle? Explain.

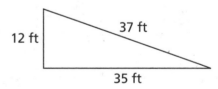

12 ft

37 ft

35 ft

2. A triangle has side lengths 1.5 inches, 2 inches, and 3 inches. Is the triangle a right triangle? Explain.

3. A triangle has side lengths 9 feet, 40 feet, and 41 feet. Is the triangle a right triangle? Explain.

Quick Review

The Pythagorean Theorem can be used to find unknown side lengths of an object that is shaped like a right triangle. It also can be used to find diagonal measures in certain two-dimensional and three-dimensional objects.

Example

A shipping box is 20 inches long along the diagonal of its base. Each diagonal of the box is 29 inches long. How tall is the box?

29 in.   ?   20 in.

Substitute 20 for a and 29 for c. Then solve for b.

$a^2 + b^2 = c^2$

$20^2 + b^2 = 29^2$

$400 + b^2 = 841$

$b = \sqrt{441}$

The height of the shipping box is 21 inches.

Practice

1. A basketball court is in the shape of a rectangle that is 94 feet long and 50 feet wide. What is the length of a diagonal of the court? Round to the nearest tenth.

2. A packaging box for a metal rod is 7.5 inches along a diagonal of the base. The height of the box is 18 inches. What is the length of a diagonal of the box?

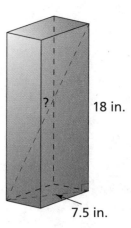

18 in.

7.5 in.

Quick Review

The Pythagorean Theorem can be used to find the distance between any two points on the coordinate plane.

Example

Find the distance between the two points on the coordinate plane. Round to the nearest tenth.

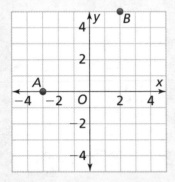

Draw a right triangle. Determine the lengths of its legs.

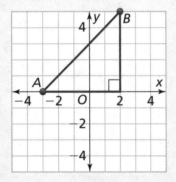

The length of the horizontal leg is 5 units.

The length of the vertical leg is 5 units.

Use the relationship $a^2 + b^2 = c^2$. Substitute 5 for a and 5 for b. Then solve for c.

$$a^2 + b^2 = c^2$$
$$5^2 + 5^2 = c^2$$
$$25 + 25 = c^2$$
$$50 = c^2$$
$$\sqrt{50} = c$$
$$7.1 \approx c$$

The distance between the two points is about 7.1 units.

Practice

1. Points C and D represent the location of two parks on a map. Find the distance between the parks if the length of each unit on the grid is equal to 25 miles. Round to the nearest mile.

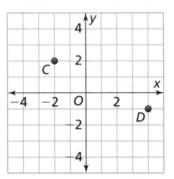

2. Find the perimeter of $\triangle ABC$. Round to the nearest tenth.

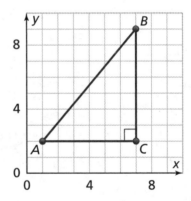

3. Triangle JKL is an equilateral triangle with two of its vertices at points J and K. What are the coordinates of point L? Round to the nearest tenth as needed.

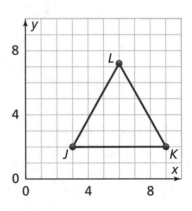

Riddle Rearranging

Solve each equation. Then arrange the answers in order from least to greatest. The letters will spell out the answer to the riddle below.

I can...
solve multistep equations.
© 8.EE.C.7b

N
$$6x - 1 = 2(2x - 3)$$

R
$$\frac{1}{5}x - 8 = 2x - 53$$

P
$$4(x + 11) = 56$$

S
$$\frac{3}{2}x + 20 = 2(x - 16)$$

A
$$11 - \frac{5}{2}x = x + 46$$

K
$$\frac{5}{8}x - 9 = 11$$

M
$$3(10 - x) = 60 - x$$

Y
$$1.9 - 7.1x = 1.9$$

E
$$7x - 14 = 5x + 17.2$$

Why did the coffee shop server love the job? Because there were so

.

TOPIC 13

SOLVE PROBLEMS INVOLVING SURFACE AREA AND VOLUME

? Topic Essential Question

How can you find volumes and surface areas of three-dimensional figures?

Topic Overview

13-1 Find Surface Area of Three-Dimensional Figures

13-2 Find Volume of Cylinders

13-3 Find Volume of Cones

13-4 Find Volume of Spheres

3-Act Mathematical Modeling: Measure Up

Topic Vocabulary

- composite figure
- cone
- cylinder
- sphere

Lesson Digital Resources

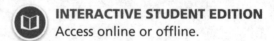

INTERACTIVE STUDENT EDITION
Access online or offline.

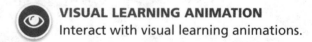

VISUAL LEARNING ANIMATION
Interact with visual learning animations.

ACTIVITY Use with *Solve & Discuss It, Explore*
and *Explain It* activities, and to explore Examp

VIDEOS Watch clips to support *3-Act
Mathematical Modeling Lessons* and *STEM Pr*

Go online

Measure
Up

Measure Up

Have you ever heard of the terms *griffin beaker*, *Erlenmeyer flask*, or *graduated cylinder*? Maybe you've used them in your science class.

Each piece of equipment in a chemistry lab has a specific purpose, so containers come in many shapes. It's sometimes necessary to pour a solution from one container to another. Think about this during the 3-Act Mathematical Modeling lesson.

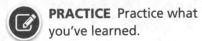 **PRACTICE** Practice what you've learned.

TUTORIALS Get help from *Virtual Nerd*, right when you need it.

MATH TOOLS Explore math with digital tools.

GAMES Play Math Games to help you learn.

KEY CONCEPT Review important lesson content.

GLOSSARY Read and listen to English/Spanish definitions.

ASSESSMENT Show what you've learned.

Did You Know?

The production of packaging is a huge industry employing over five million people with annual sales of more than 400 billion dollars.

Packaging materials protect and deliver food and products to consumers.

About **30%** of landfills are composed of polystyrene foam.

Polystyrene foam lasts forever!

A plastic bottle takes 450–1,000 years to biodegrade.

Seabirds are dying of starvation with stomachs full of plastic and Styrofoam.

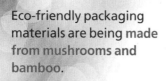

Eco-friendly packaging materials are being made from mushrooms and bamboo.

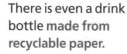

There is even a drink bottle made from recyclable paper.

New technology results in packaging materials that are both affordable and biodegradable.

Environmentally friendly companies are producing sustainable packaging. In addition to using recyclable materials, they reduce the water, natural resources, and energy needed for production. They minimize waste when designing products.

Your Task: Wrap it Up!

Engineers consider several factors when designing product packaging. These factors include cost efficiency and eco-friendly design so that materials are disposable, recyclable, biodegradable, and not wasted. Suppose you are an engineer working for Liquid Assets, an environmentally friendly company that designs, builds, and packages water purifiers. You and your classmates will use your knowledge of volume and surface area to determine an environmentally sound way to package the purifiers.

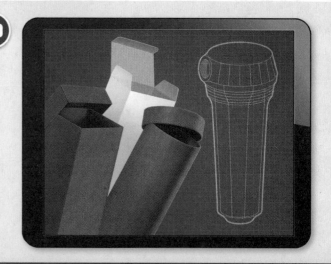

Review What You Know!

Vocabulary

Choose the best term from the box to complete each definition.

base
diameter
radius
three-dimensional
two-dimensional

1. The _____ is the distance from the center to the edge of a circle.

2. A shape that has length, width, and height is _____.

3. Any side of a cube can be considered a _____.

4. A shape that has length and width, but not height, is _____.

5. The _____ of a circle is a line segment that passes through its center and has endpoints on the circle.

Multiplying with Decimals

Find the product.

6. $14 \cdot 3.5 =$ [ ]

7. $9 \cdot 3.14 =$ [ ]

8. $4.2 \cdot 10.5 =$ [ ]

Areas of Circles

Find the area of each circle. Use 3.14 for π.

9.

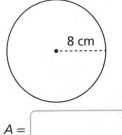

8 cm

$A =$ [ ]

10.

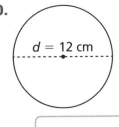

$d = 12$ cm

$A =$ [ ]

Use the Pythagorean Theorem

Find the missing side length of the triangle.

11.

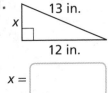

13 in.

x

12 in.

$x =$ [ ]

12.

30 m

x

24 m

$x =$ [ ]

Language Development

Complete the word web. Write key words, ideas, examples, or illustrations that connect to each new vocabulary term.

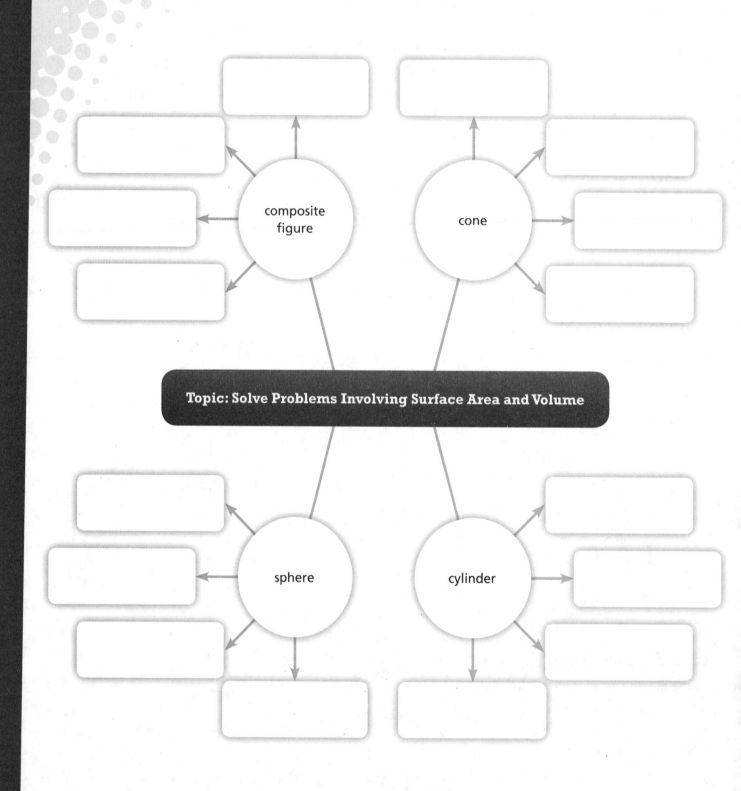

composite figure

cone

Topic: Solve Problems Involving Surface Area and Volume

sphere

cylinder

PROJECT 13A

What makes a
concert rock?

PROJECT: DESIGN PROPS OR
STAGE STRUCTURES

PROJECT 13B

What is the most
interesting museum
you have visited?

PROJECT: MAKE A MODEL
OF A MUSEUM

PROJECT 13C

Where around the United States can you find quarries?

PROJECT: POUR AND MEASURE SAND

PROJECT 13D

If you were cast in a play, would it be a comedy or a drama? Why?

PROJECT: WRITE A SKIT

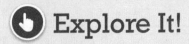 **Explore It!**

ACTIVITY

Andrea is designing the packaging for a tube-shaped container.

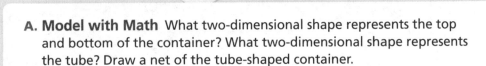

I can...
find the surface areas of cylinders, cones, and spheres.

 Common Core Content Standards
8.G.C.9

Mathematical Practices
MP.3, MP.4, MP.5, MP.6, MP.7, MP.8

A. Model with Math What two-dimensional shape represents the top and bottom of the container? What two-dimensional shape represents the tube? Draw a net of the tube-shaped container.

B. Look for Relationships The circular top and bottom fit perfectly on the ends of the container. How are the measures of the circles and the rectangle related?

Focus on math practices

Model with Math How can you check whether the net that you drew accurately represents the tube-shaped container?

VISUAL LEARNING   ASSE

EXAMPLE 1 Find the Surface Area of a Cylinder

Scan for Multimedia

A contractor builds porch columns that are painted on all surfaces with a protective sealant. If the contractor has enough sealant to cover 150 square feet, can he seal all of the surfaces of one column? Explain.

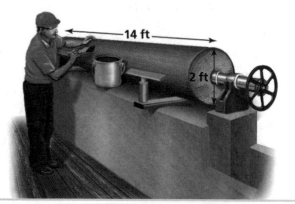

14 ft

2 ft

Look for Relationships How does knowing the area of a two-dimensional figure help you find the surface area of the column?

Draw a *cylinder* to represent the column. A **cylinder** is a three dimensional figure with two parallel circular bases that are the same size.

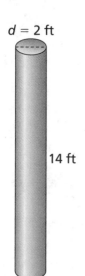

d = 2 ft

14 ft

Draw a net of the cylinder and find the area of each surface. Use 3.14 for π.

The two circles are identical.

$A = \pi r^2$
$= \pi(1)^2$
$\approx 3.14 \text{ ft}^2$

2 ft

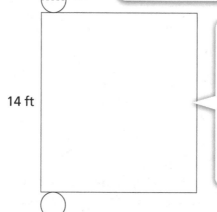

14 ft

The height, *h*, of the rectangle is the height of the cylinder and the base, *b*, is the circumference of the circle.

$A = bh$
$= 2\pi rh$
$= 2\pi(1)(14)$
$= 28\pi$
$\approx 87.92 \text{ ft}^2$

S.A. $\approx 2(3.14) + 87.92 \approx 94.2 \text{ ft}^2$

The contractor can seal all of the surfaces of one column because the surface area is less than 150 ft².

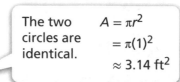 Try It!

What is the surface area of a cylinder with a height of 9.5 inches and a radius of 2.5 inches?

The surface area of the cylinder is ⬚ square inches.

Convince Me! How can you find the surface area of a cylinder if you only know its height and the circumference of its base?

S.A. = $2(\pi r^2) + (2\pi r)h$

$= 2\pi(\boxed{}^2) + 2\pi(\boxed{})(\boxed{})$

$= \boxed{}\pi + \boxed{}\pi$

$= \boxed{}\pi$

EXAMPLE 2 Find the Surface Area of a Cone

 ACTIVITY ASSESS

A manufacturer packages ice cream cones in paper. How much paper is needed to package one ice cream cone? Use 3.14 for π.

Draw the net of the *cone* to represent the packaging and find the area of each surface. A **cone** is a three-dimensional figure with one circular base and one vertex.

radius 1.5 in.

Ice Cream

6 in.

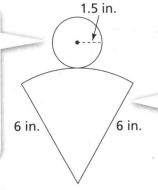

1.5 in.

6 in.   6 in.

Find the area of the circular base.

$A = \pi r^2$

$= \pi(1.5)^2$

$= 2.25\pi$

$\approx 7.065 \text{ in.}^2$

Find the area of the curved surface.

The slant height, ℓ, is 6.

$A = \pi r \ell$

$= \pi(1.5)(6)$

$= 9\pi$

$\approx 28.26 \text{ in.}^2$

S.A. $\approx 7.065 + 28.26 = 35.325 \text{ in.}^2$

About 35.325 in.² of paper are needed to package each ice cream cone.

EXAMPLE 3 Find the Surface Area of a Sphere

12 in.

James is making a model of Earth. He has enough blue paint to cover 500 in.². How can James determine whether he can paint the entire sphere blue?

Draw a *sphere* to represent the model of Earth. A **sphere** is the set of all points in space that are the same distance from a center point.

The radius, *r*, of the sphere is 6 in.

An open cylinder with the same radius as the sphere and a height of 2r has the same surface area as the sphere.

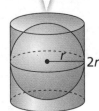

An open cylinder has no top or bottom surfaces.

r

2r

S.A. $= 2\pi rh$

$= 2\pi r(2r)$

$= 2 \cdot 2 \cdot \pi \cdot r \cdot r$

$= 4\pi r^2$

Use the formula to find the surface area of the model. Use 3.14 for π.

S.A. $= 4\pi r^2$

$= 4\pi(6)^2$

$= 4\pi(36)$

$= 144\pi$

$\approx 452.16 \text{ in.}^2$

James can paint the entire surface of his model blue.

Generalize The formula to find the surface area of a sphere with radius r is S.A. $= 4\pi r^2$.

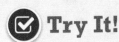 **Try It!**

a. What is the surface area of a cone with a radius of 7 feet and a slant height of 9 feet? Use $\frac{22}{7}$ for π.

b. What is the surface area of a sphere with a diameter of 2.7 inches? Use 3.14 for π.

Formulas for finding the area of polygons can be used to find the surface areas of cylinders, cones, and spheres.

Do You Understand?

1. **Essential Question** How are the areas of polygons used to find the surface area formulas for three-dimensional figures?

2. **Reasoning** Why is the length of the base of the rectangle the same as the circumference of the circles in the net of a cylinder?

3. **Construct Arguments** Aaron says that all cones with a base circumference of 8π inches will have the same surface area. Is Aaron correct? Explain.

Do You Know How?

4. What is the surface area of the cylinder? Use 3.14 for π, and round to the nearest tenth.

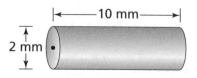

5. What is the surface area of the cone to the nearest tenth? Use 3.14 for π.

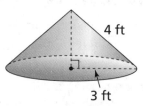

6. What is the surface area of the sphere in terms of π?

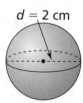

$d = 2$ cm

Practice & Problem Solving

Scan for
Multimedia

Leveled Practice In 7–8, find the surface area.

7. What is the surface area of the cylinder? Use 3.14 for π, and round to the nearest tenth.

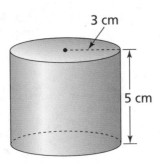

3 cm

5 cm

S.A. $= 2(\pi r^2) + (2(\pi r)h$

$= 2\pi(\quad^2) + 2\pi(\quad)(\quad)$

$= 2\pi(\quad) + 2\pi(\quad)$

$= \quad\pi + \quad\pi$

$= \quad\pi$

$\approx \quad$ cm^2

8. What is the surface area of the cone? Use $\frac{22}{7}$ for π.

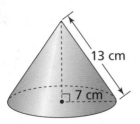

13 cm

7 cm

S.A. $= \pi r^2 + \pi \ell r$

$= \pi(\quad^2) + \pi(\quad)(\quad)$

$= \quad\pi + \quad\pi$

$= \quad\pi$

$\approx \quad$ cm^2

9. Construct Arguments Sasha incorrectly claimed that the surface area of the cylinder is about 76.9 square inches. Explain her likely error and find the correct surface area of the cylinder.

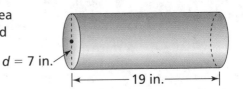

$d = 7$ in.

19 in.

10. A theme park has a ride that is located in half a sphere. The ride goes around the widest part of the sphere, which has a circumference of 514.96 yards. What is the surface area of the sphere? Estimate to the nearest hundredth using 3.14 for π.

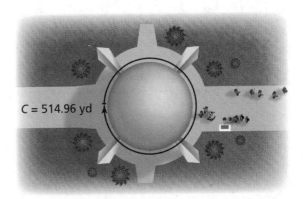

$C = 514.96$ yd

11. Find the amount of wrapping paper you need to wrap a gift in the cylindrical box shown. You need to cover the top, the bottom, and all the way around the box. Use 3.14 for π, and round to the nearest tenth.

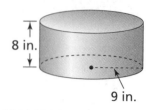

8 in.

9 in.

12. Donna paints ornaments for a school play. Each ornament is made up of two identical cones, as shown. How many bottles of paint does she need to paint 70 ornaments?

She uses one bottle of paint to cover 2,000 cm².

4.1 cm

8.9 cm

13. Higher Order Thinking

a. What is the surface area of the cone? Use 3.14 for π, and round to the nearest whole number.

b. **Reasoning** Suppose the diameter and the slant height of the cone are cut in half. How does this affect the surface area of the cone? Explain.

12 cm

$d = 6$ cm

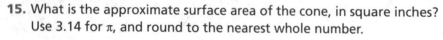

Assessment Practice

14. What is the surface area of the sphere? Use 3.14 for π, and round to the nearest tenth.

Ⓐ 254.5 cm²

Ⓑ 56.55 cm²

Ⓒ 1,017.4 cm²

Ⓓ 4,071.5 cm²

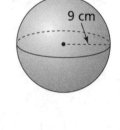

9 cm

15. What is the approximate surface area of the cone, in square inches? Use 3.14 for π, and round to the nearest whole number.

40 in.

$d = 40$ in.

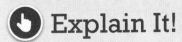 
Explain It!

Jenna and Ricardo are buying a new fish tank for the growing population of zebra fish in their science lab. Jenna says the tanks hold the same amount of water because they have the same dimensions. Ricardo says that he can fill the bottom of the rectangular tank with more cubes, so it can hold more water.

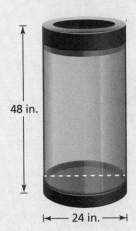

48 in.

|← 24 in. →|

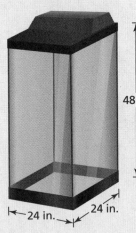

48 in.

|← 24 in. →| 24 in.

I can...
use what I know about finding volumes of rectangular prisms to find the volume of a cylinder.

Common Core Content Standards
8.G.C.9

Mathematical Practices
MP.2, MP.3, MP.5, MP.6, MP.7

A. Look for Relationships How are the shapes of the two fish tanks alike? How are they different?

B. Critique Arguments Who do you think is correct, Ricardo or Jenna? Explain.

Focus on math practices

Use Structure How can you use what you know about areas of two-dimensional figures and volumes of prisms to compare the volumes of the fish tanks?

VISUAL LEARNING ASS

EXAMPLE 1 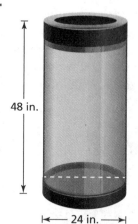 Relate Volumes of Rectangular Prisms and Cylinders

Scan for Multimedia

Jenna and Ricardo need to buy a tank that is large enough for 25 zebra fish. The tank needs to have a volume of 2,310 cubic inches. How can Jenna and Ricardo determine whether the cylindrical tank can hold the zebra fish?

Look for Relationships Remember, volume is the measure of the amount of space inside a solid figure. You can find the volume by filling the solid with unit cubes.

48 in.

24 in.

Like you did to find the volume of a prism, fill the base of the cylinder with one layer of unit cubes and stack the layers to fill the cylinder.

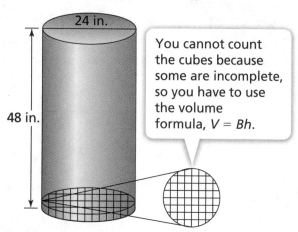

24 in.

48 in.

You cannot count the cubes because some are incomplete, so you have to use the volume formula, $V = Bh$.

Use the formula to find the volume of the cylinder. Use 3.14 for π.

$$V = Bh$$
$$= \pi r^2 \cdot h$$
$$\approx 3.14 \cdot (12)^2 \cdot 48$$
$$= 21{,}703.68 \text{ in.}^3$$

The base of a cylinder is a circle, so the area of the base $B = \pi r^2$.

The cylindrical tank is large enough for the 25 zebra fish.

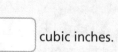 **Try It!**

The area of the base of the cylinder is 78.5 in.^{2}. What is the volume of the cylinder?

$V = Bh$

$= \boxed{} \cdot \boxed{}$

$= \boxed{}$

The volume of the cylinder is $\boxed{}$ cubic inches.

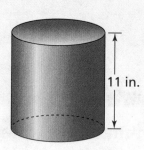

11 in.

Convince Me! Why can you use the formula $V = Bh$ to find the volume of a cylinder?

EXAMPLE 2 Find an Unknown Measure

The volume of the juice can is 300 milliliters, which is equal to 300 cubic centimeters. What is the radius of the can? Use 3.14 for π, and round your answer to the nearest tenth.

14 cm

Use the formula $V = Bh$ to find the radius of the base of the can.

$$V = Bh$$

$$300 = \pi r^2 \cdot 14$$

$$300 = 43.96r^2$$

$$6.82 \approx r^2$$

$$2.6 \approx r$$

The radius of the can is about 2.6 centimeters.

EXAMPLE 3 Solve Problems Involving Volume of a Cylinder

Safety barrels are used on some highways to cushion cars on impact. If a city manager approves the purchase of 15 cubic meters of sand, how many barrels can be filled with sand? Use 3.14 for π.

The diameter is 0.9 m.

The height is 1.2 m.

STEP 1 Find the volume of each safety barrel.

$$V = Bh$$

$$= \pi r^2 h$$

$$= \pi(0.45)^2 1.2$$

The diameter is 0.9 meter, so the radius is 0.45 meter.

$$V \approx 0.76302 \text{ m}^3$$

STEP 2 Find the number of barrels that can be filled.

$$\frac{15}{0.76302} \approx 19.7$$

The city manager purchased enough sand to fill 19 safety barrels.

Try It!

Lin is building a cylindrical planter with a base diameter of 15 inches. She has 5,000 cubic inches of soil to fill her planter. What is the height of the largest planter Lin can build? Use 3.14 for π, and round to the nearest inch.

The formula for the volume of a cylinder is the same as the formula for the volume of a prism. The formula for volume of a cylinder is $V = Bh$, where B is the area of the circular base and h is the height of the cylinder.

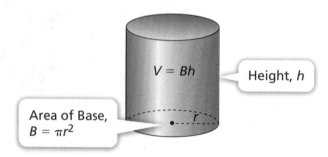

$V = Bh$

Height, h

Area of Base,
$B = \pi r^2$

r

Do You Understand?

1. **? Essential Question** How is the volume of a cylinder related to the volume of a rectangular prism?

2. **Use Structure** What two measurements do you need to know to find the volume of a cylinder?

3. **Reasoning** Cylinder A has a greater radius than Cylinder B. Does Cylinder A necessarily have a greater volume than Cylinder B? Explain.

Do You Know How?

4. What is the volume of the cylinder? Express your answer in terms of π.

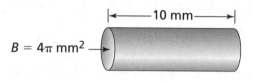

$B = 4\pi$ mm^2

|←———10 mm———→|

5. What is the approximate height of the cylinder? Use 3.14 for π, and if necessary, round to the nearest tenth.

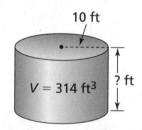

10 ft

$V = 314$ ft^3

? ft

6. What is the volume of the cylinder? Use 3.14 for π, and if necessary, round to the nearest tenth.

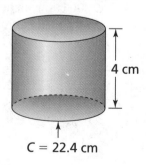

4 cm

$C = 22.4$ cm

Practice & Problem Solving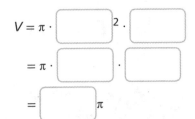

7. Leveled Practice What is the volume of a cylinder
with a radius of 5 centimeters and height of 2.5 centimeters? Use 3.14 for π.

$V = \pi \cdot \boxed{}^2 \cdot \boxed{}$

$= \pi \cdot \boxed{} \cdot \boxed{}$

$= \boxed{}\,\pi$

The volume of the cylinder is about $\boxed{}$ cubic centimeters.

---

8. Find the volume of each cylinder in terms of π.
Which cylinder has the greater volume?

Cylinder A: Area of Base = 6π ft², height = 10 ft
Cylinder B: Circumference = 6π ft, height = 6 ft

9. The volume of a cylinder is 225π cubic inches,
and the height of the cylinder is 1 inch. What
is the radius of the cylinder?

---

10. A company is designing a new cylindrical water bottle. The volume
of the bottle is 103 cubic centimeters. What is the radius of the
water bottle? Estimate using 3.14 for π, and round to the nearest
hundredth.

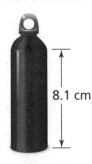

8.1 cm

---

11. Use the figure at the right.

  a. Find the volume of the cylinder in terms of π.

  b. Is the volume of a cylinder, which has the
same radius but twice the height, greater or
less than the original cylinder? Explain.

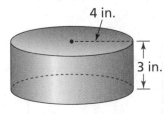

4 in.

3 in.

---

12. Reasoning A rectangular piece of cardboard with dimensions 6 inches
by 8 inches is used to make the curved side of a cylinder-shaped
container. Using this cardboard, what is the greatest volume the cylinder
can hold? Explain.

13. The cylinder shown has a volume of 885 cubic inches.

   a. What is the radius of the cylinder? Use 3.14 for π.

   b. Reasoning If the height of the cylinder is changed, but the volume stays the same, then how will the radius change? Explain.

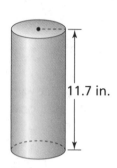

11.7 in.

---

14. Toy rubber balls are packaged in a cylinder that holds 3 balls. Find the volume of the cylinder. Use 3.14 for π, and round to the nearest tenth.

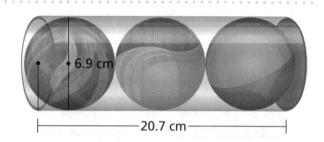

6.9 cm

20.7 cm

---

15. Higher Order Thinking An insulated collar is made to cover a pipe. Find the volume of the material used to make the collar. Let *r* = 3 inches, *R* = 5 inches, and *h* = 21 inches. Use 3.14 for π, and round to the nearest hundredth.

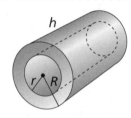

h

r *R*

✅ Assessment Practice

16. The volume of a cylinder is 1,029π cubic centimeters. The height of the cylinder is 21 centimeters. What is the radius, to the nearest centimeter, of the cylinder?

17. The diameter of a cylinder is 7 yards. The height is 12 yards. What is the volume, in terms of π and to the nearest cubic yard, of the cylinder?

18. A cylinder is shown. What statements about the cylinder are true?

   ☐ The radius of the cylinder is 2 ft.

   ☐ The diameter of the cylinder is 4 yd.

   ☐ The height of the cylinder is 8 in.

   ☐ The volume of the cylinder is 32 in.²

   ☐ The volume of the cylinder is 32π in.³

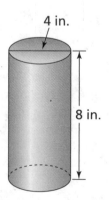

4 in.

8 in.

1. Vocabulary Select all the statements that describe surface area and volume. *Lessons 13-1 and 13-2*

☐ Surface area is the sum of the areas of all the surfaces of a figure.

☐ Volume is the distance around a figure.

☐ Surface area is a three-dimensional measure.

☐ Volume is the amount of space a figure occupies.

☐ Volume is a three-dimensional measure.

In **2–4**, use the figure at the right. Sallie packed a cone-shaped cup inside of a cylindrical package.

2. The cone-shaped cup is made out of paper. How much paper was used to make the cup, excluding the opening at the top of the cup? Use 3.14 for π, and round to the nearest tenth. *Lesson 13-1*

33 cm

|←—20 cm—→|

3. The cylindrical package is made out of cardboard. In terms of π, how much cardboard was used to make the package? *Lesson 13-1*

4. How much space does the package occupy in terms of π? *Lesson 13-1*

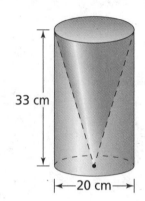

3 ft

5. What is the surface area of the sphere in terms of π? *Lesson 13-1*

6. The volume of the cylinder is 400π cm³. What is the height of the cylinder? *Lesson 13-2*

Ⓐ 5 cm

Ⓑ 16 cm

Ⓒ 25 cm

Ⓓ 80 cm

|←—10 cm—→|

How well did you do on the mid-topic checkpoint? Fill in the stars.

☆ ☆ ☆

MID-TOPIC PERFORMANCE TASK

Melissa designed a sculpture in which a cylinder-shaped section was removed from a cube.

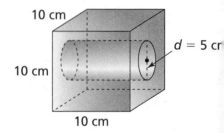

10 cm

10 cm

10 cm

d = 5 cr

PART A

Before painting the surface of the sculpture, Melissa wants to sand the surface where the cylinder section was removed. What is the surface area of the section she will sand? Use 3.14 for π. Explain how you found the surface area.

PART B

Melissa has a can of spray paint that covers about 6,500 square centimeters. Can Melissa apply two coats of paint to the entire sculpture? Explain. Use 3.14 for π.

PART C

What is the volume of the sculpture? Use 3.14 for π.

Solve & Discuss It!  ACTIVITY

A landscape architect uses molds for casting rectangular pyramids and rectangular prisms to make garden statues. He plans to place each finished pyramid on top of a prism. If one batch of concrete mix makes one prism or three pyramids, how does the volume of one pyramid compare to the volume of one prism? Explain.

Look for Relationships What do you notice about the dimensions of the bases of the pyramid and prism? How are the heights of the two solids related?

I can...
find the volume of cones.

© **Common Core Content Standards**
8.G.C.9

Mathematical Practices
MP.1, MP.2, MP.7

Focus on math practices

Make Sense and Persevere If the architect mixes 10 batches of concrete, how many sculptures combining 1 prism and 1 pyramid could he make? Explain.

VISUAL LEARNING ASSES

EXAMPLE 1 ▸ 👁 **Find the Volume of a Cone**

Scan for Multimedia

Kiara is filling a cone-shaped pastry bag with frosting from a cylinder-shaped container. How much frosting can the pastry bag hold? How can Kiara determine how many times she can fill the pastry bag?

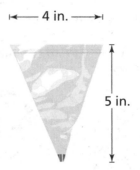
← 4 in. →
5 in.

← 4 in. →
5 in.

Look for Relationships How are a pyramid and a cone alike? How are they different?

Draw a cylinder to represent the container of frosting and a cone to represent the pastry bag.

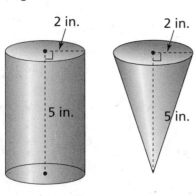
2 in.
5 in.

2 in.
5 in.

The volumes of a cone and a cylinder with the same base and height are related in the same way as the volumes of a pyramid and a prism with the same base and height.

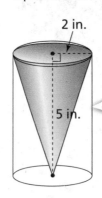
2 in.
5 in.

The volume of the cone is $\frac{1}{3}$ the volume of the cylinder. $V = \frac{1}{3}Bh$

Find the volume of the pastry bag. Use 3.14 for π.

$V = \frac{1}{3}Bh$

$= \frac{1}{3}\pi r^2 \cdot h$

$\approx \frac{1}{3} \cdot 3.14 \cdot (2)^2 \cdot 5$

$\approx 20.93 \text{ in.}^3$

The pastry bag can hold about 20.93 cubic inches of frosting. The bag can be filled three times from the container of frosting.

✅ **Try It!**

Find the volume of the cone. Use 3.14 for π.

The volume of the cone is about ☐ cubic inches.

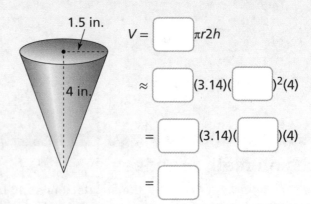
1.5 in.
4 in.

$V = \boxed{} \pi r2h$

$\approx \boxed{} (3.14)(\boxed{})^2(4)$

$= \boxed{} (3.14)(\boxed{})(4)$

$= \boxed{}$

Convince Me! If you know the volume of a cone, how can you find the volume of a cylinder that has the same height and radius as the cone?

EXAMPLE 2   ACTIVITY ASSESS

EXAMPLE 2 — Apply the Pythagorean Theorem to Solve Volume Problems

Midori has a cone full of birdseed to feed the birds at the park. What is the volume of the birdseed in the cone?

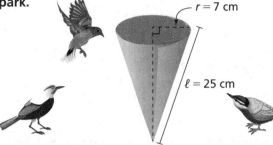

$r = 7$ cm

$\ell = 25$ cm

> **Look for Relationships** How can you use the Pythagorean Theorem to find the height of the cone?

STEP 1 Use the Pythagorean Theorem to find the height of the cone.

$$r^2 + h^2 = \ell^2$$
$$7^2 + h^2 = 25^2$$
$$49 + h^2 = 625$$
$$h^2 = 576$$
$$h = 24$$

The height of the cone is 24 centimeters.

STEP 2 Find the volume of the cone. Use $\frac{22}{7}$ for π.

$$V = \frac{1}{3}\pi r^2 h$$
$$= \frac{1}{3}\pi(7)^2(24)$$
$$\approx \frac{1}{3}\left(\frac{22}{7}\right)(49)(24)$$
$$= 1{,}232$$

> Substitute the height of the cone from STEP 1.

The cone holds about 1,232 cubic centimeters of birdseed.

EXAMPLE 3 — Find the Volume of a Cone Given the Circumference of the Base

The circumference of the base of a cone is 6π inches. What is the volume of the cone in terms of π?

13 in.

STEP 1 Use the circumference to find the radius of the base of the cone.

$$C = 2\pi r$$
$$6\pi = 2\pi r$$
$$\frac{6\pi}{2\pi} = r$$
$$3 = r$$

> Substitute 6π for the circumference C.

The radius of the cone is 3 inches.

STEP 2 Find the volume of the cone.

$$V = \frac{1}{3}\pi(3)^2(13)$$
$$= \frac{1}{3}\pi(9)(13)$$
$$= 39\pi$$

> Substitute the radius of the cone from STEP 1.

The volume of the cone is 39π inches.

✓ Try It!

Find the volume of each cone.

a. Use $\frac{22}{7}$ for π. Express the answer as a fraction.

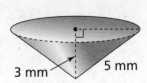

3 mm   5 mm

b. Express the volume in terms of π.

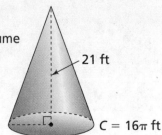

21 ft

$C = 16\pi$ ft

KEY CONCEPT

The volume of a cone is $\frac{1}{3}$ the volume of a cylinder with the same base and height. The formula for the volume of a cone is $V = \frac{1}{3} Bh$, where B is the area of the base and h is the height of the cone.

Do You Understand?

1. **Essential Question** How is the volume of a cone related to the volume of a cylinder?

2. **Use Structure** What dimensions do you need to find the volume of a cone?

3. **Look for Relationships** If you know a cone's radius and slant height, what must you do before you can find its volume?

Do You Know How?

4. Wanda found a cone-shaped seashell on the beach. The shell has a height of 63 millimeters and a base radius of 8 millimeters. What is the volume of the seashell? Estimate using $\frac{22}{7}$ for π.

63 mm

8 mm

5. What is the volume of the cone? Estimate using 3.14 for π, and round to the nearest tenth.

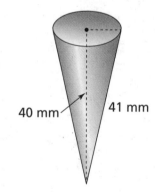

40 mm   41 mm

6. What is the volume of the cone in terms of π if the circumference of the base is 1.4π feet?

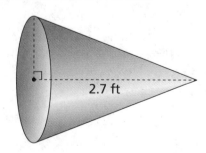

2.7 ft

Practice & Problem Solving

Leveled Practice In 7 and 8, find the volumes of the cones.

7. What is the volume of the cone? Write your answer in terms of π.

$V = \frac{1}{3}\pi(\boxed{})^2(\boxed{})$

$V = \frac{1}{3}\pi(\boxed{})(\boxed{})$

$V = \frac{1}{3}\pi(\boxed{})$

$V = \boxed{}\,\pi$ cubic meters

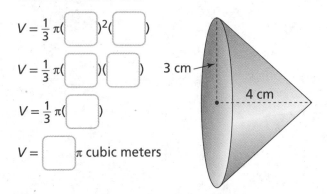
3 cm
4 cm

8. What is the volume of the cone to the nearest hundredth? Use 3.14 for π.

$V \approx \frac{1}{3}(3.14)(\boxed{})^2(\boxed{})$

$V = \frac{1}{3}(3.14)(\boxed{})(\boxed{})$

$V = \frac{1}{3}(\boxed{})$

$V = \boxed{}$ units³

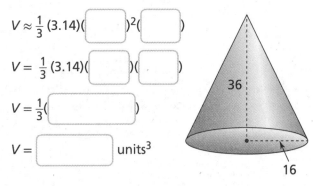
36
16

9. If a cone-shaped hole is 3 feet deep and the circumference of the base of the hole is 44 feet, what is the volume of the hole? Use $\frac{22}{7}$ for π.

10. The volume of the cone is 462 cubic yards. What is the radius of the cone? Use $\frac{22}{7}$ for π.

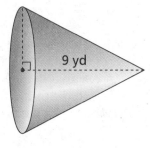
9 yd

11. A city engineer determines that 5,500 cubic meters of sand will be needed to combat erosion at the city's beach. Does the city have enough sand to combat the erosion? Use $\frac{22}{7}$ for π. Explain.

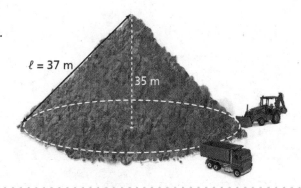
ℓ = 37 m
35 m

12. A water tank is shaped like the cone shown.

a. How much water can the tank hold? Use 3.14 for π, and round to the nearest tenth.

b. If water is drained from the tank to fill smaller tanks that each hold 500 cubic feet of water, how many smaller tanks can be filled?

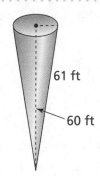
61 ft
60 ft

13. An ice cream cone is filled exactly level with the top of a cone. The cone has a 9-centimeter depth and a base with a circumference of 9π centimeters. How much ice cream is in the cone in terms of π?

14. In the scale model of a park, small green cones represent trees. What is the volume of one green cone? Use $\frac{22}{7}$ for π.

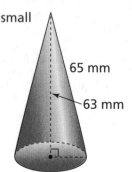

65 mm

63 mm

15. Reasoning Compare the volumes of two cones. One has a radius of 5 feet and a slant height of 13 feet. The other one has a height of 5 feet and a slant height of 13 feet.

a. Which cone has the greater volume?

b. What is the volume of the larger cone in terms of π?

16. An artist makes a cone-shaped sculpture for an art exhibit. If the sculpture is 7 feet tall and has a base with a circumference of 24.492 feet, what is the volume of the sculpture? Use 3.14 for π, and round to the nearest hundredth.

17. Higher Order Thinking A cone has a radius of 3 and a height of 11.

a. Suppose the radius is increased by 4 times its original measure. How many times greater is the volume of the larger cone than the smaller cone?

b. How would the volume of the cone change if the radius were divided by four?

Assessment Practice

18. List the cones described below in order from least volume to greatest volume.

- Cone 1: radius 6 cm and height 12 cm
- Cone 2: radius 12 cm and height 6 cm
- Cone 3: radius 9 cm and height 8 cm

Ⓐ Cone 2, Cone 3, Cone 1

Ⓑ Cone 1, Cone 3, Cone 2

Ⓒ Cone 2, Cone 1, Cone 3

Ⓓ Cone 1, Cone 2, Cone 3

19. What is the volume, in cubic inches, of a cone that has a radius of 8 inches and a height of 12 inches? Use 3.14 for π, and round to the nearest hundredth.

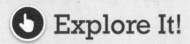 
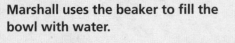 **Explore It!**

Marshall uses the beaker to fill the bowl with water.

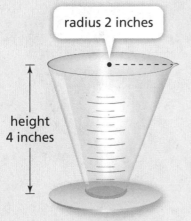

radius 2 inches

height 4 inches

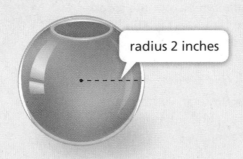

radius 2 inches

I can...
find the volume of a sphere and use it to solve problems.

© **Common Core Content Standards**
8.G.C.9

Mathematical Practices
MP.2, MP.3, MP.6, MP.7, MP.8

A. Draw and label three-dimensional figures to represent the beaker and the bowl.

B. Marshall has to fill the beaker twice to completely fill the bowl with water. How can you use an equation to represent the volume of the bowl?

Focus on math practices

Reasoning How are the volume of a sphere and the volume of a cone related? What must be true about the radius and height measurements for this relationships to be valid?

807

? **Essential Question** How is the volume of a sphere related to the volume of a cone?

EXAMPLE 1 Relate Volumes of Cones and Spheres

Scan for Multimedia

Taye fills the gumball machine using two full cone-shaped scoops. The globe of the gumball machine and the scoop have the same radius and height. How can Taye find a formula to calculate the volume of the gumball machine globe?

$r = 6$ in.

$h = 12$ in.

$r = 6$ in.

> **Look for Relationships** How can you use the formula for the volume of a cone to determine the formula for the volume of a sphere?

Draw a sphere to represent the globe of the gumball machine.

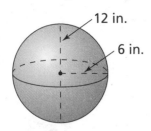

12 in.

6 in.

The volume of a sphere is the same as twice the volume of a cone with the same circular base and height.

Use the volume formula for a cone to write the volume formula for a sphere.

Volume of a sphere = 2(Volume of a cone)

$V = 2\left(\frac{1}{3} Bh\right)$

$= 2\left(\frac{1}{3} \pi r^2 h\right)$

$= 2\left(\frac{1}{3} \pi r^2 \cdot 2r\right)$ — The height of a sphere is twice its radius.

$= \frac{4}{3} \pi r^3$

> **Generalize** The formula for the volume of a sphere is $V = \frac{4}{3}\pi r^3$.

Find the volume of the globe of the gumball machine. Use 3.14 for π.

$V = \frac{4}{3} \pi r^3$

$= \frac{4}{3} \pi (6)^3$

$= \frac{4}{3} \pi (216)$

$= 288\pi$

≈ 904.32

The volume of the globe is about 904.32 cubic inches.

☑ **Try It!**

What is the volume of a ball with a diameter of 6 centimeters? Use 3.14 for π.

Convince Me! How is the volume of a sphere related to the volume of a cone that has the same circular base and height?

$V = \frac{4}{3} \pi r^3$

$= \frac{4}{3} \pi \boxed{}^3$

$\approx \boxed{} \cdot \boxed{}$

$= \boxed{}$

The volume of the ball is about $\boxed{}$ cm³.

EXAMPLE 2  Find the Volume of a Sphere Given the Surface Area

What is the volume of the soccer ball, rounded to the nearest whole number? Use 3.14 for π.

S.A. ≈ 1,519.76 cm²

STEP 1 A sphere represents the soccer ball. Find the radius of the soccer ball.

$$S.A. = 4\pi r^2$$

$$1,519.76 = 4\pi r^2$$

$$\frac{1,519.76}{4 \cdot 3.14} \approx r^2$$

$$121 = r^2$$

$$11 = r$$

The radius is about 11 centimeters.

STEP 2 Find the volume of the soccer ball.

$$V = \frac{4}{3}\pi r^3$$

$$= \frac{4}{3}\pi (11)^3$$

$$= \frac{4}{3}\pi (1,331)$$

Substitute the radius of the soccer ball from STEP 1.

$$\approx \left(\frac{5,324}{3}\right) \cdot 3.14$$

$$\approx 5,572.45$$

The volume of the soccer ball is approximately 5,572 cubic centimeters.

EXAMPLE 3 Find the Volume of a Composite Figure

A composite figure is the combination of two or more figures into one object. A corn silo is an example of a composite figure in the shape of a cylinder with a hemisphere of the same diameter on top. The diameter of this silo is 4 meters. How many cubic meters of corn can be stored in the silo? Use 3.14 for π.

4 m

10 m

STEP 1 Find the volume of the hemisphere.

$$V = \frac{1}{2} \cdot \frac{4}{3}\pi r^3$$

A hemisphere is half of a sphere.

$$= \frac{1}{2} \cdot \frac{4}{3}\pi (2)^3$$

$$= \frac{1}{2} \cdot \frac{4}{3}(8)\pi$$

$$= \frac{16}{3}\pi$$

The volume of the hemisphere is $\frac{16}{3}\pi$ cubic meters.

STEP 2 Find the volume of the cylinder.

$$V = \pi r^2 h$$

$$= \pi (2)^2 (10)$$

$$= \pi (4)(10)$$

$$= 40\pi$$

The volume of the cylinder is 40π m³.

STEP 3 Add the volumes.

$$\frac{16}{3}\pi + 40\pi = \frac{136}{3}\pi \approx 142.3$$

The volume of the silo is about 142.3 cubic meters.

 **Try It!**

What is the volume of the composite figure shown? Use 3.14 for π.

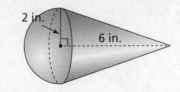

2 in.

6 in.

The volume of a sphere is twice the volume of a cone that has the same circular base and height. The formula for the volume of a sphere with radius r is $V = \frac{4}{3}\pi r^3$.

Do You Understand?

1. **? Essential Question** How is the volume of a sphere related to the volume of a cone?

2. **Critique Reasoning** Kristy incorrectly says that the volume of the sphere below is 144π cubic units. What mistake might Kristy have made?

3. **Generalize** Mehnaj has a set of blocks that are all the same height. The cone-shaped block has a volume of 125 cubic inches. The sphere-shaped block has a volume of 250 cubic inches. What do you know about the radius of the base of the cone-shaped block? Explain.

Do You Know How?

4. Clarissa has a decorative bulb in the shape of a sphere. If it has a radius of 3 inches, what is its volume? Use 3.14 for π.

5. A sphere has a surface area of about 803.84 square centimeters. What is the volume of the sphere? Use 3.14 for π and round to the nearest whole number.

6. A water pipe is a cylinder 30 inches long, with a radius of 1 inch. At one end of the cylinder there is a hemisphere. What is the volume of the water pipe? Explain.

Practice & Problem Solving

Scan for
Multimedia

7. Leveled Practice What is the amount of air, in cubic centimeters, needed to fill the stability ball? Use 3.14 for π, and round to the nearest whole number.

Use the formula $V = \frac{4}{3}\pi r^3$.

55 cm

$$V = \frac{4}{3}\pi()^3$$

$$V = \frac{4}{3}\pi()$$

$$V \approx \frac{4}{3}()()$$

$$V \approx \boxed{}$$

The volume of the stability ball is approximately $\boxed{}$ cubic centimeters.

---

8. A spherical balloon has a 22-inch. diameter when it is fully inflated. Half of the air is let out of the balloon. Assume that the balloon remains a sphere. Keep all answers in terms of π.

a. Find the volume of the fully-inflated balloon.

b. Find the volume of the half-inflated balloon.

c. What is the radius of the half-inflated balloon? Round to the nearest tenth.

9. Find the volume of the figure. Use 3.14 for π, and round to the nearest whole number.

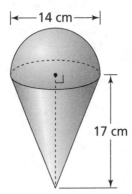

|←—14 cm—→|

17 cm

---

10. The surface area of a sphere is about 2,826 square millimeters. What is the volume of the sphere? Use 3.14 for π, and round to the nearest whole number.

11. A sphere has a volume of 1,837.35 cubic centimeters. What is the radius of the sphere? Use 3.14 for π, and round to the nearest tenth.

12. Find the volume of the solid. Use 3.14 for π, and round to the nearest whole number.

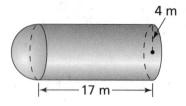
4 m

17 m

13. Your friend says that the volume of a sphere with a diameter of 3.4 meters is 164.55 cubic meters. What mistake might your friend have made? Find the correct volume. Use 3.14 for π and round to the nearest hundredth.

14. A solid figure has a cone and hemisphere hollowed out of it. What is the volume of the remaining part of the solid? Use 3.14 for π, and round to the nearest whole number.

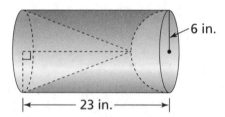

6 in.

23 in.

15. Higher Order Thinking A student was asked to find the volume of a solid where the inner cylinder is hollow. She incorrectly said the volume is 2,034.72 cubic inches.

   a. Find the volume of the solid. Use 3.14 for π. Round to the nearest whole number.

   b. What mistake might the student have made?

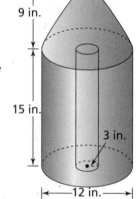

9 in.

15 in.

3 in.

12 in.

16. A spherical boulder is 20 feet in diameter and weighs almost 8 tons. Find its volume. Use 3.14 for π. Round to the nearest cubic foot.

17. A bowl is in the shape of a hemisphere (half a sphere) with a diameter of 13 inches. Find the volume of the bowl. Use 3.14 for π, and round to the nearest cubic inch.

3-ACT MATH

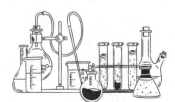

Measure
Up

3-Act Mathematical Modeling: Measure Up

Go Online

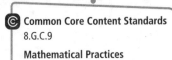
Common Core Content Standards
8.G.C.9
Mathematical Practices
MP.4, MP.1, MP.2, MP.3, MP.7, MP.8

ACT 1

1. After watching the video, what is the first question that comes to mind?

2. Write the Main Question you will answer.

3. Construct Arguments Predict an answer to this Main Question. Explain your prediction.

4. On the number line below, write a number that is too small to be the answer. Write a number that is too large.

Too small   Too large

5. Plot your prediction on the same number line.

6. What information in this situation would be helpful to know? How would you use that information?

7. **Use Appropriate Tools** What tools can you use to solve the problem? Explain how you would use them strategically.

8. **Model with Math** Represent the situation using mathematics. Use your representation to answer the Main Question.

9. What is your answer to the Main Question? Is it higher or lower than your prediction? Explain why.

10. Write the answer you saw in the video.

11. Reasoning Does your answer match the answer in the video? If not, what are some reasons that would explain the difference?

12. Make Sense and Persevere Would you change your model now that you know the answer? Explain.

Reflect

13. Model with Math Explain how you used a mathematical model to represent the situation. How did the model help you answer the Main Question?

14. Make Sense and Persevere When did you struggle most while solving the problem? How did you overcome that obstacle?

SEQUEL

15. Generalize Suppose you have a graduated cylinder half the height of the one in the video. How wide does the cylinder need to be to hold the liquid in the flask?

? Topic Essential Question

How can you find volumes and surface areas of three-dimensional figures?

Vocabulary Review

Complete each definition and then provide an example of each vocabulary word.

Vocabulary composite figure   cone   cylinder   sphere

Definition	Example
1. A three-dimensional figure with two identical circular bases is a [____] .	
2. A three-dimensional figure with one circular base and one vertex is a [____] .	
3. A [____] is the set of all points in space that are the same distance from a center point.	
4. A [____] is the combination of two or more figures into one object.	

Use Vocabulary in Writing

Draw a composite figure that includes any two of the following: a cylinder, a cone, a sphere, and a hemisphere. Label each part of your drawing. Then describe each part of your composite figure. Use vocabulary terms in your description.

Concepts and Skills Review

Quick Review

Surface area is the total area of the surfaces of a three-dimensional figure. The chart gives formulas for finding the surface area of a cylinder, a cone, and a sphere.

Shape	3-D Model	Surface Area Formula
cylinder		S.A. = $2\pi r^2 + 2\pi rh$
cone		S.A. = $\pi r\ell + \pi r^2$
sphere		S.A. = $4\pi r^2$

Example

What is the surface area of the cylinder? Use 3.14 for π.

> Radius, $r = \frac{10}{2} = 5$. Substitute 5 for r and 15 for h.

S.A. = $2\pi r^2 + 2\pi rh$

$\quad = 2\pi(5)^2 + 2\pi(5)(15)$

$\quad = 50\pi + 150\pi$

$\quad = 200\pi \approx 628$ cm²

15 cm

|← 10 cm →|

Practice

1. What is the surface area of the cone? Use 3.14 for π.

13 m

5 m

2. What is the surface area of the sphere in terms of π?

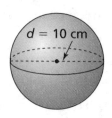

$d = 10$ cm

3. What is the surface area of the cylinder in terms of π?

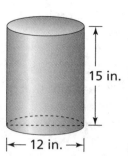

15 in.

|← 12 in. →|

Quick Review

The volume of a cylinder is equal to the area of its base times its height.

V = area of base · height, or V = πr2h

Example

What is the volume of the cylinder? Use 3.14 for π.

> Radius, $r = \frac{40}{2} = 20$. Substitute 20 for r and 60 for h.

$V = \pi r^2 h$

$\quad = \pi(20)^2(60)$

$\quad = 24{,}000\pi \approx 75{,}360 \text{ cm}^3$

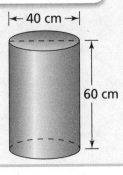

|← 40 cm →|

60 cm

Practice

1. What is the volume of the cylinder in terms of π?

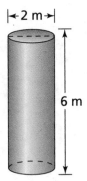

|← 2 m →|

6 m

2. The volume of the cylinder is 141.3 cubic centimeters. What is the radius of the cylinder? Use 3.14 for π.

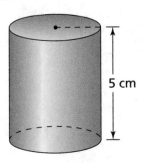

5 cm

ESSON **13-3** Find Volume of Cones

Quick Review

To find the volume of a cone, use the formula $V = \frac{1}{3}\pi r^2 h$.

Example

What is the volume of the cone? Use 3.14 for π.

> Substitute 6 for r and 9 for h.

$V = \frac{1}{3}\pi r^2 h$

$\quad = \frac{1}{3}\pi(6)^2(9)$

$\quad = 108\pi \approx 339.12 \text{ in.}^3$

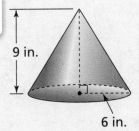

9 in.

6 in.

Practice

1. What is the volume of the cone in terms of π?

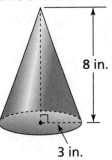

8 in.

3 in.

2. What is the volume of the cone? Use 3.14 for π.

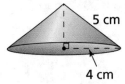

5 cm

4 cm

Quick Review

To find the volume of a sphere, use the formula $V = \frac{4}{3}\pi r^3$.

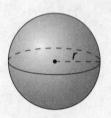

Example

Find the volume of the composite figure. Use 3.14 for π.

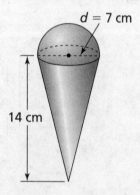

$d = 7$ cm

14 cm

First, find the volume of the sphere. Use 3.14 for π.

$V = \frac{4}{3}\pi r^3$

$= \frac{4}{3}\pi(3.5)^3$ ◁— Substitute 3.5 for r.

$= 57.17\pi \approx 179.5$ cm^3

Divide by 2 to find the volume of the hemisphere: $179.5 \div 2 \approx 89.75$ cubic centimeters.

Then, find the volume of the cone. Use 3.14 for π.

$V = \frac{1}{3}\pi r^2 h$

$= \frac{1}{3}\pi(3.5)^2(14)$ ◁— Substitute 3.5 for r and 14 for h.

$= 57.17\pi \approx 179.5$ cm^3

The volume of the composite figure is approximately $89.75 + 179.5 \approx 269.25$ cubic centimeters.

Practice

1. What is the volume of the sphere? Use $\frac{22}{7}$ for π.

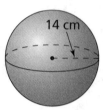

14 cm

2. The surface area of a sphere is 1,017.36 square inches. What is the volume of the sphere? Use 3.14 for π.

3. What is the volume of the composite figure? Use 3.14 for π.

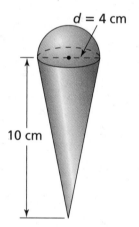

$d = 4$ cm

10 cm

Hidden Clue

For each ordered pair, solve the equation to find the unknown coordinate. Then locate and label the corresponding point on the graph. Draw line segments to connect the points in alphabetical order. Use the completed picture to help answer the riddle below.

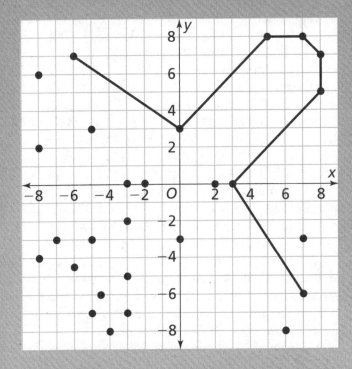

What do squares, triangles, pentagons, and octagons have in common?

A $(-13 + 6x = -x + 36, -6)$ ☐ , −6

H $(-6, y + 6 - 3y = 15)$ −6, ☐

B $(\frac{2}{3}x + 1 = 5, -8)$ ☐ , −8

I $(-8, -6y - y = -2(y - 10))$ −8, ☐

C $(0, 2.5y - 2.3 = -9.8)$ 0, ☐

J $(-7, \frac{1}{2}y + 11 + \frac{1}{6}y = 9)$ −7, ☐

D $(-3, 1.4 - 0.7y = -1.2y - 1.1)$ −3, ☐

K $(4x + 7 - x = -8, -3)$ ☐ , −3

E $(3(x + 5) = 6, -7)$ ☐ , −7

L $(-3, 7y + 11 = 4y + 11)$ −3, ☐

F $(23 - \frac{1}{2}x = 25, -8)$ ☐ , −8

M $(1.5x + 6.8 = -5.2, 6)$ ☐ , 6

G $(-4.5, 6y + 1 - 3y = -17)$ −4.5, ☐

N $(-2(3x + 4) = -5x - 2, 7)$ ☐ , 7

ACKNOWLEDGEMENTS

Photographs

CVR GLYPHstock/Shutterstock, Akugasahagy/Shutterstock, Primopiano/Shutterstock, Smach2003/Shutterstock, AlexZaitsev/Shutterstock; **398** (BCR) Photobank/Fotolia, (BR) yossarian6/Fotolia, (C) Sergiy Serdyuk/Fotolia, (CL) eranda/Fotolia, (CR) eranda/Fotolia, (TC) Gelpi/Fotolia, (TCR) iagodina/Fotolia, (TR) Yongtick/Fotolia; **401** (T) Wicked Digital/Shutterstock, (B) Veera/Shutterstock; **402** (T) Monkey Business Images/Shutterstock, (B) Galyna Andrushko/Shutterstock; **403** (C) Pack/Fotolia, (CL) annexs2/Fotolia, (TC) opka/Fotolia; **405** vladimirs/Fotolia, Taylon/Shutterstock; **409** (C) Chones/Fotolia, (CL) Claireliz/Fotolia, (T) Kurhan/Fotolia; **420** Freeskyline/Fotolia; **421** TAlex/Fotolia; **431** Mihai Simonia/Shutterstock; **435** (CR) S_Photo/Shutterstock, (CL) S_Photo/Shutterstock, (T) S_Photo/Shutterstock; **441** WavebreakMediaMicro/Fotolia; **447** Minicel73/Fotolia; **450** Ljupco Smokovski/Fotolia; **453** (CL) Razoomanetu/Fotolia, (CR) Zuzule/Fotolia, (TC) vladvm50/Fotolia; **457** kraska/Fotolia; **459** RobertoC/Fotolia; **473** Diane Keys/Fotolia; **474** (BCR) yossarian6/Fotolia, (BR) Pink Badger/Fotolia, (CL) Taras Livyy/Fotolia, (CR) Fotimmz/Fotolia, (TR) Aurielaki/Fotolia; **477** (T) Dragon Images/Shutterstock (B) Wanphen Chawarung/Shutterstock; **478** (T) Reisegraf.ch/Shutterstock (B) Stockphotofan1/Shutterstock; **479** Michael Chamberlin/Fotolia; **481** (CR) Sergei Poromov/iStock/Getty Images, (TL) David_franklin/Fotolia; **482** (C) Africa Studio/Fotolia, (TC) Elisanth/Fotolia, (TR) Sorapop Udomsri/Shutterstock; **484** (BCR) Africa Studio/Fotolia, (BR) nikkytok/Fotolia; **486** Denys Rudyi/Fotolia; **487** Photoestelar/Fotolia; **488** (TCR) Marta Jonina/Fotolia, (TR) Pixelrobot/Fotolia; **492** (BCR) Guschenkova/Shutterstock, (BR) Jayzynism/Fotolia; **493** niki2die4/Fotolia; **497** (CL) Neonshot/Fotolia, (TC) Marzanna Syncerz/Fotolia, (TCL) Blend Images/Shutterstock, (TL) Tolgatezcan/Fotolia, (TR) Monkey Business/Fotolia, CREATISTA/Shutterstock, Andy Dean Photography/Shutterstock, Atikinka/Shutterstock, Dean Drobot/Shutterstock; **499** (CR) Brian Jackson/Fotolia, (R) RedDaxLuma/Fotolia; **503** Westend61/Getty Images; **504** Auremar/Shutterstock; **505** Monkey Business/Fotolia; **506** (C) lsantilli/Shutterstock, (CR) David_franklin/Fotolia; **507** (BR) MicroOne/Shutterstock; **519** Anton Bryksin/Shutterstock; **520** (BC) jo/Fotolia, (BCR) yossarian6/Fotolia, (BR) Photobank/Fotolia, (CR) flownaksala/Fotolia, (T) pomogayev/Fotolia, (TCR) booka/Fotolia, (TL) pomogayev/Fotolia; **523** (T) Christopher Boswell/Shutterstock (B) Nidvoray/Shutterstock; **524** (T) Shift Drive/Shutterstock (B) Khakimullin Aleksandr/Shutterstock; **525** (C) Montego6/Fotolia, (CL) Natalia Merzlyakova/Fotolia, (TL) freeskyline/Fotolia; **528** (CR) Alis Photo/Fotolia, (TC) Sam Spiro/Fotolia, (TL) Grum_l/Fotolia, (TR) Chris Hill/Fotolia; **531** (Bkgrd) Sergey Nivens/Shutterstock, (C) Sascha Burkard/Fotolia; **537** (TL) Fotokostic/Shutterstock; (BR) VectorTimes/Shutterstock; **539** Jipen/Fotolia; **543** Kozini/Fotolia; **555** (CL) Windu/Fotolia, (CR) Dmytro Sandratskyi/Fotolia, (TC) Indigolotos/Fotolia, (TL) Olga Kovalenko/Fotolia, (TR) BillionPhotos.com/Fotolia; **556** (TC) Konstantin Sutyagin/Fotolia, (TR) Lisa F. Young/Fotolia; **557** (C) Maddrat/Fotolia; **559** (CL) trinetuzun/Fotolia, (TCL) Sarawutk/Fotolia, (TCR) Jenifoto/Fotolia, (TR) Kimberly Reinick/Fotolia; **561** Fotomek/Fotolia; **562** (TR) James Steidl/Shutterstock; **569** James Peragine/Shutterstock, Iconic Bestiary/Shutterstock; **579** Ryan Burke/DigitalVision Vectors/Getty Images; **582** Images-USA/Alamy Stock Photo; **583** Aboikis/Fotolia; **584** (BCR) yossarian6/Fotolia, (BR) connel_design/Fotolia, (CL) frenta/Fotolia, (CR) Gstudio Group/Fotolia, (TL) Andrew Kazmierski/Fotolia, (TR) lermannika/Fotolia; **585** (T) Darryl Brooks/Shutterstock (B) Luca Santilli/Shutterstock; **586** (T) Wes Lund/Shutterstock (B) Markus Gann/Shutterstock; **589** (TL) Dell/Fotolia, (TR) Travnikovstudio/Fotolia; **594** Adisorn Chaisan/Shutterstock; **595** (C) Westend61/Getty Images, (CR) Lisa F. Young/Shutterstock; **601** (CR) Lucy Liu/Shutterstock; **602** John Lund/Blend Images/Getty Images; **603** Sergii Moscaliuk/Fotolia; **613** Blueringmedia/Fotolia; **615** (CL) Yurakp/Fotolia, (TL) IuneWind/Fotolia; **616** (BR) Piai/Fotolia, (TR) Christian Mueller/Shutterstock; **618** Konstantinos Moraiti/Fotolia; **619** ifrpilot/Fotolia; **624** (B) SkyLine/Fotolia; **625** (CR) Denys Rudyi/Fotolia, (TCR) Cherezoff/Shutterstock, (TR) Kues/Shutterstock; **626** Macrolink/Fotolia; **628** Xijian/iStock/Getty Images; **633** (C) Miro Novak/Shutterstock, (CL) Soulart/Shutterstock, (TC) Axpitel/Fotolia; **637** (BCL) Nortongo/Fotolia, (CL) Pbnew/Fotolia; **639** (C) Rukanoga/Fotolia, (C) Rukanoga/Fotolia, (TL) Uros Petrovic/Fotolia; **644** (TCL) Darezare/Fotolia, (TL) Evdayan/Fotolia; **649** (BC) Galina Barskaya/Shutterstock, (BL) andersphoto/Fotolia; **650** Joel_420/Shutterstock, Cunico/Fotolia; leungchopan/Shutterstock; donatas1205/Fotolia; Dule964/Fotolia; Elisanth/Fotolia; Ilya Akinshin/Fotolia; Mbruxelle/Fotolia; Th3fisa/Fotolia; yossarian6/Fotolia; Željko Radojko/